2019 release

Adobe® Illustrator® CC
The Professional Portfolio

AGAINST THE CLOCK
mastering graphic technology

Managing Editor: Ellenn Behoriam
Cover & Interior Design: Erika Kendra

10 9 8 7 6 5 4 3 2 1

Print ISBN: 978-1-946396-22-8
Ebook ISBN: 978-1-946396-23-5

AGAINST THE CLOCK
mastering graphic technology

4710 28th Street North, Saint Petersburg, FL 33714
800-256-4ATC • www.againsttheclock.com

ACKNOWLEDGEMENTS

About Against The Clock

Against The Clock, long recognized as one of the nation's leaders in courseware development, has been publishing high-quality educational materials for the graphic and computer arts industries since 1990. The company has developed a solid and widely respected approach to teaching people how to effectively use graphics applications, while maintaining a disciplined approach to real-world problems.

Having developed the *Against The Clock* and the *Essentials for Design* series with Prentice Hall/Pearson Education, ATC drew from years of professional experience and instructor feedback to develop *The Professional Portfolio Series*, focusing on the Adobe Creative Suite. These books feature step-by-step explanations, detailed foundational information, and advice and tips from professionals that offer practical solutions to technical issues.

About the Author

Erika Kendra holds a BA in History and a BA in English Literature from the University of Pittsburgh. She began her career in the graphic communications industry as an editor at Graphic Arts Technical Foundation, and has been a full-time professional graphic designer since 1999.

Erika is the author or co-author of more than forty books about Adobe graphic design software. She has also written several books about graphic design concepts such as color reproduction and preflighting, and dozens of articles for industry online and print journals. Working with Against The Clock for almost twenty years, Erika was a key partner in developing *The Professional Portfolio Series* of software training books.

Contributing Editors and Artists

A big thank you to the people whose comments and expertise contributed to the success of these books:

- **Dan Cristensen,** technical editor
- **Roger Morrissey,** technical editor
- **Gary Poyysick,** technical editor
- **Amanda Gambill,** copy editor

Images used in the projects throughout this book are in the public domain unless otherwise noted. Individual artists' credit follow:

Project 5:
Einstein mural photo by Sidney Perry on Unsplash.com
DNA image by vitstudio on Publicdomainpictures.net

Project 7:
Artwork by Chance Hoffman

Project 8:
Guitar photo used to create the header background illustration by Dark Rider on Unsplash.com

Project Goals

Each project begins with a clear description of the overall concepts that are explained in the project; these goals closely match the different "stages" of the project workflow.

The Project Meeting

Each project includes the client's initial comments, which provide valuable information about the job. The Project Art Director, a vital part of any design workflow, also provides fundamental advice and production requirements.

Project Objectives

Each Project Meeting includes a summary of the specific skills required to complete the project.

Real-World Workflow

Projects are broken into logical lessons or "stages" of the workflow. Brief introductions at the beginning of each stage provide vital foundational material required to complete the task.

Step-By-Step Exercises

Every stage of the workflow is broken into multiple hands-on, step-by-step exercises.

Visual Explanations

Wherever possible, screen shots are annotated so students can quickly identify important information.

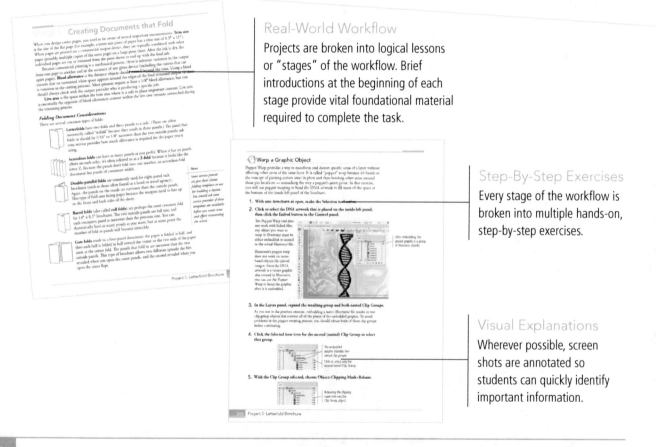

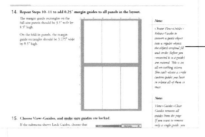

Illustrator Foundations

Additional functionality, related tools, and underlying graphic design concepts are included throughout the book.

Advice and Warnings

Where appropriate, sidebars provide shortcuts, warnings, or tips about the topic at hand.

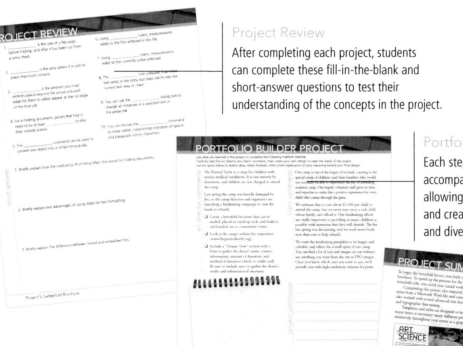

Project Review

After completing each project, students can complete these fill-in-the-blank and short-answer questions to test their understanding of the concepts in the project.

Portfolio Builder Projects

Each step-by-step project is accompanied by a freeform project, allowing students to practice skills and creativity, resulting in an extensive and diverse portfolio of work.

Visual Summary

Using an annotated version of the finished project, students can quickly identify the skills used to complete different aspects of the job.

PROJECTS AT A GLANCE

The Against The Clock *Portfolio Series* teaches graphic design software tools and techniques entirely within the framework of real-world projects; we introduce and explain skills where they would naturally fall into a professional workflow. For example, rather than an entire chapter about printing (which most students find boring), we teach printing where you need to do so — when you complete a print-based project.

The project-based approach in *The Professional Portfolio Series* allows you to get in depth with the software beginning in Project 1 — you don't have to read several chapters of introductory material before you can start creating finished artwork.

Our approach also prevents "topic tedium" — in other words, we don't require you to read pages and pages of information about text (for example); instead, we explain text tools and options as part of larger projects (in this case, beginning with placing text on corporate identity pieces).

Clear, easy-to-read, step-by-step instructions walk you through every phase of each job, from creating a new file to saving the finished piece. Wherever logical, we also offer practical advice and tips about underlying concepts and graphic design practices that will benefit students as they enter the job market.

The projects in this book reflect a range of different types of Illustrator jobs, from creating a series of icons to designing a corporate identity to building a web page interface. When you finish the eight projects in this book (and the accompanying Portfolio Builder exercises), you will have a substantial body of work that should impress any potential employer.

The eight Illustrator projects are described briefly here; more detail is provided in the full table of contents (beginning on Page viii).

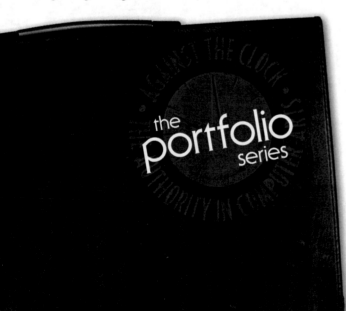

As you complete the projects in this book, our goal is to familiarize you with the tool set so you can be more productive and more marketable in your career as a graphic designer.

It is important to keep in mind that Illustrator is an extremely versatile and powerful application. The sheer volume of available tools, panels, and features can seem intimidating when you first look at the software interface. Most of these tools, however, are fairly simple to use with a bit of background information and a little practice.

Wherever necessary, we explain the underlying concepts and terms that are required for understanding the software. And we're confident that these projects provide the practice so that you'll be able to create sophisticated artwork by the end of the very first project.

CONTENTS

CONTENTS

GETTING STARTED

Prerequisites

To use *The Professional Portfolio Series,* you should know how to use your mouse to point and click, as well as how to drag items around the screen. You should be able to resize and arrange windows on your desktop to maximize your available space. You should know how to access drop-down menus, and understand how check boxes and radio buttons work. It also doesn't hurt to have a good understanding of how your operating system organizes files and folders, and how to navigate your way around them. If you're familiar with these fundamental skills, then you know all that's necessary to use the Portfolio Series.

Resource Files

All the files you need to complete the projects in this book — except, of course, the Illustrator application files — are on the Student Files Web page at againsttheclock.com. See the inside back cover of this book for access information.

Each archive (ZIP) file is named according to the related project (e.g., **Studio_AI19_RF.zip**). At the beginning of each project, you must download the archive for that project and expand it to access the resource files that you need to complete the exercises. Detailed instructions for this process are included in the Interface chapter.

Files required for the related Portfolio Builder exercises at the end of each project are also available on the Student Files page; these archives are also named by project (e.g., **Triumph_AI19_PB.zip**).

ATC Fonts

You must download and install the ATC fonts from the Student Files Web page to ensure that your exercises and projects work as described in the book. You should replace older (pre-2013) ATC fonts with the ones on the Student Files Web page.

Software Versions

This book was written and tested using the 2019 release of Adobe Illustrator CC software (version 23.0). You can find the specific version number in the Splash Screen that appears while your application is launching, or by choosing About Illustrator in the Illustrator CC/Help menu.

Because Adobe releases periodic upgrades throughout the year, some features and functionality might have changed since publication. Please check the Errata section of the Against The Clock website for any significant issues that might have arisen from these periodic upgrades.

System Requirements

The Professional Portfolio Series was designed to work on both Macintosh or Windows computers; where differences exist from one platform to another, we include specific instructions relative to each platform. One issue that remains different from Macintosh to Windows is the use of different modifier keys (Control, Shift, etc.) to accomplish the same task. When we present key commands, we always follow the same Macintosh/Windows format — Macintosh keys are listed first, then a slash, followed by the Windows key commands.

THE ILLUSTRATOR USER INTERFACE

Adobe Illustrator is the industry-standard application for creating digital drawings or **vector images** (graphics composed of mathematically defined lines instead of pixels). Our goal in this book is to teach you how to use the available tools to create different types of work that you might encounter in your professional career. Some projects in this book focus on creating graphics and illustrations — the true heart of the application. You can also use the tools in Illustrator to combine type, graphics, and images into a cohesive design — as you will do in several projects to create posters, flyers, package design, and even a website interface.

The simple exercises in this introduction are designed for you to explore the Illustrator user interface. Whether you are new to the application or upgrading from a previous version, we highly recommend that you follow these steps to click around and become familiar with the basic workspace.

Explore the Illustrator Interface

The first time you launch Illustrator, you will see the default user interface (UI) settings as defined by Adobe. When you relaunch after you or another user has quit, the workspace defaults to the last-used settings — including open panels and the position of those panels on your screen. We designed the following exercise so you can explore different ways of controlling panels in the Illustrator user interface.

1. **Create a new empty folder named WIP on any writable disk (where you plan to save your work).**

2. **Download the InterfaceAI_AI19_RF.zip archive from the Student Files web page.**

3. **Macintosh users: Place the ZIP archive in your WIP folder, then double-click the file icon to expand it.**

   Windows users: Double-click the ZIP archive file to open it. Click the folder inside the archive and drag it into your primary WIP folder.

   The resulting **InterfaceAI** folder contains all the files you need to complete the exercises in this introduction.

| **Macintosh:** Double-click the archive file icon to expand it. | **Windows:** Open the archive file, then drag the InterfaceAI folder from the archive to your WIP folder. |

4. **Macintosh users: While pressing Command-Option-Shift, launch Illustrator. Hold down the modifier keys until Illustrator opens.**

   Windows users: While pressing Control-Alt-Shift, launch Illustrator. Hold down the modifier keys until Illustrator opens.

   This step resets Illustrator to the preference settings that are defined by Adobe as the application defaults. This helps to ensure that your application functions in the same way as what we show in our screenshots.

5. If you get a warning message about GPU Performance, click OK.

GPU Performance enables faster on-screen rendering if your hardware meets the feature requirements. If you do not have the appropriate hardware, you will still be able to use all of the Illustrator toolset, but rendering will be processed by your computer's Central Processing Unit (CPU).

6. Macintosh users: Open the Window menu and make sure the Application Frame option is toggled on.

Many menu commands and options in Illustrator are **toggles**, which means they are either on or off; when an option is already checked, that option is toggled on (visible or active). You can toggle an active option off by choosing the checked menu command, or toggle an inactive option on by choosing the unchecked menu command.

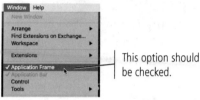

This option should be checked.

Note:

On Windows, the Application Frame menu command is not available; you can't turn off the Application Frame on the Windows OS.

Understanding the Application Frame

On Windows, each running application is contained within its own frame; all elements of the application — including the Menu bar, panels, tools, and open documents — are contained within the Application frame.

Adobe also offers the Application frame to Macintosh users as an option for controlling the workspace. When the Application frame is active, the entire workspace exists in a self-contained area that can be moved around the screen. All elements of the workspace (excluding the Menu bar) move when you move the Application frame.

The Application frame is active by default, but you can toggle it off by choosing Window>Application Frame. If the menu option is checked, the Application frame is active; if the menu option is not checked, it is inactive. (On Windows, the Application Frame menu command is not available; you can't turn off the Application Frame on the Windows OS.)

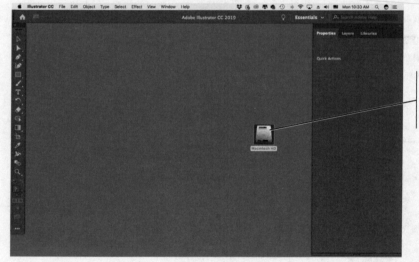

When the Application frame is not active, the desktop is visible behind the workspace elements.

7. Review the options in the Home screen.

The default user interface shows a stored "Home" workspace. No panels are visible in this workspace. When you first launch the application, you have "quick start" access to several common file sizes. After one or more files have been opened, those buttons are replaced with icons for recently opened files.

The Home workspace appears whenever Illustrator is running, but no file is open. As soon as you open or create a file, the interface reverts to show the last-used workspace arrangement.

The Macintosh and Windows workspaces are virtually identical, with a few primary exceptions:

- On Macintosh, the application bar appears below the Menu bar; the Close, Minimize, and Restore buttons appear on the left side of the application bar, and the Menu bar is not part of the Application frame.

- On Windows, the Close, Minimize, and Restore buttons appear at the right end of the Menu bar, which is part of the overall Application frame.

- Macintosh users have two extra menus (consistent with the Macintosh operating system structure). The Apple menu provides access to system-specific commands. The Illustrator menu follows the Macintosh system-standard format for all applications; this menu controls basic application operations such as About, Hide, Preferences, and Quit.

Note:

When a file is open, you can return to the Home workspace by clicking the Home icon in the left side of the Application/Menu bar.

8. **Choose Window>Workspace>Essentials.**

   Saved **workspaces** provide one-click access to a defined group of panels.

9. **Choose Window>Workspace>Reset Essentials.**

   If you or someone else changed anything, and then quit the application, those changes are remembered when Illustrator is relaunched. Because we can't be sure what your default settings show, completing this step resets the user interface to the built-in, default Essentials workspace so that your screen will match our screenshots.

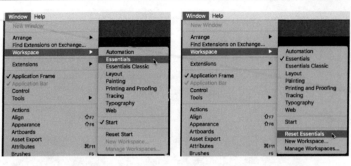

Note:

If a menu or dialog box option is grayed out, it is not available for the active selection.

10. **Macintosh users: Choose Illustrator CC>Preferences>User Interface.**

    Windows users: Choose Edit>Preferences>User Interface.

    Remember that on Macintosh systems, the Preferences dialog box is accessed in the Illustrator menu; Windows users access the Preferences dialog box in the Edit menu.

    Macintosh   **Windows**

    Preferences customize the way many of the program's tools and options function.

When you open the Preferences dialog box, the active pane is the one you chose in the Preferences submenu. Once open, however, you can access any of the Preference categories by clicking a different option in the left pane; the right side of the dialog box displays options related to the active category.

In the User Interface preferences, you control the overall appearance of the workspace:

- **Brightness.** You might have noticed the rather dark appearance of the interface background. Illustrator uses the medium-dark "theme" as the default.

- **Canvas Color.** This setting determines the color of the space around the artboard.

- **Auto-Collapse Iconic Panels.** When panels are iconic/iconized (only the panel name and icon are visible), clicking a panel button opens that panel to the left of the icon. When this option is active, iconic panels automatically collapse as soon as you click away from the panel.

- **Open Documents As Tabs.** Checked by default, each open file appears as a separate tab below the Application/Menu bar. If you uncheck this option, each file appears in its own separate floating window.

- **Large Tabs.** Checked by default, this setting enlarges the text in the various panel tabs; this is part of Adobe's overall efforts to reduce eyestrain throughout the Creative Cloud suite. If you uncheck this option, the panel tabs revert to the smaller text of previous versions.

- **UI Scaling.** When you launch Illustrator the first time (or after clearing the preferences, as you did at the beginning of this exercise), Illustrator identifies your screen resolution and adjusts the application scale so that measurements on your screen mirror real-life measurements as accurately as possible. Scale Cursor Proportionately, which is checked by default, scales cursor icons in proportion to the UI Scaling that you have selected.

Note:

We use the Light UI brightness option throughout this book because text in the interface elements is easier to read in printed screen captures.

Note:

Changes to the UI Scaling options do not take effect until you relaunch the application.

11. **In the Brightness menu, choose any option that you prefer.**

12. **Check the Auto-Collapse Iconic Panels option.**

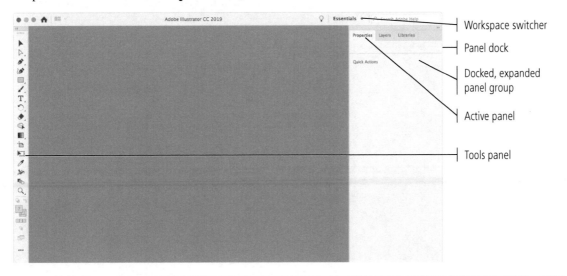

Choose a brightness setting here.

Check this option.

13. **Click OK to close the Preferences dialog box.**

14. **Continue to the next exercise.**

Explore the Arrangement of Illustrator Panels

As you gain experience and familiarity with Illustrator, you will develop personal artistic and working styles. Illustrator includes a number of options for arranging and managing the numerous panels, so you can customize and personalize the workspace to suit your specific needs.

We designed the following exercise to give you an opportunity to explore different ways of controlling Illustrator panels. Because workspace preferences are largely a matter of personal taste, the projects in this book instruct you to use certain tools and panels, but where you place those elements within the interface is up to you.

1. **With Illustrator open, review the options available in the user interface.**

The default Essentials workspace includes the Tools panel on the left side of the screen and a set of expanded panels attached to the right side of the screen. (The area where the panels are stored is called the **panel dock**.)

Workspace switcher

Panel dock

Docked, expanded panel group

Active panel

Tools panel

> **Note:**
>
> *As you work your way through this book, you will learn not only what you can do with these different collections of Preferences, but also **why** and **when** you might want to adjust them.*

2. Review the panel dock on the right side of the interface.

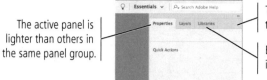

The active panel is lighter than others in the same panel group.

The area behind the panel tabs is called the **drop zone**.

Each panel in the group is represented by a tab.

Note:

Most screenshots in this book show floating panels so we can focus on the most important issue in a particular image. In our production workflow, however, we make heavy use of docked and iconized panels and take full advantage of saved custom workspaces.

3. Click the Properties panel tab and drag it away from the docked group.

You can click an individual panel tab to drag it to another location, or click the panel group drop zone to move an entire group. If you drag a panel (group) away from the dock, it **floats** freely in the workspace.

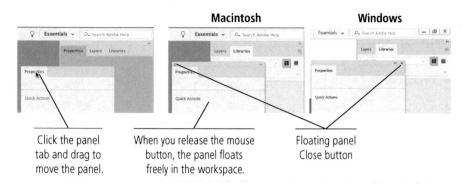

Macintosh   **Windows**

Click the panel tab and drag to move the panel.

When you release the mouse button, the panel floats freely in the workspace.

Floating panel Close button

4. Click the floating Properties panel tab and drag until a blue highlight appears to the left of the docked panel group.

You can create multiple columns of panels in the dock. This can be very useful if you want easy access to a large number of panels, and if you have a monitor with enough available screen space.

Note:

You can press the Tab key to temporarily hide all panels at one time. (Press the Tab key a second time to restore the same panels that were visible when you first pressed Tab.)

This pop-out "drawer" indicates that releasing the mouse button...

...will create a second column in the panel dock.

5. Choose Window>Artboards.

All Illustrator panels are available in the Window menu.

- If you choose a panel that is open but iconized, the panel expands left of its icon.

- If you choose a panel that is open in an expanded group, that panel comes to the front of the group.

- If you choose a panel that isn't currently open, it opens in the same position as when it was last closed.

6. In the floating panel group, Control/right-click the Asset Export panel tab and choose Close from the contextual menu.

As we explained in the Getting Started section, when commands are different for the Macintosh and Windows operating systems, we include the different commands in the Macintosh/Windows format.

Control/right-click the panel tab to access that panel's contextual menu.

In this case, Macintosh users who do not have right-click mouse capability can press the Control key and click to access the contextual menu. You do not have to press Control *and* right-click to access the menus.

Control/right-clicking opens a contextual menu, where you can change a variety of behaviors or properties of the specific object you Control/right-click. Many elements in Illustrator have contextual menus, which make it easy to access item-specific options.

In this contextual menu, you can use the Close option to close a single panel or choose Close Tab Group to close all panels in the same group. (When a panel group is floating, you can also use the floating group's Close button to close an entire floating group.)

Note:

If you're using a Macintosh with a mouse that doesn't have right-click capability, we highly recommend that you purchase one that does. They're inexpensive, available in most retail stores, and will save you significant amounts of time when accessing contextual options.

7. Click the Artboards panel tab (in the floating panel group) and drag until a blue highlight appears below the docked panel group in the right column.

Individual panels can be dragged to different locations (including into different groups) by dragging the panel's tab. The target location — where the panel will be located when you release the mouse button — is identified by the blue highlight.

- If the highlight surrounds an existing panel group, the dragged panel will become part of the highlighted group.

- If the highlight appears between existing panel groups (or at an edge of the dock), the dragged panel will create a new group at the location of the highlight.

The highlight shows where the panel will be placed if you release the mouse button.

The dragged panel is moved into the dock, in its own group.

8. Hover the mouse cursor over the bottom edge of the Layers/Libraries panel group (in the right column of the dock) until you see a two-facing arrow icon, then click and drag up.

When you drag the bottom edge of a docked group, other variable panels in the same column expand or contract to fit the available space. By "variable panels," we mean any panel that has an undefined number of options. Some panels, such as the Stroke panel, have a fixed number of options so they do not expand or contract. The Layers panel, on the other hand, can list a variable number of items so it can be made larger or smaller.

Dragging the bottom edge of a docked panel group changes the height of that group.

Note:

You can drag the left edge of a column to change the width of any docked column.

9. **Double-click the dock title bar above the docked icons to collapse the docked panels to icons.**

    You can independently iconize or expand each column of docked panels and each floating panel group .

    Double-click the title bar at the top of the dock column to collapse or expand it.

    Each column in the dock can be iconized independently.

    Note:

    You can double-click the a panel tab in an expanded group to minimize that group, or collapse it down to show only the panel tabs.

10. **Hover the mouse cursor over the left edge of the iconized dock column until you see a two-facing arrow icon, then click and drag right.**

    When panels are iconized, each panel is represented by a button that defaults to show the icon and panel name. Narrowing the iconized dock column reduces the panel buttons to show only the related icons.

    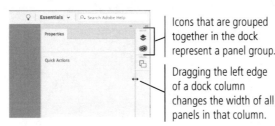

    Icons that are grouped together in the dock represent a panel group.

    Dragging the left edge of a dock column changes the width of all panels in that column.

11. **Control/right-click the title bar above either column of docked panel icons. Make sure the Auto-Collapse Iconic Panels option is toggled on (checked), then click away from the contextual menu to dismiss it.**

    Because you turned on the Auto-Collapse option in the User Interface preferences, this toggle is already checked. You can use either option — preference or contextual menu command — to toggle the option on or off at any time.

    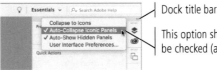

    Dock title bar

    This option should be checked (active).

12. **In the panel dock, click the top button (Layers).**

    Clicking a collapsed panel icon expands that panel to the left of the icon. If you expand a panel that is part of a group, the entire group expands; the icon you click is the active panel in the group.

    The icon you clicked is the active panel in the expanded group.

    The panel name appears in a tool tip when the cursor hovers over the icon.

13. **Click away from the expanded panel, anywhere in the workspace.**

    Because the Auto-Collapse option is active, the expanded panel group collapses back to an icon when you click away from the panel.

14. On the left side of the workspace, review the Tools panel.

The default Tools panel in the built-in Essentials workspace includes a limited set of the dozens of tools that are available in Illustrator. The More button at the bottom of the Tools panel provides quick access to the complete set, so that you can add the hidden tools into the Tools panel (see Customizing Tools Panels on Page 12).

15. Choose Window>Toolbars>Advanced.

This command restores all tools, including the nested variations, to the Tools panel.

Note:

Throughout this book, we assume you are using the Advanced Tools panel.

16. If you don't see all of the panel options, double-click the Tools panel title bar.

The Tools panel can be displayed as either one or two columns; double-clicking the Tools panel title bar toggles between these two modes.

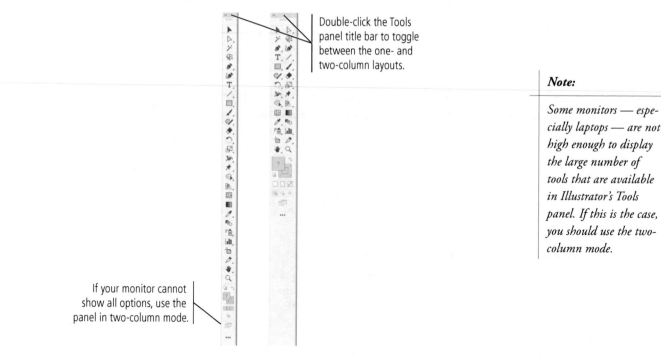

Double-click the Tools panel title bar to toggle between the one- and two-column layouts.

If your monitor cannot show all options, use the panel in two-column mode.

Note:

Some monitors — especially laptops — are not high enough to display the large number of tools that are available in Illustrator's Tools panel. If this is the case, you should use the two-column mode.

17. Continue to the next exercise.

Identifying and Accessing Illustrator Tools

In the Illustrator Tools panel, tool icons that show a small black arrow in the lower-right corner have **nested tools**. You can access nested tools by clicking the primary tool and holding down the mouse button until a pop-up menu shows the nested variations, or Control/right-clicking the tool in the panel.

If you hover your mouse over a tool, a pop-up **tool tip** shows the name of the tool, as well as

This arrow means the tool has other nested tools.

A tool tip shows the name of the tool.

the associated keyboard shortcut if one exists. If a tool has a defined shortcut, pressing that key activates the associated tool. (If you don't see tool tips, check the Show Tool Tips option in the General pane of the Preferences dialog box.)

If you drag the mouse cursor to the bar on the right of the nested-tool menu, the nested-tool options separate into their own floating toolboxes, so you can more easily access the nested variations. (The primary tool is not removed from the main Tools panel.)

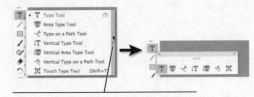

Hold down the mouse button, drag to here, then release the mouse button to tear off a separate panel with all the related tools.

The chart below offers a quick reference of nested tools, as well as the keyboard shortcut (if any) for each tool. Nested tools are shown indented.

- Selection tool (V)
- Direct Selection tool (A)
  - Group Selection tool
- Magic Wand tool (Y)
- Lasso tool (Q)
- Pen tool (P)
  - Add Anchor Point tool (+)
  - Delete Anchor Point tool (-)
  - Anchor Point tool (Shift-C)
- Curvature tool (Shift-`)
- Type tool (T)
  - Area Type tool
  - Type on a Path tool
  - Vertical Type tool
  - Vertical Area Type tool
  - Vertical Type on a Path tool
  - Touch Type tool (Shift-T)
- Line Segment tool (\)
  - Arc tool
  - Spiral tool
  - Rectangular Grid tool
  - Polar Grid tool

- Rectangle tool (M)
  - Rounded Rectangle tool
  - Ellipse tool (L)
  - Polygon tool
  - Star tool
  - Flare tool
- Paintbrush tool (B)
  - Blob Brush tool (Shift-B)
- Shaper tool (Shift-N)
  - Pencil tool (N)
  - Smooth tool
  - Path Eraser tool
  - Join tool
- Eraser tool (Shift-E)
  - Scissors tool (C)
  - Knife tool
- Rotate tool (R)
  - Reflect tool (O)
- Scale tool (S)
  - Shear tool
  - Reshape tool

- Width tool (Shift-W)
  - Warp tool (Shift-R)
  - Twirl tool
  - Pucker tool
  - Bloat tool
  - Scallop tool
  - Crystallize tool
  - Wrinkle tool
- Puppet Warp tool
- Free Transform tool (E)
- Shape Builder tool (Shift-M)
  - Live Paint Bucket tool (K)
  - Live Paint Selection tool (Shift-L)
- Perspective Grid tool (Shift-P)
  - Perspective Selection tool (Shift-V)
- Mesh tool (U)
- Gradient tool (G)
- Eyedropper tool (I)
  - Measure tool
- Blend tool (W)

- Symbol Sprayer tool (Shift-S)
  - Symbol Shifter tool
  - Symbol Scruncher tool
  - Symbol Sizer tool
  - Symbol Spinner tool
  - Symbol Stainer tool
  - Symbol Screener tool
  - Symbol Styler tool
- Column Graph tool (J)
  - Stacked Column Graph tool
  - Bar Graph tool
  - Stacked Bar Graph tool
  - Line Graph tool
  - Area Graph tool
  - Scatter Graph tool
  - Pie Graph tool
  - Radar Graph tool
- Artboard tool (Shift-O)
- Slice tool (Shift-K)
  - Slice Selection tool
- Hand tool (H)
  - Print Tiling tool
- Zoom tool (Z)

The Tools panel can be customized to show only certain tools, making it easier and quicker to find what you need to complete a given task. The built-in Essentials workspace, for example, includes only the more commonly used drawing tools.

The Find More Tools button at the bottom of the Tools panel provides access to the entire toolset, regardless of which tools are currently available in the   Find More Tools Tools panel.

Tools that are already in the Tools panel appear grayed out in the pop-up menu. You can drag additional tools into the Tools panel from the menu. A blue line between existing tools shows where the tool will be added as a new, first-level tool. A blue highlight around an existing tool indicates it will be added as a new nested tool in that location.

You can also drag to reposition existing tools within the panel. As with adding new tools, the blue highlight identifies the new location of the tool.

You can remove a tool from the Tools panel by simply dragging it away from the panel (as indicated by the minus sign in the cursor icon).

Drag a tool from the pop-up menu between existing tools to add it to the Tools panel.

Drag a tool onto another tool to add it as a nested tool in that location.

Drag a tool away from the Tools panel to remove it.

In addition to modifying the built-in Tools panels, you can also create custom Tools panels that you can recall at any time.

The New Toolbar option in the Find More Tools panel menu opens a dialog box where you can name the new panel. (You can also choose Window>Toolbars>New Toolbar.)

Click here to open the panel menu.

Clicking OK creates a new empty Tools panel; the large plus-sign icon indicates that you have not yet added any tools to it. You can click the Find More Tools button at the bottom of the new panel to add tools. The process is the same as adding reorganizing, and removing tools from the basic Tools panel.

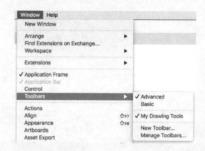

Find More Tools

Changes to a custom Tools panel are saved automatically. If you close a custom panel (by clicking the panel's Close button), the same tools appear in the same position when you reopen it. Existing custom Tools panels can always be opened in the Window>Toolbars submenu.

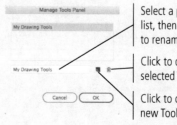

Choosing Window>Toolbars>Manage Toolbars opens a dialog box where you can rename or delete custom panels.

Select a panel in the list, then use the field to rename it.

Click to delete the selected Tools panel.

Click to create a new Tools panel.

Customizing Keyboard Shortcuts

In addition to positioning specific panels in precise locations, you can also add to or modify the keyboard shortcuts used for different functions in the application.

Choosing Edit>Keyboard Shortcuts opens a dialog box where you can modify the shortcuts for menu commands and tools. If you assign a shortcut that isn't part of the default set, you have to save a custom set of shortcuts (Illustrator won't let you modify the default set of keyboard shortcuts).

When more than one set of shortcuts exists (i.e., if you or someone else has added to or changed the default settings), you can switch between the different sets using the menu at the top of the dialog box.

Create a Saved Workspace

By now you should understand that you have virtually unlimited control over the appearance of your Illustrator workspace — what panels are visible, where and how they appear, and even the size of individual panels and panel groups.

Over time you will develop personal preferences based on your work habits and project needs. Rather than re-establishing every workspace element each time you return to Illustrator, you can save your custom workspace settings so you can recall them with a single click.

1. **Click the Workspace switcher on the right side of the Application/Menu bar and choose New Workspace.**

   Again, keep in mind that we list differing commands in the Macintosh/Windows format. On Macintosh, the Workspace switcher is in the Application bar; on Windows, it's in the Menu bar.

   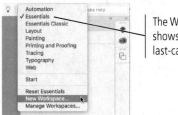

   The Workspace switcher shows the name of the last-called workspace.

2. **In the New Workspace dialog box, type Portfolio and click OK.**

   After saving the current workspace, the Workspace switcher shows the name of the new saved workspace.

   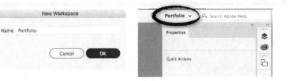

Note:

Because workspace preferences are largely a matter of personal taste, the projects in this book instruct you regarding which panels to use, but not where to place those elements within the interface.

Note:

The Manage Workspaces option opens a dialog box where you can rename or delete user-defined custom workspaces. You can't alter the default workspaces that come with the application.

3. **Click the Workspace switcher and choose Essentials from the list of available workspaces.**

   Calling a saved workspace restores the last-used state of the workspace. You have made a number of changes since calling the Essentials workspace at the beginning of the previous exercise, so calling the Essentials workspace restores the last state of that workspace — in essence, nothing changes from the saved Portfolio workspace.

4. **Open the Workspace switcher and choose Reset Essentials (or choose Window>Workspace>Reset Essentials).**

   Remember, saved workspaces remember the last-used state; calling a workspace again restores the panels exactly as they were the last time you used that workspace. For example, if you close a panel that is part of a saved workspace, the closed panel will not be reopened the next time you call the same workspace. To restore the saved state of the workspace, including opening closed panels or repositioning moved ones, you have to use the Reset option.

5. **Continue to the next exercise.**

Explore the Illustrator Document Window

There is much more to using Illustrator than simply arranging panels around the workspace. In this exercise, you open several Illustrator files and explore interface elements that will be important as you begin creating digital artwork.

Before completing this exercise, you should download and install the ATC fonts from the Student Files web page.

1. **In Illustrator, choose File>Open and navigate to your WIP>InterfaceAI folder.**

2. **Click to select butterfly.ai in the list of available files, then press Shift and click tiedye.ai.**

   The Open dialog box is a system-standard navigation dialog box. This is one area of significant difference between Macintosh and Windows users.

   On both operating systems, this step selects all files including and between the two you click. Pressing Shift allows you to select multiple consecutive files in the list. You can also press Command/Control and click to select multiple non-consecutive files.

Note:

Press Command/Control-O to access the Open dialog box.

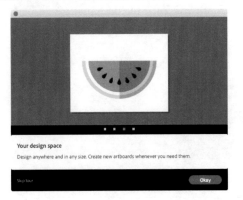

Macintosh   Windows

3. **Click Open. If you see a pop-up window with an introductory tour, click the Skip Tour option in the bottom left corner.**

4. Click the document tab for tiedye.ai if it is not already active.

Illustrator files open in the document window. Across the top of the document window, each open document is represented by a separate tab; the document tabs show the file name, current view percentage, color space, and current viewing mode.

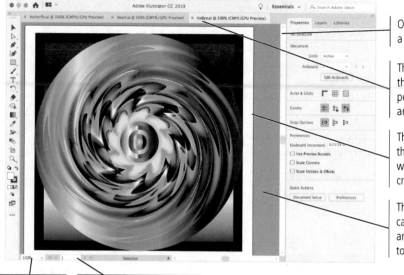

Open files appear in a document window.

The **document tab** shows the active file name, view percentage, color space, and current viewing mode.

The **artboard** is essentially the digital page, or the area where artwork should be created or placed.

The **canvas** (sometimes called the **pasteboard**) around the artboard defaults to a gray color.

View Percentage menu/field

Use these options to navigate from one artboard to another within a single file.

5. Open the View Percentage menu in the bottom-left corner of the document window and choose 200%.

Different people prefer different view percentages, depending on a number of factors, such as eyesight, monitor size, and so on. You can zoom an Illustrator document from 3.13% to 64000%.

As you complete the projects in this book, you'll see our screen shots zoom in or out as necessary to show you the most relevant part of a particular file. In most cases, we do not tell you what specific view percentage to use for a particular exercise unless it is specifically required for the work being done.

Note:

Files open in the order in which they appear in the Open dialog box. If your files are sorted in reverse alphabetical order, the tabs will appear in reverse of what you see here, and butterfly.ai will be the active file.

Note:

Macintosh users: If you turn off the Application frame (Window>Application Frame), the new document will have its own title bar.

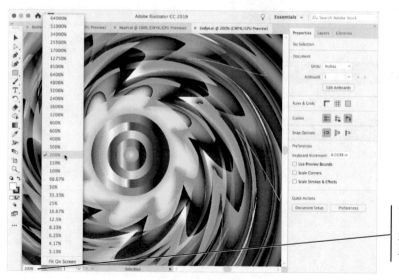

Type a specific percentage in the field or choose one of the predefined percentages from the menu.

6. Choose View>Fit Artboard in Window.

These five options affect the view percentage of a file.

The Fit Artboard in Window command automatically calculates view percentage based on the size of the document window.

7. Review the options in the Properties panel.

The Properties panel is context sensitive, which means it provides access to different options depending on which tool is active and what is selected in the document.

When nothing is selected in the file, you can use the Properties panel to change a number of settings related to the overall file. The most important options open the Document Setup dialog box and the Preferences dialog box (more about these specific elements in the projects).

Document and application-specific options are available when nothing is selected.

8. **Click the Selection tool at the top of the Tools panel to make that tool active, then click the purple square at the edge of the artwork to select that object.**

The Selection tool (the black arrow) is used to select entire objects in the file. The Control panel shows the attributes of the selected object (in this case, a path).

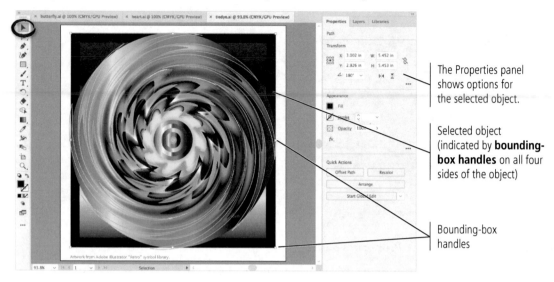

The Properties panel shows options for the selected object.

Selected object (indicated by **bounding-box handles** on all four sides of the object)

Bounding-box handles

9. **Choose Window>Control to open the Control panel.**

The Control panel, which appears at the top of the interface, is another context-sensitive tool that shows options related to the selected object.

10. **Click the text near the bottom of the artwork to select the type object.**

Like the Properties panel, the Control panel changes to show options related to type objects.

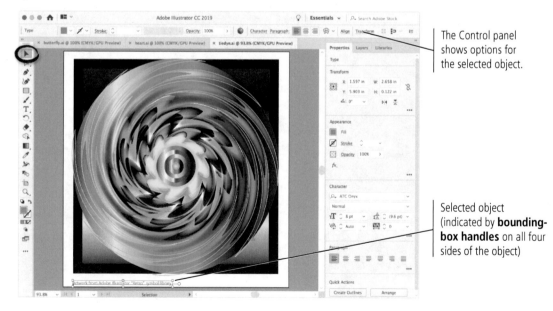

The Control panel shows options for the selected object.

Selected object (indicated by **bounding-box handles** on all four sides of the object)

11. **Continue to the next exercise.**

More about the Control Panel

What you see in the Control panel depends on the size of your monitor (or the size of your Application frame if you've made it smaller than your monitor). When working with a smaller space, some options are not available directly in the panel; instead, you have to use the hot-text links (identified by an underline) to open pop-up versions of the related panel.

In the images below, for example, you have to click the Paragraph hot-text link in the top version to open the pop-up panel and access the paragraph alignment options. In the wider version, you can access three paragraph alignment options directly in the Control panel.

Regardless of your interface width, options in the Control panel are a limited subset related to the selected object. You can click any hot-text link to open the related pop-up panel and access additional options. Clicking the Y link, for example, opens the Transform panel with additional object transformation options.

Click these hot-text links to open the related pop-up panel.

Explore the Arrangement of Multiple Documents

Because designers frequently need to work with more than one Illustrator file at once, Illustrator incorporates a number of options for arranging multiple documents. We designed the following simple exercise to allow you to explore these options.

1. **Click the butterfly.ai tab at the top of the document window.**

Clicking a specific tab makes that file active in the document window.

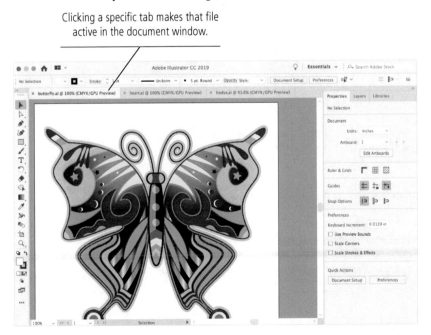

2. Choose Window>Arrange>Float in Window.

Floating a document separates the file into its own document window.

The title bar of the separate document window shows the same information that was in the document tab.

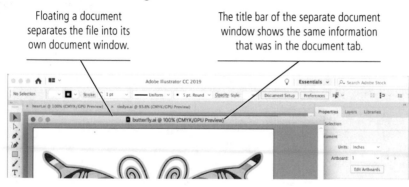

Note:

You can separate all open files by choosing Window>Arrange> Float All In Windows.

3. In the Application/Menu bar, click the Arrange Documents button to open the menu of defined arrangements.

The Arrange Documents menu includes a number of tiling options for arranging multiple open files in the workspace. (On Macintosh systems, the Application bar must be visible to access the Arrange Documents button.)

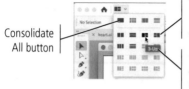

Consolidate All button

The appearance of each icon suggests the result of each option.

Rolling your mouse cursor over an icon shows the arrangement name in a tool tip.

Note:

You can drag document tabs to rearrange their order. You can also drag a floating window back to the document tab bar, or use the Consolidate All option to restore the floating document to a tabbed file.

4. Click the Consolidate All button (top-left) in the Arrange Documents panel.

The Consolidate All button consolidates all floating documents into a single tabbed document window (just like the default arrangement).

The remaining buttons in the top row separate all open files into individual document windows, and then arrange the different windows as indicated.

The lower options use a specific number of floating documents (2-Up, 3-Up, etc.); if more files are open than an option indicates, the extra files are consolidated as tabs in the first document window.

Note:

When multiple floating document windows are open, two options in the Window>Arrange menu allow you to cascade or tile the different document windows.

5. Click the button at the bottom of the Tools panel to show the screen mode options.

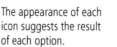

Illustrator has four different **screen modes**, which change the way the document window displays on the screen. The default mode, which you saw when you opened these three files, is called Normal Screen mode.

6. **Choose Full Screen Mode with Menu Bar from the Screen Mode menu.**

In Full Screen Mode with Menu Bar, the document tabs are hidden.

In Full Screen Mode with Menu Bar, the document window fills the entire workspace and extends behind the docked panels.

7. **Click the Screen Mode button at the bottom of the Tools panel and choose Full Screen Mode.**

All open files are listed at the bottom of the Window menu. You can use those menu options to navigate from one file to another, which is particularly useful in Full Screen Mode with Menu Bar because the document tabs are not visible in this mode.

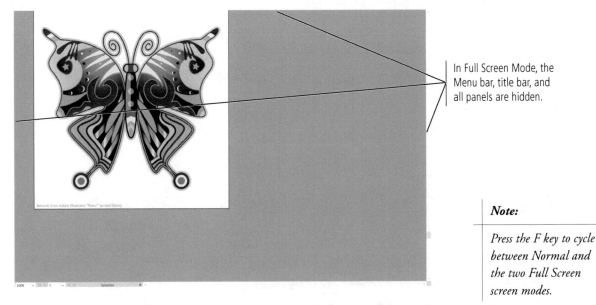

In Full Screen Mode, the Menu bar, title bar, and all panels are hidden.

Note:

Press the F key to cycle between Normal and the two Full Screen screen modes.

8. **Press the Escape key to exit Full Screen Mode and return to Normal Screen Mode.**

9. Press Shift-F to enter Presentation mode.

Presentation mode fills the entire screen with the active spread; the area around the page is solid black.

In Presentation mode, the page, surrounded by solid black, fills the entire screen.

10. Press ESC to exit Presentation mode.

11. Click the Close button on the butterfly.ai tab. If asked whether you want to save changes, click Don't Save.

Closing the Application frame closes all files open in that frame.

Clicking the Close button on a document tab closes only that file.

Macintosh

Clicking the Menu bar Close button closes all open files, and quits the application.

Windows

12. Macintosh: Click the Close button in the top-left corner of the Application bar. If asked, click Don't Save for all files.

Closing the Macintosh Application frame closes all open files, but does not quit the application.

Windows: Click the Close button on each document tab to close the files. If asked, click Don't Save for all files.

Clicking the Close button on the Windows Menu bar closes all open files *and* quits the application. To close open files *without* quitting, you have to manually close each file using the document tabs.

As we show you how to complete different stages of the workflow, we usually won't tell you when to change your view percentage because that's largely a matter of personal preference. However, you should understand the different options for navigating around an Illustrator file so you can efficiently get to what you want.

To change the file view percentage, you can type a specific percent in the **View Percentage field** of the document window or choose from the predefined options in the menu.

You can also click with the **Zoom tool** to increase the view percentage in specific, predefined intervals (the same intervals you see in the View Percentage menu in the bottom-left corner of the document window). Pressing Option/Alt with the Zoom tool allows you to zoom out in the same defined percentages.

Animated Zoom is active by default when GPU Preview is enabled; clicking and dragging with the Zoom tool dynamically changes the view percentage depending on which way you drag (right to enlarge or left to reduce).

If you turn off Animated Zoom in the Performance pane of the Preferences dialog box, you can drag a marquee with the Zoom tool to zoom into a specific location; the area surrounded by the marquee fills the available space in the document window.

The **View menu** also provides options for changing view percentage. (The Zoom In and Zoom Out options step through the same predefined view percentages as clicking with the Zoom tool.)

Zoom In	Command/Control-plus (+)
Zoom Out	Command/Control-minus (-)
Fit Artboard in Window	Command/Control-0 (zero)
Fit All in Window	Command-Option-0/ Control-Alt-0 (zero)
Actual Size (100%)	Command/Control-1

Whatever your view percentage, you can use the **Hand tool** to drag the file around in the document window. The tool changes what is visible in the window; it has no effect on objects in the file. If the insertion point is not flashing, you can press the Spacebar to temporarily access the Hand tool; when the insertion point is placed, you can press the Option/Alt key to temporarily access the Hand tool.

Using the Navigator Panel

The **Navigator panel** (Window>Navigator) is another method of adjusting what you see, including the view percentage and the specific area that is visible in the document window. The Navigator panel shows a thumbnail of the active file; a red rectangle (called the Proxy Preview Area) represents exactly how much of the document shows in the document window. You can drag the proxy in the panel to change the visible portion of the image in the document window.

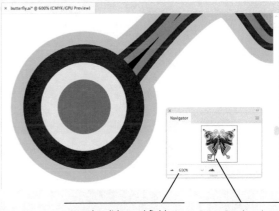

Use the slider and field to change the view percentage.

Proxy Preview Area

Working with Saved Views

Named views can be helpful if you repeatedly return to the same area and view percentage. By choosing View>New View, you can save the current view with a specific name.

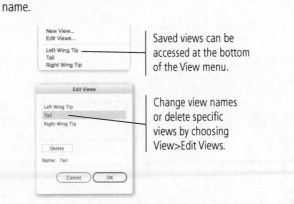

Saved views can be accessed at the bottom of the View menu.

Change view names or delete specific views by choosing View>Edit Views.

Campground Icons

Cooper's Lake Campground is a family-oriented campground that hosts individual camping, as well as large planned events at their grounds. The owner has hired you to create a digital collection of icons that they can use to create signs, print on a variety of collateral, and place on their website.

This project incorporates the following skills:

❏ Placing raster images into an Illustrator file to use as drawing templates

❏ Creating and managing simple shapes and lines

❏ Using various tools to transform objects' color, position, and shape

❏ Cloning objects to minimize repetitive tasks

❏ Using sublayers and groups to organize and manage artwork

❏ Drawing complex shapes by combining simple shapes

PROJECT MEETING

We have a set of icons on our website, but we need to use the same artwork in other places as well — signs throughout the park, flyers that we hand out to new guests, and so on.

Our printer told us that the symbols on our website are "low res," so they can't be used for print projects. The printer also said he needs vector graphics that will scale larger and still look good. The printer suggested we hire a designer to create digital versions of the icons so we can use them for a wide variety of purposes, from large signs to small cards, to anything else that might come up.

We need you to help us figure out exactly what we need, and then create the icons for us.

Basically, we have the icons, but they're low-resolution raster images, so they only work for the web, and they can't be enlarged. The good news is that you can use the existing icons as templates and, more or less, trace them to create the new icons.

The client needs files that can be printed cleanly and scaled from a couple of inches up to several feet. Illustrator vector files are perfect for this type of job. In fact, vector graphics get their resolution from the printer being used for a specific job, so you can scale them to any size you want without losing quality.

To complete this project, you will:

- ❏ Use a variety of tools and techniques to create, align, and transform basic shapes
- ❏ Control objects' fill and stroke attributes
- ❏ Import raster images to use as artwork templates
- ❏ Use sublayers and groups to manage complex artwork
- ❏ Use the Line Segment tool to create a complex object from a set of straight lines
- ❏ Edit properties of Live Shapes to create finished icon artwork
- ❏ Draw and combine basic Live Shapes using the Shaper tool
- ❏ Draw complex artwork with the Pencil tool

STAGE 1 / Setting up the Workspace

There are two primary types of digital artwork: raster images and vector graphics. (**Line art**, sometimes categorized as a third type of image, is actually a type of raster image.)

Raster images are pixel-based, made up of a grid of individual **pixels** (**rasters** or **bits**) in rows and columns (called a **bitmap**). Raster files are **resolution dependent**; their resolution is determined when you scan, photograph, or create the file. As a professional graphic designer, you should have a basic understanding of the following terms and concepts:

- **Pixels per inch (ppi)** is the number of pixels in one horizontal or vertical inch of a digital raster file.

- **Lines per inch (lpi)** is the number of halftone dots produced in a linear inch by a high-resolution imagesetter, which simulates the appearance of continuous-tone color.

- **Dots per inch (dpi)** or **spots per inch (spi)** is the number of dots produced by an output device in a single line of output.

Drawing objects that you create in Illustrator are **vector graphics**, which are composed of mathematical descriptions of a series of lines and points. Vector graphics are **resolution independent**; they can be freely scaled and are output at the resolution of the output device.

Create a New Document

In this project, you work with the basics of creating vector graphics in Illustrator, using a number of different drawing tools, adding color, and managing various aspects of your artwork. The first step is to create a new document for building your artwork.

1. **Download Camping_AI19_RF.zip from the Student Files web page.**

2. **Expand the ZIP archive in your WIP folder (Macintosh) or copy the archive contents into your WIP folder (Windows).**

   This results in a folder named **Camping**, which contains all of the files you need for this project. You should also use this folder to save the files you create in this project.

   If necessary, refer to Page 1 of the Interface chapter for specific information on expanding or accessing the required resource files.

3. **In Illustrator, choose File>New.**

   You have several options for creating a new file:

   - Choose File>New;
   - Use the associated keyboard shortcut, Command/Control-N; or
   - Click the Create New button in the Home workspace.

   If the Home workspace is visible, click the Create New button to open the New Document dialog box.

4. **Click the Print option at the top of the resulting New Document dialog box.**

The New Document dialog box offers a number of preset sizes and prebuilt starter templates, broken into categories based on the intended output.

When you choose the Print category, you see common page sizes such as Letter and Legal. The Print presets automatically default to the CMYK color mode and 300 ppi raster effects, which are required for commercial printing applications. For all other categories of presets (Mobile, Web, Film & Video, and Art & Illustration), the new document defaults to the RGB color mode and 72 ppi raster effects. (You will learn more about the importance of those options in later projects.)

Click a category name to show related presets.

Click here to define a new file name.

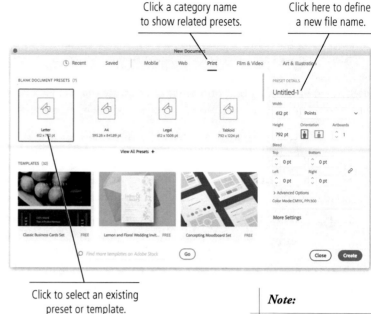

Click to select an existing preset or template.

5. **On the right side of the dialog box, type icons in the Name field.**

6. **Choose Points in the Units menu, and choose Portrait Orientation.**

Although inches is the standard unit of measurement in the United States, the default **points** option is a standard unit of measurement for graphic designers. There are 72 points in an inch. Don't worry, though, about being able to define everything in points; Illustrator can make the calculations for you.

7. **Make sure the Number of Artboards field is set to 1.**

Options on the right side of the dialog box, such as artboard orientation and units of measurement, default to the last-used settings.

Illustrator includes the ability to create multiple **artboards** (basically, Illustrator's version of "pages"). For this project, you need only a single artboard.

8. **Set all four bleed values to 0.**

Bleed is the amount an object needs to extend past the edge of the artboard or page to meet the mechanical requirements of commercial printing.

File name

Default unit of measurement

Portrait

Landscape

When linked, all four Bleed fields will have the same value.

Note:

You can change the color mode and raster effects settings by expanding the Advanced Options in the right side of the New Document dialog box.

9. **Click Create to create the new file. Immediately choose View>Fit Artboard in Window.**

   In the resulting document window, the letter-size "page" (or artboard) is represented by a dark black line.

   The color of the pasteboard (the area around the artboard) defaults to match the brightness of the user interface. You can change this setting to show a white pasteboard in the User Interface pane of the Preferences dialog box.

   As we explained in the Interface chapter, the panels you see depend on what was done the last time you (or someone else) used the application. Because workspace arrangement is such a personal preference, we tell you what panels you need to use, but we don't tell you where to place them.

Note:

Our screenshots show the Macintosh OS using the Application frame.

The name you defined appears in the document tab.

This is the artboard edge.

The artboard area is white.

The area outside the artboard is gray.

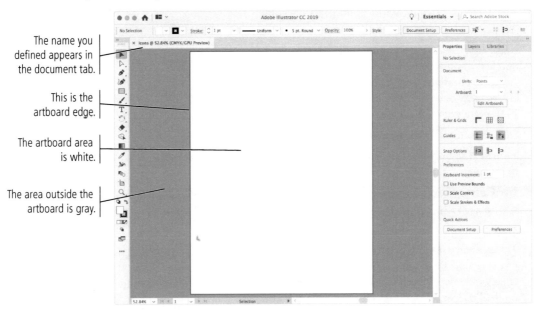

10. **Choose File>Save As and navigate to your WIP>Camping folder.**

    If you assign a name in the New Document dialog box (as you did in Step 5), that name becomes the default file name in the Save As dialog box.

    The dialog box defaults to Adobe Illustrator (.ai) format, and the extension is automatically added to the name you defined.

Note:

Feel free to work with whatever workspace settings you are most comfortable using as you complete the projects in this book.

Note:

Press Command/Control-S to save a document, or press Command/Control-Shift-S to open the Save As dialog box.

11. **Click Save in the Save As dialog box. Review the options in the resulting Illustrator Options dialog box.**

This dialog box determines what is stored in the resulting file. The default options are adequate for most files.

- Use the **Version** menu to save files to be compatible with earlier versions of the software. (Keep in mind that many features are not supported by earlier versions; if you save a file for an earlier version, some file information will probably be lost.)

- **Subset Fonts when Percent of Characters Used Is Less Than** determines when to embed an entire font instead of just the characters that are used in the file. Embedding the entire font can significantly increase file size.

- Make sure **Create PDF Compatible File** is checked if you want to use the file with other Adobe applications (such as placing it into an InDesign layout). This does not create a separate PDF file; it simply includes PDF preview data in the file.

- **Include Linked Files** embeds files that are linked to the artwork.

- **Embed ICC Profiles** stores color information inside the file for use in a color-managed workflow.

- **Use Compression** compresses PDF data in the Illustrator file.

- **Save Each Artboard to a Separate File** saves each artboard as a separate file; a separate master file with all artboards is also created.

- **Transparency** options determine what happens to transparent objects when you save a file for Illustrator 9.0 or earlier. Preserve Paths discards transparency effects and resets transparent artwork to 100% opacity and Normal blending mode. Preserve Appearance and Overprints preserves overprints that don't interact with transparent objects; overprints that interact with transparent objects are flattened.

12. **Click OK to save the file, and then continue to the next exercise.**

Define Smart Guide Preferences

Adobe Illustrator provides many tools to help you create precise lines and shapes. **Smart Guides** are dynamic snap-to guides that help you create, align, and transform objects. Smart Guides also show you when the cursor is at a precise angle relative to the original position of the object or point you're moving. In this exercise, you will make sure the correct Smart Guides are active.

1. **With icons.ai open, make sure the Control panel is visible (Window>Control).**

2. **Click the Preferences button in the Control panel or Properties panel.**

   When nothing is selected in the file, you can access the Preferences dialog box directly from either panel. If something is selected in the file, you have to choose from the Illustrator>Preferences (Macintosh) or Edit>Preferences (Windows) submenu.

3. **Choose Smart Guides in the list of categories on the left.**

4. **In the Display section, check all but the Construction Guides option.**

   The Display options determine what is visible when Smart Guides are active:

   - When **Alignment Guides** is active, Smart Guides show when a new or moved object aligns to the center or edge of a nearby object.

   - When **Object Highlighting** is active, moving the mouse over any part of an unselected object shows the anchors and paths that make up that object.

   - When **Transform Tools** is active, Smart Guides display when you scale, rotate, or shear objects.

   - When **Anchor/Path Labels** is active, Smart Guides include labels that show the type of element (path or anchor) under the cursor.

   - When **Measurement Labels** is active, Smart Guides show the distance and angle of movement.

   - When **Construction Guides** is active, Smart Guides appear when you move objects in the file at or near defined angles (0°, 45°, 90°, and 135° are the default angles). A number of common angle options are built into the related menu, or you can type up to six specific angles in the available fields.

5. **Click OK to close the Preferences dialog box.**

6. **Choose View>Smart Guides to make sure that option is toggled on (checked).**

   If the option is already checked, simply move your mouse away from the menu and click to dismiss the menu without changing the active option.

7. **Continue to the next exercise.**

Draw Rounded Rectangles

Illustrator includes a number of tools that make it easy to create basic shapes — rectangles (or squares), ellipses (or circles), and so on.

Using any of the basic shape tools, you can click and drag with the tool cursor to create a shape of any size. Pressing Shift while dragging constrains the shape to equal height and width — for example, an exact square or circle. Pressing Option/Alt while you drag creates the shape so that the center appears where you first click. In the images to the right, the red dot identifies where we first clicked to create the new shape; the yellow circle identifies the current location of the cursor.

You can also single-click using a basic shape tool to open a dialog box, where you can define settings specific to the shape. In this case, the top-left corner of the new shape will be positioned at the place where you click.

In this exercise, you are going to draw a set of simple rectangles with rounded corners to contain the icon artwork that you create throughout this project. We introduce you to a number of techniques for creating these shapes so you can be better aware of the options as you continue your professional career using Illustrator.

Click and drag

Shift-click and drag

Option/Alt-click and drag

1. **With icons.ai open, choose Window>Toolbars>Advanced.**

   This command shows the entire Illustrator toolset, including all nested variations. Throughout this book, we assume you are using the Advanced Tools panel.

2. **Click the Rectangle tool in the Tools panel and hold down the mouse button until the nested tools appear. Choose the Rounded Rectangle tool from the list of nested tools.**

   When you choose a nested tool, that variation becomes the default option in the Tools panel. You don't need to access the nested menu to select the Rounded Rectangle tool again as long as the application remains open.

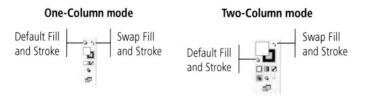

3. **Click the Default Fill and Stroke button at the bottom of the Tools panel.**

   In Illustrator, the default fill is white and the default stroke is 1-pt black. The button appears in a slightly different location depending on whether your Tools panel is in one- or two-column mode.

One-Column mode	Two-Column mode
Default Fill and Stroke — Swap Fill and Stroke	Default Fill and Stroke — Swap Fill and Stroke

Note:

You can also press D to restore the default fill and stroke colors.

4. **With the Rounded Rectangle tool active, click anywhere on the artboard.**

   In the case of the Rounded Rectangle tool, you can define the size of the shape you want to create, as well as the corner radius. The default measurement system is points, which you defined when you created this file.

The Width field is highlighted when the dialog box opens.

   When the dialog box first opens, the Width field is automatically highlighted. You can simply type to replace the highlighted value.

5. Type 1.75″ in the Width field, then press Tab to move to the Height field.

Regardless of which unit of measurement you see in the dialog box, you can enter values in whatever system you prefer, as long as you remember to type the correct unit in the dialog box fields (use ″ for inches, mm for millimeters, and pt for points). Illustrator automatically translates one unit of measurement to another.

When you move to the next field, Illustrator calculates the conversion of 1.75 inches (the value you typed in the Width field) to 126 pt (the value that automatically appears in the Width field after you move to the Height field).

The value in inches is converted to the default measurement (points).

Pressing Tab automatically highlights the next field value.

6. Type 1.75″ in the Height field.

Because you are making a shape with the same height and width, you could also click the Constrain icon (the broken chain) on the right side of the dialog box to make the Height field match the modified Width field.

7. Make sure the corner radius field is set to 12 pt.

A rounded-corner rectangle is simply a rectangle with the corners cut at a specific distance from the end (the corner radius). The two sides are connected with one-fourth of a circle, which has a radius equal to the amount of the rounding.

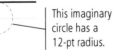

This imaginary circle has a 12-pt radius.

8. Click OK to create the new shape.

A shape appears on the artboard with its top-left corner exactly where you clicked with the Rounded Rectangle tool. (If you Option/Alt-click with any of the shape tools, the place where you click becomes the center of the new shape.)

9. Zoom in so you can clearly see the entire rectangle.

As a general rule, we don't tell you what view percentage to use unless we want to highlight a specific issue. As you work through the projects in this book, we encourage you to zoom in and out as necessary to meet your specific needs.

10. Click the Selection tool (the black arrow) at the top of the Tools panel. If the rounded rectangle is not already selected, click to select the shape.

The Selection tool is used to select entire objects.

When the object is selected, the rectangular **bounding box** marks the outermost edges of the shape. **Bounding-box handles** mark the corners and exact horizontal and vertical center of the shape. (If you don't see the bounding box, choose View>Show Bounding Box.) Because this shape has rounded corners, the corner bounding-box handles actually appear outside the shape edges.

Four small circles inside each corner of the shape are Live Corner widgets, which allow you to click and drag to change the shape of object corners.

Note:

You can choose View>Hide Corner Widget to toggle the visibility of live corner widgets, or use the Show/Hide Shape Widgets button in the Control panel when a rectangle or polygon live shape is selected.

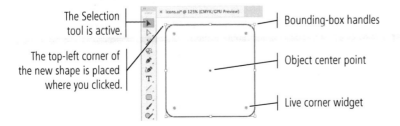

The Selection tool is active.

The top-left corner of the new shape is placed where you clicked.

Bounding-box handles

Object center point

Live corner widget

11. **Click the Rounded Rectangle tool in the Tools panel and hold down the mouse button until the nested tools appear. Choose the Rectangle tool from the list of nested tools.**

12. **Move the cursor to the right of the top edge of the existing shape. When you see a guide line connected to the top edge of the first shape, click, hold down the mouse button, and drag down and right.**

The line is a function of the Smart Guides feature, which provides instant feedback while you draw.

13. **When cursor feedbacks show both Width and Height values of 126 pt, release the mouse button to create the second shape.**

As you drag, cursor feedback shows the size of the new shape. Smart Guides identify when the new shape's bottom edge aligns with the bottom of the previous shape. The diagonal guide identifies when the shape has equal height and width, making it easy to draw a perfect square. (You can also press Shift while dragging to create a shape with equal height and width.)

Note:

If you do something wrong, or aren't happy with your results, press Command/Control-Z to undo the last action you took.

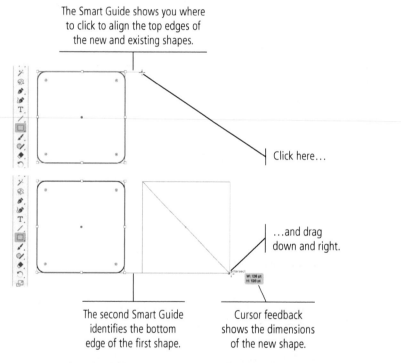

The Smart Guide shows you where to click to align the top edges of the new and existing shapes.

Click here…

…and drag down and right.

The second Smart Guide identifies the bottom edge of the first shape.

Cursor feedback shows the dimensions of the new shape.

Because you are using the Rectangle tool instead of the Rounded Rectangle tool, the second shape does not have rounded corners; the bounding-box handles match the actual shape corners.

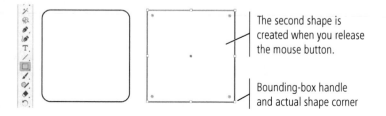

The second shape is created when you release the mouse button.

Bounding-box handle and actual shape corner

14. Click one of the Live Corner widgets and drag toward the center of the shape. When cursor feedback shows a corner radius of approximately 12 pt, release the mouse button.

The Live Corner widgets allow you to manually adjust the corner radius for all corners on the selected shape. Dragging in toward the shape center increases the corner radius; dragging out toward the corner decreases the corner radius.

Dragging the Live Corner widget affects the shape of all selected corners.

Cursor feedback shows the corner radius as you drag.

Because the entire object is selected, dragging any of the widgets applies the same change to all corners on the shape. To change only certain corners, you can use the Direct Selection tool to select the corner points you want to affect before dragging a Live Corner widget.

More about Working with Live Corners

If a shape is an actual rectangle (with all 90° corners), the Live Corner widgets appear whenever the shape is selected with either Selection tool. For any other shape, including a four-cornered polygon with different-angled corners, the widgets appear only when the shape is selected with the Direct Selection tool.

Select the shape with the Direct Selection tool to access the Live Corner widgets.

Click inside the shape to select the entire object (and all shape corners).

Click specific corner points to select only those corners.

If the entire object is selected, dragging any one Live Corner widget affects all corners on the same shape (below left). If you want to affect only specific corners, you can select those points first, and then drag any of the visible widgets to change only the selected corners (below right).

Option/Alt-clicking a Live Corner widget toggles through the available corner shapes — round, inverted round, and chamfer/beveled. Again, only selected corners are affected by the shape change.

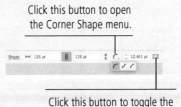

Round   Inverted Round   Chamfer

If you have a wide enough application frame, you can also use the Corner Shape button in the Control panel to change the corner shapes.

Click this button to open the Corner Shape menu.

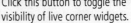

Click this button to toggle the visibility of live corner widgets.

15. **With the adjusted shape still selected, open the Transform panel (Window>Transform).**

    When a rectangle is selected, the Transform panel shows the corner radius of all four corners on the shape. If you find it difficult to achieve an exact radius by dragging, you can always use these fields to adjust the corner radius to specific values.

16. **Make sure the Constrain icon between the Corner Radius fields is active (highlighted). Highlight any of the Corner Radius fields and type 12. Press Return/Enter to finalize the change.**

    Because you are using the default unit of measurement (points), you don't need to type the unit.

    Corner radius fields are only available in the Transform panel if the shape is a rectangle (with four 90° corner angles).

    Corner Radius fields can also be accessed by clicking the Shape hot-text link in the Control panel, or by clicking the More Options button in the Transform section of the Properties panel.

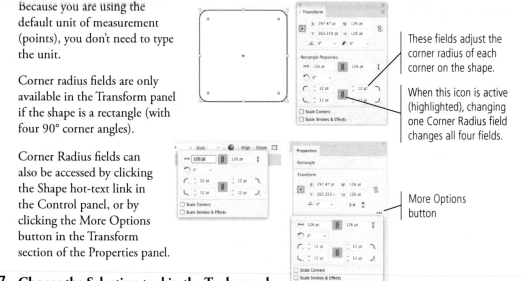

These fields adjust the corner radius of each corner on the shape.

When this icon is active (highlighted), changing one Corner Radius field changes all four fields.

More Options button

17. **Choose the Selection tool in the Tools panel.**

18. **Using the Selection tool, press Option/Alt, then click the second shape and drag right.**

    When you drag an object with the Selection tool, you move it to another location. If you press Option/Alt while dragging, you clone (make a copy of) the original object and move the clone.

    Again, Smart Guides make it easy to align objects. You can see the horizontal guide connecting the center of the original object to the center of the one you are cloning. Smart Guides also identify distances between objects, so you can place multiple objects at the same distances from one to the next. (Don't worry about the exact spaces between the objects; you will define precise object spacing in a later exercise.)

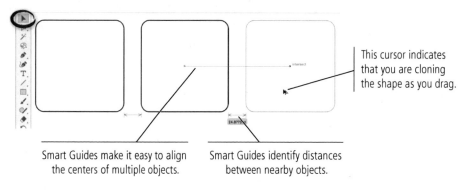

This cursor indicates that you are cloning the shape as you drag.

Smart Guides make it easy to align the centers of multiple objects.

Smart Guides identify distances between nearby objects.

19. **Save the file and continue to the next exercise.**

Understanding Selection Basics

Most Illustrator objects (including shapes like rounded-corner rectangles) contain two basic building blocks: anchor points and paths. You don't need to worry about the geometric specifics of vectors because Illustrator manages them for you — but you do need to understand the basic concept of how Illustrator works with anchor points and paths. You should also understand how to access those building blocks so you can do more than create basic shapes.

Path (line) segment

Curve handle controls the shape of the path

Anchor point

If you select an object with the **Selection tool** (the black arrow), you can see the bounding box that identifies the outermost dimensions of the shape. Bounding-box handles, which you can use to resize the shape, appear at the edges of the bounding box. (Press Command/Control-Shift-B to show or hide the bounding box of selected objects.)

When you select an object with the **Direct Selection tool** (the white arrow), you can see the anchor points and paths that make up the selected object. As you work with Illustrator, keep this distinction in mind: use the Selection tool to select an entire object; use the Direct Selection tool to edit the points and paths of an object.

Selection tool

Click any part of an object to select the entire object.

Bounding-box handles mark the outer dimensions of the selection.

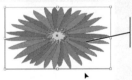

Click any part of a group to select the entire group.

Direct Selection tool

Click to select a specific line segment or point on a shape.

Click an object's fill to select the entire object, even if it is part of a group.

Clicking and dragging to draw a marquee with the Selection tool…

…selects any object touched by the marquee.

Clicking and dragging to draw a marquee with the Direct Selection tool…

…selects only points within the marquee.

Control Fill and Stroke Attributes

At the beginning of the previous exercise, you clicked the Default Fill and Stroke button in the Tools panel to apply a white fill and 1-pt black stroke to the objects you created. Obviously, most artwork requires more than these basic attributes.

As you complete the projects in this book, you will learn about styles, patterns, gradients, effects, and other attributes that can take an illustration from flat to fabulous. In this exercise, you learn about a number of options for changing the basic fill, stroke, and color attributes for objects on the page.

1. **With icons.ai open, choose the Selection tool in the Tools panel. Click the left rectangle on the artboard to select it.**

2. **Choose View>Hide Corner Widget.**

   These widgets can be distracting, so it's useful to turn them off when they are no longer needed.

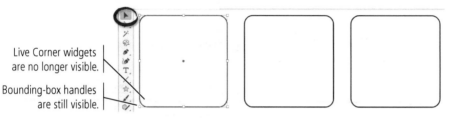

Live Corner widgets are no longer visible.

Bounding-box handles are still visible.

3. **Choose Window>Swatches to open the Swatches panel. If the panel is docked, float it away from the dock.**

   If the panel shows a list of items including the color names, open the Swatches panel Options menu and choose Small Thumbnail View.

Click here to open the panel Options menu.

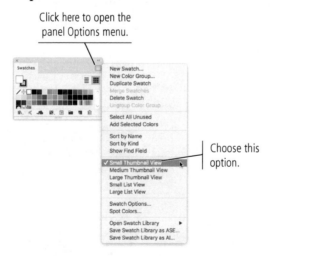

Choose this option.

Note:

Remember, panels can always be accessed in the Window menu.

The Swatches panel includes a number of predefined and saved colors, which you can use to change the color of the fill and stroke of an object. You can also save custom swatches to more efficiently apply specific colors as you create artwork.

4. At the top of the Swatches panel, click the Stroke icon to bring it to the front of the stack.

The fill and stroke icons in the Swatches panel are used to determine which attribute is active — in other words, which would be changed by clicking a swatch in the Swatches panel. Clicking one of these buttons brings it to the front of the stack, making it active, so you can change the color of that attribute.

You can also use the same icons at the bottom of the Tools panel to change the active attribute.

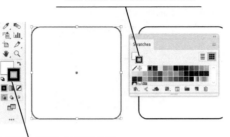

Click an icon to bring it to the top and make that attribute active.

The same options are available in the Tools panel.

Note:

You can press the X key to switch the active attribute between Stroke and Fill.

5. In the Swatches panel, click the light brown swatch in the third row.

Because the Stroke icon is active in the Tools panel, the color of the selected object's stroke (border) changes to light brown.

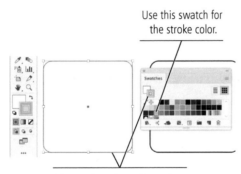

Use this swatch for the stroke color.

The top icon determines what attribute will be changed when you click a swatch in the panel.

Note:

It is very easy to forget to check which icon (fill or stroke) is on top of the stack. If you forget and accidentally change the color of the wrong attribute, simply undo the change (press Command/Control-Z), and then bring the correct attribute to the front before changing colors.

6. In the Tools or Swatches panel, click the Fill icon to bring it to the front of the stack. In the Swatches panel, click the black swatch in the first row.

Because the Fill icon is the active attribute, clicking the black color swatch changes the fill color of the selected object.

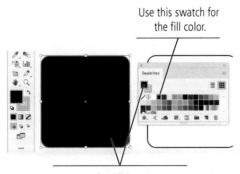

Use this swatch for the fill color.

Because the Fill icon is on top, clicking a swatch changes the object's fill color.

7. **With the rounded rectangle selected, change the Stroke Weight field in the Control panel to 3 pt. Press Return/Enter to apply the change.**

The Stroke icon in the Tools panel does not need to be active to change the stroke weight. The Tools panel icons relate only to color changes made with the stand-alone Swatches or Color panels.

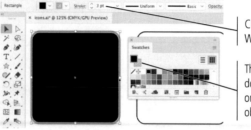

Change the Stroke Weight field to 3 pt.

The Stroke icon doesn't need to be on top to change an object's stroke weight.

8. **With the rectangle still selected, click the Swap Fill and Stroke button in the Tools panel.**

This button makes it easy to reverse the fill and stroke colors of an object; the stroke weight remains unaffected when you swap the colors.

Swap Fill and Stroke button

Note:

You can press Shift-X to swap the active Stroke and Fill colors.

9. **Using the Selection tool, click the second rectangle on the artboard.**

The Fill and Stroke icons change to reflect the colors of the selected objects.

Click these swatches to open a pop-up Swatches panel.

Note:

Fill Color, Stroke Color, and Stroke Weight fields are also available in the Control panel.

10. **In the Appearance section of the Properties panel, change the Stroke Weight value to 3 pt.**

11. **Click the Fill color swatch to open the pop-up Swatches panel. Choose the light brown swatch in the third row to change the fill color for the selected object.**

When an object is selected with the Selection tool, the Properties panel provides quick access to the stroke and fill colors for the selected object; you don't need to worry about which icon is active in the Tools panel.

Clicking the Fill color swatch opens an attached Swatches panel so you can change the fill for the selected object without opening the separate Swatches panel.

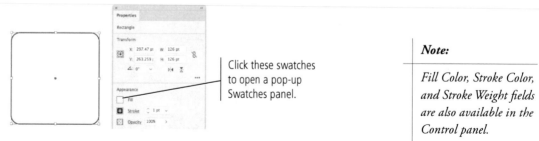

12. **Using the Selection tool, click the third rectangle on the artboard.**

Again, the Fill and Stroke icons in the Tools panel change to reflect the colors of the selected object.

13. **Select the Eyedropper tool in the Tools panel, and then click the first or second rectangle on the artboard.**

The Eyedropper tool copies fill and stroke attributes from one object (the one you click) to another (the one you first selected).

Note:

You can double-click the Eyedropper tool in the Tools panel to define which attributes are picked up and applied by clicking with the tool.

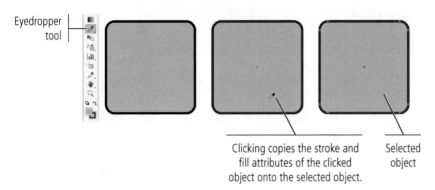

Eyedropper tool

Clicking copies the stroke and fill attributes of the clicked object onto the selected object.

Selected object

14. **Press and hold the Command/Control key, and click anywhere on the artboard away from the three rectangles.**

Pressing Command/Control temporarily switches to the last-used Selection tool (Selection or Direct Selection). By clicking on the empty artboard area while holding down the modifier key, you can quickly deselect the selected object(s). When you release the Command/Control key, the tool reverts to the one you last used — in this case, the Eyedropper tool.

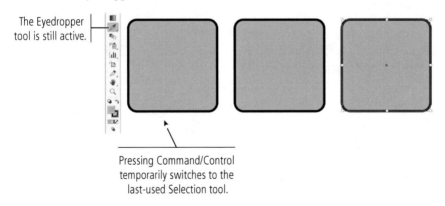

The Eyedropper tool is still active.

Pressing Command/Control temporarily switches to the last-used Selection tool.

15. **Release the Command/Control key.**

16. **Choose the Rounded Rectangle tool in the Tools panel.**

17. **To the right of the third shape on the artboard, draw a fourth rounded rectangle that is 126 pt square.**

The Fill and Stroke swatches remember the last-used options, so the new rectangle has the same heavy black stroke and brown fill as the others. Don't worry if your shapes aren't entirely on the artboard; you will define their precise positions in the next exercise.

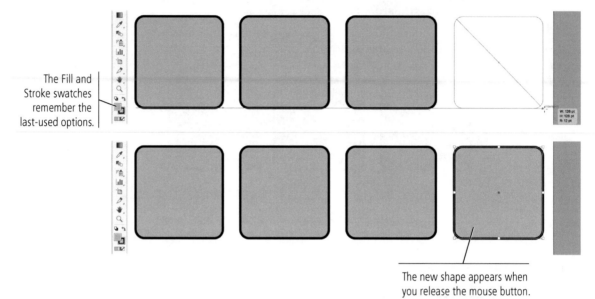

The Fill and Stroke swatches remember the last-used options.

The new shape appears when you release the mouse button.

18. **Save the file (File>Save or Command/Control-S) and continue to the next exercise.**

Control Object Positioning

The ability to move objects around on the artboard is one of the advantages of digital drawing. On paper, you have to manually erase items and then redraw them in their new locations. Illustrator offers a number of tools that make it easy to move objects around the artboard, either as isolated objects or in relation to other elements on the page. In this exercise, you learn several techniques for moving objects on the artboard.

1. **With icons.ai open, change your zoom percentage so you can see all four shapes and the entire top of the artboard.**

2. **Choose View>Rulers>Show Rulers to show the rulers at the top and left edges of the document window.**

Because you created this file using points as the default unit of measurement, the rulers — and fields in dialog boxes and panels — show measurements in points.

Note:

The Change to Global Rulers option is only relevant when you work with multiple artboards.

3. **Control/right-click the top ruler and choose Inches from the contextual menu.**

Rulers on the top and left edges show measurements in the default units of measurement.

4. **Choose the Selection tool at the top of the Tools panel, then click the left rectangle on the artboard to select it.**

5. **In the Properties panel, review the Transform options for the active selection.**

Transform options in the Properties panel are the same as those that are available in the stand-alone Transform panel (Window>Transform).

Note:

If you have a wide monitor, the reference point proxy and the X, Y, W, and H fields are available directly in the Control panel.

If you have a smaller application frame, the Control panel includes a hot-text link to a pop-up Transform panel.

The **reference points** correspond to the bounding box handles of the selected object. The selected square in this icon identifies which point of the object is being measured.

Reference point
around which numeric
transformations are based

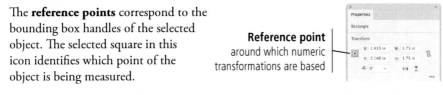

If you use the W or H fields to resize an object, you can constrain the object's height-to-width aspect ratio by clicking the chain icon (to the right of the W and H fields in the Transform panel, or between the W and H fields in the Control panel).

In Illustrator, the default **zero point** (the source of measurements) is the top-left corner of the artboard; the X and Y positions of an object are measured relative to that location. The X axis is the horizontal value and the Y axis is the vertical value. You can change the zero point by clicking where the horizontal and vertical rulers meet, and dragging to a new position; if you do reposition the zero point, you can double-click the intersection of the rulers to restore the default zero point.

Keep these ideas in mind when you move something in an Illustrator file:

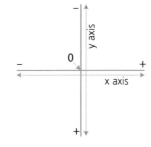

- Moving up requires subtracting from the Y value.
- Moving down requires adding to the Y value.
- Moving left requires subtracting from the X value.
- Moving right requires adding to the X value.

6. **Click the top-left reference point to select it.**

The X and Y fields now show the exact position of the top-left bounding box handle for the selected object.

7. **Highlight the X field and type .25. Press Return/Enter to apply the change.**

You don't need to type the measurement unit (″) or the preceding zero (0). Because the rulers are showing inches, Illustrator automatically applies inches as the unit of value.

The top-left reference
point is selected.

Measurements
correspond to this point
of the selected shape.

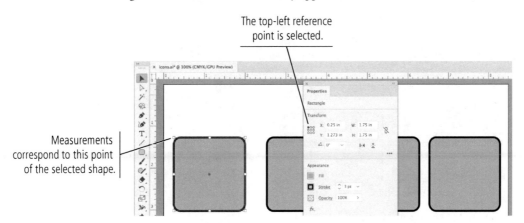

8. **Highlight the Y field and type .25. Press Return/Enter to apply the change.**

The top-left handle of the selected object is now 1/4″ from the top and left edges. The numbers you typed correspond to the measurements you see on the rulers.

Rulers show that the selected point of the object is at the position you just defined.

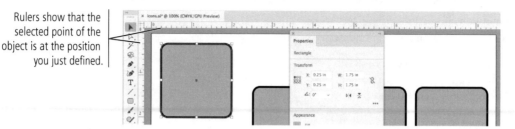

9. **Using the Selection tool, click the second rectangle and drag until a guide line appears, connecting the center points of the first and second shapes.**

As you drag, the cursor feedback shows the relative position of the object. In other words, you can see the change (<u>difference</u>) in the object's position, both horizontally (<u>X</u>) and vertically (<u>Y</u>) — hence the "dX" and "dY" values.

As we explained previously, Smart Guides can be very useful for aligning objects on the artboard. Illustrator identifies and highlights relative alignment as you drag, and snaps objects to those alignment points.

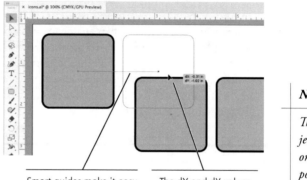

Smart guides make it easy to align multiple objects.

The dX and dY values show the changes to the object's X and Y values.

Note:

The X position is an object's horizontal position on the artboard; the Y position is the object's vertical position.

10. **Release the mouse button while the center Smart Guide is visible.**

If you don't see the alignment guides as you drag, make sure that option is checked in the Smart Guides preferences.

11. **Click the fourth shape on the page. Select the top-right reference point, type 8.25 in the X field, and type .25 in the Y field.**

Because you changed the reference point, you defined the X/Y position for the top-right bounding-box handle of the fourth rectangle.

Note:

When a field value is highlighted in a panel or dialog box, you can use the Up Arrow and Down Arrow keys to increase or decrease (respectively) the highlighted value.

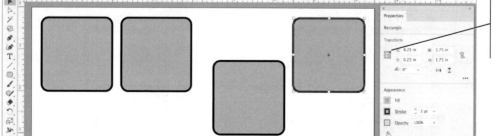

The top-right reference point means the X and Y values refer to the top-right corner of the selected shape.

12. **Save the file and continue to the next exercise.**

As you have already seen, there is almost always more than one way to accomplish a specific task. Although Smart Guides make alignment very easy, the Align panel is useful for certain functions that are not enabled by Smart Guides. You can use the Align panel to align multiple objects relative to one another within a selection, to a specific object in the selection, or to the active artboard.

The **Align Object options** are fairly self explanatory; when multiple objects are selected, the objects align based on the edge(s) or center(s) you click. Icons on the various buttons indicate the function of each.

- Align Left Edges
- Align Horizontal Centers
- Align Right Edges
- Align Top Edges
- Align Vertical Centers
- Align Bottom Edges

You can use the Align To menu to determine how selected objects will align. If you don't see the Align To menu, open the panel Options menu and choose Show Options.

Align To:

✓ Align to Selection
Align to Key Object
Align to Artboard

The **Align To Selection** option aligns selected objects to one another based on the outermost edge of the entire selection. In other words, aligning the top edges moves all objects to the same Y position as the highest selected object.

If you use the **Key Object** option, you can click any object in the selection to designate it as the key. (The key object shows a heavier border than other objects in the selection.)

Because you can align objects relative to the document, the align buttons are also available when only one object is selected, allowing you to align any single object to a precise location on the page or spread.

By default, Align options apply based on the outermost edge of the active selection. In the following image, dashed lines indicate the original top edges of the objects:

Using the **Align To Key Object** option, the middle image was selected as the key. The Align options apply to the edges of the defined key object:

The **Distribute Objects options** enable you to control the positions of multiple objects relative to each other. By default, objects are equally distributed within the dimensions of the overall selection.

- Distribute Top Edges
- Distribute Vertical Centers
- Distribute Bottom Edges
- Distribute Left Edges
- Distribute Horizontal Centers
- Distribute Right Edges

The following images show the original placement, followed by the result of applying the Distribute Vertical Centers and Distribute Horizontal Centers options to evenly space the three fish.

You can use the Distribute Spacing option to align objects to one another by a specific amount based on the selected key object. To access the measurement field for these options, you must first click one of the selected objects to define the key. You can then type a value in the field, then click the Horizontal or Vertical options (or both, as we did in the following image):

If you don't see the Distribute Spacing options, open the panel Options menu and choose Show Options.

Align and Distribute Objects

In addition to dragging objects around the artboard, the Illustrator Align panel makes it very easy to align and distribute selected objects relative to one another, to a specific key object in the file, or to the overall artboard. In this exercise, you learn how to use the Align panel to align shapes.

Note:

When multiple objects are selected, you can access the basic Align options in the Properties panel. Click the More Options button to access the full pop-up panel.

More Options

1. **With icons.ai open, click and drag with the Selection tool to draw a marquee that touches some part of all four objects on the artboard.**

   The Selection tool selects objects, so the selection marquee only needs to touch the objects you want to select. The marquee doesn't need to surround the objects entirely.

   Start at the outside of the existing shapes to avoid moving them.

   Selection marquee

   The bounding box shows the outer edges of the entire selection (the four shapes collectively).

2. **Open the Align panel (Window>Align) and click the Vertical Align Top button.**

   By default, alignment and distribution functions occur relative to the selected objects. In other words, when you click the Vertical Align Top button, Illustrator determines the topmost edge of the selected objects, and then moves the top edges of all other selected objects to that position.

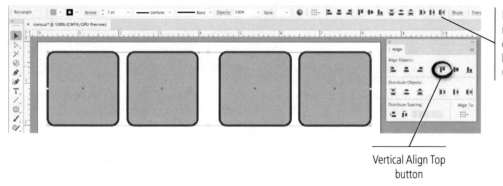

   Depending on your monitor width, Align options might also be available in the Control panel.

   Vertical Align Top button

3. **With all four objects selected, click the Horizontal Distribute Center button.**

   By default, the distribution functions create equal distance between the selected point of the selected objects. In this case, Illustrator distributes the center points along the horizontal axis by determining the center positions of the outermost selected objects, and then moving the middle two objects to create equal distance between the centers of all four selected objects; the positions of the two outer objects remain unchanged.

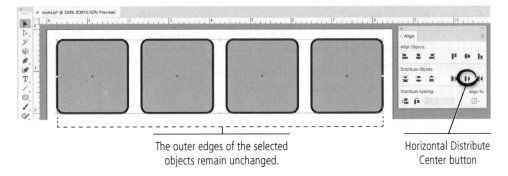

The outer edges of the selected
objects remain unchanged.

Horizontal Distribute
Center button

4. **Click inside any of the selected objects. While still holding down the mouse button, press Option/Alt and drag down.**

5. **Use the Smart Guides and cursor feedback to drag exactly vertical (the dX value should be 0). When the dY value in the cursor feedback is 2 in, release the mouse button.**

   Remember, pressing Option/Alt while you drag clones the original selection.

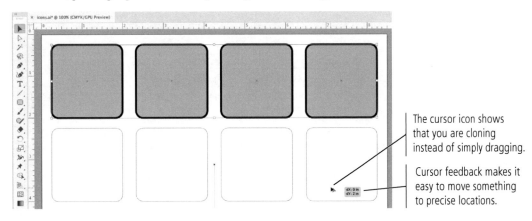

The cursor icon shows
that you are cloning
instead of simply dragging.

Cursor feedback makes it
easy to move something
to precise locations.

6. **Click anywhere outside the selected shapes to deselect all objects.**

7. **Save the file and continue to the next exercise.**

Import Template Images

Many Illustrator projects require you to start with something that has already been captured — a sketch, for example, or low-resolution image (which is the case in this project). In this exercise you will place files to use as templates for your new artwork.

1. **With icons.ai open, choose File>Place. Navigate to your WIP>Camping folder and click picnic.jpg to select that file.**

2. **Macintosh users: If you don't see a series of check boxes across the bottom of the dialog box, click the Options button.**

   The dialog box button remembers the last-used state, so the actual options might already be visible. We do not repeat the instruction to click the Options button whenever you place a file throughout the projects in this book.

3. **At the bottom of the Place dialog box, check the Link and Template options.**

   When you check the Link option, the placed file does not become a part of the actual file where you're working; for the file to output properly, Illustrator must be able to locate the linked file in the same location (hard drive, flash drive, etc.) as when you placed it. If the Link option is *not* checked, the placed file is **embedded** — it becomes part of the file where it's placed; the original external file is not necessary for the artwork to output properly.

   In the case of this project, you are going to delete the template images after you create the artwork; it doesn't matter if the images are embedded.

   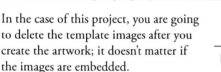

   Macintosh users: Click the Options button to reveal the actual options.

   Make sure this option is checked.

4. **Click Place.**

   When you place an object into Illustrator as a Template, it is automatically centered in the current document window. In our example, you can see that the placed image is mostly hidden by the background shapes; regardless of where your template images appear, you will correct this issue in the next exercise.

   The Control panel shows information about the placed image.

   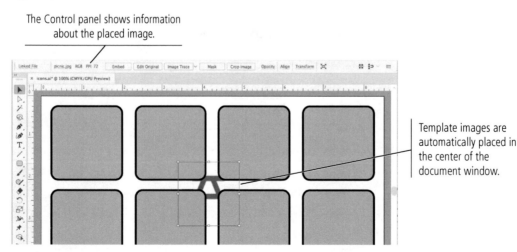

   Template images are automatically placed in the center of the document window.

5. **Choose File>Place a second time. Select hiking.jpg in the list, check the Template option, and click Place.**

   The Place dialog box remembers the last-used location, so you don't have to re-navigate to the Camping folder. The Link option also remembers the last-used settings. The Template option, however, always defaults to off, so you have to manually check this box for each template object.

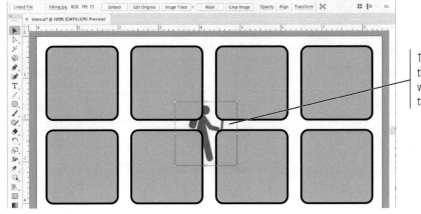

This image is also placed in the center of the document window, directly on top of the first placed image.

6. **Repeat Step 5 to place campfire.jpg and tents.jpg into your file as template images.**

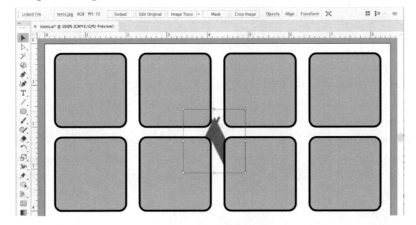

Note:

If you change the view percentage or scroll the document in the window before placing the second image, the second file will not be centered over the first. Instead, it will be centered in the document window based on the current view.

7. **Click an empty area of the artboard to deselect the last-placed template image.**

8. **Save the file and continue to the next exercise.**

Manage Multiple Layers

When you create artwork in Illustrator, you almost always end up with more than one object on the artboard. In many cases, a completed file has dozens or hundreds of objects, arranged in specific order on top of one another. As files become more and more complex, it can be difficult to find and work with exactly the pieces you need. Illustrator layers are one of the most powerful tools available for solving this problem.

1. **In the open icons.ai file, open the Layers panel.**

   By default, all files have a single layer, named Layer 1.

   When you place an object as a template, it's added to the file on a separate, non-printing layer that is partially grayed, making it easier to work with. Below Layer 1, your file has four additional layers — the template layers. Template layers are locked by default, which means you can't select or modify objects on those layers.

Note:

If you don't see all four locked template layers, you forgot to check the Template option when you placed one of the images. You can select and delete the placed file from the artboard, and then replace the necessary image as a template.

   Click in this column to show or hide a layer.

   Click in this column to lock or unlock a layer.

   Double-click the layer thumbnail to open the Layer Options dialog box.

   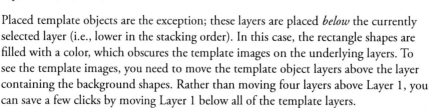

2. **In the Layers panel, click the Layer 1 name and drag it below all four template layers in the stack.**

   The top-to-bottom position of objects or layers is called the **stacking order**. Objects and layers typically appear in the stack based on the order in which they are created — the first-created is at the bottom, the last-created is at the top, and so on, in between.

   Click and drag a layer to move it in the stacking order.

   Placed template objects are the exception; these layers are placed *below* the currently selected layer (i.e., lower in the stacking order). In this case, the rectangle shapes are filled with a color, which obscures the template images on the underlying layers. To see the template images, you need to move the template object layers above the layer containing the background shapes. Rather than moving four layers above Layer 1, you can save a few clicks by moving Layer 1 below all of the template layers.

   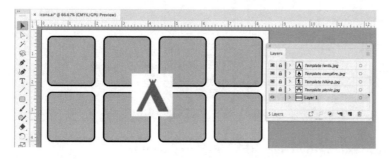

Note:

For a template layer, the Visibility icon is a small square instead of an eye.

3. **In the Layers panel, click the Lock icon for the Template picnic.jpg layer to unlock that layer.**

   Because you need to move the placed template object into the correct position, you first need to unlock the layer where that object resides.

   Click here to unlock the template layer.

4. **Using the Selection tool, click the top-left rounded rectangle to select it.**

5. **With the Selection tool active, press Shift and click anywhere inside the area where the template images are placed.**

   Pressing Shift allows you to add objects to the current selection. The first rectangle and the image should both be selected. (Remember, the other three template object layers are still locked. Even though you can't see it, you can select the picnic.jpg image by clicking in the area where it is placed.)

6. **With both objects selected, click the Align To button in the Control panel.**

   The Align and Distribute options in the Control panel are the same as the options in the Align panel.

Click this button to access the Align To options.

The placed template images are stacked on top of each other in the order in which you placed them.

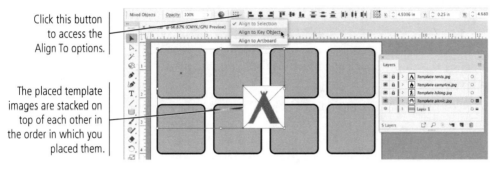

7. **Choose Align to Key Object in the menu.**

The default key object is identified with a heavy border.

8. **Click the selected rounded rectangle on the artboard.**

   Key Object alignment allows you to define where you want other objects to align. By selecting the key object, you're telling Illustrator which object to use as the basis for alignment.

Click any selected object to define the key object for the alignment.

The border colors match the defined layer colors.

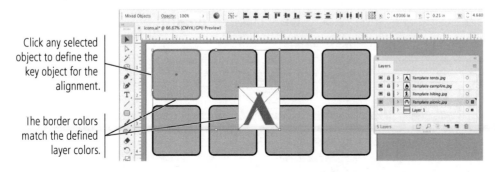

9. **Click the Horizontal Align Center and Vertical Align Center buttons in the Control panel.**

   Because you selected the rounded rectangle as the key object, the placed template image moves to the horizontal and vertical center of the rounded rectangle; the rectangle — the key object — remains in the same place.

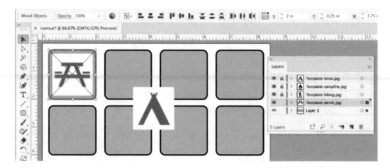

10. **In the Layers panel, click the empty space to the left of the Template picnic.jpg layer to relock that layer.**

    Now that the template object is in place, it's a good idea to lock it again so you don't accidentally move the object.

11. **Double-click the layer thumbnail of the Template picnic.jpg layer.**

    Double-clicking a layer thumbnail opens the Layer Options dialog box for that layer, where you can change a number of attributes for the selected layer.

12. **Change the Dim Images To field to 30, and then click OK to close the Layer Options dialog box.**

    Dimming the template image will make it easier to see your artwork when you draw.

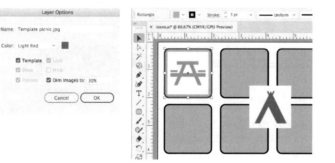

Note:

The Color menu in the Layer Options dialog box determines the color of bounding box handles and other visual indicators for objects on a layer.

13. **Repeat Steps 3–12 to position the other three template images in the first-row rectangles (as shown in the following image).**

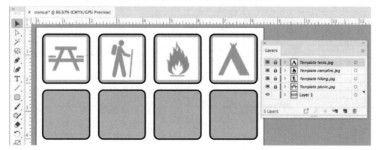

14. In the Layers panel, double-click the Layer 1 name to highlight it. Type `Backgrounds` to change the layer name, then press Return/Enter.

Whenever you have more than one working layer, it's a good idea to use names that tell you what is on each layer. Doing so prevents confusion later when you or someone else needs to change a particular item.

Double-click the layer name to highlight it.

Type a new layer name, then press Return/Enter to finalize it.

15. In the Layers panel, click the empty space immediately left of the Backgrounds layer.

This step — locking the Backgrounds layer — is simply a safeguard to avoid accidentally changing the background rectangles while you're drawing the icon artwork.

Lock the Backgrounds layer to protect the objects on that layer.

16. In the Layers panel, click the Create New Layer button.

In the next stage of the project, you will start tracing the objects in the templates. The completed icon will be a series of black icons on top of the rounded rectangles with the brown background color.

Create New Layer button

At this point, most of the brown color in the background shapes is obscured by the placed images, because the template layers are above the layer containing the rectangles. If you tried to draw the icon shapes on the existing non-template layer, you would be drawing *behind* the template — in other words, you wouldn't be able to see what you were drawing. Instead, you need a layer above the template layers, where you can create the icon artwork.

17. In the Layers panel, drag Layer 6 to the top of the layer stack.

New layers are automatically placed immediately above the selected layer. You need this new layer to be above the template layers so you can see what you're drawing.

18. Double-click the Layer 6 name in the Layers panel. Type `Icon Art` and press Return/Enter to finalize the new layer name.

19. Save the file and continue to the next stage of the project.

STAGE 2 / Drawing with Basic Shapes

A number of tools and utilities can be used to create complex Illustrator artwork. Creating the icons in this project gives you an opportunity to experiment with some of these options. As you complete the other projects in this book, you will dig deeper into complex drawing techniques.

Numerically Transform Drawing Objects

Basic shapes, such as rectangles, can be used as the basis for a wide variety of drawings. In the next two exercises, you will use basic rectangles to create the picnic table art.

1. **With icons.ai open, make sure the Icon Art layer is active, and then zoom into the picnic table template image.**

2. **Choose the Rectangle tool in the Tools panel.**

3. **With nothing selected on the artboard, change the fill color to black and the stroke color to None.**

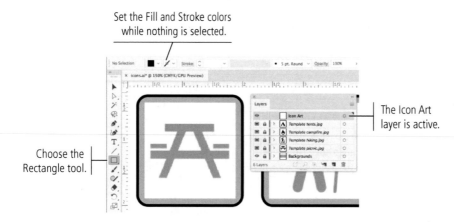

Set the Fill and Stroke colors while nothing is selected.

Choose the Rectangle tool.

The Icon Art layer is active.

4. **Click and drag to create the shape that represents the top of the picnic table.**

5. **Click and drag again to create the second horizontal shape in the artwork.**

6. **Using the Selection tool, click the top rectangle to select it.**

7. **Open the Transform panel (Window>Transform). Make a note of the H (height) field in the Transform panel.**

   We use the stand-alone Transform panel in this exercise because it eliminates the need to constantly reopen the panel using the Control panel hot-text link.

Note:

We changed the layer color of the Icon Art layer to magenta so that the visual indicators on the layer will be more visible in our printed screen captures.

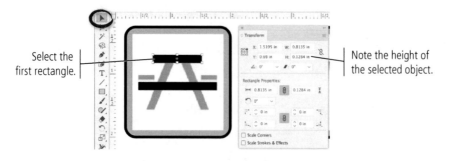

Select the first rectangle.

Note the height of the selected object.

8. Click to select the second shape (from Step 5).

9. If necessary, click the Constrain Width and Height Proportions button in the Transform panel to turn off that option.

   When this button is active, changing the height or width field makes a proportional change to the other dimension. When it is inactive, you can change one dimension of a shape without affecting the other dimension.

   | W: 1.3111 in | The Constrain option |
   | H: 0.1389 in | is turned on. |

   | W: 1.3111 in | The Constrain option |
   | H: 0.1389 in | is turned off. |

10. With the second shape selected, change the H (height) field to the same value that you noted in Step 7.

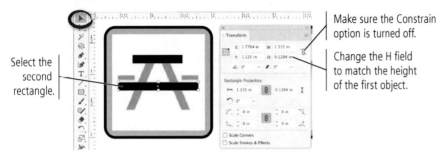

Select the second rectangle.

Make sure the Constrain option is turned off.

Change the H field to match the height of the first object.

11. Using the Rectangle tool, click and drag to create the seat shape on the left side of the template.

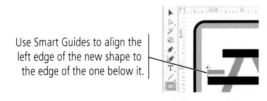

Use Smart Guides to align the left edge of the new shape to the edge of the one below it.

12. Choose the Selection tool. Press Option/Alt, then click the new shape and drag right to clone it.

13. Continue dragging until Smart Guides show the right edge of the cloned shape aligned to the right edge of the bottom rectangle (as shown here).

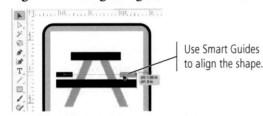

Use Smart Guides to align the shape.

14. Save the file and continue to the next exercise.

Shear and Reflect Drawing Objects

Illustrator includes four transformation options — Rotate, Reflect, Scale, and Shear. Each of these transformations can be applied either by hand, using the related tool in the Tools panel; or numerically, using either the fields in the Transform panel or the appropriate dialog box from the Object>Transform menu. In this exercise, you will use these methods to finish the picnic table artwork.

1. **With icons.ai open, choose the Rectangle tool in the Tools panel.**

2. **Draw a vertical rectangle beginning at the bottom of the artwork and ending at the bottom edge of the top horizontal shape (as shown after Step 3).**

   Illustrator recognizes certain basic shapes, including rectangles, ellipses, and lines. When one of these shapes — called Live Shapes — is selected, the lower half of the Transform panel includes properties specific to the type of shape. For a rectangle, you can change the height, width, rotation angle, and corner radius for each corner.

3. **With the Constrain option turned off, change the W field in the Transform panel to the same value you used for the height of the horizontal shapes in the previous exercise.**

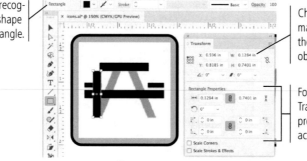

Illustrator recognizes this shape as a rectangle.

Change the W field to match the height of the longer horizontal objects.

For a Live Shape, the Transform panel includes properties specific to the active type of shape.

4. **Select the Shear tool (nested under the Scale tool) in the Tools panel.**

   When you select one of the transformation tools, an **origin point** appears by default at the center of the selected object. This origin point acts as an anchor when using the transformation tools; it is the point around which transformations occur. You can single-click anywhere to define a different origin point.

5. **Move the cursor to the bottom-right anchor point of the vertical rectangle. When you see the word "anchor" in the cursor icon, click to reposition the origin point.**

   The word "anchor" is another function of Illustrator's Smart Guides. When you move the cursor near an existing anchor point, Illustrator identifies that point so you can click exactly on the existing point.

Shear tool

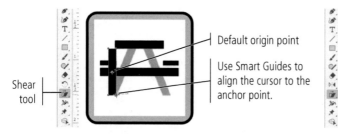

Default origin point

Use Smart Guides to align the cursor to the anchor point.

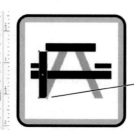

Click to relocate the origin point.

6. **Click the top edge of the selected shape and drag right until the shape matches the table leg shape in the template image.**

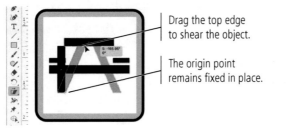

Drag the top edge to shear the object.

The origin point remains fixed in place.

After you shear a Live Shape, it is no longer recognized as the original Live Shape; the specific shape properties are no longer available in the Transform panel.

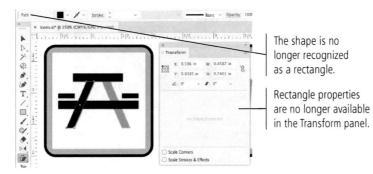

The shape is no longer recognized as a rectangle.

Rectangle properties are no longer available in the Transform panel.

Note:

The Illustrator transformation tools all use this same origin point concept as the basis for transformations. You can click without dragging to reposition the origin point before applying the transformation.

7. **Choose the Reflect tool (nested under the Rotate tool) in the Tools panel.**

8. **Double-click the Reflect tool in the Tools panel.**

    Double-clicking a transformation tool in the Tools panel opens a dialog box, where you can numerically define the transformation. (This dialog box is the same one you would see by choosing Object>Transform>Reflect.)

9. **Check the Preview option at the bottom of the dialog box.**

    When the Preview option is active, you can see the result of your choices before finalizing them.

10. **Choose the Vertical option in the Axis section.**

    Reflecting vertically flips the object around the Y axis. Reflecting horizontally flips the object around the X axis.

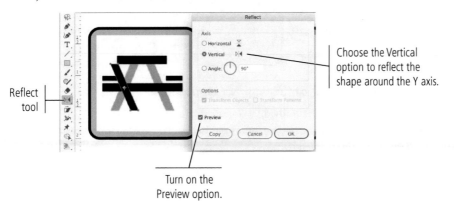

Reflect tool

Choose the Vertical option to reflect the shape around the Y axis.

Turn on the Preview option.

Note:

Transformation dialog boxes default to the last-used settings for that transformation.

11. Click Copy.

If you simply clicked OK, the original object would have been reflected. By clicking Copy, you create the second table leg shape; the original remains in place.

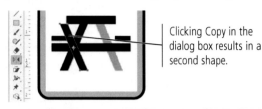

Clicking Copy in the dialog box results in a second shape.

12. Using the Selection tool, click the reflected shape and drag right. Use Smart Guides to keep the dragged shape aligned to the original.

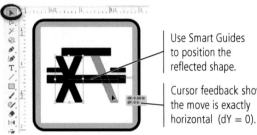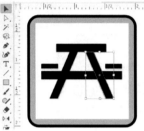

Use Smart Guides to position the reflected shape.

Cursor feedback shows the move is exactly horizontal (dY = 0).

13. Save the file and continue to the next exercise.

Manage Artwork with Groups

The artwork for this icon consists of six separate shapes (seven, if you count the background rectangle). Because these distinct objects make up one piece of artwork, you should create a group so that all pieces can be treated as a single unit.

1. With **icons.ai** open, select the Template picnic.jpg layer in the Layers panel.

2. Click the panel's Delete Selection button. When asked to confirm the deletion, click Yes.

Since the picnic table artwork is complete, you no longer need the template image.

Delete Selection button

3. In the Layers panel, click the arrow to the left of the Icon Art layer.

When you expand a layer in the panel, you can see the individual objects that exist on that layer (called **sublayers**). You drew six shapes in the previous exercise; the expanded Icon Art layer lists each of those objects separately.

Objects are listed in the order you created them; the first object you create appears at the bottom of the list and the last object appears at the top. This bottom-to-top arrangement is called **stacking order**.

4. **With the Selection tool active, choose Select>All.**

This command selects all unlocked objects in the file. Because the Backgrounds layer is locked, the rectangle behind the artwork is not selected.

Click these arrows to expand a layer.

Each separate object is listed individually.

These squares identify selected objects.

Note:

The Select>All on Artboard command selects only unlocked objects on the active artboard.

5. **With all the objects selected, choose Object>Group.**

The six individual objects are components of a single thing — the "picnic" icon. Grouping them allows all the pieces to be treated as a single object on the artboard.

Grouping allows you to treat the icon artwork as a single object.

6. **Click the arrow to the left of the Backgrounds layer to expand that layer.**

Because you locked the entire layer, all objects on that layer are also locked.

Because the parent layer is locked, all objects on that layer are also locked.

7. **Click the Lock icon for the Backgrounds layer to unlock it.**

When you unlock a layer, all objects on that layer are also unlocked.

8. **Using the Selection tool, Shift-click the brown background shape to add it to the active selection.**

If you used the Select All method, you would select all eight background shapes because the Backgrounds layer is now unlocked. Manually clicking is a better choice to select only the one you want.

Objects on multiple layers can be selected at the same time.

9. **Choose Object>Group.**

10. **In the Layers panel, click the arrow to the left of the resulting group.**

When you group objects that exist on different layers, all objects in the group are moved to the top-most layer in the selection. In this case, the background rectangle is moved from the Backgrounds layer to the group on the Icon Art layer.

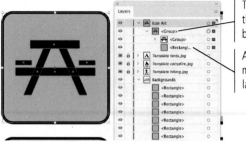

The parent group contains the icon group and the background rectangle.

All grouped objects are moved to the top-most layer in the selection.

Note:

You can choose Object>Ungroup, or press Command/Control-Shift-G, to ungroup objects in a group.

11. **Click the arrow to collapse the Backgrounds layer, and then click the empty space to the left of the Backgrounds layer to relock that layer.**

12. **With the group on the Icon Art layer selected, choose Object>Lock>Selection.**

The lock icon in the Layers panel shows that the group is locked, but the parent Icon Art layer is not. You can draw more artwork on the same layer without accidentally affecting the existing artwork.

Click this space to lock or unlock only a specific sublayer.

13. **In the Layers panel, double-click the parent <Group> name to highlight it.**

14. **Type Picnic Table, then press Return/Enter to finalize the new name.**

You can assign specific names to sublayers, just as you do to regular layers. Meaningful names for each group will make it easier to manage the various icons if you need to make changes at a later date.

15. **Click the arrows to collapse the Picnic Table sublayer and the Icon Art layer.**

16. **Save the file and continue to the next exercise.**

Using the Group Selection Tool

You can create more than one level of group, called **nesting**, by selecting an existing group, and then grouping it with other objects or groups. You can use the **Group Selection tool** to help navigate complex levels of nested groups.

The first click with the Group Selection tool selects an individual object in a group. The second click selects that object's containing group. The third click adds the next containing group to the selection, and so on, until the entire parent group is selected.

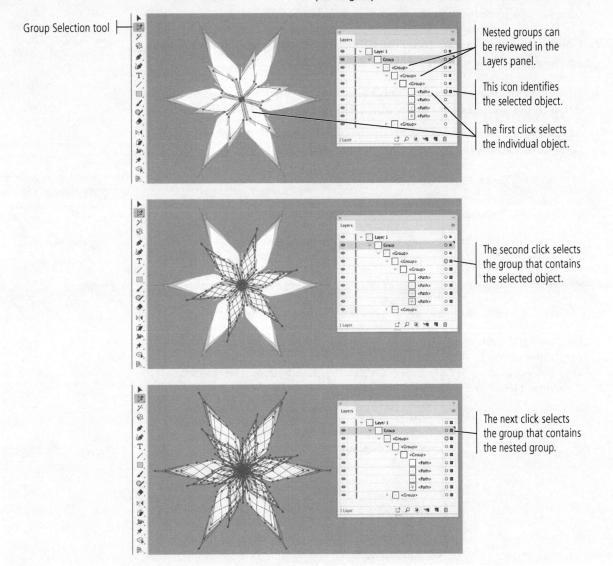

Group Selection tool

Nested groups can be reviewed in the Layers panel.

This icon identifies the selected object.

The first click selects the individual object.

The second click selects the group that contains the selected object.

The next click selects the group that contains the nested group.

Create Artwork with Lines

The Hiker icon is a perfect candidate for drawing with lines — which makes it ideal for introducing the Line Segment tool. In this exercise, you combine simple lines with other basic shapes to create the final icon.

1. **With icons.ai open, make sure the Icon Art layer is active. Make the hiker template art prominent in the document window.**

2. **Choose the Line Segment tool in the Tools panel. Using the Control panel, set the Fill to None and the Stroke to 1-pt Black.**

3. **Click near the top of the figure's neck, hold down the mouse button, and drag down to the bottom of the figure's back leg (as shown in the following image).**

   As you drag, the cursor feedback shows the distance (D) or length, as well as the angle of the line you're drawing.

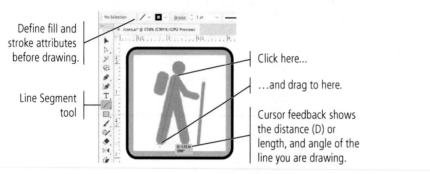

Define fill and stroke attributes before drawing.

Line Segment tool

Click here...

...and drag to here.

Cursor feedback shows the distance (D) or length, and angle of the line you are drawing.

Note:

If you don't see the cursor feedback, choose View>Smart Guides to toggle on that option.

When you release the mouse button, the line appears with the 1-pt black stroke that you defined in Step 2. The Control panel shows that Illustrator recognizes this object as a Line — a function of Live Shapes capability. The Transform panel includes Line Properties of length and rotation.

The object is recognized as a Line.

You can use the Properties panel to change the length and angle of a Line.

4. **Using the Control panel, change the Stroke Weight field to 12 pt.**

5. **Open the Stroke panel (Window>Stroke). If you only see the Stroke Weight field, open the panel's Options menu and choose Show Options.**

   Stroke properties are not limited to simply the stroke weight. The panel includes a number of options for customizing the appearance of a line.

Click here to open the panel Options menu.

6. **With the line selected on the artboard, choose the Round cap style in the Stroke panel.**

By default, lines have flat ends that stop at the anchor points that mark the ends of the lines. If you choose the Round or Square cap styles, the caps extend beyond the ending anchor points by one half the defined stroke weight.

In this case, you defined a 12-pt stroke, so the caps extend 6 points beyond the ending anchor points. Because the round caps essentially make the line longer, you have to change the line length to match the icon artwork.

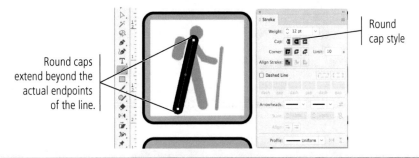

Round caps extend beyond the actual endpoints of the line.

Round cap style

The Stroke Panel in Depth

The **Cap** options define the appearance of a stroke beyond the endpoint of the line.

None cap style

Round cap style

Square cap style

The **Corner** options define the appearance of corners where two lines meet. When Miter Join is selected, you can define a miter limit in the Limit field. A miter limit controls when the corner switches from a pointed joint to a beveled joint as a factor of the stroke weight. If you define a miter limit of 2 for a 2-point line, the corner is beveled if the pointed corner extends beyond 4 points (2 × 2).

Miter join   Round join   Bevel join

The **Align Stroke** options determine where the stroke is placed relative to the actual path.

Align Stroke to Center   Align Stroke to Inside   Align Stroke to Outside

When the **Dashed Line** option is checked, you can define a specific pattern of dashes and gaps in the related fields. The two buttons to the right of the check box determine how a dash pattern is stretched (or not) so that line ends or object corners have the same appearance.

Aligns Dashes to Corners and Path Ends is active

Preserves Exact Dash and Gap Lengths is active

The **Arrowheads** options can be used to control end treatments on each end of a line. You can choose an arrowhead shape from the menus, and change the scale of applied arrowheads (relative to the applied stroke weight).

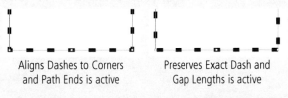

The Align [Arrowheads] options determine how arrowhead treatments are positioned relative to the path endpoint.

Place Arrow Tip at End of Path   Extend Arrow Tip Beyond End of Path

7. **Using the Transform panel, change the Line Length field to 1 in. Press Return/Enter to finalize the change.**

When you use the Line Properties options, the change always orients around the center of the line. The selected reference point at the top of the panel has no effect on the change.

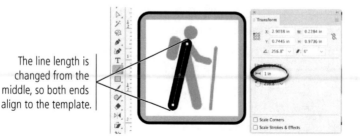

The line length is changed from the middle, so both ends align to the template.

8. **Press Command/Control to temporarily access the Selection tool and click away from the active line to deselect it.**

If you don't deselect the first line, clicking at the same spot as an existing, selected anchor point would actually drag the existing point instead of drawing a new line. This function of Live Shapes means you can edit existing line points and properties without switching tools, but it also means you can't begin a new line at the same point without first deselecting the original line.

Press Command/Control to temporarily access the last-used Selection tool.

The Line Segment tool is still technically active.

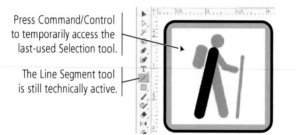

9. **With the Line Segment tool still active, move the cursor over the top end of the existing line until you see the word "anchor" in the cursor.**

The "anchor" label, a function of Smart Guides, indicates that clicking will create a new point at the same location as the existing one. Because you are using the Line Segment tool, the two lines will remain separate; they are not connected at the overlapping anchor points.

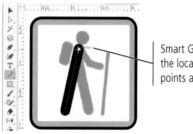

Smart Guides identify the location of existing points and paths.

10. **Click and drag down to the bottom of the front leg in the template artwork. When the cursor feedback shows the line is 1 in long, release the mouse button.**

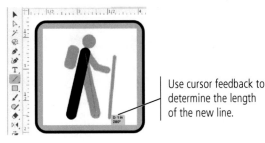

Use cursor feedback to determine the length of the new line.

11. **Command/Control-click away from the selected line to deselect it.**

12. **Click again at the point where the lines meet, and drag to create the figure's top arm segment.**

The new line uses the same stroke attributes as the previous ones unless you change those settings before drawing. In this case, the 12-pt stroke is too heavy, so you need to reduce it.

13. **Using the Control panel or the Stroke panel, change the line weight to 8 pt.**

14. **Deselect the new line, then draw the lower segment of the figure's arm.**

15. **Using the Line Segment tool, click and drag to create the walking stick. Define the line to have a 4-pt stroke with round caps.**

16. **Save the file and continue to the next exercise.**

Draw with Live Shapes

In addition to using the Transform panel to edit the properties of Live Shapes, you can also use the tool cursor to edit those shapes without the need to constantly switch tools. In this exercise, you will create and edit two more live shapes to complete the Hiking icon artwork.

1. **With icons.ai open, deselect everything on the artboard.**

2. **Choose the Rectangle tool, and define a 1-pt black stroke with no fill.**

Note:

Zooming in to the artwork can be helpful for completing the next two exercises.

3. **Click and drag to create a rectangle that is approximately the same size as the backpack in the template art.**

The shape is recognized as a Rectangle.

4. **Click the object's center point and drag to move the shape until its center approximately matches the center of the shape in the template art.**

Because this is a Live Shape, you do not need to change tools to rotate, move, or transform the shape.

Click the center point and drag to move the Live Shape.

The Rectangle tool is still active.

Dragging the center point changes the shape's position.

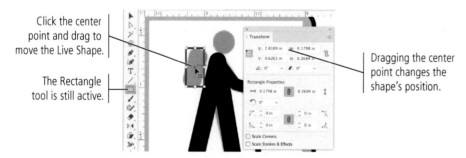

5. **Move the cursor near the corner of the resulting shape. When you see the rotation cursor, click and drag to rotate the shape to match the angle of the same shape in the template art.**

Click just outside a corner point and drag to rotate the Live Shape.

The Rectangle tool is still active.

Dragging outside the corner handle changes the rotation property.

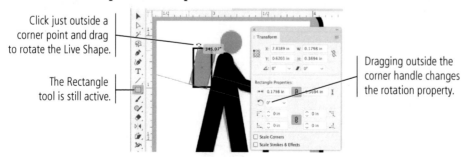

6. **Click and drag any of the bounding-box handles until the shape's height and width matches the template art.**

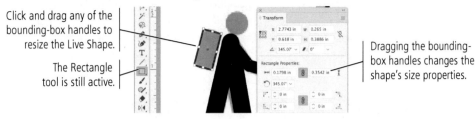

Click and drag any of the bounding-box handles to resize the Live Shape.

The Rectangle tool is still active.

Dragging the bounding-box handles changes the shape's size properties.

7. **In the Transform panel, make sure the link between the Corner Radius fields is active, then change any of the fields to 0.05 in.**

   Remember, you hid the Corner Widgets in an earlier exercise. If they were visible, you could drag the live widgets to change the shape's corner radius.

Note:

To show corner widgets, choose View>Show Corner Widgets.

The Rectangle tool is still active.

Use these fields to change the corner radius if the on-screen widgets are not visible.

8. **With the object selected, click the Swap Fill and Stroke button at the bottom of the Tools panel.**

Swap Fill and Stroke button

9. **Choose the Ellipse tool (nested under the Rectangle tool).**

10. **Press Option/Alt, then click at the center of the figure's head and drag out. Use the Smart Guides to create a shape with equal height and width.**

   Pressing Option/Alt while you draw creates the new shape with its center at the point where you click. You can press Shift to constrain the new shape to a circle, or simply use the Smart Guides.

   Again, ellipses are recognized by Illustrator's Live Shapes functionality. The Transform panel shows options that are relative to an ellipse.

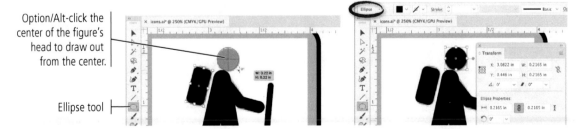

Option/Alt-click the center of the figure's head to draw out from the center.

Ellipse tool

11. **If necessary, adjust the circle's size and position until you are satisfied with the results.**

12. **Save the file and continue to the next exercise.**

Transforming Objects with the Bounding Box

Bounding-box handles make it easy to transform an object on the artboard. When the Selection tool is active, you can resize an object by dragging any handle, and even rotate an object by placing the cursor directly outside a corner handle. If Smart Guides are active, cursor feedback helps if you want to make specific transformations, or you can work freestyle and drag handles until you're satisfied with the results.

Drag a left- or right-center handle
to change the object's width.

Shift-drag to maintain an object's original
height-to-width aspect ratio as you transform it.

Drag a top- or bottom-center handle
to change the object's height.

Option/Alt-drag a handle to transform
the object around its center point.

Drag a corner handle to change both the
height and shape of an object at once.

Click directly outside an object's
corner handle to rotate the object.

Artwork used in these examples is taken from the built-in Adobe symbol libraries.

Understanding the Free Transform Tool

The Free Transform tool [icon] allows you to change the shape of selected objects by dragging transformation handles.

The **Touch widget**, which you can use to change the active transformation mode, appears when the Free Transform tool is active. To move the Touch bar in the workspace, click away from the three buttons and drag to another location.

Moving the cursor over a handle shows the transformation that can be made by dragging that handle. Clicking one of the handles shows a larger icon to indicate the possible transformation.

Transformation handles

When the cursor is over a transformation handle, the icon shows which distortions can be made.

Constraint
Free Transform
Perspective Distort
Free Distort

When you first select the Free Transform tool, the widget shows that the **Free Transform** mode is active. Larger transformation handles appear over all eight of the selected object's bounding-box handles. In this case, most of the available transformations are the same as those you can make when the Selection tool is active.

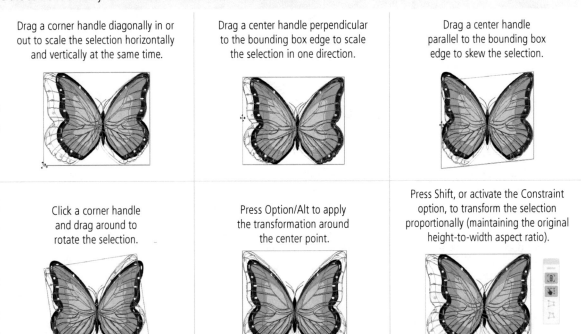

Drag a corner handle diagonally in or out to scale the selection horizontally and vertically at the same time.

Drag a center handle perpendicular to the bounding box edge to scale the selection in one direction.

Drag a center handle parallel to the bounding box edge to skew the selection.

Click a corner handle and drag around to rotate the selection.

Press Option/Alt to apply the transformation around the center point.

Press Shift, or activate the Constraint option, to transform the selection proportionally (maintaining the original height-to-width aspect ratio).

If you activate the **Perspective Distort** option in the Touch widget, you can drag the object's corner transformation handles to change the object's perspective. (The Constraint option is not available when Perspective Distort is active.)

When the Free Transform mode is active, you can accomplish the same goal by clicking a corner handle, then pressing Command-Option-Shift/Control-Alt-Shift and dragging.

If you activate the **Free Distort** option, you can drag the corner transformation handles to distort the selection. When Constraint is active, you can only drag the corner exactly horizontal or vertical from its previous position.

When the Free Transform mode is active, you can accomplish the same goal by clicking a corner handle, then pressing Command/Control and dragging.

Explore Artwork Outlines

As you develop complex artwork, it can be helpful to view the basic artwork structure without applied fill and stroke attributes. Illustrator's Outline mode makes this possible.

1. **With icons.ai open, deselect everything in the file.**

2. **Choose View>Outline.**

Regardless of the defined stroke weight, lines are still just lines. Outline mode shows you a wireframe of your artwork; fill and stroke attributes are not visible.

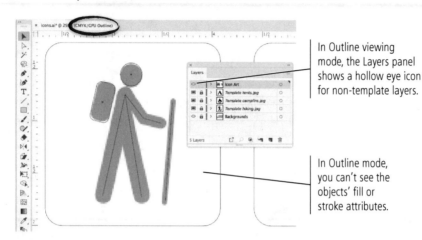

In Outline viewing mode, the Layers panel shows a hollow eye icon for non-template layers.

In Outline mode, you can't see the objects' fill or stroke attributes.

Note:

By default, objects on template layers remain visible in outline mode. You can convert a template layer to outlines by Command/Control-clicking the template layer icon.

3. **Choose the Join tool in the Tools panel (nested under the Shaper tool).**

The Join tool is an easy way to connect open line segments.

4. **Click and drag with the Join tool to paint an area over the point where the figure's elbow meets.**

Because these lines have rounded caps, outline mode makes it easier to see the actual ends of the lines.

Paint over the open endpoints to join them.

Note:

You can also select open endpoints and choose Object>Path>Join. If the selected points overlap, as in this exercise, the two points are simply combined into a single corner endpoint. If the selected endpoints do not overlap, this command creates a straight, connecting segment between the points.

5. **Choose the Selection tool in the Tools panel, and click either of the arm segments to select them.**

You can now see the bounding box of the selected object — both angled lines, which have been joined into a single Path object (as you can see in the Control panel). After joining the endpoints of the two lines, they no longer function independently.

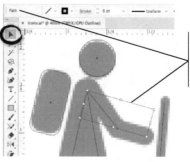

Joining the endpoints combines the two separate lines into a single path with multiple segments.

6. **With the new Path object selected, choose Object>Lock>Selection.**

When an object is locked, you can't select or change it — just as locking a layer protects the objects on that layer.

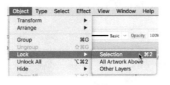

Note:

The Join tool works even when the line's endpoints do not overlap — simply paint from one endpoint to another. If lines overlap and the endpoints do not connect, you can paint to remove extra line segments past where the lines overlap.

7. **Choose the Join tool again. Click and drag over the top endpoints of the lines that make up the figure's legs.**

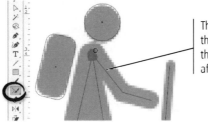

This shape is locked, so the upper endpoint of this line segment is not affected.

8. **Choose View>Preview or View>Preview on CPU to exit Outline mode and display the normal artwork.**

The available options depend on whether GPU Performance is enabled on your device.

- If GPU Performance is enabled, you can use the View menu to toggle between the Outline and Preview mode. A separate menu option allows you to choose View Using CPU, which does not use the GPU to display graphics.

- If GPU Performance is not enabled, you can only toggle between Outline and Preview on CPU mode.

When Outline mode is turned off, you can see the result of joining the endpoints. By default, connected line segments use the Miter Join method. This is obviously not appropriate for the icon artwork in this exercise.

9. **Click either unlocked line with the Selection tool to select the Path object.**

Again, joining the open endpoints combined the two Lines into a single Path object.

10. **With the Path object selected, click the Round Join Corner option in the Stroke panel.**

11. **In the Layers panel, expand the Icon Art layer.**

As you can see, the Picnic Table artwork group is locked from the earlier exercise. The second path object that makes up the figure's arm is also locked from Step 6.

These five objects make up the Hiker artwork.

Working with GPU Preview

The Graphics Processing Unit (GPU) is a specialized processor that can quickly execute commands for displaying images, which allows faster artwork rendering in Illustrator.

If your computer meets the hardware and software requirements*, GPU Performance is enabled by default. You can temporarily disable Illustrator's GPU Preview mode by choosing View>Preview on CPU. You can also permanently disable the feature in the GPU Performance pane of the Preferences dialog box.

When GPU Performance is enabled and the Zoom tool is active, you can also use the animated zoom feature:

- Hold down the mouse button to dynamically zoom in on the spot where you click.
- Click and drag right to dynamically zoom in.
- Click and drag left to dynamically zoom out.

*A complete list of requirements can be found at https://helpx.adobe.com/illustrator/kb/gpu-performance-preview-improvements.html

12. Click the Lock icon for the Path object to unlock only that object.

The Object>Unlock All menu command unlocks all individually locked objects on unlocked layers (it does not affect objects on locked layers). When a layer is expanded, however, you can use the Lock column in the Layers panel to lock and unlock individual objects without unlocking everything.

Use this column to lock or unlock specific objects on a layer.

13. Use what you learned in the previous exercise to finalize the icon artwork:

- **Delete the Template hiking.jpg layer**
- **Choose Select>All**
- **Choose Object>Group**
- **Unlock the Backgrounds layer**
- **Press Shift, then click the background shape to add it to the active selection**
- **Choose Object>Group**
- **Lock the Backgrounds layer**
- **Rename the parent group Hiker in the Layers panel**
- **Lock the Hiker sublayer**

14. Save the file and continue to the next exercise.

Draw with the Shaper Tool

The Shaper tool allows you to easily create basic shapes, almost as you would with a pencil on paper. The software automatically translates your drawing into rectangles, polygons with other than four sides, ellipses, or straight lines. In this exercise you will use this tool to create the tent artwork.

1. With **icons.ai open, expand the Icon Art layer, and then zoom into the tent template artwork.**

2. Make sure the Icon Art layer is active, then choose the Shaper tool in the Tools panel.

If you continued directly from the previous exercise, the tool is nested under the Join tool.

3. If you see a window appear with advice on using the Shaper tool, click the window's Close button.

Illustrator includes a number of these pop-up "helper" dialog boxes that explain certain features. Feel free to explore those dialog boxes when they appear.

4. **Click and drag to draw a triangle that represents the outer shape of the tent.**

   For some reason, the Shaper tool always defaults to a light gray fill, even if you define a different fill color before drawing.

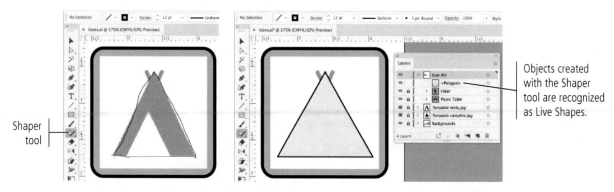

Shaper tool

Objects created with the Shaper tool are recognized as Live Shapes.

5. **Click and drag again to draw the inner triangle.**

6. **Click and drag again to draw two straight lines that represent the tent poles.**

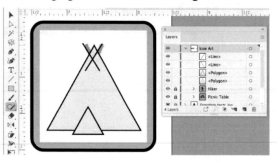

7. **Using the Shaper tool, scribble a path that begins below both rectangles and touches the overlapping area of the two triangles.**

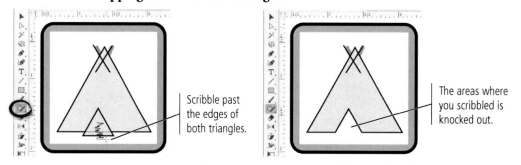

Scribble past the edges of both triangles.

The areas where you scribbled is knocked out.

8. **In the Layers panel, expand the Shaper Group sublayer.**

Scribbling over an area of overlapping objects converts those objects into a Shaper Group. All overlapping objects become part of the group, even it they were not affected by the scribbling motion.

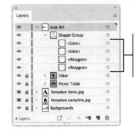

All overlapping shapes are included in the Shaper Group.

How you scribble with the tool determines what will happen:

- Scribble past the outer edges of the shapes to remove (knock out) both the fill and stroke attributes of the area.

- Scribble entirely within an overlap area to knock out that area.

- Scribble from an overlap area to a non-overlap area to merge the shapes where you scribble. The resulting shape is the color of the front shape in the stacking order.

- Scribble from a non-overlap area to an overlap area to create shapes that depend on where you start to scribble:

  - Start in the back object to create a merged shape with the same color as the back shape.

  - Start in the front object to knock out the areas where you scribble.

9. **Move the Shaper tool cursor over overlapping shapes to reveal the overlapping paths.**

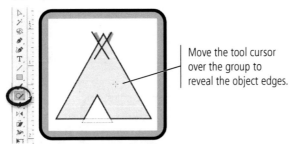

Move the tool cursor over the group to reveal the object edges.

10. **Click the group to select it.**

Clicking inside a Shaper Group selects the entire group object. It is surrounded by a single bounding box, and an arrow widget appears on the right edge. When the entire Shaper Group is selected, changes to the fill or stroke attributes affect all visible elements of the group.

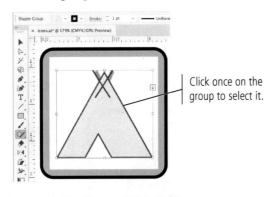

Click once on the group to select it.

11. In the Control panel, change the Stroke color to None.

Because the entire group is selected, this affects all objects in the group — including the two lines that are supposed to represent the tent poles.

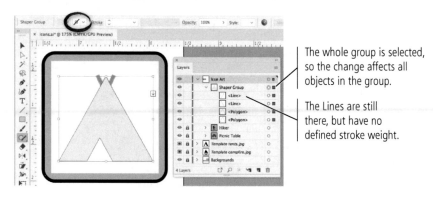

The whole group is selected, so the change affects all objects in the group.

The Lines are still there, but have no defined stroke weight.

12. Click once on the surface of the visible (back) triangle shape.

Clicking any of the filled shapes in the Shaper Group enters into Face Selection mode, in which the selected surface is identified with a crosshatch overlay. You can use this method to edit the fill color — but not the stroke color — of only the selected element within the group.

13. Using the Control panel, change the selected shape's fill color to Black.

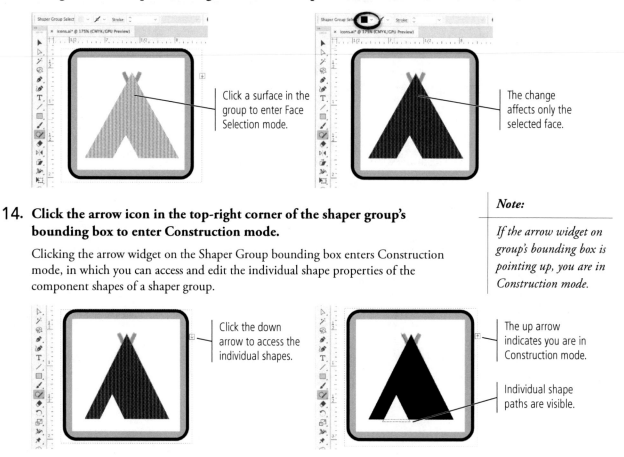

Click a surface in the group to enter Face Selection mode.

The change affects only the selected face.

14. Click the arrow icon in the top-right corner of the shaper group's bounding box to enter Construction mode.

Clicking the arrow widget on the Shaper Group bounding box enters Construction mode, in which you can access and edit the individual shape properties of the component shapes of a shaper group.

Note:

If the arrow widget on group's bounding box is pointing up, you are in Construction mode.

Click the down arrow to access the individual shapes.

The up arrow indicates you are in Construction mode.

Individual shape paths are visible.

15. **Click the black filled area again to reveal the triangle's bounding box. Adjust the bounding-box handles until it approximately matches the outer shape in the template image.**

    It is important to realize that Shaper Groups maintain the original shapes, even after you knock out or merge specific areas of those shapes.

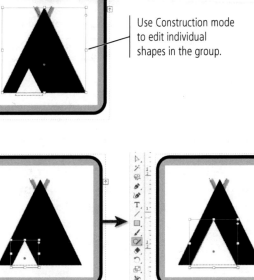

Use Construction mode to edit individual shapes in the group.

16. **Click the edge of the inner triangle to select that element of the group. Adjust the bounding-box handles until you are satisfied with the inner shape's size and position relative to the template artwork.**

    Because that shape has no fill, you have to click the edge to select it.

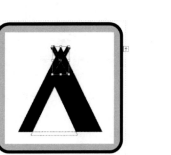

17. **Select each of the tent pole lines and define a 4-pt black stroke.**

    You can edit the lines individually, or Shift-click to select both before changing the stroke weight.

18. **Click away from the Shaper Group to exit Construction mode and deselect the group.**

19. **Delete the Template tents.jpg layer from the file.**

20. **Use what you learned in previous exercises to create a final locked group named Campsites for the tent artwork and its background.**

    In this case you do not need to create a separate group for the icon because it is already combined in a special Shaper Group.

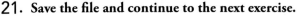

21. **Save the file and continue to the next exercise.**

Note:

You can also single-click an object's stroke or double-click an object's fill to enter into Construction mode.

Note:

To remove an object from a Shaper Group, enter into Construction mode for that group. Click the center point of the shape you want to remove, then drag it out of the Shaper Group's bounding box.

Draw with the Pencil Tool

As you might already realize, not all artwork can be created from basic shapes and lines. Illustrator includes everything you need to create artwork in any form, including irregular shapes. The Pencil tool is one method for creating custom shapes. Like a regular pencil on a piece of paper, the Pencil tool creates lines that follow the path of your cursor.

Note:

If you have a digital drawing tablet, the Pencil tool can be particularly useful for drawing custom artwork.

1. **With icons.ai open, make sure the Icon Art layer is selected in the Layers panel. Zoom in to the campfire template artwork.**

2. **Choose the Pencil tool (nested under the Shaper tool) in the Tools panel, and click the Default Fill and Stroke button in the Tools panel.**

3. **Double-click the Pencil tool in the Tools panel.**

    Double-clicking certain tools in the Tools panel opens an Options dialog box, where you can control the behavior for the selected tool. The Pencil tool options include:

    *   **Fidelity.** This option determines how far apart anchor points are added as you drag. Smooth results in fewer points and smoother curves, but also less accuracy matching the path you draw. More accurate means more anchor points and a path closer to what you draw (this can make the lines appear choppy).

    *   **Fill New Pencil Strokes.** By default, pencil paths are not filled, regardless of the fill color defined in the Tools panel.

    *   **Keep Selected.** If this option is checked, the line you draw is automatically selected when you release the mouse button.

    *   **Option Key Toggles to Smooth Tool.** As the name suggests, this allows you to quickly and temporarily switch to the Smooth tool while drawing with the Pencil tool. The Smooth tool can be used to remove unnecessary points along a pencil-drawn path, removing small or jagged jumps in the path.

    *   **Close Paths when Ends are within __ Pixels.** When this option is active, dragging back near the original starting point creates a closed path when you release the mouse button. If this option is not checked, dragging near the original point does not create a closed path.

    *   **Edit Selected Paths.** If this option is checked, drawing near a selected path (based on the Within value) can change the existing path. This is an important distinction — especially when Keep Selected is checked — because you can accidentally edit the first path instead of creating a second shape.

4. Define the following settings in the Pencil Tool Options dialog box:

   - Set the Fidelity slider to the midpoint.
   - Check the Close Paths... option
   - Uncheck all other options

5. Click OK to apply your changes and return to the artboard.

6. Click at the bottom-left point of the fire icon. Hold down the mouse button and begin dragging around the shape of the fire.

7. When you get near your original starting point and a hollow circle appears in the cursor icon, release the mouse button.

   As you drag, a colored line indicates the path you're drawing. Don't worry if the path isn't perfect; when you release the mouse button, Illustrator automatically smooths the path.

   When you release the mouse button, the shape shows the defined stroke color, but not the fill color, because you unchecked the Fill New Pencil Strokes option in Step 4.

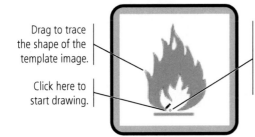

Drag to trace the shape of the template image.

Click here to start drawing.

The hollow circle in the cursor icon indicates that releasing the mouse button will create a closed shape.

8. Click near the top point of the white flame area (inside the first path) and drag to create the white inner shape in the fire icon.

Use the Pencil tool to draw this shape.

9. Using the Rectangle tool, draw the gray bar below the fire shape.

10. In the Layers panel, delete the Template campfire.jpg layer.

11. Expand the Icon Art layer if necessary.

Note:

Pressing the Option/Alt key while you drag with the Pencil tool places an anchor point at the location of the cursor when you press the key.

If you hold down the Option/Alt key while dragging, you can draw a straight line. When you release the modifier key, an anchor point ends the straight segment; continuing to drag resumes drawing a path in whatever shape you drag.

12. **Use the Selection tool to select all three shapes of the icon art. Change the fill color to black and the stroke color to None.**

When all three objects are filled, you can't see the inner shape at the top of the flame.

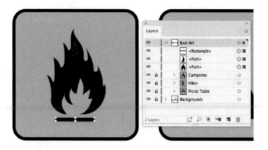

13. **Choose Object>Compound Path>Make.**

A **compound path** is a single shape made up of more than one path. Compound paths usually have inner "empty" areas, such as the letter O or Q.

This option combines all three selected shapes into one; the area of the smaller top shape is removed from the larger shape behind it.

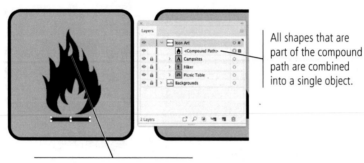

All shapes that are part of the compound path are combined into a single object.

As a compound path, the top shape is knocked out from the bottom shape.

14. **Use what you learned in previous exercises to create a locked group named Campfire for the final icon artwork.**

In this case you do not need to create a separate group for the icon because it is already combined in the Compound Path object.

15. **Save the file and continue to the final exercise.**

Edit Individual Grouped Elements

The client has decided that the icons should be white artwork on green backgrounds, so the final step in this exercise requires changing the colors of both the background shapes and the icon artwork. This is a fairly easy process, but because each of the icons are grouped, it will require a few extra steps.

1. **With icons.ai open, change your view percentage so you can see all the artwork in the file.**

2. **In the Layers panel, unlock all layers and sublayers in the file.**

3. **Choose the Selection tool, then click the picnic table artwork.**

   Because the artwork is grouped, the Selection tool selects the entire group. You need to use a different method to select only certain elements within the group.

The smaller icon indicates that only some objects on the layer (or in the group) are selected.

The large icon indicates that the entire group is selected.

Clicking with the Selection tool selects the entire group.

4. **Click anywhere outside the rectangle shapes to deselect the group, then choose the Direct Selection tool in the Tools panel.**

   The Direct Selection tool selects pieces of an object — specific paths, anchor points, or individual elements in a grouped object.

5. **Click the brown fill of the background shape behind the picnic table artwork to select it.**

   Because you clicked the fill, you selected the entire object. If you had clicked along the object's stroke, you would have selected that particular segment of the shape's edge.

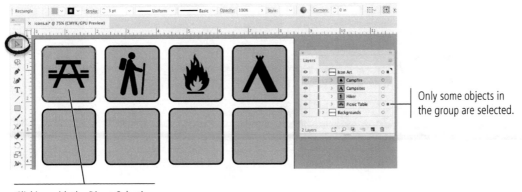

Only some objects in the group are selected.

Clicking with the Direct Selection tool selects only that object.

6. **Choose Select>Same>Fill Color.**

   The options in this menu are very useful for finding objects that share specific attributes. They select all similar unlocked objects on the entire artboard. The Select>Same menu options select objects regardless of which layer they occupy.

7. **With all eight brown shapes selected, use the Control panel to change the Stroke color to None and the Fill color to a medium green.**

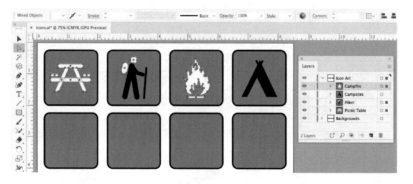

Note:

You can also use the Select Similar Objects menu in the Control panel to select objects with like attributes.

8. **Using the Direct Selection tool, click any of the black shapes that make up the picnic table icon.**

9. **Choose Select>Same>Fill Color.**

10. **With all the black-filled objects selected, change the Fill color to White.**

    As you can see, there are two problems. First, the lines in the Hiker icon are still black because they are lines and not filled shapes. Second, the elements in the Campsite icon are still black because the Select>Same commands cannot access individual pieces of a Shaper Group.

11. Choose the Selection tool in the Tools panel, and click away from all artwork to deselect everything.

12. Double-click the Hiker artwork. In the Layers panel, expand the Hiker group.

Double-clicking a group enters into **Isolation mode**, where only objects within the selected group are available. Basically, Isolation mode provides access to objects in the group without ungrouping the objects on the main artboard. Other elements outside the group are dimmed and visible, but you can't access or edit them.

13. Using the Selection tool, click to select the Hiker artwork.

Remember, you created a group from the icon artwork, and then grouped that with the background shape. Because there are two levels of grouping, you have to enter into Isolation mode for the second (nested) group to access the individual paths that make up the actual icon artwork.

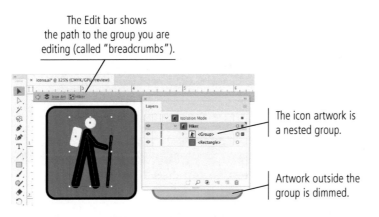

The Edit bar shows the path to the group you are editing (called "breadcrumbs").

The icon artwork is a nested group.

Artwork outside the group is dimmed.

14. Double-click the icon artwork on the artboard to enter into the nested group. In the Layers panel, expand the Group sublayer.

15. Shift-click to select the two Path objects and the Line object.

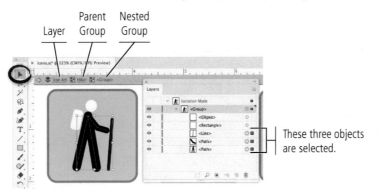

Layer   Parent Group   Nested Group

These three objects are selected.

16. Choose Object>Path>Outline Stroke.

This command converts lines to filled shapes. You can no longer access the actual paths that made up the original Line or Path objects.

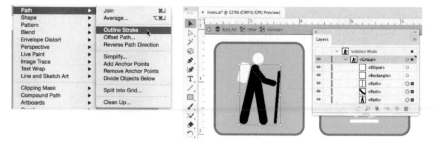

17. With all three shapes selected, change the Fill color to White.

18. At the top of the document window, click the arrow button three times to return to the main artboard.

The first click closes the nested group. The second click closes the Hiker group. The third click exits the layer and returns to the main artboard.

19. Using the Shaper tool, click to select the Campsite icon artwork.

The Shaper tool selects the Shaper Group, even though it is grouped with the background rectangle.

20. Using the Control panel, change the Fill and Stroke colors to White.

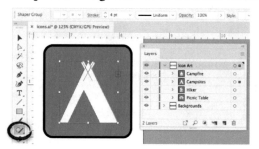

21. Save the file and close it.

Note:

You can also press the ESC key, or double-click an area outside the group, to exit Isolation mode.

Editing Similar Shapes with Global Edit

In this project, you used the Select>Similar menu to select and edit all shapes with the same fill color at one time. Illustrator includes a related option to identify similar shapes based on their appearance, size, or both.

Start Editing Similar Shapes Together

Click the arrow button to define the parameters of the search.

When an object is selected on the artboard, you can click the Start Global Edit button in the Quick Actions section of the Properties panel, or click the Start Editing Similar Shapes Together button in the Control panel to find other objects that match the current selection.

Clicking the arrow button to the right of either button opens a pop-up panel of preferences, where you can define the attributes you want to include in the search.

Appearance refers to attributes listed in the Appearance panel — fill and stroke, opacity, effects, and so on. Size refers to the physical dimensions (height and width) of the object. You can also determine which artboards to include in the search, as well as whether to include objects on the canvas (pasteboard) outside the artboard boundaries

When you enter the Global Edit mode, the software highlights other shapes that match the attributes of the original selection. (The highlight can be difficult to see, depending on the actual artwork you are building.) Changes to the selected object are also reflected in the highlighted shapes.

When you are finished editing, you can click the Stop Global Edit button or simply click away from the original selection to exit this mode.

In this example, we selected Shape 1 and chose the Match Appearance option. Five objects are not highlighted:

Shapes 2 and 6	Different fill color
Shape 7	Different stroke weight
Shape 9	Different shape
Shape 11	Applied drop shadow

Note that Shape 5 is selected even though it is a different size than Shape 1.

Shape 6 is not selected because different types of objects are not considered to match; a 1″ × 1″ ellipse will not be identified if the original selection is a 1″ × 1″ rectangle.

Changing the fill color of the selected shape also changes the fill color of all highlighted shapes.

Match Appearance is active

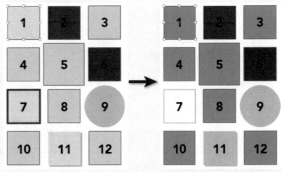

In this second example, we selected Shape 1 and chose the Match Size option. Only Shapes 6 and 11 are not highlighted.

Because the identified objects have different appearance attributes in this case, a warning notes that attributes of the selected item will be copied to all highlighted objects.

After changing the fill color of Shape 1 and dismissing the warning message, all highlighted objects now have a green fill color and no stroke color. The drop shadow effect that was previously applied to Shape 11 has been removed because Shape 1 has no applied drop shadow.

Match Size is active

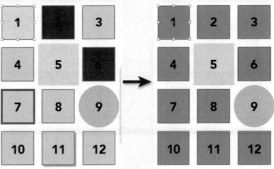

PROJECT REVIEW

1. _____ are composed of mathematical descriptions of a series of lines and points; they are resolution independent, can be freely scaled, and are automatically output at the resolution of the output device.

2. _____ are pixel-based, made up of a grid of individual pixels (rasters or bits).

3. The _____ is a rectangle that marks the outermost edges of an object, regardless of the actual object shape.

4. _____ is the relative top-to-bottom order of objects on the artboard, or of layers in the Layers panel.

5. The _____ is used to select entire objects or groups.

6. The _____ is used to select individual paths and points of a shape, or to select component pieces within a group.

7. The _____ is used to draw freeform paths defined by dragging the mouse cursor.

8. Press _____ to temporarily access the Selection tool; releasing the modifier key restores the previously selected tool.

9. A(n) _____ combines multiple Live Shapes, but maintains the original shapes in a special group.

10. A(n) _____ is a single object that is made up of more than one shape.

1. Briefly explain the difference between vector graphics and raster images.

2. Briefly explain the difference between the Selection tool and the Direct Selection tool.

3. Briefly explain how the Fill and Stroke icons at the bottom of the Tools panel affect your work.

PORTFOLIO BUILDER PROJECT

Use what you have learned in this project to complete the following freeform exercise.
Carefully read the art director and client comments, then create your own design to meet the needs of the project.
Use the space below to sketch ideas. When finished, write a brief explanation of the reasoning behind your final design.

art director comments

The client is pleased with the first four icons, and they want you to complete the rest of the set. They also want you to create an additional set of icons for athletic activities that they offer during their special holiday weekend events.

To complete this project, you should:

❑ Complete the remaining campsite icons. The bitmap versions are in your WIP>Camping folder.

❑ Carefully consider the best approach for each icon and use whichever tool (or tools) you feel is most appropriate.

❑ Create a second Illustrator file for the five new tournament icons.

client comments

Holidays are one of our busiest times, and we host a number of family-oriented special events during those weekends. To help keep everyone happy, we always set up organized tournaments for families with children of all ages, and we want to be able to post signs directing guests to those activities.

Since you did such a good job on the first four icons, we would like you to finish those first.

For the second set, we need icons for badminton, bocce, relay races, horseshoes, and volleyball. We don't have the images for these ones, so we would like you to come up with something. Remember, icons need to be easily recognizable, so they should clearly convey each activity.

project justification

PROJECT SUMMARY

The skills that you learned in this project will serve as the foundation for most work you create in Illustrator. You learned how to place raster images as templates, from which you created scalable vector graphics that will work in virtually any printed application. You learned a number of techniques for selecting objects and component pieces of objects, as well as various options for aligning objects relative to one another and to the artboard.

You learned how to draw primitive geometric shapes, and how to control the color of objects' fill and stroke attributes. You used a number of transformation options, including cloning methods to copy existing objects. Finally, you learned how to draw freeform shapes to suit more complex needs. As you move forward in this book, you will build on the basic skills you learned in this project to create increasingly complex artwork.

Draw, shear, reflect,
and clone basic shapes

Use stroke properties to
create unique artwork

Create and align
basic rectangles with
rounded corners

Use the Shaper tool to
combine and manage
Live Shapes

Use the Pencil tool and
compound paths to draw
complex shapes

Use various techniques to
select objects, groups, and
the component pieces of
those objects and groups

Regatta Artwork

Your client is the marketing director for the Long Beach Regatta, which attracts tens of thousands of visitors to the beach community throughout the four-day event. You have been hired to create the primary artwork for this year's event, which will be used in a variety of different products (ads, posters, etc.).

This project incorporates the following skills:

❏ Drawing complex custom shapes with the Pen tool

❏ Editing points and handles to control the position of vector paths

❏ Drawing irregular shapes by painting with the Blob Brush tool

❏ Creating a custom color scheme using saved swatches

❏ Adding interest and depth with color gradients

❏ Adjusting color, both globally and in specific selections

❏ Saving a PDF file for print distribution

PROJECT MEETING

client comments

The poster to promote the Regatta is basically the "play bill," and we will place it in store windows, public sites, and on bulletin boards all over the city. It will also be placed in local newspapers and entertainment magazines, and used as the cover for the souvenir program that we produce for the event.

We want the artwork to be very colorful and vivid, so the main focus — and most of the poster real estate — should be on the graphics. The only text for the poster is the event name, date, and location.

art director comments

I sketched a mock-up of a sailboat that you can use as the basis for the artwork. You should use the Pen tool to draw the necessary paths because simple shapes won't work and the Pencil tool doesn't provide fine enough control to efficiently achieve what you need.

I assigned the ocean background artwork to another designer, so you will have to incorporate your artwork into that file. This is going to be a complex piece of artwork, so you should pay close attention to the layer content when you organize the various pieces. That will make it far easier to edit specific components as necessary if the client decides to make changes.

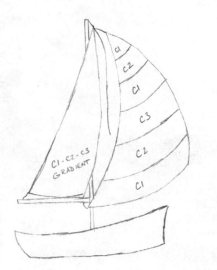

project objectives

To complete this project, you will:

❏ Use the Pen tool to draw precise curves

❏ Adjust anchor points and handles to precisely control the shape of vector objects

❏ Reshape line segments with the Anchor Point tool

❏ Use the Blob Brush tool to "paint" the area of vector shapes

❏ Define custom color swatches to allow easy universal changes

❏ Create color gradients to blend multiple colors in a single object

❏ Adjust gradients in context on the artboard

❏ Manage artwork with sublayers

❏ Save the file as a PDF

STAGE 1 / Drawing Complex Artwork

Much of the artwork you create will require far more complexity than simple lines and geometric shapes. When you need to produce custom artwork — whether from scratch or by tracing a hand-drawn sketch or photo — Illustrator includes a powerful set of tools to create and manipulate every point and path in the illustration. In the first stage of this project, you begin exploring the Pen tool, as well as other options for building and controlling custom shapes.

Prepare the Drawing Workspace

As with any project, setting up the workspace is an important first step. This project requires a single artboard to contain the entire illustration.

1. Download **Regatta_AI19_RF.zip** from the Student Files web page.

2. **Expand the ZIP archive in your WIP folder (Macintosh) or copy the archive contents into your WIP folder (Windows).**

   This results in a folder named **Regatta**, which contains the files you need for this project. You should also use this folder to save the files you create in this project.

3. **In Illustrator, choose File>New. Choose the Print option at the top of the dialog box, and choose the Letter document preset.**

   Remember, using the Print category of presets automatically applies the CMYK color mode and 300 ppi raster effects.

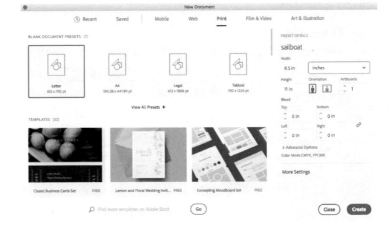

4. **Define the following settings in the Preset Details section:**

Name:	**sailboat**
Units:	**Inches**
Orientation:	**Portrait**
Artboards:	**1**

5. **Click Create to create the file.**

6. **Choose View>Fit Artboard in Window.**

   On Macintosh, the artboard of a new file is automatically centered in the document window. On some Windows systems, the artboard might be slightly off-center. The Fit Artboard in Window command centers the artboard in the document window, so the template image you place in the next step will be automatically centered on the artboard.

7. **Choose File>Place. Navigate to the file sketch.jpg in your WIP>Regatta folder. Check the Link and Template options at the bottom of the dialog box, and then click Place.**

Macintosh users: remember, you might have to click the Options button to reveal the options check boxes at the bottom of the Place dialog box.

You will use this client-supplied sketch to create the primary artwork for this illustration.

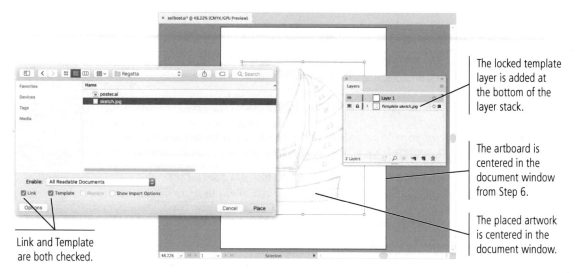

The locked template layer is added at the bottom of the layer stack.

The artboard is centered in the document window from Step 6.

The placed artwork is centered in the document window.

Link and Template are both checked.

8. **Double-click the template layer icon in the Layers panel to open the Layer Options dialog box. Uncheck the Dim Images option and click OK.**

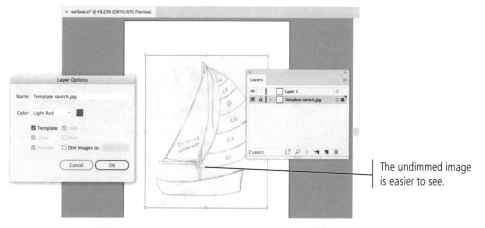

The undimmed image is easier to see.

9. **Double-click the Layer 1 name in the Layers panel to highlight it. Rename the layer Boat Drawing, then press Return/Enter to finalize the new name.**

10. **Click away from the placed sketch image to deselect it.**

11. **Save the file as an Illustrator file named sailboat.ai in your WIP>Regatta folder using the default Illustrator options, and then continue to the next exercise.**

Use the Pen Tool to Trace the Sketch

In this project, you use the Pen tool, which provides far more power to control the precise position of every line in a drawing. In fact, many believe the Pen tool is the most powerful and important tool in the Illustrator Tools panel.

An **anchor point** marks the end of a line **segment**, and the point **handles** determine the shape of that segment. That's the basic definition of a vector, but there is a bit more to it than that. Fortunately, you don't need to be a mathematician to master the Pen tool because Illustrator handles the underlying geometry for you.

Understanding Anchor Points and Handles

Each segment in a path has two anchor points, and can have two associated handles.

You can create corner points by simply clicking with the Pen tool instead of clicking and dragging. Corner points do not have their own handles; the connected segments are controlled by the handles of the other associated points. (Using the Convert Direction Point tool, click a smooth point to convert it to a corner point; click and drag from a corner point to add handles, converting it to a smoother point.)

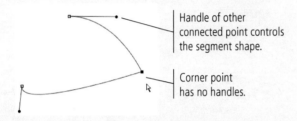

Handle of other connected point controls the segment shape.

Corner point has no handles.

In the image to the right, we clicked to create Point A and dragged (without releasing the mouse button) to create Handle A1. We then clicked and dragged to create Point B and Handle B1; Handle B2 was automatically created as a reflection of B1 (Point B is a **symmetrical point**).

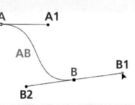

The next image shows the result of dragging Handle B1 to the left instead of to the right when we created the curve. Notice the difference in the curve here and the curve above. When you drag a handle, the connecting segment arcs away from the direction you drag.

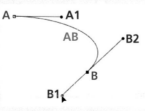

It's important to understand that every line segment is connected to two handles. In this example, Handle A1 and Handle B2 determine the shape of Segment AB. Dragging either handle affects the shape of the connected segment.

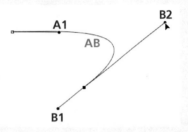

When you use the Pen tool, clicking and dragging a point creates a symmetrical (smooth) point; both handles start out at equal length, directly opposite one another. Changing the angle of one handle of a symmetrical point also changes the opposing handle of that point. In the example here, repositioning Handle B1 also moves Handle B2, which affects the shape of Segment AB. You can, however, change the length of one handle without affecting the length of the other handle.

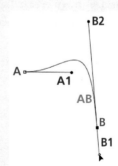

1. **With sailboat.ai open, zoom in so you can clearly see the shape of the boat in the sketch.**

2. **Open the View menu. If the menu command near the bottom of the menu says "Hide Corner Widget," choose that option.**

   This menu command toggles between "Show" and "Hide." If the command already says "Show Corner Widget," then these widgets are already hidden; you can simply click away from the menu to dismiss it.

   Live Corner widgets can be distracting when you don't need them; turning them off allows you to focus on only what you need to see to complete these exercises.

Note:

As you draw, zoom in as necessary to view different parts of the sketch.

3. **Choose the Pen tool in the Tools panel. Using the Control panel, set the stroke to 1-pt black and the fill to None.**

4. **Click with the Pen tool to place the first anchor point on the top-left corner of the boat shape.**

   We typically find it easier to start drawing at a corner (if one exists).

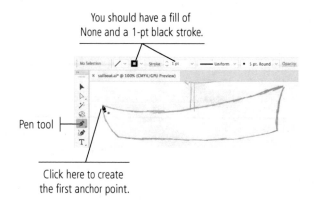

   You should have a fill of None and a 1-pt black stroke.

   Pen tool

   Click here to create the first anchor point.

5. **Click again at the bottom-left corner of the boat shape and immediately drag down and right to create handles for the second point. When the preview of the connecting segment matches the sketch, release the mouse button.**

   When you click and drag without releasing the mouse button, you create symmetrical handles, which determine the shape of the segment that connects the two points.

Note:

When we say "click and drag," you should hold down the mouse button until the end of the step.

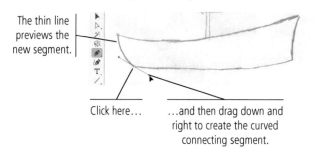

   The thin line previews the new segment.

   Click here... ...and then drag down and right to create the curved connecting segment.

6. **Click and drag again from the bottom-right corner of the boat shape.**

   Again, clicking and dragging creates a smooth, symmetrical point. Equal-length, exactly opposing handles are created on both sides of the point.

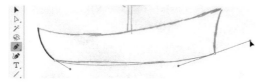

Note:

Don't worry if the connecting segment doesn't exactly match the sketch. The bottom of the boat will be obscured by other artwork in the final poster.

7. **Click again on the third anchor point and release the mouse button without dragging.**

   Clicking a smooth point as you draw converts it to a corner point, removing the outside handle from the point; the inside handle that defines the shape of the connecting segment remains in place. This allows you to change direction as you draw.

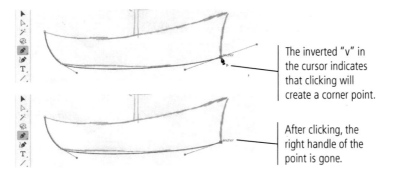

The inverted "v" in the cursor indicates that clicking will create a corner point.

After clicking, the right handle of the point is gone.

Note:

While drawing with the Pen tool, you can Option/Alt-click an anchor point, hold down the mouse button, and drag to add a non-symmetrical handle to one side of a corner point.

8. **Click and drag to create a new point (with handles) from the top-right corner of the boat shape. Drag the handles until the connecting segment matches the shape of the sketched line.**

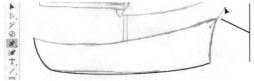

Click here and drag up and right until the connecting segment matches the shape of the sketched line.

9. **Click the original point without dragging to close the shape.**

   When you return to the original point, the cursor shows a small hollow circle. This indicates that clicking the existing point will close the shape.

Note:

The words "anchor" and "path" near the cursor icon are a function of Illustrator Smart Guides.

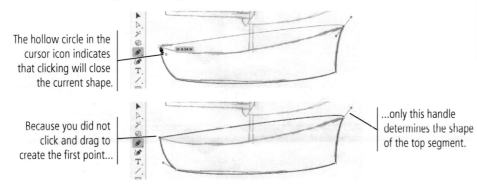

The hollow circle in the cursor icon indicates that clicking will close the current shape.

Because you did not click and drag to create the first point...

...only this handle determines the shape of the top segment.

10. **Using the Direct Selection tool, click the top-right point on the shape to select only that anchor point.**

    You can use the Direct Selection tool to edit any specific anchor point or segment.

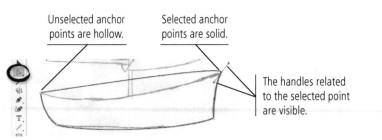

Unselected anchor points are hollow.

Selected anchor points are solid.

The handles related to the selected point are visible.

11. **Press Option/Alt, then click and drag the top handle of the selected point. Drag the handle left until the top segment matches the line in the sketch.**

    Remember, the Direct Selection tool allows you to adjust individual anchor points and handles. Option/Alt-dragging one handle of a smooth point converts the point to a corner point, but leaves both handles in place. This method allows you to change the direction of an existing point, but leaves the opposite curve intact.

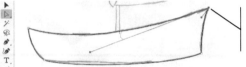

Option/Alt-dragging the handle converts the point to a corner point.

12. **Save the file and continue to the next exercise.**

Understanding Anchor Point and Bézier Curve Tools

Keep the following points in mind as you work with the Pen tool (and its nested variations) and Bézier curves.

Using the Direct Selection tool:

Click a specific anchor point to select it and show all handles that relate to that point.

Option/Alt drag a handle of a smooth point to convert it to a corner point.

Click a segment on a selected path and drag to bend the path; connected segments might also be affected.

Using the Pen tool:

Place the cursor over an existing point to temporarily access the Delete Anchor Point tool.

Place the cursor over an existing segment to temporarily access the Add Anchor Point tool.

Press Option/Alt and place the cursor over an existing point to temporarily access the Anchor Point tool.

Reshape Line Segments

In Illustrator, you have numerous options to create, select, and modify shapes — or parts of shapes — so you can create exactly what you need, regardless of what is already on the artboard. In this exercise you use a convenient method to easily bend line segments into the shapes you need.

1. **With sailboat.ai open, make the right sail in the sketch visible in the document window.**

2. **Using the Pen tool, click to place three connected anchor points at the corners of the sail.**

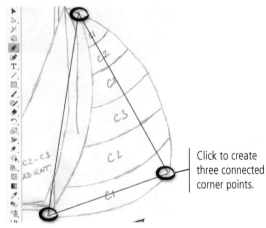

Click to create three connected corner points.

Note:

As a general rule, use as few points as necessary to create a shape with the Pen tool.

3. **Press the Option/Alt key to temporarily access the Anchor Point tool.**

The Anchor Point tool, nested under the Pen tool, can be used to change anchor points from corner to smooth (or vice versa):

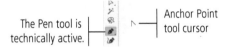

The Pen tool is technically active.

Anchor Point tool cursor

- Click a smooth point to convert it to a corner point.
- Click and drag a corner point to convert it to a smooth point with symmetrical handles.
- Option/Alt-click a handle to move only that handle, even if the point has an opposing handle; a smooth point is converted to a corner point as you drag.

4. **While holding down the Option/Alt key, click the right segment of the sail and drag until the segment matches the sketch.**

You can click and drag a segment to bend it into a different shape; handles are added to, or adjusted as necessary for the related points. This method of reshaping a line segment makes it very easy to edit your artwork without manually manipulating anchor points or handles.

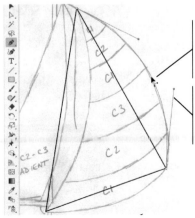

Using the Anchor Point tool, click a segment and drag to push it into a different shape.

Handles are added or adjusted as necessary when you reshape a line segment.

5. **Still holding down the Option/Alt key, adjust the other two lines that make up the sail shape.**

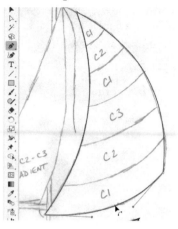

6. **Repeat Steps 2–4 to create the shape of the left sail.**

Editing Anchor Points with the Control Panel

When you are working with Bézier paths, the Control panel provides options for editing selected anchor points.

A B   C D   E F G H   I   J

A Convert Selected Anchor Points to Corner removes direction handles from both sides of the selected point(s).

B Convert Selected Anchor Points to Smooth adds symmetrical handles to both sides of the selected point(s).

C Show Handles for Multiple Selected Anchor Points. If this option is toggled on, direction handles display for all selected points.

D Hide Handles for Multiple Selected Anchor Points. If this option is toggled on, direction handles are not visible when more than one point is selected.

E Remove Selected Anchor Points removes the selected point from the path. If the removed point was between two other points, the connecting segment is not removed.

F Connect Selected End Points has the same effect as the Object>Path>Join command.

G Cut Path at Selected Anchor Points results in two overlapping, open endpoints where the selected point was previously a single point.

H Align To. Use this menu to align a selected point to the active selection or relative to the artboard.

I Point Position. Use the X and Y fields to define a specific position for the selected point. You can also use mathematical operations to move a point relative to its current position (e.g., move it left by typing "-1" after the X value).

J Isolate Selected Object enters isolation mode with the object containing the selected point(s). If points are selected on more than one object, this button is not available.

7. **Using the Pen tool, click to place a new anchor point to the left of the bottom horizontal line in the right sail, starting and stopping past the edges of the sail shape (as shown in the following image).**

You are going to use the Shape Builder tool to divide the sail into the necessary shapes. For this process to work properly, the dividing lines need to be at least on top of the outside shape; to be sure, you should extend the lines farther than they need to be.

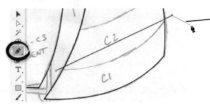

The Pen tool preview shows that clicking again will create another connected segment.

When you move the mouse cursor away from the last point you created, a thin line previews the segment that would be created by clicking again. You can turn this preview on and off using the Enable Rubber Band for Pen Tool option in the Selection and Anchor Display pane of the Preferences dialog box.

8. **Press Option/Alt, then use the Anchor Point tool to reshape the segment to match the line in the sketch.**

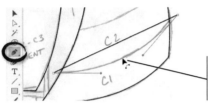

Press Option/Alt and bend the connecting segment into shape.

9. **While the Pen tool is still active, press Command/Control to temporarily access the Selection tool and click away from the line to deselect it.**

You can simply click away from selected objects with the Selection or Direct Selection tool to deselect the current selection. You can also press Command/Control-Shift-A to deselect the current selection.

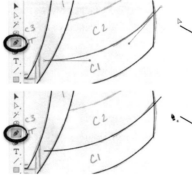

Pressing Command/Control temporarily switches to the last-used Selection tool.

Pressing Command/Control while drawing temporarily switches to the last-used Selection tool. This technique allows you to easily deselect the current path, and then continue to draw another unconnected path, all without manually switching tools.

This Pen tool cursor shows that clicking begins a new shape.

10. **Still using the Pen tool, draw the second horizontal line on the sail.**

If you don't deselect the previous path before clicking to draw the next line, the third click would create a segment that is connected to the last place you clicked (on the first line). In the context of this exercise, a single line with multiple anchor points is much more difficult to control than two separate lines with open endpoints.

11. **Press Option/Alt, then use the Anchor Point tool to reshape the segment to match the line in the sketch.**

12. Move the cursor away from the existing line, then press the ESC key.

When drawing with the Pen tool, this key disconnects your drawing from the current shape. You can then click to begin a new shape that is not part of the previously suggested shape.

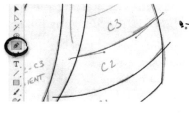

Pressing the ESC key disconnects the tool from the previous shape.

13. Repeat Steps 10–12 to draw the rest of the curved horizontal lines on the sail.

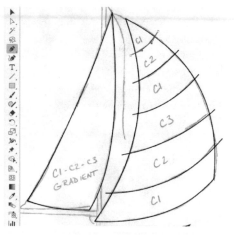

14. Save the file and continue to the next exercise.

Drawing with the Curvature Tool

The Curvature tool can be used to create and edit complex paths without manually manipulating anchor points.

Using the Curvature tool, begin by clicking to place points in a new path. As you drag after creating the first two points, the software shows a rubber-band preview of the path that will be created by clicking again. (You can turn this preview behavior off in the Selection and Anchor Display pane of the Preferences dialog box.)

As long as the Curvature tool is active, you do not need to change tools to edit the path:

- Option/Alt-click click to create a corner point.
- Click anywhere along an existing path to add a new anchor point.
- Double-click any point to toggle it between a smooth and corner point.
- Click a point to select it.
- Drag a selected point to move it.
- Press Delete to remove the selected point; the existing curve is maintained.
- Press the Esc key to stop drawing the current shape.

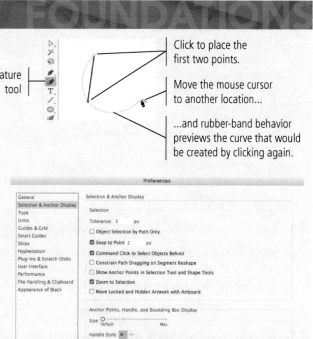

Curvature tool

Click to place the first two points.

Move the mouse cursor to another location...

...and rubber-band behavior previews the curve that would be created by clicking again.

Build Shapes from Overlapping Paths

The Shape Builder tool makes it easy to break apart overlapping objects into component pieces. This tool offers similar functionality as the Pathfinder, but on a piece-by-piece basis, rather than for entire selected shapes. In this exercise, you will use the Shape Builder tool to break the sail into the individual strips that are shown on the sketch.

1. **With sailboat.ai open, use the Selection tool to draw a marquee that selects all lines that make up the right sail.**

2. **Choose the Shape Builder tool in the Tools panel, and then reset the default fill and stroke colors.**

3. **Move the cursor over the bottom section of the sail.**

   The Shape Builder tool identifies overlapping areas of selected objects, which is why you had to select the pieces in Step 1.

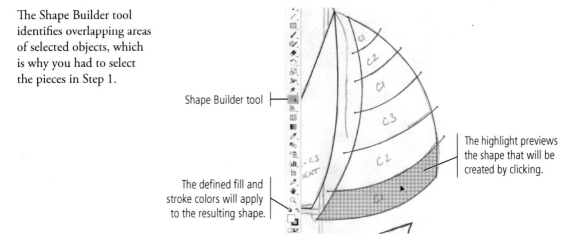

Shape Builder tool

The defined fill and stroke colors will apply to the resulting shape.

The highlight previews the shape that will be created by clicking.

4. **Click the highlighted area to create the new shape.**

   Clicking with the Shape Builder tool changes the fill of the resulting shape to the active fill color — white, in this case, because you reset the default fill and stroke colors in Step 2. The resulting shape now obscures the sketch behind it; this helps to identify which pieces you have already created.

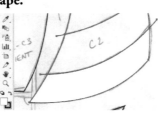

5. **Repeat Steps 3–4 for the remaining five strips on the sail.**

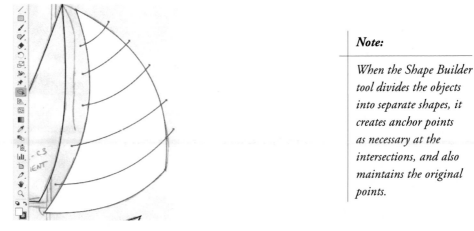

Note:

When the Shape Builder tool divides the objects into separate shapes, it creates anchor points as necessary at the intersections, and also maintains the original points.

6. **Press Option/Alt, and move the cursor over the bottom line segment outside the right sail edge. When the line segment is highlighted and the cursor shows a minus sign in the icon, click the segment to remove it.**

   The Shape Builder tool can be used to both create and remove shapes. Pressing Option/Alt switches the tool into Erase mode so you can remove paths or shapes.

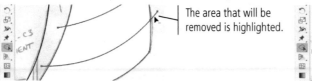

The area that will be removed is highlighted.

After clicking, the segment is gone.

7. **Repeat Step 6 to remove the remaining extraneous line segments.**

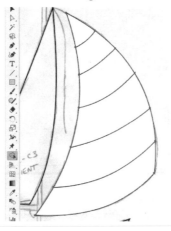

8. **Command/Control-click away from the sail to deselect everything.**

9. **Using the Direct Selection tool, click the right edge of the top shape to select that segment. Click the selected segment and drag slightly out to create a slightly bulged appearance.**

   When the Direct Selection tool is active, you can click and drag a selected segment on a closed path to access the same path-reshaping functionality as you have using the Anchor Point tool.

10. **Repeat Step 9 to adjust the right edges of the other shapes in the sail.**

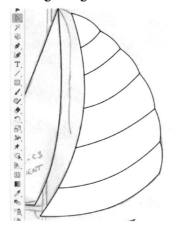

11. **Save the file and continue to the next exercise.**

More about the Shape Builder Tool

Click and drag with the Shape Builder tool to combine multiple pieces into a single shape:

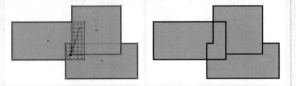

Option/Alt-click and drag with the Shape Builder tool to remove multiple pieces at once:

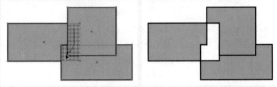

When In Merge Mode, Clicking Stroke Splits the Path is active, click a path to cut apart the path at the nearest anchor points:

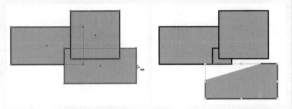

When Cursor Swatch Preview is active, three available swatches appear above the tool cursor. Use the Left and Right Arrow keys to move through those swatches:

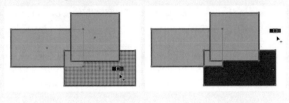

Double-clicking the Shape Builder tool in the Tools panel opens the Shape Builder Tool Options dialog box, where you can change the tool's behavior.

If a small opening exists in a path, you can activate **Gap Detection** settings to overlook small, medium, large, or custom-sized gaps in open paths. This option is especially useful if the Consider Open Filled Paths as Closed option is not checked.

The **Pick Color From** menu determines whether the tool recognizes all swatches in the file or only colors that are actually used in the artwork.

The **Selection** option defines how you can click and drag to connect shapes. The default option (Freeform) means you can drag in any direction to select objects to join. If Straight Line is active, you can only drag a straight path to combine shapes.

You can also use the **Highlight** options to determine what, if anything, is highlighted when you move the tool cursor over a shape.

Use the Draw Behind Mode

Illustrator's three drawing modes allow you to create new shapes in different ways relative to other existing shapes. In the Draw Normal method (the default), new objects are simply created on top of one another in sequential order; you can rearrange them using commands in the Object>Arrange submenu, or drag them in the Layers panel. Alternatively, you can use the Draw Behind mode to automatically create new shapes behind existing objects, which eliminates a few steps in reaching the accurate object stacking order.

1. With **sailboat.ai** open, use any method you prefer to fill the left sail with white and fill the boat shape with black.

2. Deselect everything on the artboard.

3. **Choose the Pen tool in the Tools panel. In the Control panel, set the fill color to a dark brown from the built-in swatches and the stroke to None.**

4. **At the bottom of the Tools panel, choose the Draw Behind option.**

If your Tools panel is in one-column mode, the Drawing Mode options are available in a pop-up menu. If your Tools panel is in two-column mode, the Drawing Mode options are presented as three buttons (from left to right: Draw Normal, Draw Behind, and Draw Inside).

When you use the Draw Behind mode, new objects are automatically placed behind the selected object(s), or at the bottom of the stacking order if nothing is selected.

5. **Using the sketch as a guide, use the Pen tool to click four times without dragging to create the mast shape (use the following image as a guide).**

Remember, when you see a small round circle in the cursor icon, clicking creates a closed shape. Because you aren't dragging when you click to place the anchor points, you are creating four corner points and a closed polygon shape.

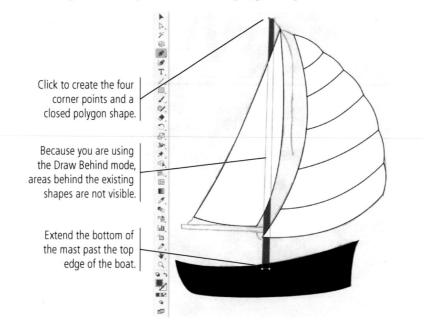

Click to create the four corner points and a closed polygon shape.

Because you are using the Draw Behind mode, areas behind the existing shapes are not visible.

Extend the bottom of the mast past the top edge of the boat.

6. **Use the Pen tool to create the boom (the horizontal pole sticking out from the mast).**

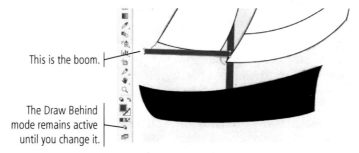

This is the boom.

The Draw Behind mode remains active until you change it.

7. **Deselect the shape you just created.**

8. **At the bottom of the Tools panel, choose the Draw Normal option.**

   The drawing mode remains at the last-used setting. To draw the rope shapes in font of the sails and mast, you need to restore the Draw Normal mode.

9. **Choose the Pencil tool in the Tools panel. In the Control panel, change the fill color to None, choose a medium brown swatch as the stroke color, and define a stroke weight of 2 pt.**

10. **Use the Pencil tool to draw the ropes on the sketch.**

11. **If necessary, adjust the anchor points of the ropes until you are satisfied with the results.**

12. **Save the file and continue to the next stage of the project.**

Using the Draw Inside Mode

The Draw Inside mode, which is only available when an existing object is selected, is an easy way to create new objects inside a **clipping path** (a shape that defines areas of other objects that will be visible; anything outside the area of the clipping path is not visible).

If you select the clipped object with the Selection tool, you can use the Edit Clipping Path and Edit Contents buttons in the Control panel to edit either shape without ungrouping and without entering isolation mode.

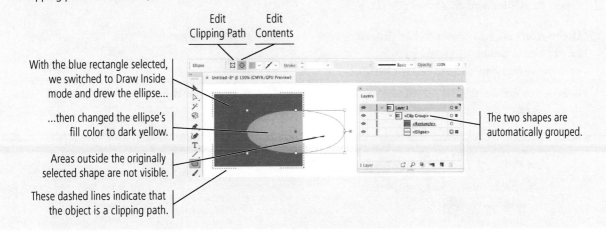

Edit Clipping Path   Edit Contents

With the blue rectangle selected, we switched to Draw Inside mode and drew the ellipse...

...then changed the ellipse's fill color to dark yellow.

Areas outside the originally selected shape are not visible.

These dashed lines indicate that the object is a clipping path.

The two shapes are automatically grouped.

STAGE 2 / Coloring and Painting Artwork

The CMYK color model, also called "process color," recreates the range of printable colors by overlapping layers of cyan, magenta, yellow, and black inks in varying (0–100) percentages.

Using theoretically pure pigments, a mixture of equal parts of cyan, magenta, and yellow would produce black. Real pigments, however, are not pure; the actual result of mixing these three colors usually appears as a muddy brown. The fourth color, black (K), is added to cyan, magenta, and yellow to extend the range of printable colors and allow purer blacks to be printed. Black is abbreviated as "K" because it is the "key" color to which others are aligned on the printing press. Using K for black also avoids confusion with blue in the RGB color model, which is used for digitally distributed files.

In process-color printing, each of the four process colors — cyan, magenta, yellow, and black — is imaged, or separated, onto an individual printing plate. Each color separation is printed on a separate unit of a printing press. When printed on top of each other in varying percentages, the semi-transparent inks produce the range of colors in the CMYK **gamut**. Other special colors (called spot colors) are printed using specifically formulated inks as additional color separations.

Different color models have different ranges or gamuts of possible colors. A normal human visual system is capable of distinguishing approximately 16.7 million different colors; color reproduction systems, however, are far more limited. The RGB model has the largest gamut of the output models. The CMYK gamut is much more limited; many of the brightest and most saturated colors that can be reproduced using light (in the RGB model) cannot be reproduced using CMYK inks.

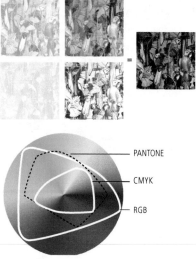

Create Global Custom Color Swatches

As you saw in the original sketch, the sail in this project will be filled using three different colors (indicated as C1, C2, and C3). In this exercise, you are going to create these colors and then save them as swatches that can be changed at any time to dynamically modify the colors in the artwork.

1. **With sailboat.ai open, deselect everything on the artboard.**

2. **Open the Color and Swatches panels.**

   If you don't see four color fields/sliders in the Color panel, open the panel options menu and choose Show Options.

   Click here to open the panel Options menu.

   Because you defined CMYK as the color mode for this document, the Color panel shows ink value sliders for those four primary colors.

   Show List View

   Show Tile View

   The default Swatches panel includes a number of default swatches.

Note:

We dragged both panels out of the panel dock so we could work with both panels at once.

3. **Open the Swatches panel Options menu and choose Select All Unused.**

The default Swatches panel includes a number of basic swatches that provide a good starting point for some artwork; you already used two of these to color the mast, boom, and rope shapes. When you build custom swatches, it can be a good idea to delete any default swatches that you don't need so your panel isn't too cluttered.

The List views show the color name as well as the swatch.

The heavy border identifies the selected swatches.

Delete Swatch button

Note:

The default swatches appear in every new file you create, even if you delete them from a specific file.

4. **Click the Swatches panel Delete button, and then click Yes in the resulting warning dialog box.**

You used two of the built-in swatches to create the mast and ropes, so those swatches remain in the panel and file.

Note:

If you delete a swatch that you applied to objects in a project, there is no effect on the existing objects; you simply can't apply that color to any new objects in the project.

5. **Using Selection tool, click to select any of the white-filled shapes and then choose Select>Same>Fill Color.**

Alternatively, you can Shift-click each white-filled object to select them individually.

6. **With all the white shapes selected, change the Opacity field in the Control panel to 50%.**

Opacity defines the transparency of the selected object. In this case, you're reducing the opacity from 100% (entirely solid or opaque) so you can see the color indicators on the original sketch.

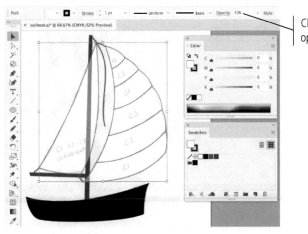

Change the shapes' opacity to 50%.

7. **Deselect everything, and then use the Selection tool to select only the top stripe in the sail (labeled C1 in the sketch).**

8. **Press Shift and click the other two C1 shapes to add them to the selection.**

   By pressing Shift, you can click to add other objects to the current selection. Shift-clicking an object that is already selected removes it from the active selection.

9. **In the Color panel, make sure the Fill icon is on top of the Stroke icon.**

   Like the options in the Tools panel, the Fill and Stroke icons determine which attribute you are currently changing. Whichever icon is on top will be affected by changes to the color values.

10. **In the Color panel, click a green area in the color spectrum bar.**

    All three selected objects fill with the green color you clicked. They seem lighter because they are still semi-transparent.

Note:

Press Shift while dragging any of the sliders in the Color panel to drag all four sliders at once. Their relative relationship to each other remains the same while you drag.

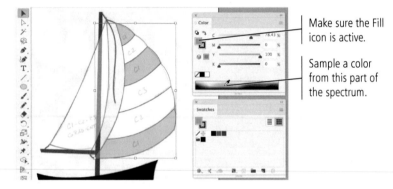

Make sure the Fill icon is active.

Sample a color from this part of the spectrum.

11. **With the Fill icon still active in the Swatches panel, click the New Swatch button at the bottom of the panel.**

Because the Fill icon is active, the fill color is the one that will be stored in the new swatch.

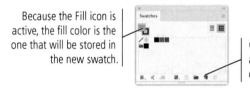

Click this button to make a new swatch from the currently active color.

12. **Check the Global option in the New Swatch dialog box.**

13. **Uncheck the Add to My Library option, then click OK.**

Note:

If you have an individual user account for the Adobe Creative Cloud, CC Libraries are a way to share assets between Adobe applications. They are explained in Project 4: Ski Resort Map.

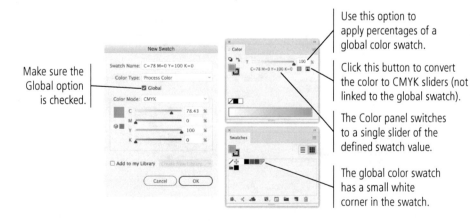

Make sure the Global option is checked.

Use this option to apply percentages of a global color swatch.

Click this button to convert the color to CMYK sliders (not linked to the global swatch).

The Color panel switches to a single slider of the defined swatch value.

The global color swatch has a small white corner in the swatch.

14. Select the two shapes marked C2 in the sketch.

15. Repeat the process from Steps 9–13 to fill the C2 shapes with a blue color and then create a global swatch from the color.

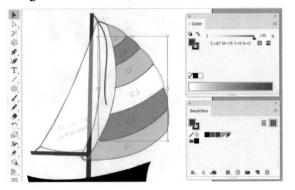

16. Select the shape marked C3 in the sketch, fill it with a purple color, and then create a third global swatch from the color.

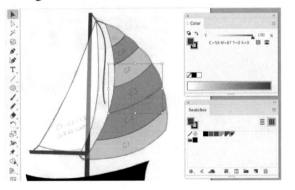

17. With the purple shape still selected, choose Select>Same>Opacity. Return the selected objects' opacity to 100%.

You no longer need to see the color markers on the sketch, so you can return these objects to full opacity.

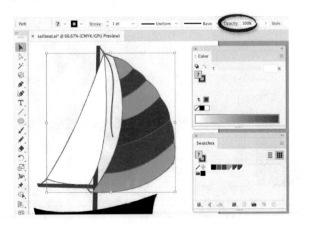

18. Deselect all objects in the file, save the file, and then continue to the next exercise.

Add a Color Gradient

Illustrator supports three types of gradient fills. When an object is selected, clicking one of the gradient types at the top of the Gradient panel (Window>Gradient) applies the default gradient to the active attribute (fill or swatch). The Gradient panel remembers the last-used gradient as the default sample, so that gradient is applied to the selected object when you apply a gradient.

Note:

A fourth type, called a gradient mesh, is explained in Project 3: Identity Package.

Linear gradient

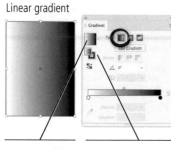

Radial gradient

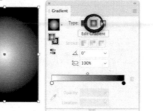

Freeform gradient

Default gradient   Fill is the active attribute

When a linear or radial gradient is applied, you can use the Gradient panel to change the gradient colors. Defined stops appear as large circles below the ramp. You can change the stop colors, move stops along the gradient, change the midpoints between adjacent stops, and add new stops. To remove a stop, simply drag it off the gradient ramp. You can also use the Gradient panel to change the angle of the applied gradient, as well as the aspect ratio of radial gradients.

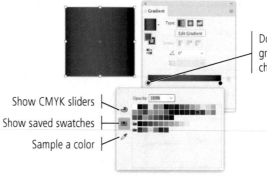

Double-click a gradient stop to change its color.

Show CMYK sliders

Show saved swatches

Sample a color

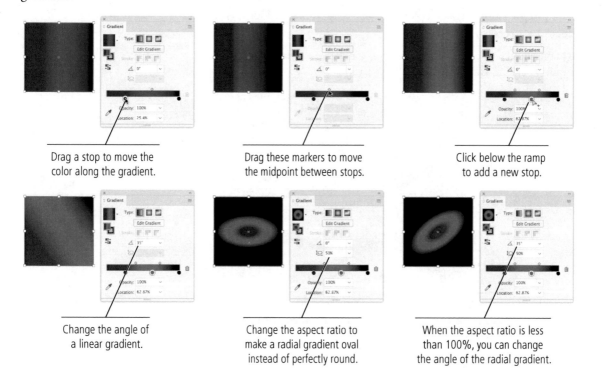

Drag a stop to move the color along the gradient.

Drag these markers to move the midpoint between stops.

Click below the ramp to add a new stop.

Change the angle of a linear gradient.

Change the aspect ratio to make a radial gradient oval instead of perfectly round.

When the aspect ratio is less than 100%, you can change the angle of the radial gradient.

When a linear or radial gradient is applied, you can click the Edit Gradient button in the Gradient panel to automatically activate the Gradient tool and show the Gradient Annotator controls. You can use this on-screen widget to dynamically change the applied gradient in immediate relation to the selected object.

When the Gradient tool is active, you can click and drag to change the position and angle of the gradient. The place where you first click is the beginning of the gradient, or the left end of the ramp in the Gradient panel; the end color of the gradient, or the right end of the ramp, exists where you release the mouse button.

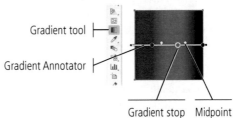

Gradient tool

Gradient Annotator

Gradient stop   Midpoint

The same color stop controls you see on the ramp in the Gradient panel appear on the Gradient Annotator. You can also change the gradient angle and aspect ratio (for radial gradients) by dragging the annotator handles.

Note:

You can also click the Edit Gradient button in the Gradient panel to access the Gradient Annotator.

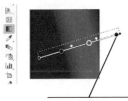

Click and drag to define the gradient.

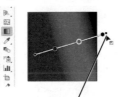

Drag the Annotator endpoint to change the gradient length.

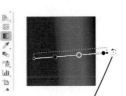

Move the cursor slightly away from the endpoint to rotate the gradient.

Note:

You can turn off the Gradient Annotator in the View menu (View>Hide Gradient Annotator).

Drag the aspect ratio handle to change a radial gradient away from round.

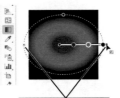

Drag either endpoint to change the size of a radial gradient.

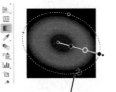

Drag the radial gradient boundary to rotate the gradient.

The original sketch shows that the left sail needs to be a gradient of the three colors in the other sail. Because the sketch shows the look of a sail billowing in the wind, a straight linear gradient would not accurately reflect the way blended colors would appear in a real sail. Instead, you will use the third type of gradient— a freeform gradient — to create the necessary effect.

1. **With sailboat.ai open, use the Selection tool to select the left sail shape.**

2. **Open the Gradient panel (Window>Gradient). If you see only a gradient sample in the panel, open the panel Options menu and choose Show Options.**

3. **If you see a pop-up window about working with Gradients, click the Skip Tour button.**

4. **With the left sail shape selected, click the Freeform Gradient button at the top of the Gradient panel.**

Freeform gradients use color points to define the location of various colors in the gradient. When you first apply a freeform gradient, the software evaluates the shape and adds stop points where it determines they might be needed.

By default, freeform gradients are created in [Draw] Points mode, which means the individual color points in the gradient are not connected.

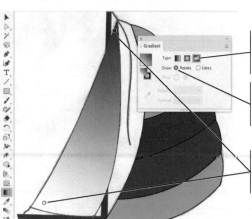

Click here to apply a freeform gradient.

Draw Points mode is active by default.

Color points are automatically added to the selected shape.

5. **Click to select the top color point in the sail shape.**

When a color point is selected, you can drag it to a new location, or press the Delete key to remove it from the gradient. You can also click the Delete button in the Gradient panel to remove the selected point.

If you move the cursor over a selected point, the dotted line identifies the spread of that point's color within the overall gradient. You can click the dotted line and drag to change the spread percentage.

Click to select a specific color point in the gradient.

The spread control widget appears when the cursor hovers over a gradient point.

Note:

You can change the opacity of the selected gradient point in the Gradient panel.

6. **Press the Delete key to remove the selected point from the gradient.**

7. **Click to select the remaining point in the gradient. Double-click the selected stop to open the pop-up color selector for that stop.**

You can change the color of stops by double-clicking the circles, which opens the color panel for that stop (the same as when you change the color for a linear or radial gradient).

8. **Choose the custom green swatch, then press Return/Enter to dismiss the panel.**

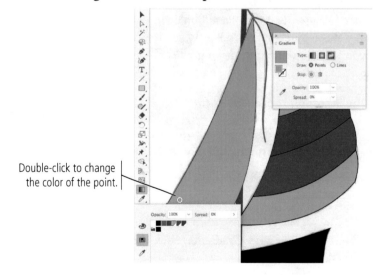

Double-click to change the color of the point.

9. **Choose the Lines option in the Gradient panel.**

   The Lines option allows you to draw a path that defines the precise shape of a gradient, rather than simply blending from one point to another.

10. **Click the existing color point to connect to it, then move the cursor halfway up the left edge of the sail. Click near the left edge of the shape to place a new color point.**

    Although it can be difficult to see on the green background a thin blue line connects each color point on the same line. This preview shows the curve that will be created when you click to place a new point.

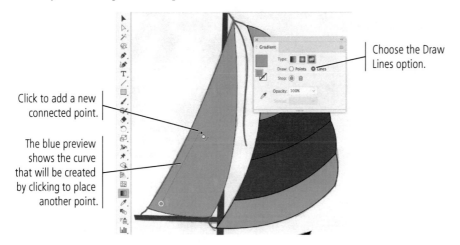

Click to add a new connected point.

The blue preview shows the curve that will be created by clicking to place another point.

Choose the Draw Lines option.

11. **Move the cursor to the top of the sail shape. Click just inside the sail shape to place a third color point on the same line.**

    Color points in a gradient line are automatically created with smooth points; you can Option/Alt-click a point on the gradient line to convert it to a corner point.

Click to place the third connected point.

The cursor and preview show that you are still connected to the existing line.

12. **Press the ESC key to disconnect from the current gradient line.**

    As with the Pen tool, the cursor remains connected to the existing line until you intentionally disconnect.

The cursor shows that clicking creates a new point not connected to the previous line.

13. **Click near the middle of the bottom line in the sail shape to create a new color point.**

14. **Double-click the new point to open the color selector. Choose the custom blue swatch as the stop color, then press Return/Enter to dismiss the panel.**

15. **Move the cursor to the middle of the shape, then click to place a new point.**

16. **Move the cursor near the top of the shape, then click to place a third point on the middle line.**

Make sure you don't click directly on top of the top point of the left line; doing so would actually connect to the existing line, which is not what you want.

You can always use the Undo command (Command/Control-Z) to undo the last click if you accidentally connect to another existing point.

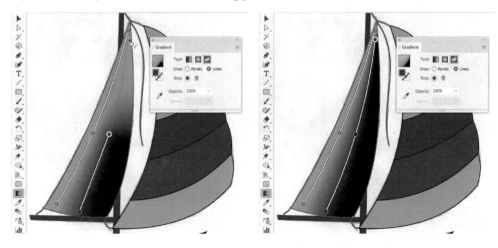

17. **Press the ESC key to disconnect from the current gradient line.**

18. **Repeat Steps 13–17 on the right side of the shape to add a third gradient line, using the custom purple swatch as the color for the stops.**

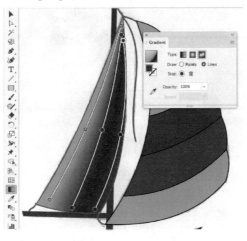

19. **Save the file and continue to the next exercise.**

Edit Global Color Swatches

Global swatches offer a particular advantage when you need to change the colors used in your artwork. In the case of this project, you are going to place this artwork into a stylized ocean illustration, in which blues are the predominant color. To make the boat more prominent in the final poster, you are going to use a yellow-orange scheme — complementary colors to blue — for the boat sails.

1. **With sailboat.ai open, deselect all objects on the artboard.**

2. **In the Swatches panel, double-click the green custom swatch.**

3. **In the resulting Swatch Options dialog box, make sure the Preview option is checked.**

4. **Change the color values to C=0 M=75 Y=75 K=10, and then click OK to change the swatch definition.**

   Because this is a global color swatch, any objects that use the color (including the gradient) reflect the new swatch definition. Locked objects are also affected by the change.

Note:

Complementary color refers to opposing colors on a color wheel.

Everything that was colored with the green swatch is now orange.

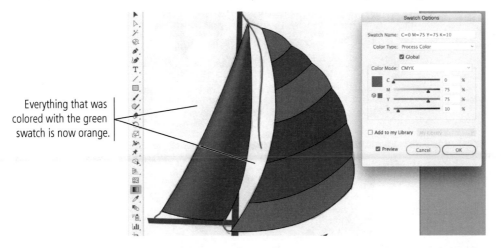

5. **Repeat Steps 2–4 to change the blue swatch definition to C=0 M=10 Y=100 K=0.**

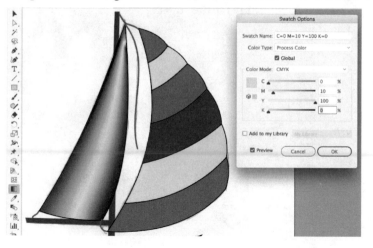

6. **Repeat Steps 2–4 to change the purple swatch definition to C=0 M=60 Y=100 K=0.**

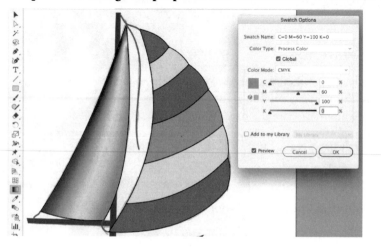

7. **Save the file and continue to the next exercise.**

Understanding Color Terms

Many vague and technical-sounding terms are mentioned when discussing color. Is hue the same as color? The same as value? As tone? What's the difference between lightness and brightness? What is chroma? And where does saturation fit in?

This problem has resulted in several attempts to normalize color communication. A number of systems have been developed to define color according to specific criteria, including Hue, Saturation, and Brightness (HSB); Hue, Saturation, and Lightness (HSL); Hue, Saturation, and Value (HSV); and Lightness, Chroma, and Hue (LCH). Each of these models, or systems, plots color on a three-dimensional diagram, based on the elements of human color perception — hue, intensity, and brightness.

Hue is what most people think of as color — red, green, purple, and so on. Hue is defined according to a color's position on a color wheel, beginning at red (0°) and traveling counterclockwise around the wheel.

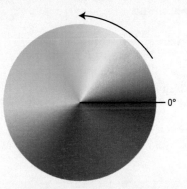

Saturation (also called "intensity") refers to the color's difference from neutral gray. Highly saturated colors are more vivid than those with low saturation. Saturation is plotted from the center of the color wheel. Color at the center is neutral gray and has a saturation value of 0; color at the edge of the wheel has the most intense saturation value (100) of that hue.

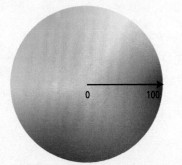

If you bisect the color wheel with a straight line, the line creates a saturation axis for two complementary colors. A color is dulled by the introduction of its complement. Red, for example, is neutralized by the addition of cyan (blue and green). Near the center of the axis, the result is neutral gray.

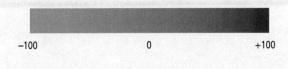

Chroma is similar to saturation, but chroma factors in a reference white. In any viewing situation, colors appear less vivid as the light source dims. The process of chromatic adaptation, however, allows the human visual system to adjust to changes in light and still differentiate colors according to the relative saturation.

Brightness is the amount of light reflected off an object. As an element of color reproduction, brightness is typically judged by comparing the color to the lightest nearby object (such as an unprinted area of white paper).

Lightness is the amount of white or black added to pure color. Lightness (also called "luminance" or "value") is the relative brightness based purely on the black-white value of a color. A lightness value of 0 means there is no addition of white or black. Lightness of +100 is pure white; lightness of −100 is pure black.

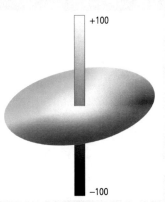

All hues are affected equally by changes in lightness.

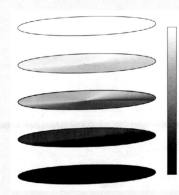

STAGE 3 / Creating the Finished Poster

The final step in the process is to place your finished sailboat in the background illustration that was created by a colleague; this type of collaborative workflow is common in the graphic design world. Although there are many ways to accomplish this task, you are going to use the most basic — copying and pasting — in this project. When all of the pieces are together in the same file, you will make necessary adjustments to make all pieces of the file work together as a single composition.

Manage Artwork with Sublayers

In the first stage of this project you created the entire sailboat on a single layer. When you paste it into the background artwork, you need to be able to manage the sailboat as a single object. In this exercise, you work with sublayers to accomplish this goal.

1. **With sailboat.ai open, make the Section tool active and make sure nothing is selected on the artboard.**

2. **In the Layers panel, click the arrow to the left of the Boat Drawing layer to reveal the sublayers.**

   Individual objects are listed as sublayers in the Layers panel. Because you created all of the artwork in this file on a single layer, every object appears as a sublayer of the Boat Drawing layer.

Click this arrow to expand the layer.

Each object is listed as a sublayer of its parent layer.

3. **Click the empty space to the right of any of the available sublayers.**

   You can use sublayers to select individual objects on a specific layer; the Selected Art icon (the larger rectangle) identifies selected objects. The parent layer of selected art shows a smaller Selected Art icon, which makes it easier to identify which layer contains a specific object.

   Note:

   This technique also works to select individual components of a group.

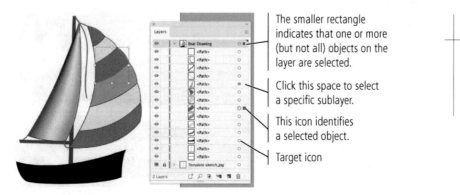

The smaller rectangle indicates that one or more (but not all) objects on the layer are selected.

Click this space to select a specific sublayer.

This icon identifies a selected object.

Target icon

Note:

You can also click the Target icon for a specific layer or sublayer to select specific objects.

4. Choose Select>All.

This command selects all unlocked objects on the artboard. The Layers panel now shows a Selected Art icon for all objects on the Boat Drawing layer. The Selected Art icon for the parent layer is now larger, which means all objects on that layer are selected.

Note:

Press Command/Control-A to select all objects in the file.

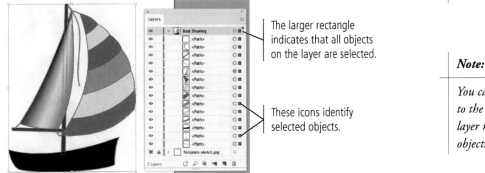

The larger rectangle indicates that all objects on the layer are selected.

These icons identify selected objects.

Note:

You can click the space to the right of a specific layer name to select all objects on that layer.

5. Choose Object>Group. In the Layers panel, click the arrow to expand the Group.

Grouping multiple objects creates a second level of nesting: the Boat Drawing layer is the parent of the Group, which is the parent of the individual objects in the artwork. You can use the Selected Art icons in the Layers panel to select individual objects in a group, just as you can to select those objects when they are not grouped.

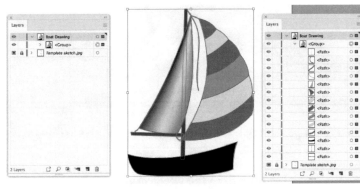

6. In the Layers panel, double-click the <Group> name to highlight it. Type Sailboat to rename the group, then press Return/Enter to finalize the new name.

You can rename sublayers — including groups and individual objects — just as you would rename actual layers. This type of descriptive naming can help you to better organize and manage the elements in a complex file.

7. With the group selected on the artboard, choose Edit>Copy.

8. Save the sailboat.ai file, then choose File>Open. Navigate to poster.ai in the WIP>Regatta folder and click Open.

9. Choose View>Fit Artboard in Window.

This command not only shows you the entire artboard, but also centers the artboard in the active document window.

Note:

You can press Command/Control-C to copy the selected objects.

10. Choose Edit>Paste.

The group you copied in Step 7 is pasted into the poster file, in the center of the document window.

Because you grouped the sailboat objects before you copied them, they are pasted as a group. If you had not grouped them, each object that makes up the sailboat artwork would be pasted as a separate sublayer in the poster file.

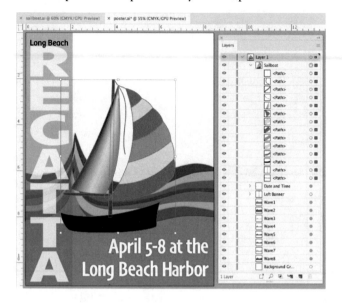

11. In the Layers panel, click the arrow to the left of the Sailboat sublayer to collapse it (if necessary).

12. Using the Selection tool, drag the selected group into the empty space at the top-right section of the poster (use the following image as a guide).

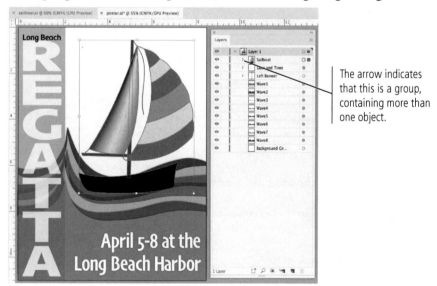

The arrow indicates that this is a group, containing more than one object.

13. **In the Layers panel, drag the Sailboat sublayer down. When a heavy line appears below the Wave6 sublayer, release the mouse button.**

When you use the Edit>Paste command, the pasted objects are placed at the top of the stacking order on the active layer. You can use this method to easily reorder sublayers as necessary.

Changing the stacking-order position of the sublayer means the bottom of the Sailboat group is hidden by sublayers higher in the stack.

14. **If necessary, adjust the position of the sailboat artwork so the entire bottom edge is hidden by the third wave from the top.**

15. **Save the file and continue to the next exercise.**

Lock and Hide Artwork

The final required adjustment for this poster is to change the shape of the highest wave so it looks like a splash. If you review the existing artwork and Layers panel, you can see that the wave nearest the top of the artboard is also the lowest in the sublayer stacking order — Wave8, according to the object names assigned in the Layers panel. To make this task easier, you are going to lock and hide certain sublayers to avoid accidentally changing elements that you don't want to change.

1. **With `poster.ai` open, click the empty space to the left of the Date and Time sublayer. Hold down the mouse button and drag down the same column to lock all other sublayers.**

Individual objects in a file can be locked by clicking the empty space immediately left of the object name in the Layers panel. If a Lock icon already appears in that space, you can click the lock icon to unlock a specific object.

You can also select an object on the artboard and choose Object>Lock.

Click here and drag down over the empty space to lock all sublayers.

2. Click the Lock icon to the left of the Wave8 sublayer to unlock only that element.

The Object>Unlock All menu command is an all-or-nothing option; it unlocks all locked objects on all layers. The Layers panel allows you to unlock only certain objects, which provides better control over your workflow.

Because all other objects in the file are locked, you can now edit the Wave8 shape without affecting the other elements.

Click the lock icon to unlock only the Wave8 sublayer.

3. In the Layers panel, click the Eye icon for the Left Banner sublayer.

The Eye icons identify visible layers and sublayers. You can click any Eye icon to hide an entire layer, or hide only specific sublayers. If an element is already hidden, you can click the empty space in the Layers panel to show that element.

Note:

When an object is locked, you can't select it, which means you also can't change it.

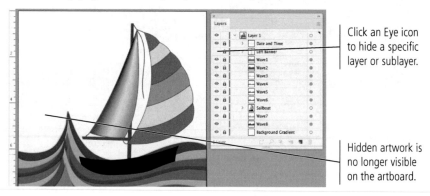

Click an Eye icon to hide a specific layer or sublayer.

Hidden artwork is no longer visible on the artboard.

You can also select an object on the artboard and choose Object>Hide>Selection. The Object>Show All command, however, shows all hidden objects on all layers in the file. As with locking and unlocking objects, it is often better to use the icons in the Layers panel to show and hide exactly (and only) the elements you need.

4. Choose Select>All.

Because all the other sublayers are locked and/or hidden, you selected only the artwork on the Wave8 sublayer.

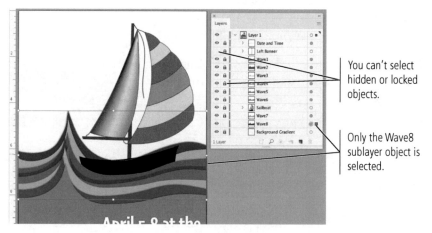

You can't select hidden or locked objects.

Only the Wave8 sublayer object is selected.

5. Save the file and continue to the next exercise.

Create Shapes with the Blob Brush Tool

The Blob Brush tool is used to paint filled shapes, which you can manipulate just as you would any other shape made up of anchor points and handles. In this exercise, you use the Blob Brush tool to paint a splashing wave shape, which you will then merge with the top wave shape to create a single object.

1. **With sailboat.ai open, deselect everything on the artboard.**

2. **Choose the Blob Brush tool (nested under the Paintbrush tool).**

3. **Double-click the Blob Brush tool in the Tools panel to open the Blob Brush Tool Options dialog box.**

4. **Check the Keep Selected option and uncheck Merge Only with Selection.**

   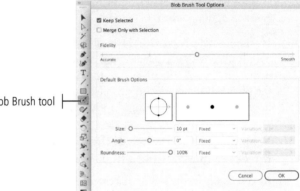

   Overlapping Blob Brush strokes merge to create a single object. If Merge Only with Selected is active, overlapping strokes will not merge unless the previous strokes are selected.

   Blob Brush tool

5. **Set the Fidelity slider to the halfway point.**

   Like the Pencil tool, the Blob Brush tool Tolerance options determine the accuracy of the resulting shape. Fidelity settings nearer the Accurate end of the scale result in more points to better match the path you drag with the tool; a setting closer to the Smooth end of the scale results in fewer points and smoother edges on the shape you draw.

6. **Leave the remaining options at their default values, then click OK.**

   The lower half of the dialog box defines the size, angle, and roundness of the brush cursor.

7. **Reset the default fill and stroke colors, then move the Blob Brush tool cursor near the peak of the top wave shape. Align the right side of the brush to the right side of the wave peak, as shown here:**

Reset the default fill and stroke colors.

When you draw with the Blob Brush tool, the cursor shows the size and shape of the defined brush.

Align the right edge of the cursor to the right edge of the wave shape.

Note:

Press the right bracket key ( ]) to increase the brush size by one point. Press the left bracket key ([ ) to decrease the brush size by one point.

8. **Click and drag to create an arch shape that approximately matches the curve of the existing wave.**

You are essentially painting a shape that matches the brush stroke you see while you drag. As you paint, the path might look a bit sketchy; however, the resulting path is smoothed based on the Fidelity setting defined in the tool options.

When you release the mouse button, the result is a single shape that fills the entire area where you drew. The shape is still selected because you activated the Keep Selected option in the tool options.

It is important to note that the resulting path is filled with the default *stroke* color you defined in Step 7. When you "paint" with the Blob Brush tool, the defined fill color has no effect on the resulting shape unless the stroke color is set to None.

The previous Stroke color becomes the Fill color of the resulting shape.

When you release the mouse button, the result is a filled shape based on where you dragged the brush cursor.

Anchor points are automatically created to define the outside edge of the shape.

9. **With the path still selected, click and drag to create another path near the top of the splash, using a slightly different arch.**

As you complete the rest of this exercise, use our images as a guide. You do not have to match the exact shape you see in our images, but your end result should be similar.

Draw a second arched shape that braches off of the first shape.

The second path is merged with the previous (selected) path.

10. **Continue adding brush strokes to the selected path to create more branches off the splash shape.**

As you draw, you can press the right bracket key ( ]) to increase the brush size by one point; press the left bracket key ([ ) to decrease the brush size by one point. Feel free to enlarge or reduce the brush size to create different thicknesses throughout the shape.

11. **Where the splash shape meets the top wave, make sure the left edge of the splash shape matches the left edge of the wave shape.**

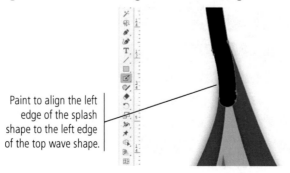

Paint to align the left edge of the splash shape to the left edge of the top wave shape.

12. Paint several shapes that do not overlap the main splash shape.

When you paint a shape that does not overlap the existing selection, it is created as a new, separate shape.

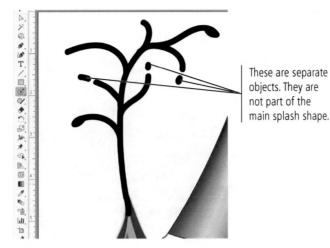

These are separate objects. They are not part of the main splash shape.

13. Deselect everything in the layout.

14. Save the file and continue to the next exercise.

Combine Shapes with the Pathfinder

Using the Illustrator Pathfinder panel, you can combine multiple shapes in a variety of ways, or you can use one object as a "cookie cutter" to remove or separate one shape from another. As you work with more complicated artwork in Illustrator, you will find many different ways to use the Pathfinder functions, alone or in combination.

1. With poster.ai open, open the Pathfinder panel (Window>Pathfinder).

2. In the Layers panel, click the top <Path> sublayer to select it in the panel. Press Shift and click the bottom <Path> object to add it, and all in-between sublayers, to the previous selection.

Selecting an element in the Layers panel is not the same as selecting it on the artboard. The right side of the panel shows no Selected Art icons, which means nothing is selected on the artboard.

Note:

You can Command/ Control-click to select multiple, nonconsecutive layers or sublayers in the Layers panel.

3. In the Layers panel, click any of the selected elements and drag them below the Wave8 sublayer.

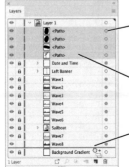
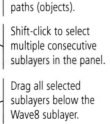

Our splash shape includes four separate paths (objects).

Shift-click to select multiple consecutive sublayers in the panel.

Drag all selected sublayers below the Wave8 sublayer.

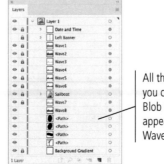

All the path objects you created with the Blob Brush tool should appear below the Wave8 layer.

4. Choose Select>All.

Because most objects are locked, only the top wave and splash shapes are selected.

5. In the Pathfinder panel, click the Unite button.

Options in the Pathfinder panel allow you to cut shapes out of other shapes and merge multiple shapes into a single shape.

Unite button

The Unite function merges overlapping shapes into a single object; non-overlapping objects are grouped with the merged shape. All elements affected by the unification adopt the appearance attributes (fill color, opacity, etc.) of the top-most selected object — which is why you reordered the sublayers in Step 3.

The resulting group contains all objects in the wave shape.

6. Choose Select>Deselect to turn off any active selection.

7. In the Layers panel, click the empty space to the left of the Left Banner sublayer to show that layer.

Click here to reshow the Left Banner sublayer.

8. Save the file and continue to the final exercise.

In the Pathfinder panel, the top row of buttons — the Shape Modes — create complex shapes by combining the originally selected shapes. You can press Option/Alt and click a Shape Mode to maintain the paths from the original objects.

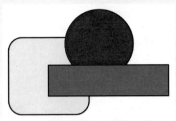

Original objects

Unite combines all selected objects into a single shape. By default, the Shape options result in a single new object.

If you Option/Alt-click a shape mode button, the result maintains the original paths unless you manually expand it.

Minus Front removes overlapping areas from the backmost shape in the selection.

Intersect creates a shape of only areas where all selected objects overlap.

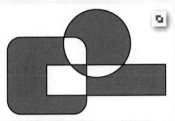

Exclude removes any areas where two objects overlap.

The second row of options — the Pathfinders — do exactly that. The resulting shapes are some combination of the paths that made up the originally selected objects.

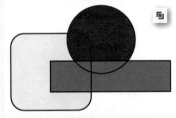

Divide creates separate shapes from all overlapping areas of selected objects.

Trim removes underlying areas of overlapping objects. Objects of the same fill color are not combined.

Merge removes underlying areas of overlapping objects. Objects of the same fill color are combined.

Crop returns the areas of underlying objects that are within the boundary of the topmost object.

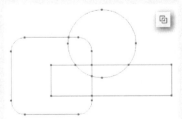

Outline divides the selected objects, then returns unfilled, open paths.

Minus Back removes the area of underlying objects from the front object.

Save the File as PDF

Adobe PDF (or simply PDF, for Portable Document Format) has become a universal method of moving files to virtually any digital destination. One of the most important uses for the PDF format is the ability to create perfectly formatted digital documents, exactly as they would appear if printed on paper. You can embed fonts, images, drawings, and other elements into the file so all the required bits are available on any computer. The PDF format can be used to move your artwork to the web as a low-resolution RGB file or to a commercial printer as a high-resolution CMYK file.

1. **With `poster.ai` open, choose File>Save As.**
   If necessary, navigate to your WIP>Regatta folder as the target location.

2. **Choose Adobe PDF in the Format/Save As Type menu and click Save.**

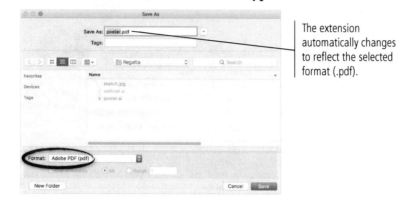

The extension automatically changes to reflect the selected format (.pdf).

3. **Choose Illustrator Default in the Adobe PDF Preset menu.**

4. **Review the options in the General pane.**

   Read the description area to see what Adobe has to say about these options.

Use this menu to call a group of saved settings (called a preset).

Choose a category from this menu to see related options.

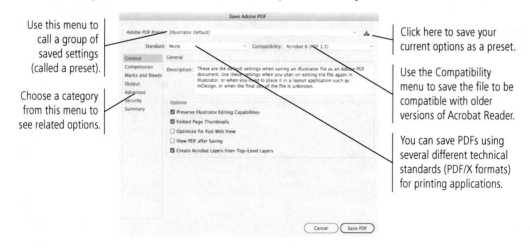

Click here to save your current options as a preset.

Use the Compatibility menu to save the file to be compatible with older versions of Acrobat Reader.

You can save PDFs using several different technical standards (PDF/X formats) for printing applications.

5. Click Compression in the list of categories on the left and review the options.

These options allow you to reduce the resulting file size by compressing color, grayscale, and/or monochrome bitmap (raster) images. You can also compress text and line art by clicking the check box at the bottom.

6. Review the Marks and Bleeds options.

These options add different marks to the output page:

- **Trim marks** indicate the edge of the page, where a page printed on a larger sheet will be cut down to its final size. You can also define the thickness (weight) of the trim marks, as well as how far from the page edge the lines should appear (offset).

- **Registration marks** resemble a small crosshair. These marks are added to each ink unit on a printing press to make sure the different inks are properly aligned to one another.

- **Color bars** are rows of small squares across the sheet, used to verify press settings for accurate color reproduction.

- **Page information** adds the file name, date, and time of output.

- **Bleeds** define how much of elements outside the page boundaries will be included in the final output. Most printers require at least a 0.125″ bleed on each side, but you should always ask before you create the final file.

Note:

Most printers require trim marks to be created outside the bleed area. Always check with your service provider when saving a PDF for commercial output.

Note:

The other categories of options are explained in later projects that discuss transparency and color management.

7. Click Save PDF.

8. Close any open Illustrator files.

PROJECT REVIEW

fill in the blank

1. The _____ tool is used to place anchor points that are connected by line segments.

2. The _____ tool is used to change a smooth anchor point to a corner anchor point (and vice versa).

3. The _____ tool is used to edit individual anchor points (and their related handles) on a vector path.

4. _____ is the range of possible colors within a specific color model.

5. _____ are the four component colors in process-color output.

6. The _____ panel includes value sliders for each component in the defined color model.

7. The _____ is used to paint shapes of solid color based on the defined brush size and the area you drag with a single mouse click.

8. The _____ appears over a gradient-filled object when selected with the Gradient tool; you can use it to control the position and direction of color in the gradient-filled object.

9. Changes made to a _____ color swatch are reflected in all elements where that color is applied.

10. Individual objects on a layer appear as _____ in the Layers panel.

short answer

1. Describe three ways to deselect the current selection on the artboard.

2. Briefly explain the significance of "process color" related to Illustrator artwork.

3. Briefly explain the advantage of using the PDF format for creating printable files.

PORTFOLIO BUILDER PROJECT

Use what you have learned in this project to complete the following freeform exercise.
Carefully read the art director and client comments, then create your own design to meet the needs of the project.
Use the space below to sketch ideas. When finished, write a brief explanation of the reasoning behind your final design.

art director comments

Your local animal shelter hosts an annual fundraising gala on the first Saturday in October. You have been hired to create a poster advertising this year's theme — a classic, black-tie masquerade ball.

❑ Design an 11″ × 17″ poster to promote the event in local storefronts and public venues.

❑ Develop a creative type treatment for the event name: "Barking Mad for the Masquerade."

❑ Find or create imagery and graphics to support the event theme.

❑ Include the event date (look at this year's calendar to find the exact date) prominently in the poster design.

❑ Include the contact information (phone number and web address) for your local animal shelter.

client comments

We raise a considerable portion of our annual operating budget during this annual event. This year, the theme is a very classic masquerade in the style of Victorian-England opulence — think "Phantom of the Opera," the state dining room on the Titanic, that sort of thing. Men in tuxes and women in flowing gowns, everyone masked in some fashion until the traditional "reveal" at midnight.

Every year, the event includes a silent auction with some incredible prizes that are donated by local businesses, as well as a gourmet four-course meal prepared by a celebrity chef.

If there is any way you could tastefully incorporate a couple of animal photos in the poster, we would like that. However, it isn't really a requirement as long as the shelter's name and contact information is clearly displayed.

project justification

PROJECT SUMMARY

This project incorporated more advanced drawing techniques that allow you to exercise precise control over every point and path in a file. The Pen tool is arguably one of the most important tools you will use throughout your career as an illustrator; although it can be challenging at first, practice is the best way to master this skill.

This project also explored working with color in Illustrator: applying color, saving global color swatches to make changes more efficiently, and using gradients to add visual interest.

Finally, you saved your artwork in a file format that is commonly used to share Illustrator artwork with other applications. The PDF format is an invaluable part of design workflows using software applications that can't import native Illustrator files.

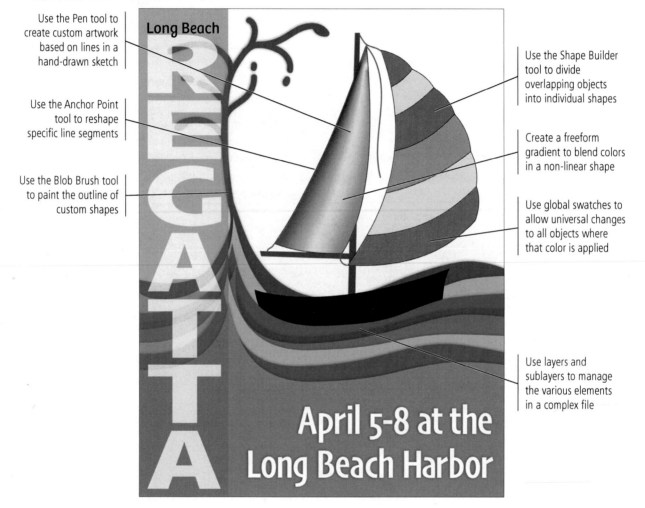

Use the Pen tool to create custom artwork based on lines in a hand-drawn sketch

Use the Anchor Point tool to reshape specific line segments

Use the Blob Brush tool to paint the outline of custom shapes

Use the Shape Builder tool to divide overlapping objects into individual shapes

Create a freeform gradient to blend colors in a non-linear shape

Use global swatches to allow universal changes to all objects where that color is applied

Use layers and sublayers to manage the various elements in a complex file

Identity Package

3

Your client is rebranding and relaunching a local cafe that has been open since 1982. She has hired you to create a logo for the establishment's new name, as well as stationery that can be used for various purposes throughout the business operations.

This project incorporates the following skills:

❑ Developing custom logo artwork based on an object in a photograph

❑ Using a gradient mesh to create realistic color blends

❑ Manipulating letter shapes to create a finished logotype

❑ Using layers to easily manage complex artwork

❑ Creating multiple artboards to contain specific projects and layouts

❑ Building various logo versions to meet specific output requirements

❑ Printing desktop proofs of individual artboards

PROJECT MEETING

In six weeks, Home Town Diner will officially become Cafe Limon. First, we need a logo for the new name. I want the words to be clearly styled — not just regular type — using a lemon in place of the letter "o."

We want to have everything in place for the Grand Reopening, so we need to make things as versatile as possible. Once the logo is created, we need a letterhead-style page that we're going to have printed in large quantities. We'll use those preprinted blanks for everything, including daily menus, invoices, and correspondence.

The printer I spoke with said I could do this for less money if I go "four-color" for the letterhead, but "two-color" for the envelope; I really don't know what that means — I'm hoping you do.

The logo is the first part of this project because you will use it on the other two pieces. The client told you exactly what she wants, so that part is done. I had our photographer take a good picture of a lemon; use that as the basis for the one you draw in the logo art.

The client wants to print the letterhead in four-color and the envelope in two-color, so you will have to create two different versions of the logo. Since logos are used on far more than just these two jobs in this one application, you should also create a one-color version because the client will inevitably ask for it at some point.

To complete this project, you will:

- ❏ Use the Pen tool to trace the outline of a photograph
- ❏ Create a gradient mesh
- ❏ Use Smart Guides to manage a gradient mesh
- ❏ Use effects to add object highlights
- ❏ Create and control point-type objects
- ❏ Convert text to outlines so you can manipulate the letter shapes
- ❏ Use the Appearance panel to revert gradient mesh objects back to regular paths
- ❏ Apply spot-color inks for special printing applications
- ❏ Create versions of the final logo for one-color, two-color, and four-color printing
- ❏ Print desktop proofs of the completed identity pieces

STAGE 1 / Working with Gradient Meshes

There are several important points to keep in mind when you design a logo. First, logos need to be scalable. A company might place its logo on the head of a golf tee or on the side of a building. Vector graphics — the kind you typically create in Illustrator — can be scaled as large or small as necessary without losing quality. Photographs are raster images, and they typically can't be greatly enlarged or reduced without losing quality. That's why you're converting a photograph (a raster image) into a vector graphic in this project.

Second, you almost always need more than one version of a logo. Different kinds of output require different formats (specifically, one set of files for print and one for the web), and some types of jobs require special options saved in the files, such as the four-color, two-color, and one-color versions that you will create in this project.

Set up the Workspace

Illustrator includes a number of tools ideally suited for creating lifelike illustrations. In this project, you will work from a photograph to create a vector-based lemon graphic that will be part of your client's logo. You will start with the full-color version, and then work from there to create variations that are part of a typical logo package.

1. Download **Cafe_AI19_RF.zip** from the Student Files web page.

2. **Expand the ZIP archive in your WIP folder (Macintosh) or copy the archive contents into your WIP folder (Windows).**

   This results in a folder named **Cafe**, which contains the files you need for this project. You should also use this folder to save the files you create in this project.

3. **In Illustrator, choose File>New. Choose the Print option at the top of the dialog box, and then choose the Letter document preset.**

   Remember, using the Print category of presets automatically applies the CMYK color mode and 300 ppi raster effects.

   Because the CMYK gamut is smaller than the RGB gamut, you are starting with the smaller gamut to avoid the color shift that could occur if you started with RGB and converted the colors to CMYK. You are also creating the file to meet the high-resolution requirements of commercial printing.

4. **Define the following settings in the Preset Details section:**

Name:	**cafe-logo**
Units:	**Inches**
Orientation:	**Portrait**
Artboards:	**1**

   You are simply using this artboard as a drawing space, so you only need to make it large enough to draw. Later, you will adjust the artboard to meet the specific needs of the finished logo. You will also add multiple artboards to hold various versions of the logo.

5. **Click Create to create the file.**

6. **Choose View>Fit Artboard in Window.**

   The Fit Artboard in Window command centers the artboard in the document window, so the template image you place in the next step will be automatically centered on the artboard.

7. **Choose File>Place. Navigate to lemon.jpg in your WIP>Cafe folder. Make sure the Template option is checked, and then click Place.**

   Macintosh users might need to click the Options button to access the actual Options at the bottom of the dialog box.

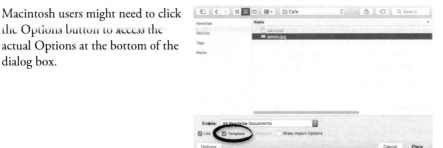

8. **In the Layers panel, double-click the template layer icon to open the Layer Options dialog box. Uncheck the Dim Images option, then click OK.**

   Choosing the Template option places an image onto a template layer that is automatically dimmed. You want the photograph to appear at full visibility so you can extract colors from the photo.

Uncheck this option.

   For most of the drawing process, you will use the lemon photo as the basis of your artwork. You will draw on other layers, and then delete the template layer when your lemon graphic is complete. You're starting with a letter-size artboard. After you finish the logo graphic, you will resize the artboard to fit the artwork.

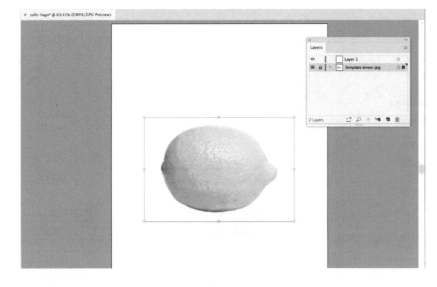

9. **Save the file as a native Illustrator file named cafe-logo.ai in your WIP>Cafe folder, and then continue to the next exercise.**

Note:

Whenever you save an Illustrator file throughout this book, use the default Illustrator options.

Create a Gradient Mesh

A gradient mesh is basically a special type of fill. Each point in the mesh can have a different color value. Areas between mesh lines are gradients of the surrounding point colors; connecting lines between mesh points control the shape of related gradients.

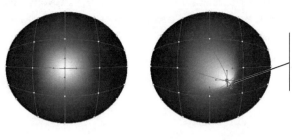

Moving a mesh point or changing its handles affects the position and shape of the associated gradient areas.

1. With **cafe-logo.ai** open, double-click the Layer 1 name and type **Lemon**. Press Return/Enter to finalize the new layer name.

2. Using the Pen tool with a 1-pt black stroke and no fill, draw the outline of the lemon in the template image.

3. If necessary, use the Direct Selection tool to adjust the anchor points and handles until the outline matches the lemon shape.

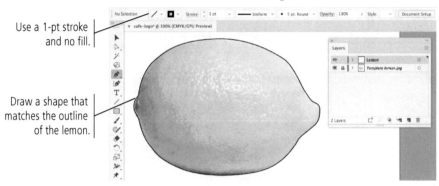

Use a 1-pt stroke and no fill.

Draw a shape that matches the outline of the lemon.

Note:

Refer back to Project 2: Regatta Artwork for details about drawing and editing Bézier curves.

4. Using the Selection tool, select the outline shape on the Lemon layer.

5. Using the Eyedropper tool, click a medium-yellow color in the template image to fill the selected shape with the sampled color.

You can add a gradient mesh to a path without filling it with color first, but if you don't choose a color, the mesh will automatically fill with white.

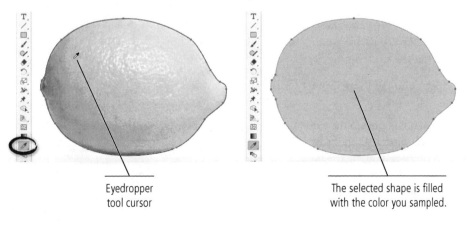

Eyedropper tool cursor

The selected shape is filled with the color you sampled.

6. **Choose Object>Create Gradient Mesh.**

7. **In the Create Gradient Mesh dialog box, activate the Preview option. Set the Rows value to 8 and the Columns value to 7, and make sure the Appearance menu is set to Flat.**

   The Rows and Columns settings determine how many lines make up the resulting mesh.

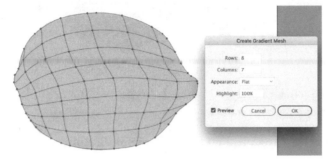

Note:

When you convert a path to a mesh, the shape is no longer a path. You cannot apply a stroke attribute to a gradient mesh object.

8. **Click OK to create the mesh.**

9. **Save the file and continue to the next exercise.**

Understanding Gradient Mesh Options

The Appearance option in the Create Gradient Mesh dialog box determines how colors affect the mesh you create.

Flat spreads a single color to all points in the mesh. If you don't fill the shape with a color before creating the mesh, the mesh object will fill with white.

To Center creates a white highlight at the center and spreads the highlight color outward toward the object edges. The Highlight (%) field controls the strength of white in the resulting mesh.

To Edge is essentially the opposite of the To Center option; the white highlight appears around the edges of the mesh, blending to the solid color in the center of the mesh object.

  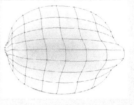

Work in Outline Mode

Outline mode allows you to see the points and paths of an object without the colors and fills. This viewing mode can be very useful when you need to adjust anchor points of one shape while viewing the underlying objects.

1. **With cafe-logo.ai open, choose View>Smart Guides to make sure that option is turned on.**

   When Smart Guides are active, you can see the entire mesh wireframe as soon as your cursor touches any part of the object —even if that object is not selected. The cursor feedback also identifies specific points along the mesh.

2. **Make sure the Snap to Point option is toggled off in the View menu.**

Turn on Smart Guides.

Turn off Snap to Point.

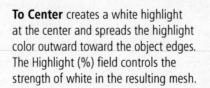

Note:

When using Smart Guides, make sure the Snap to Point option is toggled off. If Snap to Point is active, Smart Guides will not work (even if you have the command selected in the menu).

3. **Choose View>Outline.**

   In Outline mode, you see only the edges, or **wireframes**, of the objects in the file.

   Template layers are not affected when you view the file in Outline mode. You can now see the mesh wireframe and the actual pixels of the lemon image, enabling you to sample colors directly from the lemon image, and then use those colors to paint the mesh points.

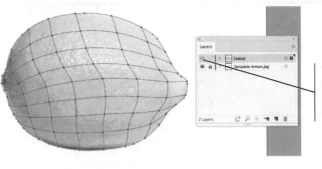

The iris in the icon is missing when a layer displays in Outline mode.

4. **Using the Direct Selection tool, click the left anchor point on the bottom horizontal mesh line to select only that mesh point.**

   Your mesh might appear different than ours, based on where you placed your anchor points on the shape edges. You will still be able to achieve the same overall effect as what you see in our examples.

5. **With the mesh point selected, choose the Eyedropper tool in the Tools panel, and then click next to the selected mesh point to sample the color from the lemon photo.**

   Because the mesh object is still displayed in Outline mode, you can't see the effect of the color sampling.

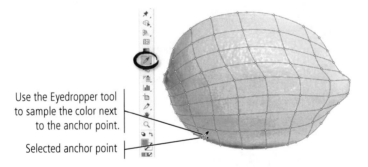

Use the Eyedropper tool to sample the color next to the anchor point.

Selected anchor point

6. **Press and hold the Command/Control key to temporarily access the Direct Selection tool, and then click to select the next point along the bottom line of the mesh.**

   Remember, pressing Command/Control with another tool selected temporarily accesses the last-used Selection tool.

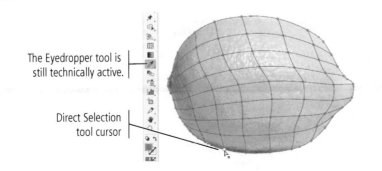

The Eyedropper tool is still technically active.

Direct Selection tool cursor

Note:

In our screen shots, we have the bounding box turned off to better show only the mesh points. You can turn off the bounding box by choosing View>Hide Bounding Box.

7. **Release the Command/Control key to return to the Eyedropper tool, and then click to sample the color next to the selected mesh point.**

When you release the Command/Control key, you return to the previously active tool.

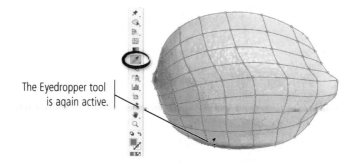

The Eyedropper tool is again active.

8. **Continue this process to change the color of all mesh points on the bottom three rows of points on the mesh.**

As you progress, keep an eye on which point is actually selected when you click with the Direct Selection tool. The handles of one mesh point might overlap the actual anchor point; you might actually be clicking the handle of another point and, ultimately, selecting the point related to the handle instead of the point you want to affect. If this is the case, you can click and drag a marquee to select the actual mesh point instead of simply clicking.

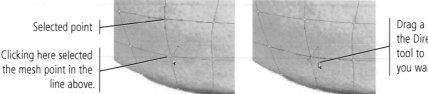

Selected point

Clicking here selected the mesh point in the line above.

Drag a marquee with the Direct Selection tool to select the point you want to affect.

9. **Command/Control-click the eye icon for the Lemon layer to change only that layer back to Preview mode.**

When working in Outline mode, Command/Control-clicking a layer's visibility icon (the eye icon) returns only that layer to Preview mode.

10. **Deselect the mesh object and review your progress.**

When you change the color of a mesh point, you change the way surrounding colors blend into that point's color. After painting only the bottom three rows of mesh points, you can already see how the shadows and highlights are starting to blend naturally.

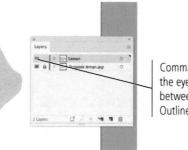

Command/Control-click the eye icon to toggle between Preview and Outline modes.

11. **Command/Control-click the eye icon for the Lemon layer to change that layer back to Outline mode.**

12. **Using the same technique from the previous steps, finish painting all the mesh points in the mesh object.**

   This task might seem tedious because there are so many points in the mesh, but with this process, you can create realistic depth in a flat vector object in a matter of minutes. To accomplish the same result using manual techniques would require many hours of time and a high degree of artistic skill.

13. **Deselect the mesh object. Command/Control-click the Lemon layer eye icon to return that layer to Preview mode, then review your results.**

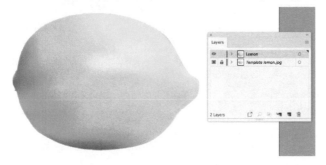

14. **Select the template layer in the Layers panel, then click the Delete Selection button at the bottom of the panel to remove the template layer. When asked to confirm the deletion, click Yes.**

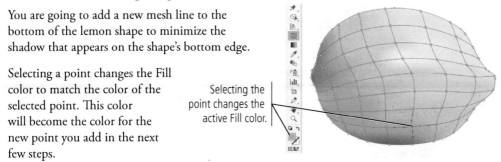

15. **Save the file and continue to the next exercise.**

Edit the Gradient Mesh Lines

In addition to simply painting the points that were created when you defined the mesh, you can add to or remove lines from the mesh, move existing points, and even adjust the point handles to change the blending direction. In this exercise, you will adjust the mesh to manipulate the shadows that appear in the lemon artwork.

1. **With cafe-logo.ai open, make sure the Direct Selection tool is active.**

2. **Click to select the center point along the bottom internal mesh line (as shown in the following image).**

   You are going to add a new mesh line to the bottom of the lemon shape to minimize the shadow that appears on the shape's bottom edge.

   Selecting a point changes the Fill color to match the color of the selected point. This color will become the color for the new point you add in the next few steps.

   Selecting the point changes the active Fill color.

3. **Click away from the shape to deselect it, then choose the Mesh tool in the Tools panel.**

   The Mesh tool adds new gridlines to an existing mesh, or it creates a mesh if you click inside a basic shape that doesn't currently have a mesh. You can also press Option/Alt and click an existing gridline to remove it from the mesh.

4. **Move the cursor over the center vertical gridline, between the bottom edge and the first internal horizontal gridline.**

   Because Smart Guides are active, you can see the mesh lines as soon as the tool cursor enters the shape area.

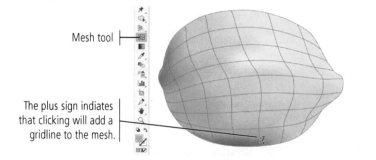

Mesh tool

The plus sign indiates that clicking will add a gridline to the mesh.

> **Note:**
>
> *If you don't see the plus sign in the Mesh tool cursor, clicking simply selects an existing point or handle on the mesh.*

5. **When you see a plus sign in the tool cursor, click to add a new gridline to the mesh.**

   When you see the plus sign in the cursor, clicking adds a new line to the mesh. Clicking a horizontal gridline adds a new vertical one; clicking a vertical gridline adds a new horizontal one.

   The point where you click uses the fill color you defined in Step 2. The darker color on the bottom edge now only extends as far as the new line; you have effectively reduced the shadow area in half by adding the new gridline.

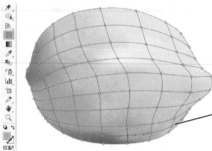

This line was added to our mesh.

6. **Using the Eyedropper method from the previous exercise, change the color of each mesh point on the new row to match the point immediately above it.**

7. **Using the Direct Selection tool, move down the points in the new horizontal mesh line to further reduce the shadow distance on the shape's bottom edge.**

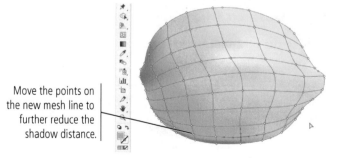

Move the points on the new mesh line to further reduce the shadow distance.

8. **Continue adjusting the positions and colors of the mesh points until you are satisfied with the result.**

9. **Save the file and continue to the next stage of the project.**

STAGE 2 / Working with Type

In this stage of the project, you will use some of Illustrator's basic type formatting options to set your client's company name. You will also use illustration techniques to manipulate the individual letter shapes in the company name to create the finished logotype.

Before you begin the exercises in the second stage of this project, you should understand the terms that are commonly used when people talk about type. Keep the following terms in mind as you work through the next exercises.

Baseline ⊢ Never tell people how to do things. ⊣ Serif font

Tell them what to do and they will

Leading ⊢ surprise you with their ingenuity. ⊣ Body clearance

– George Smith Patton, *War as I Knew It*, 1947 ⊣ Sans-serif font

Type is typically divided into two basic categories: serif and sans serif. **Serif type** has small flourishes on the ends of the letterforms; **sans-serif** has no such decorations (*sans* is French for "without"). There are other categories of special or decorative fonts, including script, symbol, dingbat, decorative, and image fonts.

The actual shape of letters is determined by the specific **font** you use; each character in a font is referred to as a **glyph**. Fonts can be monospaced or proportionally spaced. In a monospace font, each character takes up the same amount of space on a line; in other words, a lowercase i and m occupy the same horizontal space. In a proportionally spaced font, different characters occupy different amounts of horizontal space as necessary.

The **x-height** of type is the height of the lowercase letter x. Elements that extend below the baseline are called **descenders** (as in g, j, and p); elements that extend above the x-height are called **ascenders** (as in b, d, and k).

The size of type is usually measured in **points**; there are approximately 72 points in an inch. When you define type size, you determine the distance from the bottom of descenders to the top of ascenders (plus a small extra space above ascenders called the **body clearance**).

When you set type, it rests on a non-printing line called the **baseline**. If a type element has more than one line in a single paragraph, the distance from one baseline to the next is called **leading** (pronounced "ledding"). Most applications set the default leading as 120% of the type size.

Create Point-Type Objects

Creating type in Illustrator is fairly simple; just click with the Type tool and begin typing. Many advanced options are also available, such as importing type from an external file, using type areas to control long blocks of text, and so on. In this project, you concentrate on the basic type formatting controls.

1. **With `cafe-logo.ai` open (from your WIP>Cafe folder), choose View>GPU Preview.**

   Although you changed the Lemon layer back to the Preview mode in the previous exercise, the overall file is still technically in Outline mode.

   Note:

   If you can't use GPU preview, choose View>Preview on CPU.

2. **Lock and hide the Lemon layer. Create a new layer named `Type` at the top of the layer stack, and make sure the new layer is selected.**

3. **Choose the Type tool in the Tools panel, and then click an empty area of the artboard to create a new point-type object.**

When you single-click with the Type tool, you create **point type**. The type object is automatically filled with placeholder text, which is highlighted. The type automatically defaults to black fill and no stroke, set with the last-used character and paragraph formatting options.

Depending on the width of your application frame, basic character and paragraph formatting options might be available in the Control panel. If not, you can use the Character and Paragraph hot-text links to open the pop-up panels.

You can also access character and paragraph formatting options in the Properties panel whenever a type object is selected.

Note:

You can turn off the automatic placeholder text in the Type Preferences dialog box by unchecking the Fill New Type Objects with Placeholder Text option.

Highlighted placeholder text

The Control panel might include basic text formatting options.

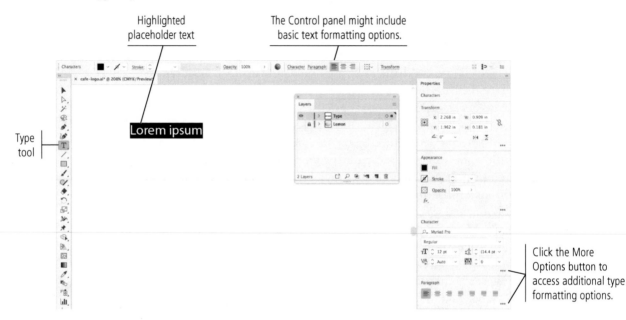

Type tool

Click the More Options button to access additional type formatting options.

4. **With the placeholder text highlighted, type** `cafe`**.**

When the type tool is active and text is not highlighted, the insertion point flashes in the type object. This insertion point marks the location where text will be added if you continue typing.

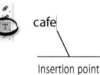

cafe

Insertion point

5. **Choose the Direct Selection tool in the Tools panel.**

When selected with the Direct Selection tool, you can see the point and path that make up the type object.

6. **Open the Character panel (Window>Type>Character).**

The Character panel provides access to all character formatting options that can be applied in Illustrator. Character formatting options can also be accessed in the Properties panel, or by clicking the Character hot-text link in the Control panel.

Note:

Hot text *is any text in the user interface that appears underlined in a panel. Clicking these hot-text links opens a panel or dialog box where you can change the related settings.*

You can create two basic kinds of type (or text) objects in Illustrator: **point-type objects** (also called **path type**), where the text usually resides on a single line or path, and **area-type objects**, where the text fills a specific shape (usually a rectangle).

Clicking with the Type tool creates a point-type object. Clicking and dragging with the Type tool creates an area-type object.

Point type (or path type) starts at a single point and extends along or follows a single path. **Area type** fills up an area (normally a rectangle).

The difference between the two kinds of type becomes obvious when you try to resize them or otherwise modify their shapes using the Selection tool. Area type is contained within an area. If you resize that area, the type doesn't resize; it remains within the area but simply flows (or wraps) differently. If you scale or resize point type by dragging a bounding box handle, the type within the object resizes accordingly.

Point-Type Objects

When selected with the Direct Selection tool, you can see the paths that make up the type object.

This is a point type object, which is created by clicking once with the Type tool.

When selected with the Selection tool, you can see the object's bounding-box handles.

This is a point type object, which is created by clicking once with the Type tool.

Using the Selection tool, resizing the bounding box resizes the text in the point-type object.

This is a point type object, which is created by clicking once with the Type tool.

Area-Type Objects

When selected with the Direct Selection tool, you can see the edges of the type object, but no bounding-box handles appear.

This is an area type object, which is created by clicking and dragging with the Type tool.

You can see the edges of the type object, as well as the object's bounding-box handles.

This is an area type object, which is created by clicking and dragging with the Type tool.

Using the Selection tool, resizing the bounding box resizes the object; the text rewraps inside the new object dimensions.

This is an area type object, which is created by clicking and dragging with the Type tool.

Path Alignment

Another consideration is where the "point" sits on the type path. When you change the paragraph alignment of point type, the point remains in the same position; the text on the point moves to the appropriate position, relative to the fixed point.

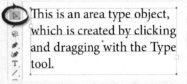

Point (path) type — Left-aligned text

Point (path) type — Center-aligned text

Point (path) type — Right-aligned text

The point for path type is determined by where you click to place the object.

Converting Type Objects

When the Selection tool is active, the handle on the right side of the type-object bounding box indicates whether that object contains point type or area type. A hollow handle identifies a point-type object; a solid handle identifies an area-type object. When you move the cursor over a type object, an icon in the cursor indicates that double-clicking will convert the object to the other kind of type object.

This is an area type object, which is created by clicking and dragging with the Type tool.

Double-click the hollow handle to convert to an area-type object.

This is an area type object, which is created by clicking and dragging with the Type tool.

Double-click the solid handle to convert to a point-type object.

7. **Click the Font Family field to highlight the active font. Type atc.**

When you type in the Font Family field, a menu shows all fonts that include the letters you type. By default, the menu includes any font containing those letters, regardless of the position of the letters within the font name. In other words, typing "gar" would show fonts named both "Garamond" and "Adobe Garamond."

If you click the Magnifying Glass icon to the left of the field, you can choose Search First Word Only. In that case, the letters you type automatically scroll the Font Family list to the first font with the typed letters at the beginning of the name; typing "gar" would scroll to Garamond and skip over Adobe Garamond.

8. **Move your mouse cursor over various fonts in the menu.**

You can use this method in the font menu to show a live preview of various fonts before actually applying them to the selected text.

Individual characters do not need to be selected to change text formatting. Changes made while a type *object* is selected apply to all text in that type object.

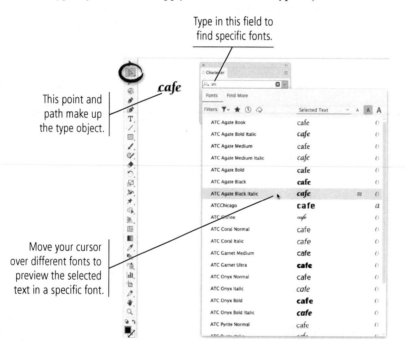

Type in this field to find specific fonts.

This point and path make up the type object.

Move your cursor over different fonts to preview the selected text in a specific font.

9. **Click ATC Garnet Medium in the Font menu to select that font.**

After you select the font, you should notice that the Font Family menu shows "ATC Garnet" and the secondary Font Style menu shows "Medium." When you use the Font Search option (as in Step 7), the resulting menu shows all font variations that include the letters you type — including different styles within the same family.

Font Family
Font Style

10. **Click the Selection tool in the Tools panel.**

When the Selection tool is active, you can see the bounding-box handles of the type object. (If you don't see the bounding box, choose View>Show Bounding Box to toggle it on.) Like any other object, you can use the handles to stretch, scale, or rotate the type object.

11. Click any of the type object's corner handles and drag out to make the type larger. When the cursor feedback shows the object's height of approximately 0.5 in, release the mouse button.

You can press Shift after you begin dragging to constrain the object's original proportions.

We turned Smart Guides on (View>Smart Guides) to show the cursor feedback in our screen shots.

12. If you only see four fields below the Font Style menu in the Character panel, open the panel Options menu and choose Show Options.

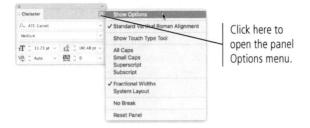

Click here to open the panel Options menu.

13. Review the extended character formatting options in the Character panel.

The Size menu shows the new size that results from resizing the object by dragging its bounding-box handles. If you do not constrain the resizing, you might have a horizontal or vertical scale other than 100%.

14. In the Character panel, change the Size field to 72. Make sure both the horizontal and vertical scale values are set to 100%.

Pressing Tab moves through the panel fields; as soon as you move to a new field, your changes in the previous field are reflected in the document. You can also press Return/Enter to finalize a change.

15. Using the Type tool, double-click the word "cafe" to select all the letters in the word.

16. In the Character panel, change the Tracking field to -10 to tighten the space between all selected letters.

Tracking and kerning are two terms related to the horizontal spacing between characters in a line of text. **Kerning** is the spacing between two specific characters; **tracking** refers to the spacing between all characters in a selection.

Smaller type does not usually pose tracking and kerning problems; when type is very large, however, spacing often becomes an issue. To fix spacing problems, you need to adjust the kerning and/or tracking values.

You can change the field manually, choose a pre-defined value from the Tracking menu, or click the up- or down-arrow button to change the tracking by 1 unit with each click.

The Character Panel in Depth

The Character panel includes all the options you can use to change the appearance of selected text characters.

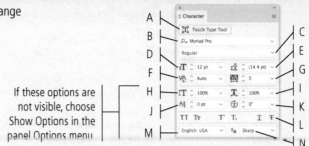

If these options are not visible, choose Show Options in the panel Options menu

A The **Touch Type tool** is used to change the shape and position of individual characters in a text object. If this tool is not visible at the top of the panel, you can choose Show Touch Type Tool in the panel Options menu.

B **Font Family** is the general font that is applied, such as Minion or Warnock Pro.

C **Font Style** is the specific variation of the applied font, such as Italic, Bold, or Light.

D **Font Size** is the size of the type in points.

E **Leading** is the distance from one baseline to the next. Adobe applications treat leading as a character attribute, even though leading controls the space between lines of an individual paragraph. (Space between paragraphs is controlled using the Space Before and Space After options in the Paragraph panel.) To change leading for an entire paragraph, you must first select the entire paragraph.

If you change the leading for only certain characters in a line, keep in mind that the adjusted leading applies to the entire line where adjusted characters exist; for example:

> In this sentence, we changed the leading for only the <u>underlined</u> word; all text in the same line moves to accommodate the adjusted leading of the characters.

F **Kerning** increases or decreases the space between pairs of letters. Kerning is used in cases where particular letters in specific fonts need to be manually spread apart or brought together to eliminate a too-tight or too-spread-out appearance. Manual kerning is usually necessary in headlines or other large type elements. Many commercial fonts have built-in kerning pairs, so you won't need to apply much hands-on intervention with kerning. Adobe applications default to the kerning values stored in the **font metrics**.

G **Tracking**, also known as "range kerning," refers to the overall tightness or looseness across a range of characters. Tracking and kerning are applied in thousandths of an **em** (or the amount of space occupied by an uppercase "M," which is usually the widest character in a typeface).

H, I **Vertical Scale** and **Horizontal Scale** artificially stretch or contract the selected characters. This scaling is a quick way of achieving condensed or expanded type if those variations of a font don't exist. Type that has been artificially condensed or expanded too much looks bad because the scaling destroys the type's metrics. If possible, use a condensed or expanded version of a font before resorting to horizontal or vertical scaling.

J **Baseline Shift** moves the selected type above or below the baseline by a specific number of points. Positive numbers move the characters up; negative values move the characters down.

K **Character Rotation** rotates only selected letters, rather than rotating the entire type object.

L Type Styles — **All Caps**, **Small Caps**, **Superscript**, **Subscript**, **Underline**, and **Strikethrough** — change the appearance of selected characters.

M **Language Dictionary** defines the language that is used to check spelling in the story.

N **Anti-aliasing** can be used to help smooth the apparent edges of type that is exported to a bitmap format that does not support vector information.

17. **Click with the Type tool to place the insertion point between the "c" and the "a".**

   This is a good example of a **kern pair** that needs adjustment. The Auto setting built into the font leaves a little too much space between the two characters, even after you have tightened the tracking considerably.

18. **Change the Kerning value to -20.**

   Like tracking, you can change this value manually, choose a value from the pop-up menu, or use the Kerning field buttons to change kerning by 1 unit.

   These slight modifications to tracking and kerning improve the overall appearance and readability of the logo. Later in the project, you will use a different technique to adjust letter spacing. For now, however, you should become familiar with making this type of manual adjustment.

Insertion point

Note:

Kerning and tracking are largely matters of personal preference. Some people prefer much tighter spacing than others.

19. **Save the file and continue to the next exercise.**

Manipulate Type Objects

When you work with type in Illustrator, you need to be aware of a few special issues that can affect the way you interact with the application. This exercise explores some common problems that can arise when you work with type, as well as some tricks you can use to work around them.

1. **With cafe-logo.ai open, select the Type tool in the Tools panel. Click anywhere in the existing type object to place the insertion point.**

2. **Move the Type tool cursor away from the existing type object. Click to deselect the existing type object.**

   When the insertion point is already flashing in a type object, the exact position of the cursor determines what happens if you click. When the cursor is within the bounds of the existing type object, clicking simply places the insertion point where you click. If you move the cursor outside the bounds of the active type object (where the insertion point is flashing), clicking deselects the previously active type object; you can then click again to create a new point-type object.

Note:

When the insertion point is flashing in a type object, you can't use the keyboard shortcuts to access tools; instead, pressing a key adds that letter to the current type object, at the location of the insertion point.

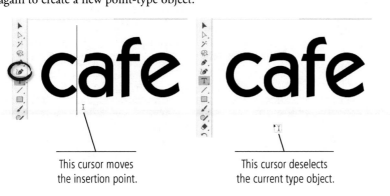

This cursor moves the insertion point.

This cursor deselects the current type object.

More about Working with Fonts

You can click the arrow to the right of the Font Family menu to open the Font panel, which provides a number of options for finding fonts you want to use in your design. (The same options are available wherever you see a Font Family menu — the Character panel, the Control panel, and the Properties panel.)

The top section of the menu lists up to ten most recently used fonts. These appear in the order in which they were used, with the most recent at the top of the menu. (You can change the number of displayed fonts in the Type pane of the Preferences dialog box.)

The second and third sections list Variable and SVG fonts, respectively. The fourth section lists all other fonts that are available to Illustrator.

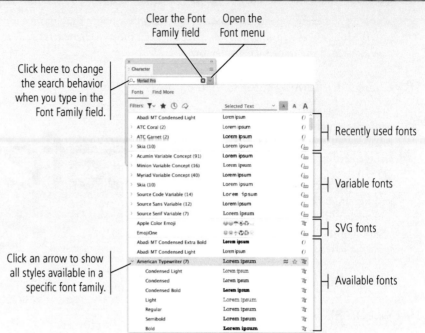

Clear the Font Family field

Open the Font menu

Click here to change the search behavior when you type in the Font Family field.

Click an arrow to show all styles available in a specific font family.

Recently used fonts

Variable fonts

SVG fonts

Available fonts

The font family names in each section appear in alphabetical order. An arrow to the left of a font name indicates that a specific font family includes more than one style. You can click the arrow to show all possible styles in the panel.

If you apply a font that includes more than one style, the style you choose appears in the Font Style menu. You can open the Font Style menu to change the style without changing the font family.

Each font in the panel includes a sample of the font, which defaults to show the currently selected text. If no text is selected, the sample text simply shows the word "Sample." You can choose a different sample text from the menu at the top of the panel. You can also change the size of the sample text using the three icons to the right of the menu

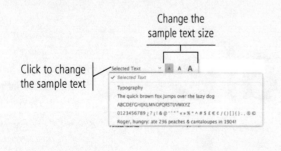

Click to change the sample text

Change the sample text size

The right column in the Font menu shows an icon to identify the type of font:

a **PostScript (Type 1) fonts** have two file components (outline and printer) that are required for output.

Tr **TrueType fonts** have a single file, but (until recently) were primarily used on the Windows platform.

O **OpenType fonts** are contained in a single file that can include more than 60,000 glyphs (characters) in a single font. OpenType fonts are cross-platform; the same font can be used on both Macintosh and Windows systems.

OpenType SVG fonts allow font glyphs to be created as SVG (scalable vector graphics) artwork, which means glyphs can include multiple colors and gradients. These fonts, which are relatively new, are most commonly used for emojis.

OpenType Variable fonts, introduced in 2016, were developed jointly by Adobe, Apple, Google, and Microsoft to allow a single font file to store a continuous range of variants. If you apply a variable font, you can adjust the width and weight of the applied font without the need for different font files for variations such as Bold, Black, Condensed, or Extended.

Typekit fonts are those that have been activated from Adobe Typekit through your Creative Cloud account.

Above the list of fonts in the Font panel, you can use the Filters options to show only certain fonts in the panel. Clicking the Filter Fonts by

▼˅   Filter Fonts by Classification

★   Show Favorite Fonts

🕔   Show Recenly Added Fonts

🗘   Show Activated (Typekit) Fonts

Classification button opens a menu where you can find fonts of a certain style (serif, sans serif, etc.), as well as fonts with specific properties:

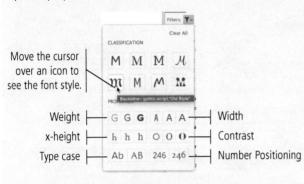

Move the cursor over an icon to see the font style.

- Weight, or the thickness of strokes in the letterforms
- Width of the individual letterforms
- x-height, or the ratio of lowercase letter height compared to uppercase
- Contrast, or the ratio of thin strokes compared to thick strokes in individual letterforms
- Type case, or whether a font includes both upper- and lowercase, or all capitals/small caps and all caps
- Number positioning, which refers to whether numbers all align to the baseline or extend above or below the baseline

When you use any of the filtering options, the Font panel shows only fonts that match the selected filter. You can click the Clear All link in the top-right corner of the panel to restore the default font list.

When the mouse cursor hovers over a font in the list, two additional icons appear on the right side of the panel for the highlighted font.

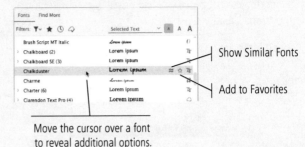

Show Similar Fonts

Add to Favorites

Move the cursor over a font to reveal additional options.

You can click the Show Similar Fonts ≈ button to show only fonts similar to one you selected; clicking the Back hot-text link returns to the full Font panel.

Clicking the Add to Favorites ☆ button designates a font as a Favorite. Favorite fonts are identified by a solid star icon even when the cursor is not hovering over that particular font. You can also use the Filtering option at the top of the panel to show only Favorite fonts.

Working with Adobe Typekit

Adobe Typekit is an online library of high-quality fonts. The Typekit Portfolio Plan, which provides access to the full font library and allows you to sync up to 100 fonts at a time to your desktop, is included in your individual user subscription to the Adobe Creative Cloud.

The Find More option at the top of the Font panel provides a link to Adobe Typekit fonts from directly in the Illustrator interface.

When you find a font you want to use, move your mouse over that font to show the Activate icon ⬆; click that icon to activate it in your Creative Cloud account. (A separate icon shows that a particular font is currently being activated ⟲.) Synced fonts will be available for use in any application on your device.

If only certain fonts in a family are active, you can click the Active Remaining icon ⬆ to activate all fonts in that family.

If a font is already active, move your mouse over the Active icon ⟲ to access the Deactivate icon ⟲; click that icon to unsync that font.

Verifying your Adobe ID

To use Typekit fonts in an Adobe application, you must first verify that you are signed in using the username and password that is associated with your individual user subscription. (Typekit functionality is not available if you are working on a computer that has an Adobe software Device license instead of an individual user subscription.)

If you open the Help menu, you will see an option to either Sign In or Sign Out. If you see the words "Sign Out," the

menu option also shows the email address (username) that is currently signed in.

If you see your own username, you are already signed in, and can use the Typekit functionality. If you see a different username, you should choose the Sign Out option, and then sign in with your own username. If you see the words "Sign In," you should choose that menu option and follow the on-screen directions to sign in with your own username.

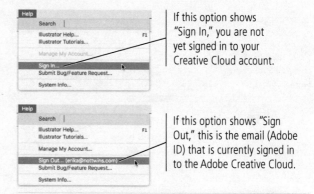

If this option shows "Sign In," you are not yet signed in to your Creative Cloud account.

If this option shows "Sign Out," this is the email (Adobe ID) that is currently signed in to the Adobe Creative Cloud.

Using the Adobe Creative Cloud Application

On Macintosh, the Adobe Creative Cloud application is accessed on the right side of the Menu bar at the top of the screen. On Windows, it is accessed on the right side of the Taskbar at the bottom of the screen.

Macintosh

Windows

Font syncing through Adobe Typekit is managed through the Assets:Fonts pane of the application. Any fonts that are already synced in your account are listed in this pane. (If you have not yet synced fonts in your account, you see a default screen.)

3. **With the Type tool active, click to create a new point-type object.**

When you add a new type object, the placeholder text is automatically set using the last formatting options that you defined in the Character panel. (Settings that were altered by scaling the type object, such as font size and horizontal scale, are not maintained.)

Note:

You can press the ESC key to switch to the Selection tool, which effectively removes the insertion point and selects the type object.

4. **With the placeholder text highlighted, type Limon.**

5. **With the insertion point flashing, press Command/Control.**

As you know, this modifier key temporarily switches the active tool to the last-used Selection tool. The bounding box of the type object remains visible as long as you hold down the Command/Control key. If you release the Command/Control key, you return to the previously active tool (in this case, the Type tool).

6. **While still holding down the Command/Control key, click within the bounding box of the type object.**

When you click, you select the actual type object. The point and path become active, and the insertion point no longer flashes. You can use this method to move or modify a type object without switching away from the Type tool.

Pressing Command/Control temporarily accesses the last-used Selection tool and reveals the type object's bounding box.

7. **Press Command/Control. Click the second type object and drag it until the "i" in Limon aligns with the "f" in cafe.**

You might want to zoom in to better align the two type objects. Use the following image as a guide.

The layer color previews the new position of the type object.

Note:

When you're working with type, it can be easier to work with bounding boxes turned off. You can turn off the bounding boxes for all objects — including type objects — by choosing View>Hide Bounding Box.

Managing Missing Fonts

It is important to understand that fonts are external files of data that describe the font for the output device. The fonts you use in a layout need to be available on any computer that opens the file. Illustrator stores a reference to used fonts, but it does not store the actual font data.

When you open a file that uses fonts you don't have installed on your computer, a Missing Fonts dialog box shows which fonts should be installed.

Fonts available in Typekit are checked in the list.

Click here to sync fonts checked in the list.

The software scans the Typekit library to locate missing fonts; missing fonts that exist in the Typekit library are automatically checked in the list. Clicking the Activate Fonts button syncs the required Typekit fonts in your Creative Cloud (CC) account, making them available in your desktop version of Illustrator.

Using the Find Font Dialog Box

You can also use the Find Font dialog box (accessed by clicking the Find Fonts button in the Missing Fonts dialog box or by choosing Type>Find Font) to replace one font with another throughout a layout.

The top half of the dialog box lists every font used in the file; missing fonts are identified by a warning icon in the list. If a missing font is available in the Typekit library, it is automatically checked in the top list. You can click the Activate Fonts button to sync those fonts in your CC account.

The lower half shows fonts that can be used to replace fonts in the top list. Document shows only fonts used in the file. Recent shows fonts you have recently used in Illustrator. System shows all fonts that are active on your computer.

If you click the Change or Change All button, the font selected in the top list will be replaced with the font selected in the bottom list. You can also use the Find button to locate instances of the selected font without making changes.

8. **Release the mouse button to reposition the type object.**

9. **Press the Command/Control key again, click the type object, then press Shift and drag up or down until there is only a small space between the bottom of the "e" in cafe and the top of the "m" in Limon.**

10. **Release the Command/Control key to return to the Type tool.**

11. **Save the file and continue to the next exercise.**

Convert Type to Outlines

In Illustrator, fonts — and the characters that compose them — are like any other vector objects. They are made up of anchors and paths, which you can modify just as you would any other vector object. To access the anchor points, however, you must first convert the text to outlines.

1. **With `cafe-logo.ai` open, expand the Type layer in the Layers panel.**

   Each type object exists as a separate sublayer.

2. **Use the Selection tool to select both type objects in the file.**

3. **Choose Type>Create Outlines.**

   When you convert the type to outlines, the anchor points and paths that make up the letter shapes appear. Each type object (in this case, one for "cafe" and one for "Limon") is a separate group of letter shapes.

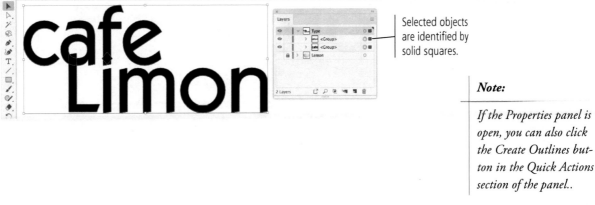

Selected objects are identified by solid squares.

Note:

Press Command/Control-Shift-O to convert type to outlines.

Note:

If the Properties panel is open, you can also click the Create Outlines button in the Quick Actions section of the panel..

4. **In the Layers panel, click the arrow to the left of the each group on the Type layer to expand them.**

By expanding the individual layers and sublayer groups, you can use the Layers panel to access and work with individual objects in a group, without ungrouping the objects.

5. **In the Layers panel, click the space to the right of the Target icon of the "m" to select only that object.**

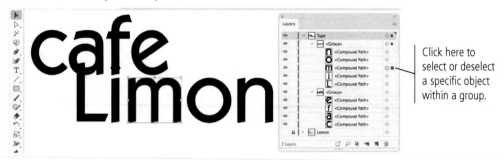

Click here to select or deselect a specific object within a group.

6. **With the Selection tool active, press the Left Arrow key three times to nudge the selected object left, narrowing the space between the letter shapes.**

You can open the General pane of the Preferences dialog box to change the distance an object moves when you press the arrow keys (called the **keyboard increment**). Press Shift and an arrow key to move an object 10 times the default keyboard increment.

You could have fine-tuned the letter spacing with tracking and kerning before you converted the letters to outlines. Since you're working with these letters as graphics, you are nudging individual pieces of a group to adjust the spacing in the overall logotype.

7. **Repeat Steps 5–6 to move the "o" and "n" shapes closer to the other letters in the same word.**

    As mentioned previously, letter spacing is largely a matter of personal preference. You might prefer more or less space between the letters than what you see in our images.

8. **Repeat Steps 5–6 to move the "e" closer to the "f" in the word cafe.**

9. **In the Layers panel, click the space to the right of the Target icon of the "a" to select only that object.**

10. **Press Shift, and click the same space for the "c" to add that object to the active selection.**

    You can Shift-click the icons in the panel to add or subtract sublayers from the active selection. In this case, however, Shift-clicking does not select all in-between sublayers when you add more than one object to the selection.

    You can also Shift-click the icon for a selected object to remove it from the active selection.

11. **Press the Right Arrow key one time to nudge both selected objects closer to the "f" in the same word.**

    Shift-click to select multiple sublayers.

12. Use the Layers panel to select only the "L" in Limon, then drag it until the vertical section appears immediately below the vertical line in the "a" (use the following image as a guide).

Although the individual letter shapes are parts of various groups, selecting sublayers in the Layers panel means you don't need to switch to the Direct Selection tool to move only the selected objects.

13. Save the file and continue to the next exercise

Create Custom Graphics from Letter Shapes

Because you converted the letter shapes to outlines, the logo text no longer behaves as type. You can now apply your drawing skills to adjust the vector shapes and create a unique appearance for your client's logotype. Remember, you can use the Add Anchor Point tool to add points to a vector path, use the Delete Anchor Point tool to remove points from a vector path, and use the Anchor Point tool to convert smooth points to corner points (and vice versa). All three of these tools are nested below the Pen tool in the Tools panel.

1. With `cafe-logo.ai` open, click the Eye icon to hide the "cafe" sublayer.

2. Select only the "i" object, and then choose Object>Compound Path>Release.

A compound path is simply a single object that is made up of more than one path. Where multiple objects overlap, the top object knocks out (removes) underlying objects without destructively changing the underlying shapes.

In this case, releasing the compound path simply breaks the two shapes that make up the "i" into separate objects.

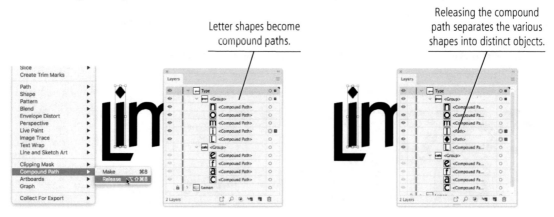

Letter shapes become compound paths.

Releasing the compound path separates the various shapes into distinct objects.

3. Using what you know about anchor points, edit the dot over the "i" to resemble a leaf character.

We converted the bottom, left, and right points to smooth points, then adjusted the position of the top point to achieve the leaf shape.

4. Change the fill color of the selected object to a medium green from the built-in swatches.

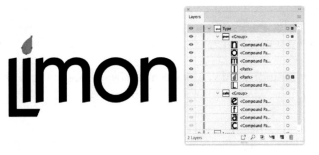

5. Show the "cafe" sublayer, then edit the bottom of the "f" to align with the leaf shape you just created.

6. Using the Direct Selection tool, select the two right anchor points on the "L" shape. Drag them right until the shape creates an underline below all the other letters in the word "Limon."

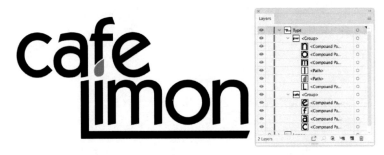

7. Select and delete the "o" object from the "Limon" sublayer.

8. Show and unlock the Lemon layer. Transform the gradient-mesh object and move it to fill the space left by deleting the "o" letter shape.

9. Save the file and continue to the next stage of the project.

For all intents and purposes, the Cafe Limon logo is now complete. However, you still need to create the alternate versions that can be used in other applications. You need a two-color version for jobs that will be printed with spot colors, and you need a one-color version for jobs that will be printed with black ink only.

Rather than generating multiple files for individual versions of a logo, you can use Illustrator's multiple-artboard capabilities to create a single file that manages the different logo variations on separate artboards.

In this stage of the project, you adjust the artboard to fit the completed logo. You then duplicate the artwork on additional artboards, and adjust the colors in each version to meet the specific needs of different color applications.

Adjust the Default Artboard

When you place an Illustrator file into another file (for example, a page-layout file in InDesign or even another Illustrator file) you can decide how to place that file — based on the artwork boundaries (the outermost bounding box), on the artboard boundaries, or on other specific dimensions. To make the logo artwork more placement-friendly, you should adjust the Illustrator artboard to fit the completed logo artwork.

1. **With cafe-logo.ai open, make the Selection tool active, then choose Select>All to select all elements on the artboard.**

2. **Using the Properties panel, choose the top-left reference point in the Transform section. Change the X and Y positions to 0.125 in.**

Position the selection based on the top-left reference point.

3. **Make sure the W and H fields are linked, then type 250% in the W field.**

Type the percentage, including the % character, to scale the selection.

Note:

Your W and H values might be slightly different than what you see in our screenshots, but they should be in the same general ballpark.

4. **Press Return/Enter to finalize the transformation.**

When you press Return/Enter (or simply click away from the panel field), the selection is scaled proportionally to 250% of its original size.

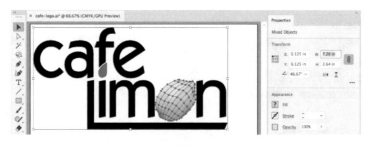

5. **Select the Artboard tool in the Tools panel.**

   When the Artboard tool is active, the artboard edge is surrounded by marching ants; you can drag the side and corner handles to manually resize the artboard in the workspace.

Drag the handles to manually resize the artboard.

Artboard tool

6. **Click the bottom-right handle of the artboard, then drag up and left until the artboard is approximately 1/8″ larger than the artwork on all four sides.**

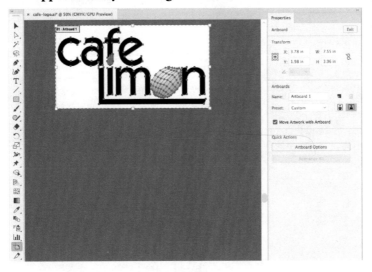

7. **Click the Selection tool to exit the Artboard-editing mode.**

8. **Save the file and continue to the next exercise.**

When the Artboard tool is active, the Control panel presents a number of options for adjusting the active artboard.

A   Use this menu to change the artboard to a predefined size (letter, tabloid, etc.).

B   Click to change the artboard to portrait orientation.

C   Click to change the artboard to landscape orientation.

D   Click to add a new artboard at the currently defined size. The cursor is "loaded" with the new artboard; you can click to place the new artboard in the workspace.

E   Click to delete the active artboard.

F   Type here to define a name for the active artboard.

G   Click to toggle the Move/Copy Artwork with Artboard option. When active, objects on the artboard move along with the artboard being moved (or cloned).

H   Click to open the Artboard Options dialog box.

I   Choose a registration point for changes in size or position.

J   Use these fields to define the position of the artboard. (The first artboard always begins at X: 0, Y: 0.)

K   Use these fields to change the size of the artboard. If the link icon is active, the height and width will be constrained.

L   If a file includes more than one artboard, you can click this button to open a dialog box in which you can define a grid pattern for all existing artboards. You can determine the number of columns in the grid, as well as the exact space between individual artboards.

Clicking the Artboard Options button opens a dialog box where you can further manage and control the selected artboard. Most of these options (Preset, Width, Height, Orientation, and Position) are the same as those available in the Control panel.

The remaining choices are explained here:

- **Constrain Proportions** maintains a consistent aspect ratio (height to width) if you resize the artboard.

- **Show Center Mark** displays a point in the center of the crop area.

- **Show Cross Hairs** displays lines that extend into the artwork from the center of each edge.

- **Show Video Safe Areas** displays guides that represent the areas inside the viewable area of video.

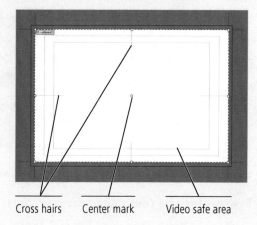

Cross hairs   Center mark   Video safe area

- **Video Ruler Pixel Aspect Ratio** specifies the pixel aspect ratio used for artboard rulers.

- **Fade Region Outside Artboard** displays the area outside the artboard darker than the area inside the artboard.

- **Update While Dragging** keeps the area outside the artboard darker as you move or resize the artboard.

Use the Layers Panel to Organize Artwork

Your goal is to create three separate versions of the logo — the four-color version that's already done, a two-color version for spot-color applications, and a one-color version that will be used in jobs that are printed black-only.

As you created the artwork, you used two layers and a variety of sublayers to manage the arrangement and stacking order of the various elements. Now that the drawing is complete, however, you will use layers for a different purpose — to create, isolate, and manage multiple versions of the logo in a single file.

1. **With `cafe-logo.ai` open, choose Select>All to select all objects on the artboard.**

2. **Choose Object>Group. In the Layers panel, expand the resulting group.**

   When you group objects, the resulting group is placed on the top-most layer in the active selection. All objects in the group are moved to the same layer containing the group. The original stacking order is maintained, so the mesh object from the Lemon layer still appears at the bottom of the list in the resulting group

The new group exists on the top-most layer in the previous selection.

The mesh object is moved from its original layer into the group.

The mesh object is still below other objects in the stacking order.

3. **Collapse the Type layer in the panel to hide the sublayers.**

4. **Double-click the Type layer name to highlight it. Type `Four-Color Logo`, then press Return/Enter to finalize the new name.**

5. **Select the Lemon layer in the Layers panel, then click the Delete Selection button.**

   Because this layer no longer has any artwork, you are not asked to confirm the deletion.

Delete Selection button

6. **Save the file and continue to the next exercise.**

Copy the Artboard and Artwork

The final step in this project is to create the two alternate versions of the logo. This process is largely a matter of cloning the existing artboard and artwork — but you need to complete a few extra steps to convert the mesh objects to standard filled paths.

1. **With cafe-logo.ai open, choose the Artboard tool in the Tools panel.**

2. **With the only artboard currently active, highlight the contents of the Name field in the Control panel and type Four Color.**

3. **Make sure the Move/Copy Artwork with Artboard option is toggled on.**

Note:

You might want to zoom out so you can see the entire original artboard and the empty space below it.

The Artboard name appears in the Name field and in the artboard tag.

The Move/Copy Artwork with Artboard option should be toggled on.

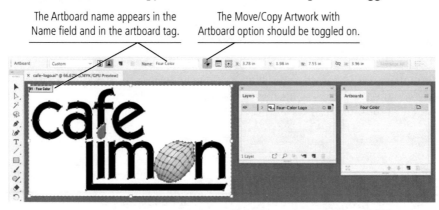

4. **Place the cursor inside the artboard area. Press Option/Alt and then click and drag down to clone the existing artboard.**

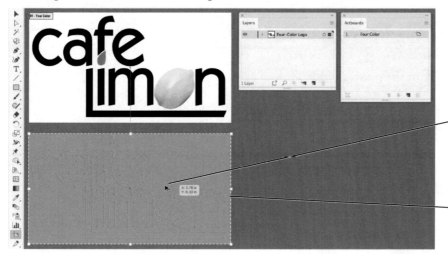

Pressing Option/Alt clones the existing artboard, just as you would clone a regular drawing object.

Because Move/Copy Artwork with Artboard is toggled on, the logo artwork and the artboard are cloned at the same time.

5. **When the new artboard/artwork is entirely outside the boundaries of the first artboard, release the mouse button.**

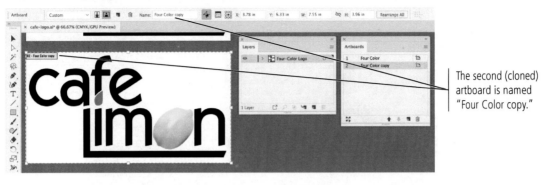

The second (cloned) artboard is named "Four Color copy."

6. **With the second artboard active, change the Name field to Two Color.**

7. **In the Layers panel, click the Create New Layer button.**

New layers are added above the previously selected layer. Because the Four Color layer was the only layer in the file, the new layer is added at the top of the layer stack.

Create New Layer button

8. **Double-click the new layer name in the panel, then type Two-Color Logo to rename the layer.**

9. **Using the Selection tool, drag a marquee to select all the objects on the second artboard.**

10. **In the Layers panel, drag the Selected Art icon from the Four-Color Logo layer to the Two-Color Logo layer.**

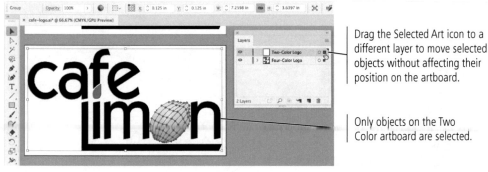

Drag the Selected Art icon to a different layer to move selected objects without affecting their position on the artboard.

Only objects on the Two Color artboard are selected.

When you release the mouse button, the selected objects are moved to the Two-Color Logo layer.

11. **Save the file and continue to the next exercise.**

Convert Mesh Objects to Regular Paths

When you created the gradient meshes in the first stage of this project, you saw that adding the mesh removed the original path you drew. When you worked on the mesh, you might have noticed that the Control panel showed that the selected object was transformed from a path object to a mesh object.

To create the flat two-color version of the logo, however, you need to access the original paths you drew to create the mesh objects. There is no one-step process to convert the mesh object back to a flat path object, so you need to take a few extra steps to create the flat version of the logo.

Because the black-only version of the logo is also flat, you are going to create the flat two-color version first, and then clone it. Doing so avoids unnecessary repetition of the process presented in this exercise.

1. **With `cafe-logo.ai` open, deselect everything in the file and then open the Artboards panel (Window>Artboards).**

The Artboards panel can be used to access and arrange the various artboards in a file.

2. **In the Artboards panel, double-click the Two Color artboard (away from the artboard name).**

   This forces the selected artboard to fill the space available in the document window.

3. **Expand the Two-Color Logo layer in the Layers panel. If necessary, expand the first group so you can see the three sublayers in the group.**

4. **Use the Layers panel to select the mesh object on the Two-Color Logo layer.**

5. **Open the Appearance panel (Window>Appearance).**

6. **With the mesh object selected, click the Add New Stroke button at the bottom of the Appearance panel.**

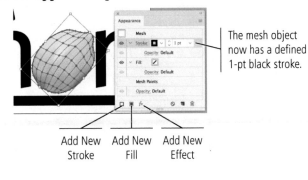

The mesh object now has a defined 1-pt black stroke.

Add New Stroke   Add New Fill   Add New Effect

The Appearance panel allows you to review and change the appearance attributes of objects, including stroke, fill, transparency, and applied effects.

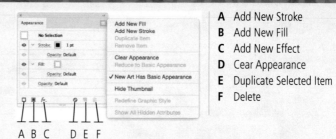

A Add New Stroke
B Add New Fill
C Add New Effect
D Cear Appearance
E Duplicate Selected Item
F Delete

As you know, the last-used settings for fill color, stroke color, and stroke weight are applied to new objects. Other attributes, such as the applied brush or effects, are not automatically applied.

If you need to create a series of objects with the same overall appearance, you can turn off the **New Art Has Basic Appearance** option in the Appearance panel Options menu.

Clicking the **Clear Appearance** button reduces the selected object to a fill and stroke of None.

Choosing **Reduce to Basic Appearance** in the panel Options menu resets an object to only basic fill and stroke attributes; fill color and stroke weight and color are maintained, but all other attributes are removed.

You can use the **Duplicate Selected Item** button to create multiple versions of the same attribute for an object, such as two stroke weights/colors, allowing you to compound the effect without layering multiple objects.

New appearance attributes are created on top of the currently selected appearance. You can drag the appearance names in the panel to change their stacking sequence, which can have a significant impact on the end result.

If you want to remove a specific attribute, simply select that item and click the panel's **Delete** button.

7. **With the mesh object still selected, choose Object>Expand Appearance.**

   This command converts the selected object into separate constituent objects — one path for the shape's stroke attribute and one for the object's mesh fill — which are automatically grouped together.

8. **In the Layers panel, expand the new group.**

Expanding the appearance creates separate (grouped) objects for each attribute.

9. **Use the Layers panel to select only the mesh object in the group.**

10. **Press Delete/Backspace to remove the selected mesh object.**

   You now have a simple path object that is essentially the lemon shape. However, you need to complete one more step because the path is still part of the group that was created by the Expand Appearance command.

After deleting the mesh, the remaining path is still part of the group.

11. **Use the Layers panel to select the path in the group, and then choose Object>Ungroup.**

After ungrouping, the selected path is a regular sublayer (it is not grouped).

12. **Save the file and continue to the next exercise.**

Add Spot Color to the Two-Color Logo

Spot colors are created with special premixed inks that produce a certain color with one ink layer; they are not built from the standard CMYK process inks. Each spot color appears on its own separation. Spot inks are commonly used to reproduce colors you can't get from a CMYK build, in two- or three-color documents, or as additional separations when exact colors are needed.

You can choose a spot color directly from the library on your screen, but you should look at a printed swatch book to verify that you're using the color you intend. Special inks exist because many of the colors can't be reproduced with process inks, nor can they be accurately represented on a monitor. If you specify spot colors and then convert them to process colors later, your job probably won't look exactly as you expect.

1. **With cafe-logo.ai open, choose Window>Swatch Libraries>Color Books>Pantone+ Solid Coated.**

    Illustrator includes swatch libraries of all the common spot-color libraries. You can open any of these libraries to access the various colors available in each collection.

Note:

In the United States, the most popular collections of spot colors are the Pantone Matching System (PMS) libraries. TruMatch and Focoltone are also used in the United States. Toyo and DICColor (Dainippon Ink & Chemicals) are used primarily in Japan.

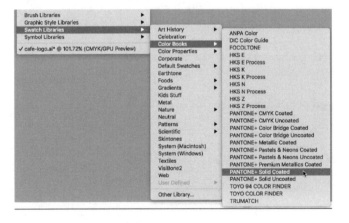

2. **In the Pantone+ Solid Coated library Options menu, choose Small List View to show the color names for each swatch.**

It is often easier to view swatches with their names and samples, especially when you need to find a specific swatch (as in this exercise).

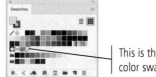
Note:

The View options in the panel Options menu are available for all swatch panels, including colors, patterns, and brushes.

Note:

To restore all spot color to the panel, simply delete the characters from the panel's Search field.

3. **On the Two Color artboard/layer, select the path that represents the lemon.**

4. **In the Find field of the color library panel, type 102.**

You could simply scroll through the panel to find the color you want, but typing a number in the Find field shows only colors that match what you type.

5. **Make sure the Fill icon is active in the Tools panel, and then click Pantone 102 C in the swatch Library panel.**

The Fill is the active attribute.

6. **Review the Swatches panel (Window>Swatches).**

When you apply a color from a swatch library, that swatch is added to the Swatches panel for the open file.

This is the Pantone color swatch.

7. **Using whichever method you prefer, change the stroke color of the selected object to None.**

8. **Select only the leaf shape that you created from the dot over the "i."**

Use the Direct Selection tool or the icons in the Layers panel to select only that shape.

9. **Change the fill color to None and change the stroke to 2-pt Black.**

10. **Choose the Artboard tool. With the Move/Copy Artwork with Artboard option still active, press Option/Alt and then click and drag down to clone the flat version. Rename the new artboard** One Color**.**

11. **Move the artwork on the third artboard to a new layer named** One-Color Logo**. Change the lemon shape to a fill of None with a 2-pt Black stroke.**

12. **Save the file, close it, and then continue to the next stage of the project.**

STAGE 4 / Combining Text and Graphics

The final stage of this project requires two additional layouts: a letterhead and a business envelope. Rather than adding more artboards to the logo file, you are going to create a new file that will contain both pieces of stationery. This means you must place the logos from the original cafe-logo.ai file, and understand how to work with objects that are placed from external files.

Work with Placed Graphics

Some production-related concerns dictate how you design a letterhead. In general, there are two ways to print a letterhead: commercially in large quantities, or one-offs on your desktop laser or inkjet printer. The second method includes a letterhead template, which you can use to write and print your letters from directly within a page-layout program; while this method is common among designers, it is rarely done using Illustrator.

If your letterhead is being printed commercially, it's probably being printed with multiple copies on a large press sheet, from which the individual letterhead sheets will be cut. Most commercial printing happens this way. This type of printing typically means that design elements can run right off the edge of the sheet; this is called **bleeding**. If you're using a commercial printer, always ask the output provider whether it's safe (and cost-effective) to design with bleeds, and find out how much bleed allowance to include.

If you're designing for a printer that can only run letter-size paper, you need to allow enough of a margin area for your printer to hold the paper as it moves through the device (called the **gripper margin**); in this case, you can't design with bleeds.

1. **Open the New Document dialog box (File>New). Define the following settings:**

Intent:	**Print**
Preset:	**Letter**
Name:	**stationery**
Units:	**Inches**
Orientation:	**Portrait**
Artboards:	**1**
Bleed:	**0.125 in (all four sides)**

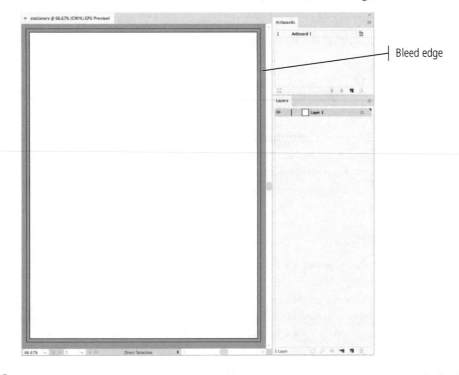

2. **Click Create to create the new file.**

The red line indicates the defined bleed (1/8″ outside the artboard edge).

Bleed edge

3. **Choose File>Place. Navigate to the file cafe-logo.ai in your WIP>Cafe folder, and make sure Link and Template are both unchecked. Check the Show Import Options box, then click Place.**

Until now, you have placed raster images in the JPEG format. Different types of files, however, have different options that determine what is imported into your Illustrator file.

4. Review the options in the Place PDF dialog box.

Although you're placing a native Illustrator (.ai) file, the dialog box shows options for placing PDF files. Illustrator files use PDF as the underlying structure (which is what enables multiple artboard capability), so the options are the same as those you would see if you were placing a PDF file.

Use these arrows to select which artboard you want to place.

The **Crop To** option determines exactly what is placed into an Illustrator file. (If you are placing an Illustrator file, many of these options produce the same result.)

- The **Bounding Box** setting places the file's bounding box, or the minimum area that encloses the objects on the page or artboard.

- The **Art** setting crops incoming files relative to the size and position of any objects selected at the time of the cropping. For example, you can create a frame and use it to crop an incoming piece of artwork.

- Use the **Crop** setting when you want the position of the placed file to be determined by the location of a crop region drawn on the page, when placing an Illustrator file, this refers to the defined artboard.

- The **Trim** setting identifies where the page will be physically cut in the production process, if trim marks are present.

- The **Bleed** setting places only the area within bleed margins (if a bleed area is defined). This is useful if the page is being output in a production environment. The printed page might include page marks that fall outside the bleed area.

- The **Media** setting places the area that represents the physical paper size of the original PDF document (for example, the dimensions of an A4 sheet of paper), including printers' marks.

Note:

If Show Import Options is not checked in the Place dialog box, the Illustrator file is placed based on the last-used Crop To option.

5. Choose Bounding Box in the Crop To menu, and then click OK to place the four-color logo.

6. If you get a warning about an unknown image construct, click OK to dismiss it.

For some reason, gradient mesh objects *created in Illustrator* are unrecognized *by Illustrator*, which is the case with this logo file. Gradient meshes are imported into the new file as "non-native art" objects that can't be edited in the new file unless you use the Flatten Transparency command to turn them into embedded raster objects.

After dismissing the warning message, the selected file is loaded into the Place cursor. A small preview of the loaded file appears in the cursor.

The selected file is loaded into the Place cursor.

7. **Click near the top-left corner of the artboard to place the loaded image.**

8. **Open the General pane of the Preferences dialog box. Make sure the Scale Strokes & Effects option is checked, and then click OK.**

Note:

On Macintosh, open the Preferences dialog box in the Illustrator menu. On Windows, open the Preferences dialog box in the Edit menu.

If this option is checked, scaling an object also scales the applied strokes and effects proportionally to the new object size. For example, reducing an object by 50% changes a 1-pt stroke to a 0.5-pt stroke. If this option is unchecked, a 1-pt stroke remains a 1-pt stroke, regardless of how much you reduce or enlarge the object.

9. **With the placed artwork selected, use the Transform panel to scale the artwork to 3 in wide (constrained). Using the top-left reference point, position the artwork 0.25 in from the top and left edges (as shown in the following image).**

Constrain the width and height before changing the object size.

10. **Using the Type tool, click to create a new point-type object. Type 47653 Main Street, Pittsburgh, PA 05439. Format the type as 9-pt ATC Coral Normal.**

11. **Using the Selection tool, position the type object directly below the stylized L (use the following image as a guide).**

Note:

Remember, your original artwork might be a slightly different size than ours, so your resized height might also be slightly different than what is shown here.

12. Activate the Selection tool, then choose File>Place. Navigate to the file leaves.ai in your WIP>Cafe folder and click Place.

The Show Import Options check box remembers the last-used setting, so it should still be checked. After clicking Place, the Place PDF dialog box automatically appears.

The Place PDF dialog box also defaults to the last-used option, so Bounding Box should already be selected in the Crop To menu.

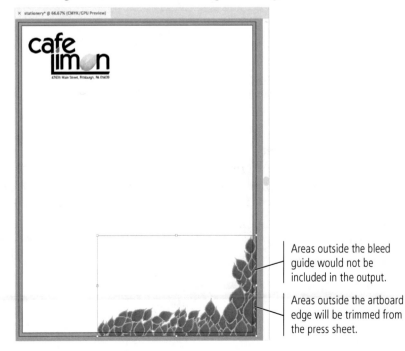

13. Click OK to close the Place PDF dialog box.

Again, the selected file is loaded into the Place cursor.

14. Click the loaded Place cursor to place the leaves.ai file.

15. Using the Selection tool, drag the placed graphic so the edges of the artwork align with the bottom and right bleed guides.

Areas outside the bleed guide would not be included in the output.

Areas outside the artboard edge will be trimmed from the press sheet.

16. **Choose View>Trim View.**

    The Trim view hides any elements that extend beyond the artboard edge. This allows you to more accurately preview the finished job as it will appear when output.

Areas outside the trim edge are hidden.

17. **Choose View>Trim View to toggle off that option.**

18. **Save the file as an Illustrator file named stationery.ai in your WIP>Cafe folder, and then continue to the next exercise.**

Create the Envelope Layout

In general, printed envelopes can be created in two ways. You can create and print the design on a flat sheet, which will be specially **die cut** (stamped out of the press sheet), and then folded and glued into the shape of the finished envelope. Alternatively (and usually at less expense), you can print on pre-folded and -glued envelopes.

Both of these methods for envelope design have special printing requirements, such as ensuring no ink is placed where glue will be applied (if you're printing on flat sheets), or printing far enough away from the edge (if you're printing on pre-formed envelopes). Whenever you design an envelope, consult with the output provider that will print the job before you get too far into the project.

In this case, the design will be output on pre-folded #10 business-size envelopes (4-1/8″ by 9-1/2″). The printer requires a 1/4″ gripper margin around the edge of the envelope where you cannot include any ink coverage.

1. **With stationery.ai open, zoom out until you can see the entire artboard and an equal amount of space to the right.**

2. **Choose the Artboard tool. With the current artboard active, type Letterhead in the Name field of the Control panel.**

Note:

The **live area** is the "safe" area inside the page edge, where important design elements should remain. Because printing and trimming are mechanical processes, there will always be some variation, however slight. Elements too close to the page edge run the risk of being accidentally trimmed off.

3. **Place the cursor to the right of the existing artboard, then click and drag to create a new artboard.**

Click and drag to create a new artboard.

4. **With the second artboard active, type Envelope in the Name field of the Control panel.**

5. **With the second artboard active, use the fields in the Control panel to change the artboard dimensions to W: 9.5 in, H: 4.13 in.**

If the W and H fields are not visible in your Control panel, click the Artboard Options button in the Control panel and use the resulting dialog box to change the artboard size.

Depending on where you created the second artboad, and which reference point was active when you changed the artboard size, your two artboards might end up overlapping.

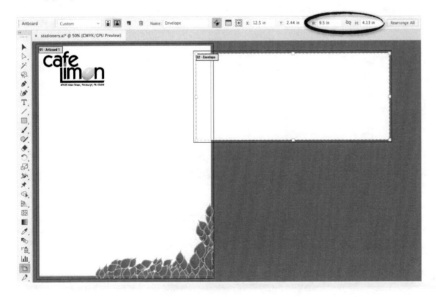

6. **Click the Rearrange All button in the Control panel.**

This dialog box allows you to align multiple artboards to one another in a specific, defined grid.

The Grid-by-Row ( ) option aligns the top edge of each artboard in a single row. If the number of artboards is greater than the allowed number of columns (in the Columns field), additional rows of artboards are created as necessary to accommodate all artboards in the file.

Grid by Column   Grid by Row

The Grid-by-Column ( ) option aligns the left edge of each artboard in a single row. If the number of artboards is greater than the allowed number of rows (in the Rows field), additional columns of artboards are created as necessary to accommodate all artboards in the file.

The Spacing field determines how much space appears between individual artboards in a row or column.

The Arrange by Row (↔) and Arrange by Column (↕) options place all artboards in a single row or column, respectively.

The Layout Order defaults to use the Left-to-Right (→) option, which places artboards left-to-right (for example, Artboard 1, then 2, then 3). If you select the Change to Right-to-Left Layout option (←), artboards are placed in reverse order (for example, Artboard 3, then 2, then 1).

7. **Change the Spacing field to 0.25 in and click OK.**

The top edges of the two artboards are aligned, with 0.25″ between the two artboards.

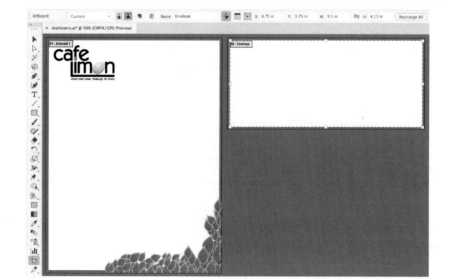

Note:

Press Shift and drag a marquee to select multiple artboards in the document window.

8. Choose File>Place. Navigate to the file **cafe-logo.ai** in your WIP>Cafe folder. Make sure Show Import Options is checked, then click Place.

9. In the Place PDF dialog box, click the right-arrow button to show 2 of 3, then click OK.

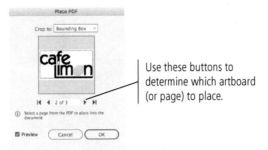

Use these buttons to determine which artboard (or page) to place.

10. Click with the loaded Place cursor to place the loaded file on the Envelope artboard.

11. Make the Selection tool active. If rulers are not visible in your document window, choose View>Rulers>Show Rulers.

12. Choose View>Rulers and make sure the menu option reads "Change to Global Rulers".

When Artboard rulers are active — which you want for this exercise — the menu command reads "Change to Global Rulers."

Artboard rulers show all measurements from the zero-point of the active artboard. Global rulers show all measurements from the zero-point of Artboard 1 (unless you reset the zero-point when a different artboard is active).

Note:

You can't switch between Artboard and Global rulers while the Artboard tool is active.

13. Select the placed object with the Selection tool. Scale it to **2.5 in** wide (constrained) and place it **0.25 in** from the top and left edges of the envelope artboard.

Because Artboard rulers are active, each artboard has its own zero point.

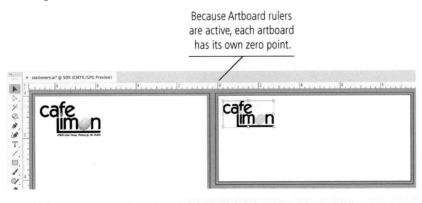

14. Copy the type object from the letterhead and paste it onto the envelope layout. Change the size of the type in the pasted object to 7.5 pt.

15. Save the file and continue to the next exercise.

Print Desktop Proofs of Multiple Artboards

Before you send a file to a commercial output provider, it's a good idea to print a sample to see how the artwork looks on paper. Illustrator provides a large number of options for outputting files.

There are two important points to remember about using inkjet and laser proofs. First, inkjet printers are usually not PostScript driven. Because the commercial output process revolves around the PostScript language, proofs should be created using a PostScript-compatible printer, if possible. Second, inkjet and laser printers typically do not accurately represent color.

1. With stationery.ai open, choose File>Print.

The Print dialog box is divided into eight sections or categories, which display in the window on the left side of the dialog box. Clicking one of the categories in the list shows the associated options on the right side of the dialog box.

2. In the Printer menu, choose the printer you want to use, and then choose the PPD for that printer in the PPD menu (if possible).

If you are using a non-PostScript printer, complete as much of the rest of this exercise as possible based on the limitations of your output device.

The most important options you'll select are the Printer and PPD (PostScript printer description) settings at the top of the dialog box. Illustrator reads the information in the PPD to determine which of the specific print options are available for the current output.

3. With the General options showing, choose the Range radio button and type 1 in the field.

By default, all artboards in the file are output when you click Print.

If your printer can only print letter-size paper, you need to tile the letterhead artboard to multiple sheets, so you can output a full-size proof. Tiling is unavailable when printing multiple artboards, so in this exercise you are printing each artboard separately.

4. In the Options section, make sure the Do Not Scale option is selected.

As a general rule, proofs — especially final proofs that would be sent to a printer with the job files — should be output at 100%.

Note:

A print preset is a way to store many different settings in a single menu choice. You can create a print preset by making your choices in the Print dialog box, and then clicking the Save Preset button.

5a. **If your printer is capable of printing oversize sheets, choose Tabloid/A3/11×17 in the Media menu. Choose the Portrait orientation option.**

Note:

The Tile options are not available if you are printing multiple artboards at one time.

5b. **If you can only print to letter-size paper, turn off the Auto-Rotate option and choose the Landscape orientation option. Choose Tile Full Pages in the Scaling menu and define a 1 in Overlap.**

To output a letter-size page at 100% on letter-size paper, you have to tile to multiple sheets of paper. Using the landscape paper orientation allows you to tile to 2 sheets instead of 4 (as shown in the preview area).

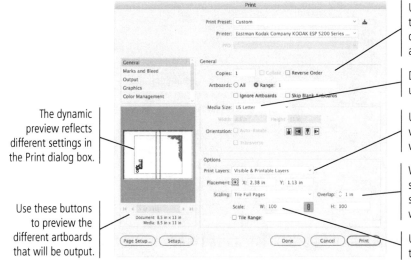

The dynamic preview reflects different settings in the Print dialog box.

Use these buttons to preview the different artboards that will be output.

Use these options to print more than one copy and reverse the output order of the multiple artboards (last to first).

Define the paper size used for the output.

Use this menu to output visible and printable layers, visible layers, or all layers.

When tiling a page to multiple sheets, you can define a specific amount of space that will be included on both sheets.

Use these options to scale the output (if necessary).

6. **Click the Marks and Bleed option in the list of categories on the left. Activate the All Printer's Marks option, and then change the Offset value to 0.125 in.**

If you type the value in the Offset field, Illustrator rounds up to the nearest two-decimal value. Since 0.13″ is larger than the 0.125″ bleed, this offset position is fine.

7. **In the Bleeds section, check the Use Document Bleed Settings option.**

When you created the stationery file, you defined 1/8″ bleeds on all four sides of the artboard. Checking this box in the Print dialog box includes that same 1/8″ extra on all four sides of the output.

Note:

The Auto-Rotate option is useful if you are printing multiple artboards; when this option is active, the application automatically positions each artboard to take best advantage of the available paper.

Use these options to select individual printer's marks or print all marks.

The Offset value determines how far from the page edge the printer's marks will be placed.

The preview now includes all selected printer's marks and the defined bleed area.

Note:

Some output providers require printer's marks to stay outside the bleed area, which means the offset should be at least the same as or greater than the defined bleed area.

8. **Click the Output option in the list of categories on the left.**

   Depending on the type of output device you are using, you can print all colors to a single sheet by choosing Composite in the Mode menu, or print each color to an individual sheet by choosing Separations (Host-based). The third option — In-RIP Separation — allows the file data to be separated by the output device instead of by the software.

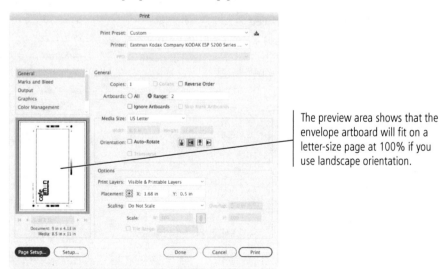

Note:

The other options in this dialog box (Emulsion and Image) are reserved for high-end commercial output to a filmsetter or imagesetter.

When printing separations, click any of these icons to stop that ink separation from outputting.

If a job includes spot colors, click the icon in this column to convert the spot color to process color for the output.

9. **Click Print to output the artwork.**

10. **Choose File>Print again. Choose the Range radio button and type 2 in the field to print the envelope layout.**

11. **Choose US Letter in the Size menu and choose the Landscape orientation option. Choose Do Not Scale in the Scaling menu.**

   In this case, a letter-size sheet is large enough to print the envelope artboard without scaling. Some of the printer's marks might be cut off by the printer's gripper margin, but that is fine for the purpose of a desktop proof.

The preview area shows that the envelope artboard will fit on a letter-size page at 100% if you use landscape orientation.

12. **Click Print to output the envelope proof.**

13. **When the document comes back into focus, save and close it.**

PROJECT REVIEW

fill in the blank

1. The _____ provides access to handles that you can use to manually resize the artboard in the workspace.

2. Press _____ and click the eye icon on a specific layer to switch only that layer between Preview and Outline mode.

3. When _____ are active, moving your cursor over an unselected object reveals the paths that make up that object.

4. The _____ tool is used to sample colors from an object already placed in the file.

5. The _____ is used to monitor and change the individual attributes (fill, stroke, etc.) of the selected object.

6. The _____ is the imaginary line on which the bottoms of letters rest.

7. _____ is the spacing between specific pairs of letters (where the insertion point is placed).

8. The _____ command makes the vector shapes of letters accessible to the Direct Selection tool.

9. A _____ is a special ink used to reproduce a specific color, typically used for one- or two-color jobs.

10. Click the _____ in the Layers panel to select a specific sublayer.

short answer

1. Explain the advantages of using a gradient mesh, compared to a regular gradient.

2. Briefly explain two primary differences between point-type objects and area-type objects.

3. Explain the potential benefits of using multiple artboards rather than different files for different pieces.

PORTFOLIO BUILDER PROJECT

Use what you have learned in this project to complete the following freeform exercise.
Carefully read the art director and client comments, then create your own design to meet the needs of the project.
Use the space below to sketch ideas. When finished, write a brief explanation of the reasoning behind your final design.

art director comments

The Cincinnati Zoo has hired you to create a series of graphics that will be used to rebrand the facility at next spring's Grand Reopening. Your work will be used for everything from printed collateral and park signage, to the zoo's website, and even embroidery on clothing.

❏ Create a new logo to identify the redesigned zoo.

❏ Create a series of icons for each of the zoo's seven main sections: Tropics, Desert, Arctic, Forest, Ocean, Sky, and Kids Kingdom.

❏ Create an invitation for the Grand Reopening celebration incorporating the new logo. Research the best size for a printed invitation that will be sent through the U.S. Postal Service. Include placeholder text for the date and time of the event, as well as the zoo's phone number and web address.

client comments

Our facility received a significant grant from an anonymous donor to update the entire facility — everything from the animal enclosures and guest facilities, to the walking paths and water fountains. Basically, we've rebuilt from the ground up, and are very excited to reveal our efforts to the public next spring at the Grand Reopening.

Since everything is new, we felt it was also time to update our corporate identity. The previous logo was designed more than 20 years ago and is little more than the words, "Cincinnati Zoo." We want something fresh that incorporates more than just two words in a fancy typeface. Remember though, it has to look good on a 15-foot sign or embroidered on the pocket of a T-shirt.

For the section icons, try to keep them simple. We don't want visitors to have to work to figure out what they mean. You can include the actual words, but we're an international facility, so not everyone will be able to read the English explanations.

project justification

PROJECT SUMMARY

Logos are one of the most common types of artwork that you will create in Illustrator. These can be as simple as text converted to outlines, or as complex as a line drawing based on an object in a photograph. Most logos will actually be some combination of drawing and text-based elements. As you learned throughout this project, one of the most important qualities of a logo is versatility. A good logo can be used in many different types of projects, and output in many different types of print processes. To accomplish this goal, logos should work equally well in grayscale, four-color, and spot-color printing.

By completing this project, you worked with complex gradients to draw a realistic lemon, then added creative type treatment to build the finished logotype. After completing the initial logo, you converted it to other variants that will work with different output processes (two-color and one-color). Finally, you incorporated the logo artwork into completed stationery for your client's communication needs as he expands his business.

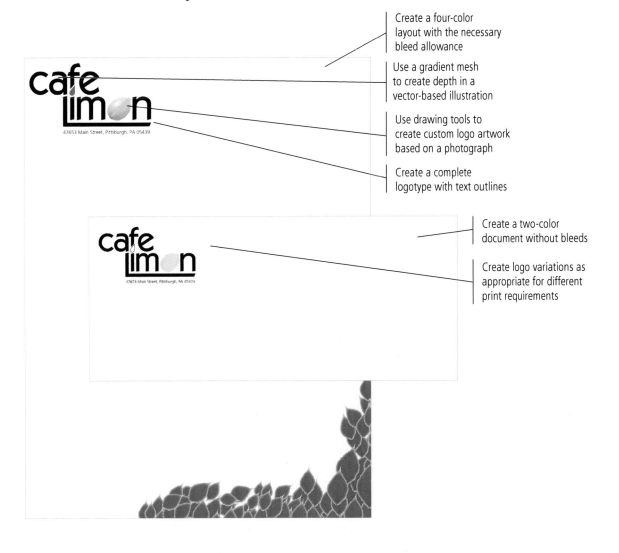

Create a four-color layout with the necessary bleed allowance

Use a gradient mesh to create depth in a vector-based illustration

Use drawing tools to create custom logo artwork based on a photograph

Create a complete logotype with text outlines

Create a two-color document without bleeds

Create logo variations as appropriate for different print requirements

Ski Resort Map

Your client manages a ski resort. He wants to create a basic map of the resort to show the locations of various resort features and amenities. The map will be printed independently, but also placed into other projects, such as the local entertainment magazine and local restaurant menus.

This project incorporates the following skills:

❏ Managing built-in libraries of swatches, brushes, and symbols
❏ Defining custom art and pattern brushes for specific applications
❏ Saving user-defined libraries of custom assets
❏ Understanding and creating symbols and symbol instances
❏ Transforming symbol instances and editing symbol artwork
❏ Replacing symbols in placed instances
❏ Creating a clipping mask

PROJECT MEETING

This map will be available on kiosks around the resort, but it is also going to be used in advertising and cross-promotional marketing. We'll be placing it in the local entertainment magazine and papers, along with some coupons, and we also have some interest from local restaurants to print the map on their placemats and menus.

I started to create the map I want, but I need you to finish it. I did find some nice graphics for the resort lodge, but I realized that I don't have the time or skills to create something that looks good.

When you see what he gave us, you can see what needs to be done. He didn't get any further than different colored lines and some text telling where a few things are.

I already showed the client some ideas for icons instead of text to identify different amenities. He approved those, so I created a library for you to use when you build the completed file. You'll need to include the icons both in the legend and wherever they are indicated by the existing text.

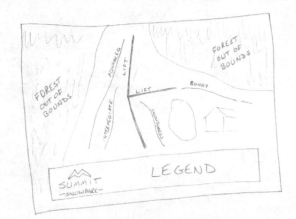

To complete this project, you will:

- ❏ Open and use built-in swatch libraries
- ❏ Define custom gradient swatches
- ❏ Modify a stroke width profile
- ❏ Create a new custom pattern swatch based on existing artwork
- ❏ Define custom art and pattern brushes
- ❏ Save a custom brush library
- ❏ Open and use an external symbol library
- ❏ Place and control symbol instances
- ❏ Edit symbols to change all placed instances
- ❏ Break the link from placed instances to the original symbols
- ❏ Replace symbols in placed instances
- ❏ Spray multiple symbol instances
- ❏ Create a clipping mask to hide unwanted parts of the artwork

STAGE 1 / Working with Custom Swatches

The default Swatches panel (Window>Swatches) includes a seemingly random collection of swatches from various built-in libraries. Illustrator also includes a large number of built-in swatch libraries, many of which contain thematic color schemes (such as Earthtone, Metal, and Nature). These libraries are accessed by choosing Window>Swatch Libraries, or by opening the Swatch Libraries menu at the bottom of the Swatches panel.

If you open more than one swatch library from the Window>Swatch Libraries menu, each library opens as a new panel, grouped with other open swatch libraries. Library panels open in the same location and state as the last time they were used. If a panel is not automatically grouped with other library panels, it was already used and repositioned.

If you open a different library using the Swatch Libraries menu at the bottom of an open panel, the new library replaces the one that was active when you opened the new library. You can drag a panel out of the group to manage it independently.

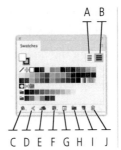

A Show List View
B Show Thumbnail View
C Swatch Libraries menu
D Open Color Themes panel
E Add to Current Library
F Show Swatch Kinds menu
G Swatch Options
H New Color Group
I New Swatch
J Delete Swatch

A Swatch Libraries menu
B Load Previous Swatch Library
C Load Next Swatch Library

Manage the Swatches Panel

In this project, your client created the basic elements, but was unable to complete the entire map. The first logical step in any project where you are provided with an existing file is to review the supplied artwork.

1. **Download Skiing_AI19_RF.zip from the Student Files web page.**

2. **Expand the ZIP archive in your WIP folder (Macintosh) or copy the archive contents into your WIP folder (Windows).**

   This results in a folder named **Skiing**, which contains the files you need for this project. You should also use this folder to save the files you create in this project.

3. **Open the file summit-map.ai from your WIP>Skiing folder.**

   The file includes a very basic map, with mostly plain text, basic solid lines, and a few graphics that have been placed by the client. Your job is to add visual interest using a variety of methods, including custom gradients, patterns, brush strokes, and symbols.

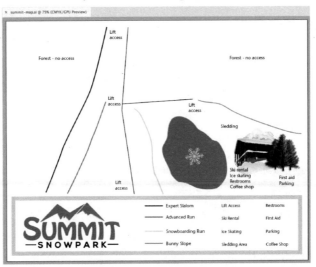

4. **Open the Swatches panel (Window>Swatches).**

   The default Swatches panel (Window>Swatches) includes a seemingly random collection of swatches from the various built-in libraries. Every new file includes these swatches, plus any custom swatches that have been created in the file.

   The file you were provided for this project also includes four custom global swatches.

5. **Open the Swatches panel Options menu and choose Select All Unused.**

6. **Click the Delete Swatch button at the bottom of the panel. When asked, click Yes to confirm the deletion.**

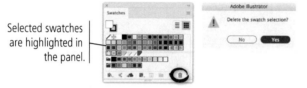

   Selected swatches are highlighted in the panel.

7. **Click the Show List View button at the top of the Swatches panel. Click the bottom-right corner of the panel and drag until you see the entire list of swatches.**

   The Swatches panels appear by default in Thumbnail mode. In the list view, you see the name of the color, as well as an icon that indicates the type of the color. You can also choose Small List View or Large List view in the panel's Options menu.

   CMYK color icon

   Click here and drag to resize the panel.

8. **Click the Grays folder in the panel and drag to the Delete Swatch button.**
   The only swatch in this color group is 100% Black — the same as the basic Black swatch that is not in the group; there is no reason to maintain two swatches with the same color make-up, so you are deleting the extra black swatch.

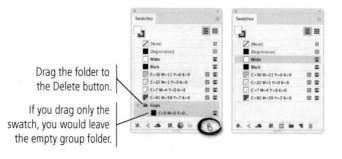

   Drag the folder to the Delete button.

   If you drag only the swatch, you would leave the empty group folder.

9. **Save the file and continue to the next exercise.**

Note:

We recommend using floating panels throughout this project to avoid problems created by auto-collapsing docked panels.

Note:

Deleting a used swatch does not affect objects where the color is applied.

Note:

When a library displays in Thumbnail mode, you can roll the mouse over a specific swatch to see the swatch name in a tool tip. The same option is available for brush libraries, graphic style libraries, and symbol libraries.

Note:

The Registration swatch, which can't be deleted, is a special color that outputs at 100% of all inks. It is typically used for file information on a printing plate, outside the trim area. You should never use the registration color inside the artboard boundaries.

Define Gradient Swatches

A gradient smoothly merges one color into another. Illustrator supports both linear gradients, which move in a line from one color to another, and radial gradients, which move from one color at the center of a circle to another color at the outer edges.

Illustrator includes a number of built-in pattern and gradient swatch libraries, which can be accessed in the Window>Swatch Libraries>Gradients or >Patterns submenus. You can also create your own gradient and pattern swatches, which are stored in the file's Swatches panel. In this exercise, you will create two custom gradient swatches that you can apply to any object in the file.

1. **With summit-map.ai open, open the Gradient panel (Window>Gradient).**

2. **Choose the Radial option at the top of the Gradient panel.**

3. **Drag the C=7 M=4 Y=0 K=0 swatch from the Swatches panel onto the left stop of the gradient ramp (in the Gradient panel).**

   The gradient-stop color changes from white to blue, and the sample swatch now shows the effect of the new stop color.

Drag this swatch onto the left gradient stop.

Choose the radial type of gradient here.

The swatch shows a sample of the gradient with the current settings.

4. **Drag the C=36 M=11 Y=0 K=0 swatch from the Swatches panel onto the right stop of the gradient ramp.**

Drag this swatch onto the right gradient stop.

5. **Drag the C=22 M=1 Y=0 K=0 swatch from the Swatches panel to the middle of the gradient ramp.**

6. **With the new stop selected, change the Location field to 67%.**

Drag this swatch to the midpoint of the gradient ramp to add a new stop...

...then change the Location to 67%.

7. **Drag the C=36 M=11 Y=0 K=0 swatch in the Swatches panel to the 33% location on the gradient ramp.**

Note:

Several gradient swatches are also available in the default Swatches panel. If you use a gradient or pattern swatch from one of the built-in library collections, it is automatically added to the file's Swatches panel.

Note:

Delete specific stops from the gradient by dragging the stops down and away from the gradient ramp.

8. Double-click the new stop to open the options for that stop. Change the tint slider to 70%.

If the pop-up panel shows swatches instead of the tint slider, click the Color button on the left side of the panel.

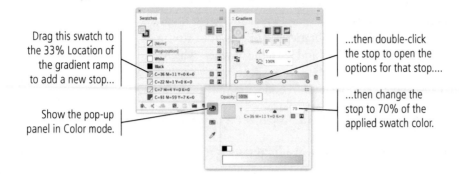

Drag this swatch to the 33% Location of the gradient ramp to add a new stop...

Show the pop-up panel in Color mode.

...then double-click the stop to open the options for that stop....

...then change the stop to 70% of the applied swatch color.

9. Click the sample swatch in the Gradient panel and drag it into the main Swatches panel.

Drag this sample into the Swatches panel.

10. Double-click the new swatch name in the Swatches panel. Type Ice Radial to rename the swatch, then press Return/Enter to finalize the new name.

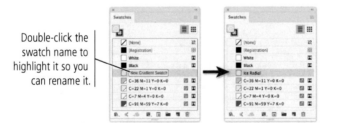

Double-click the swatch name to highlight it so you can rename it.

Note:

You can also double-click the swatch thumbnail to open the Swatch Options dialog box, where you can rename the swatch.

11. In the Gradient panel, click the Linear button to change the Gradient type.

Changing the type of gradient does not change the color-stop settings.

12. Repeat Steps 9–10 to create a new gradient swatch named Ice Linear.

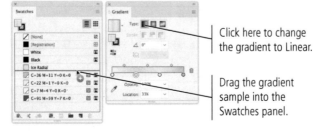

Click here to change the gradient to Linear.

Drag the gradient sample into the Swatches panel.

13. Save the file and continue to the next exercise.

Using Spot Colors in Gradients

If you create a gradient that blends from a spot color to a process-color build, the results will be unpredictable at best, and disastrous at worst. In short, we strongly discourage this practice. It is possible, however, to create a gradient that blends from a spot color to white; doing so just requires a simple trick to avoid output problems.

The images to the right show the components of a basic linear gradient that blends from white to Pantone 484C. By default, the White stop is actually a CMYK build, with all four ink components set to zero. When a Pantone color blends into the CMYK white, the intermediate steps of the gradient will be created with CMYK builds instead of shades of the Pantone color.

To solve the problem, apply the spot color to both stops, and define the white stop as 0% of the spot color. When both stops are tints of a Pantone color, the intermediate shades of the gradient will be created as shades of the Pantone color instead of CMYK percentages.

Color makeup of the first gradient stop

Color makeup of the second gradient stop

Apply and Control Gradients

Once you have created gradient swatches, you can apply them by simply selecting an object, selecting the target attribute (fill or stroke), and then clicking the appropriate swatch. You can then use the Gradient panel and Gradient tool to control the position of an applied gradient.

1. **With summit-map.ai open, use the Selection tool to select the lake shape on the artboard.**

2. **Open the Fill Color panel from the Control panel, and click the Ice Radial swatch.**

   The Fill and Stroke Color panels include the same swatches that are available in the document's Swatches panel. Because you deleted the unused swatches from the default set, you see only the few colors that were part of the original file and the two gradient swatches that you defined in the previous exercise.

The same swatches in the Swatches panel are available in the Control panel's pop-up panels.

The applied radial gradient is centered in the selected object.

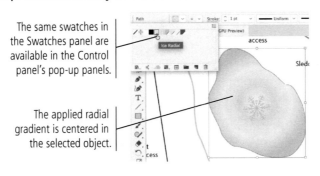

Note:

You can Shift-click the Fill or Stroke icons in the Control panel to show an alternate color panel UI:

3. **Using the Gradient tool, click near the top area of the lake object and drag to the bottom area.**

When you first choose the Gradient tool, the Gradient Annotator appears; by default, it is exactly horizontal. After you complete this step, the Gradient Annotator matches the line you drag with the Gradient tool.

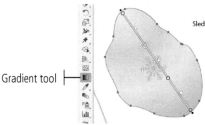

Gradient tool

Note:

If you are not satisfied with the length and angle of your gradient, simply click and drag again to change it.

When you are using a radial gradient, the first place you click with the Gradient tool defines the center point (the starting color) of the applied gradient. The location where you release the mouse button marks the outer edge of the radial gradient. The area beyond the outer edge of the gradient fills with the end-stop color of the gradient. The direction to drag defines the angle of the gradient.

4. **In the Gradient panel, change the Aspect Ratio field to 45%.**

Changing the aspect ratio of a radial gradient converts the gradient shape to an ellipse instead of a circle. A 45% aspect ratio means the gradient's height is 45% of its width.

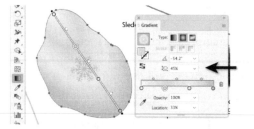

5. **Using the Selection tool, select the rectangle shape around the logo.**

6. **Open the Stroke Color panel from the Control panel, then click the Ice Linear swatch.**

When you apply a gradient to a stroke, the default option (Apply Gradient within Stroke) basically "fills" the stroke with the gradient.

By default, gradients are applied within the stroke.

7. **In the Gradient panel, bring the Stroke attribute to the front of the stack.**

8. **Click the Apply Gradient Along Stroke button.**

Using the Apply Gradient Along Stroke option, the gradient is applied in a linear fashion. Depending on the shape of the path, this option might not make a noticeable difference. For this rectangle, however, you can see that the starting point of the gradient is located at the bottom-right corner of the stroke; the gradient then travels around the shape, until the ending point of the gradient meets the same corner.

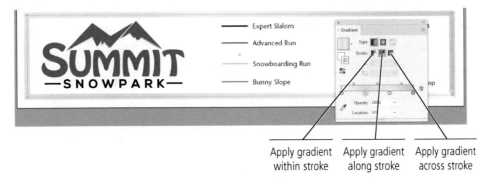

Apply gradient within stroke   Apply gradient along stroke   Apply gradient across stroke

9. **Click the Apply Gradient Across Stroke button.**

Using the Apply Gradient Across Stroke option, the gradient begins at the outside edge of the path and ends on the inside edge.

10. **Save the file and then continue to the next exercise.**

Edit a Path Profile

In addition to simply applying stroke attributes to a path, you can use the Width tool to adjust the shape of a stroke at any point along a specific path. This moves beyond the ability to manipulate the points and segments that make up a shape. In this exercise, you will modify the path that surrounds the legend.

1. **With summit-map.ai open, choose the Width tool in the Tools panel.**

2. **Move the cursor over the top-left corner of the legend box.**

It might help to zoom in so you can more clearly see the anchor points that make up the shape.

3. **When you see the word "anchor" in the cursor feedback, click and drag away from the point. When the overall width is approximately 0.28 in, release the mouse button.**

When a path is selected, clicking the path with the Width tool adds a width point. You can drag out from the width point to add symmetrical width handles, which change the stroke width at that point along the path. If you click and drag an existing width handle, the opposite handle is also affected.

When the Width tool cursor is over an existing stroke, the cursor feedback shows the overall width of the stroke at that point, as well as the width of each side of the stroke.

Clicking and dragging with the Width tool adds symmetrical handles on both sides of the path. Cursor feedback shows the width of each side, and the overall width of the point.

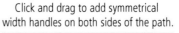
Click and drag to add symmetrical width handles on both sides of the path.

Width tool

Cursor feedback shows the width of the stroke, and each side of the stroke.

4. **Move the cursor along the path until the feedback shows an "intersect" with the center of the placed logo.**

The path is still just a path, even though you edited its width.

Note:

Don't worry if the measurements are not exact; you will learn how to define precise side widths in the next few steps.

5. **Press Option/Alt, then click and drag down until cursor feedback shows that Side 2 is approximately 0.08 in.**

If you press Option/Alt while dragging from a width point, you add non-symmetrical width handles. You can also Option/Alt-click an existing width handle and drag to adjust it independently of the opposing handle.

Option/Alt-click and drag to create non-symmetrical handles.

Note:

To remove a width point from a stroke, click with the Width tool to select a particular point, then press Delete/Backspace.

6. **About half-way across the stroke, click and drag down slightly to initiate the width points, then drag up until the overall width of the point is approximately 0.1 in.**

In this case, the two sides of the stroke are already different because you created non-symmetrical handles on the previous point. Dragging the handles of this point maintains the proportional relationship between the two sides.

7. **Double-click the new point from Step 6. In the resulting Width Point Edit dialog box, activate the link icon to force the Side 1 and Side 2 fields to symmetrically proportional lengths.**

   You can numerically manipulate the length of width handles by double-clicking a particular width point. When the link icon is active, changing one side has a proportional effect on the other side.

Note:

If multiple points are selected when you double-click, this dialog box will include fields for each point.

8. **Change the Side 1 field to 0.04 in, then press Tab to highlight the Side 2 field.**

   Because you linked the two fields, the width of Side 2 is also changed proportionally (from 0.034 to 0.024 in our example).

Make this link active.

9. **Click OK to close the Width Point Edit dialog box.**

10. **Click the point you added in Step 6 (the one in the middle of the top edge) and drag right until that point is approximately two-thirds of the way across the frame edge.**

    You can move a specific width point by clicking and dragging; other width points are not affected.

Note:

If you Shift-click and drag a width point, other points on the path adjust proportionally.

Click and drag an existing width point to move it along the path.

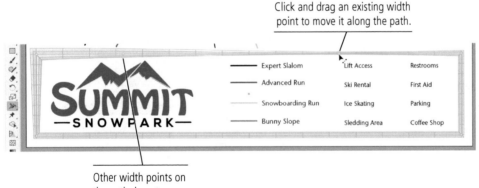

Other width points on the path do not move.

When you release the mouse button, you can see the effect of moving one width point on the overall path shape. The lower edge of the path is very close to the logo, so you should edit the path width at that point to provide a slightly larger gap between the logo and the path.

11. Double-click the width point above the logo on the top of the frame edge. Unlink the two Side fields, change the Side 2 field to 0.07 in, then click OK.

Because you did not link the two Side fields, changing one does not affect the other. In this case, you are modifying the width on only Side 2 — the side nearest the logo.

Turn off this link.

12. Add and adjust width points along the bottom path of the shape until you are satisfied with the overall result.

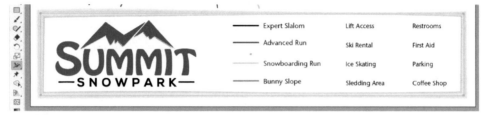

13. Save the file and continue to the next exercise.

Creating Variable-Width Stroke Profiles

Once you have edited the shape of a path, you can save your work as a custom stroke profile so you can apply that same stroke appearance to other paths.

The Variable Width Profile menu is available in both the Control and Stroke panels. Stroke profiles do not include the initial stroke width; the profile is applied proportionally based on the defined width of the stroke where you apply the profile.

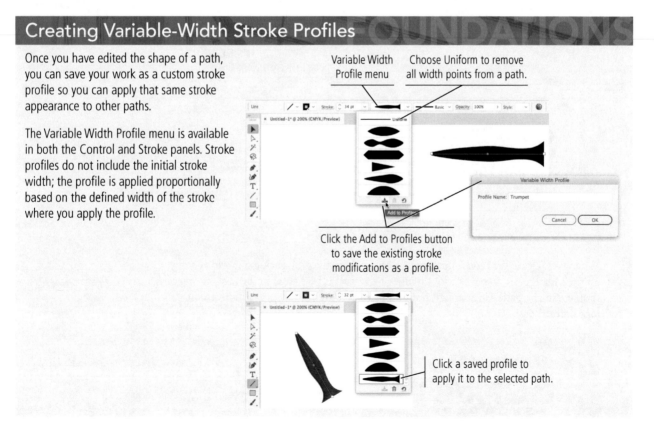

Variable Width Profile menu

Choose Uniform to remove all width points from a path.

Click the Add to Profiles button to save the existing stroke modifications as a profile.

Click a saved profile to apply it to the selected path.

Create a Custom Pattern

Illustrator includes a Pattern Options panel, which makes it very easy to create a custom pattern from any artwork. In this project, you will create a snowflake pattern that fills the background of the entire artboard.

1. **With summit-map.ai open, make sure nothing is selected on the artboard.**

2. **Using the Selection tool, click the snowflake artwork and drag it to the Swatches panel.**

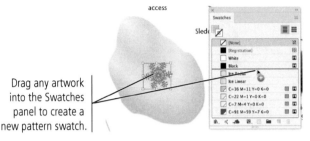

Drag any artwork into the Swatches panel to create a new pattern swatch.

3. **Double-click the new swatch name in the panel. Type Snowflake, then press Return/Enter to finalize the new name.**

4. **Choose View>Fit Artboard in Window.**

    This command changes the view percentage to match the available space, and centers the current artboard in the document window.

    When you enter Edit Pattern mode in the next step, the pattern artwork appears in the center of the document window. If the artboard is not centered in the document window before you enter Edit Pattern mode, the pattern artwork might not appear entirely within the artboard boundary.

    It doesn't matter where the pattern artwork appears relative to the artboard; however, it can be confusing if the pattern appears partially inside and partially outside the artboard edge. Using the View>Fit Artboard in Window command works around this problem.

5. **Double-click the Snowflake swatch thumbnail to enter into Edit Pattern mode.**

    Edit Pattern mode is a special interface where you can define specific parameters of the pattern. The Pattern Options panel includes a number of options that make it easy to define a custom pattern from any artwork. You can define the repeating area (the "tile") and the manner in which it is repeated, and see an instant on-screen preview of each change you define.

    Artboards in the active file are also visible in the document window while working in Edit Pattern mode. The pattern artwork defaults to appear in the center of the document window. However, the actual pattern has no relation to the artboard.

> **Note:**
>
> *Do not move the artboard (with the Artboard tool) when working in Edit Pattern mode.*

> **Note:**
>
> *You can also click the Edit Pattern button at the bottom of the Swatches panel.*

6. If necessary, zoom in so you can more clearly see the pattern.

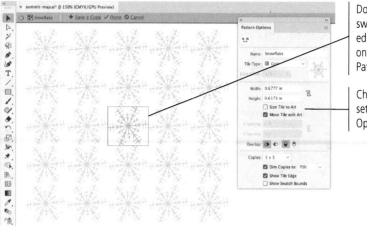

Double-click the pattern swatch thumbnail to edit the pattern settings on the special Edit Pattern artboard.

Change the pattern settings in the Pattern Options panel.

7. At the bottom of the Pattern Options panel, uncheck the Show Swatch Bounds option (if necessary).

The Copies menu defines how many copies of the pattern artwork appear in the pattern preview. The Dim Copies To field reduces the opacity of the copies so you can more easily distinguish the actual pattern artwork.

The Tile Edge, which appears as a solid black line on the artboard, is the area that is repeated when you apply the pattern. The Swatch Bounds is simply the storage space surrounding the pattern artwork. If you change the tile size, the swatch boundary grows or shrinks to accommodate the new tile size.

When you first create a pattern, the tile size matches the size of the pattern artwork. You can use the Width and Height fields in the Pattern Options panel to change the tile size, or click the Pattern Tile tool at the top of the panel to manually resize the tile on the artboard.

Note:

Don't confuse changing the tile size with changing the artwork size.

8. Activate the link icon to link the Width and Height fields. Change the Width field to 0.5 in, then press Return/Enter.

If you use the fields in the panel to change the tile size, you can activate the link icon to maintain the original aspect ratio of the tile; changing one field applies a proportional change to the other field.

Changing the tile size changes the way individual objects interact when the pattern is repeated. Artwork outside the tile area is still included in the pattern, overlapping the other repeating objects.

If you change the size of the artwork, you can check the Size Tile to Art option to force the tile to match the resized artwork. When this option is active, you can use the H Spacing and V Spacing fields to add or remove a specific amount of space around the artwork when it is repeated in the panel. You can also use the Overlap options to determine how individual objects affect others in the repeated pattern, which is useful if pattern artwork has applied effects or transparency.

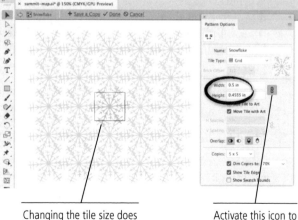

Changing the tile size does not change the size of the actual pattern artwork.

Activate this icon to constrain the tile size aspect ratio.

9. **In the Tile Type menu, choose Brick by Row. Choose 1/3 in the Brick Offset menu.**

The Tile Type menu determines how the pattern artwork repeats. When you choose one of the Brick options, you can use the Brick Offset menu to determine how the "bricks" are stacked in the repeating pattern.

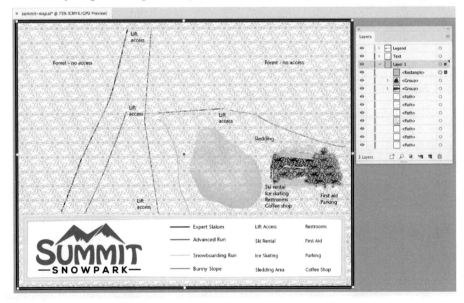

10. **Click the Done option at the top of the document window.**

Clicking Done saves the changes to the existing pattern. If you had already applied the pattern anywhere in the file, those objects would reflect the new pattern.

You can also click Save a Copy to save your changes as a new pattern; in this case, the changes would not be reflected in any objects where the original pattern had been applied.

If you click Cancel, the changes are not saved and the existing pattern is not affected.

11. **Select and delete the snowflake from the middle of the lake.**

12. **Using the Rectangle tool, create a shape that fills the entire artboard. Apply a 6-pt black stroke, then apply the Snowflakes pattern as the shape's fill.**

13. **In the Layers panel, expand Layer 1 and locate the pattern-filled rectangle.**

Note:

You can double-click a specific object in the layers panel to name it, just as you name specific layers. For example, you could rename the "Rectangle" item as "Background filled rectangle."

14. Create a new layer named `Background`, and move it to the bottom of the layer stack.

15. Click the Selected Art icon and drag to the Background layer.

The pattern now appears behind the other artwork, but it is still too strong compared to other objects in the file.

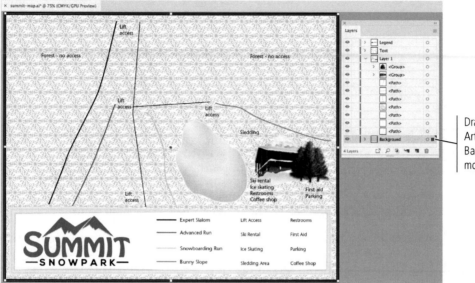

Drag the Selected Art icon to the Background layer to move the rectangle.

16. Deselect everything on the artboard.

17. In the Swatches panel, double-click the Snowflakes pattern swatch to re-enter Edit Pattern mode. At the bottom of the Pattern Options panel, uncheck the Dim Copies option.

Turning off the Dim Copies option allows you to better see the actual pattern that will result from your changes.

18. Using the Selection tool, click to select the snowflake artwork in the pattern tile. Change the fill tint to 25% in the Color panel.

Pattern artwork is still artwork, which means you can modify it just as you would any other artwork.

Because the fill is a global swatch, you can apply a percentage of the swatch.

19. Click the Done link at the top of the document window.

When you click Done, the changes are reflected anywhere the pattern has been applied. As you can see, lightening the color in the pattern artwork makes the overall background pattern much more subtle.

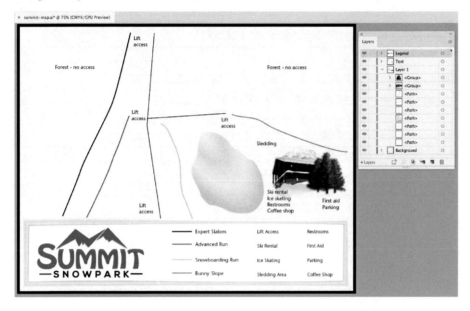

20. Save the file and then continue to the next stage of the project.

STAGE 2 / Working with Brushes

Brushes enhance or (as Adobe puts it) decorate paths. The default Brushes panel (Window>Brushes) includes several basic brushes of different types. You can use the Brushes panel Options menu to change the panel display, manage brushes, and load different brush libraries.

The Brushes panel appears by default in Thumbnail mode. If you choose List View in the panel Options menu, you see the name of the brush, as well as an icon that indicates the type of brush.

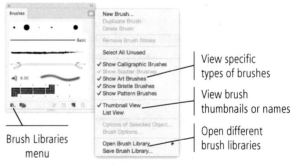

- **Art brushes** apply a brush stroke or object shape across the length of a path.

- **Bristle brushes** create strokes that mimic the behavior of a real artist's brushes.

- **Calligraphic brushes** create strokes that resemble what you would draw with the angled tip of a calligraphic pen.

- **Pattern brushes** paint a pattern of defined tiles along the length of a path, on inner and outer corners, and the beginning and end of a path.

- **Scatter brushes** scatter copies of an object along a path.

Beyond the few brushes in the default Brushes panel, you can also open a number of built-in brush libraries using the Brush Libraries menu at the bottom of the Brushes panel or at the bottom of the Window menu.

Note:

Brush libraries open in the same position as when they were last used. If you open more than one brush library, the new library opens as a separate tab in the existing panel group unless it has already been moved into a different panel group.

Create a New Art Brush

An art brush applies an object along the length of a path. You will use this type of brush to create the ski lift paths. To create an art brush, you must first create the object(s) you want to use as the brush stroke.

1. **With summit-map.ai open, create a new layer named Ski Lift immediately above Layer 1.**

2. **Select the two ski-lift paths on the artboard. In the Layers panel, click the Selected Art icon for Layer 1, then drag it to the Ski Lift layer.**

   If you dragged the Selected Art icon for any specific path, only that path would be moved to the new layer. Because you dragged the Selected Art icon for the active layer that contained both paths, both are moved to the new layer.

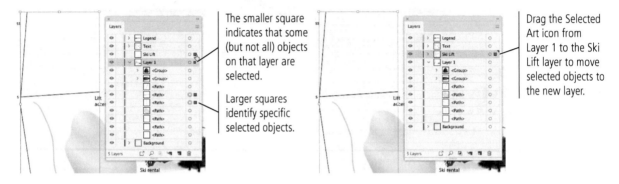

The smaller square indicates that some (but not all) objects on that layer are selected.

Larger squares identify specific selected objects.

Drag the Selected Art icon from Layer 1 to the Ski Lift layer to move selected objects to the new layer.

3. **Option/Alt-click the eye icon for the Ski Lift layer to hide all but that layer.**

4. **Click away from the two paths to deselect everything.**

5. **Anywhere on the artboard, create a 5-pt horizontal black line that is approximately 1″ long. Change the stroke color to 75% black.**

6. **With the line selected, choose Edit>Copy.**

7. **Choose Edit>Paste in Front to paste a copy of the line directly on top of the original.**

   The Paste options are very useful for positioning copied objects.

   - **Paste** puts the copy in the center of the document window.
   - **Paste in Front** puts the copy in the same place as the copied object, one level higher in the object stacking order than the current selection.
   - **Paste in Back** puts the copy in the same place as the copied object, one level lower in the object stacking order than the current selection.
   - **Paste in Place** puts the copy on the selected artboard in the same position as it was on the original artboard.
   - **Paste on All Artboards** puts a copy on all artboards in the document, in the same position as the original artboard. A copy is also placed on the original artboard, so you might want to remove the duplicate copy from the original active artboard.

8. **With the pasted line still selected, change the stroke weight to 2.5 pt and change the stroke color to 30%.**

9. **Select both lines, then choose Object>Path>Outline Stroke.**

   This command converts a stroked path to a filled object. The original stroke color becomes the fill color of the resulting shape.

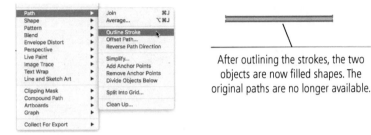

   After outlining the strokes, the two objects are now filled shapes. The original paths are no longer available.

10. **Select both rectangles and group them (Object>Group or Command/Control-G).**

11. **Make sure the basic Brushes panel is open (Window>Brushes), and then drag the grouped rectangles into the Brushes panel.**

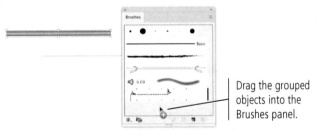

   Drag the grouped objects into the Brushes panel.

12. **In the resulting New Brush dialog box, choose the Art Brush radio button and then click OK.**

13. **Type** Ski Lift **in the Name field of the resulting dialog box, and then click OK.**

After you click OK in the dialog box, the new brush appears in the Brushes panel.

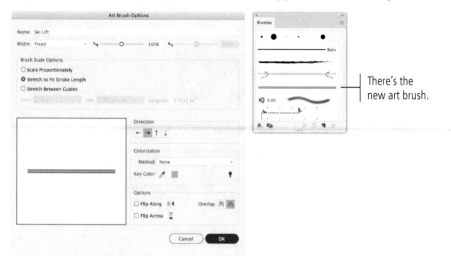

There's the new art brush.

14. **Delete the grouped lines from the artboard, save your work, then continue to the next exercise.**

Understanding Art Brush Options

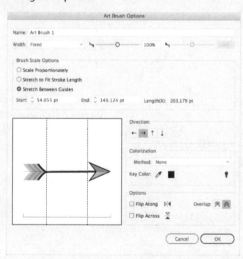

The Art Brush Options dialog box opens automatically when you create a new art brush. You can also double-click an existing art brush to change its options.

The **Width** field defines the width of the brush stroke relative to the applied stroke weight. For example, a 200% Width value would result in a 2-pt apparent stroke if the path has a 1-pt defined stroke weight.

The **Fixed** menu can be used to allow a variable stroke width based on a number of factors, including pressure and tilt from drawing tablet hardware.

In the Brush Scale Options, **Scale Proportionally** stretches the artwork both horizontally and vertically to match the stroke length.

Stretch to Fit Stroke Length stretches the brush artwork horizontally across the entire length of the stroke (in only the direction of the stroke).

Stretch Between Guides can be used to define areas of the brush artwork that do not stretch. Areas between the defined Start and End guides (dashed lines in the Preview) will stretch across the stroke length.

Direction controls the direction of brush artwork relative to the path. The active button matches the direction of the arrow in the preview; both of these indicate which side of the original artwork will be the end of the stroke.

Colorization options determine how colors in the paths are affected by colors in the brush artwork.

Flip Along and **Flip Across** reverse the orientation of art relative to the path.

Overlap controls how the artwork is treated on corners.

Control an Art Brush Stroke

Applying a brush stroke is simple — draw a path (or select an object), then click the brush you want to apply (either in the Brushes panel or in the Control panel menu). Once a brush stroke is applied, however, you should also understand how to control it.

1. **With summit-map.ai open, select the two paths that represent the ski lifts.**

2. **Click the Ski Lift brush in the Brushes panel.**

   The paths immediately take on the appearance of the brush you created earlier. You created the original darker-line stroke as 5 pt. When you created a brush from the grouped rectangles, you left the Width field (in the Art Brush Options dialog box) at 100%.

   The width of the path stroke is important when using brushes. When you apply artistic brush strokes, the width of the path's stroke actually defines the percentage of the brush width that will be applied. In this case, the width of the path stroke is 1 pt, so the applied brush stroke is 100% of the brush size. In other words, applying the brush to a 1-pt path results in a brush stroke with a 5-pt width.

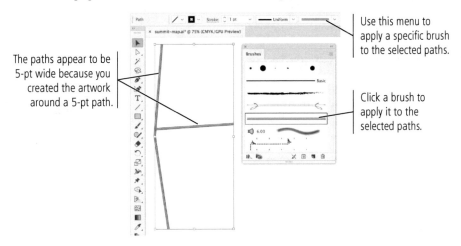

The paths appear to be 5-pt wide because you created the artwork around a 5-pt path.

Use this menu to apply a specific brush to the selected paths.

Click a brush to apply it to the selected paths.

3. **With the brushed path selected, double-click the Ski Lift brush in the Brushes panel to open the Art Brush Options dialog box.**

4. **In the Art Brush Options dialog box, change the Width field to 200% and then click OK.**

   The Width field defines brush stroke width as a percentage of the applied stroke weight.

   You could accomplish the same result by changing the path strokes to 2 pt. Every job has different requirements, so it's important to understand your options.

Note:

You can also click the Options of Selected Object button at the bottom of the Brushes panel to edit the brush options.

5. **In the resulting dialog box, click Apply to Strokes.**

When you change the options for a specific brush, you can determine what to do for strokes where the brush has already been applied.

- If you click Apply to Strokes, the changes will be applied to any path where the brush has been applied.

- If you click Leave Strokes, existing paths are unaffected; a copy of the changed brush is added to the Brushes panel.

- If you click Cancel, the Brush Options dialog box closes without applying the new brush options.

6. **Save the file and continue to the next exercise.**

Note:

If you try to delete a brush that has been used in the open file, you must decide what to do with strokes where the brush has been applied.

If you click Expand Strokes, the applied brush strokes are converted to filled objects.

If you click Remove Strokes, objects that include the deleted brush strokes are reduced to their basic appearance (fill color, stroke color, and weight).

If you click Cancel, your artwork is unaffected and the brush remains in the Brushes panel.

Expand Brush Strokes into Objects

If you look at the map as it is now, you might notice a problem where the ski lift paths connect — the dark gray of the horizontal path overlaps the light gray of the vertical path. To more accurately reflect the appearance of a single path that branches off in a different direction, you need to convert the path strokes to regular objects so you can manipulate selected parts of the paths (i.e., where the lines intersect).

1. **With summit-map.ai open, zoom in so you can more clearly see where the two paths meet.**

2. **Select both paths, then choose View>Hide Bounding Box.**

When the bounding box is hidden, you can better see the selected paths without the bounding box that marks the outer bounds of the active selection.

3. **Open the Appearance panel (Window>Appearance).**

The Appearance panel shows the properties of the selected objects, including the applied stroke and fill attributes. You can see here that the stroke attribute is Ski Lift.

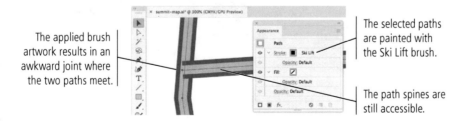

The applied brush artwork results in an awkward joint where the two paths meet.

The selected paths are painted with the Ski Lift brush.

The path spines are still accessible.

4. **With the paths still selected, choose Object>Expand Appearance.**

In the Appearance panel, you now see that the selection is a group. When you expand the appearance of a selection, Illustrator simplifies the selection (as much as possible) into basic filled and stroked shapes; the resulting shapes are grouped.

Objects that make up the brush patterns are accessible and the path spines are gone.

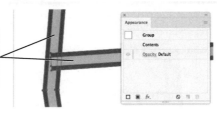

5. **In the Layers panel, expand the Ski Lift layer.**

As a result of expanding the strokes, each path is now a group.

6. **Click the arrows to expand each group.**

Each group contains the two paths in the artwork that made up the brush stroke.

The resulting groups are each made up of two paths — the lighter one and the darker one.

7. **With the expanded paths still selected, choose Object>Ungroup.**

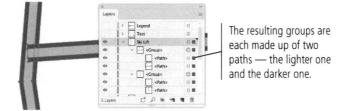

8. **Deselect everything, and then select the lighter path of the horizontal ski lift.**

9. **Choose Select>Same>Fill Color to select the other object that has the lighter fill.**

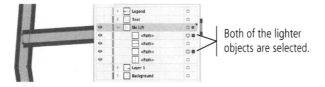

Both of the lighter objects are selected.

10. **In the Pathfinder panel (Window>Pathfinder), click the Unite button.**

All the selected shapes are now a single object. When you use the Pathfinder, the merged objects move to the stacking-order position of the highest object in the original selection, as you can see in the Layers panel. This is unlike the Shape Builder tool, which moves the merged object to the stacking-order position of the first object you click.

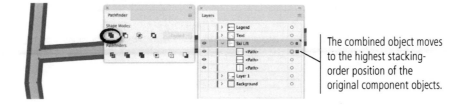

The combined object moves to the highest stacking-order position of the original component objects.

11. **Repeat Steps 8–10 to unite the darker objects into a single shape.**

You don't need to send the combined object to the back of the stacking order because it is already behind the lighter object.

12. **In the Layers panel, collapse the Ski Lift layer.**

13. **Save the file and continue to the next exercise.**

Create Pattern Brush Tiles

While an art brush stretches a specific piece of artwork along a path, a pattern brush repeats specific artwork along the path. You can even define different artwork to use for sides, corners, and endpoints of a specific path. In this exercise, you will use an art brush to define the four different ski runs at the resort.

1. **With summit-map.ai open, hide the Ski Lift layer and show Layer 1.**

2. **Create a new layer named Ski Runs immediately above the Ski Lift layer.**

3. **Select the four ski-run paths on the artboard. In the Layers panel, click the Selected Art icon for Layer 1, then drag it to the Ski Runs layer.**

4. **Hide Layer 1, then deselect everything on the artboard.**

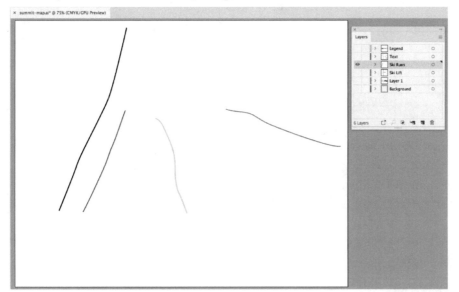

5. **Choose the Rectangle tool, then click and drag anywhere on the page to create a rectangle that is 0.4″ square. Fill the new rectangle with black and apply a stroke of None.**

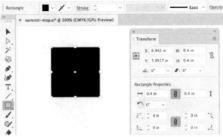

Depending on which selection tool was last used, the shape might appear differently on your screen than what you see here. If you last used the Selection tool, you will see eight bounding-box handles surrounding the shape (as in our screen shots). If you last used the Direct Selection tool, you will only see the new shape's anchor points.

6. **Rotate the rectangle 45°.**

When you rotate the object, the bounding box remains attached to the original object dimensions.

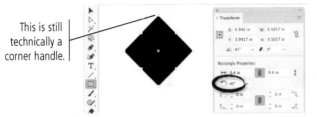

This is still technically a corner handle.

7. **In the Transform panel, make sure the W and H fields are not linked, then change the H field to 0.35 in.**

This icon should show broken links before you change the H field value.

8. **With the object still active, click the Selection tool in the Tools panel to reveal the shape's bounding-box handles.**

If you don't see all eight bounding-box handles on the shape, choose View>Show Bounding Box.

The bounding box is rotated because you rotated the shape in Step 6.

9. **Choose Object>Transform>Reset Bounding Box.**

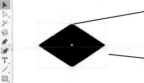

This is now the top-center handle.

Resetting the bounding box restores it to a horizontal rectangle.

When you rotated the shape in Step 6, the bounding box rotated along with the shape; the corners are still the corners. If you drag what appears to be the top handle, you would change the height and width of the shape.

The Reset Bounding Box command restores the bounding box to a horizontal rectangle. If you drag the top-center handle, you will affect only the height of the shape.

10. Using the Selection tool, press Option/Alt, then click and drag the shape to the right to clone it.

11. Using the Line Segment tool with the default stroke weight, draw a vertical line that bisects the second diamond.

Smart guides make it easy to create a path that exactly aligns to the center of the diamond.

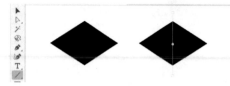

12. Using the Selection tool, press Shift and click the diamond shape to add it to the selection.

13. In the Pathfinder panel, click the Divide button.

14. In the Layers panel, expand the Ski Runs layer, then expand the group at the top of that layer.

When a pathfinder option results in more than one shape, the resulting shapes are automatically grouped together. You are going to use the halves individually, so you need to ungroup them.

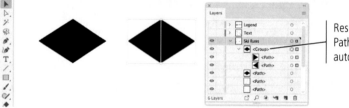

Resulting shapes from the Pathfinder operation are automatically grouped.

15. With the group still selected, transform the selected artwork to 140% proportionally.

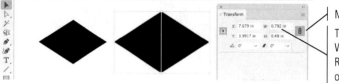

Make the link icon active.

Type **140%** in the W field, then press Return/Enter to scale the objects proportionally.

16. With the entire group selected, choose Object>Ungroup.

17. Save the file and continue to the next exercise.

Create a New Pattern Brush

Now that you have the three objects you need to create the pattern brush, you have to convert those objects to patterns, and then define the pattern brush.

1. **With summit-map.ai open, deselect all objects on the artboard.**

2. **Using the Selection tool, drag the right-facing triangle shape into the Swatches panel.**

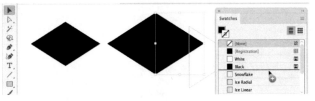

3. **In the Swatches panel, double-click the new swatch to highlight the name. Type Run Start and press Return/Enter.**

4. **Delete the right-facing triangle from the artboard.**

5. **Repeat Steps 2–4 to create a pattern swatch named Run End from the left triangle shape, and a swatch named Run Path from the diamond shape.**

   Make sure you delete the shapes from the artboard after you create the necessary pattern swatches.

6. **Use the Show Swatch Kinds menu at the bottom of the panel to show only pattern swatches.**

Note:

On some Windows systems, there is a bug that prevents some custom swatches from appearing in the Pattern Brush Options dialog box until you save the file where you created the swatches.

7. **If the panel changes to thumbnail view, click the Show List View button at the top of the panel to restore the panel to Small List view.**

8. **With nothing selected on the artboard, click the New Brush button at the bottom of the Brushes panel.**

   If anything is selected when you click the New Brush button, Illustrator tries to create a new brush based on the current selection.

9. **In the New Brush dialog box, select the Pattern Brush option and click OK.**

New Brush button

10. In the Pattern Brush Options dialog box, name the brush Ski Runs.

11. **Click the menu for the Side Tile icon, and then choose Run Path from the list of available pattern swatches.**

    Pattern brush tiles must be saved as pattern swatches (as you did in Steps 2–5) before you can access them in the Pattern Brush Options dialog box.

    After you choose the Side Tile pattern, the preview area shows how the pattern tile will appear along a path.

Note:

Pattern brushes can consist of five possible tiles: side, outer corner, inner corner, start, and end. You can define different patterns for any or all of these tiles.

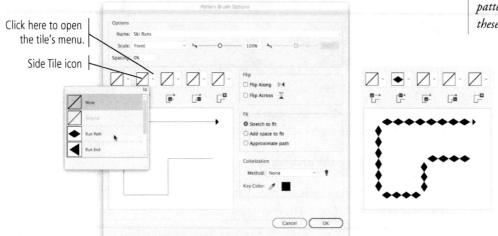

Click here to open the tile's menu.

Side Tile icon

12. **Open the Start Tile menu, and then click Run Start in the list of patterns.**

13. **Open the End Tile menu, and then click Run End in the list of patterns.**

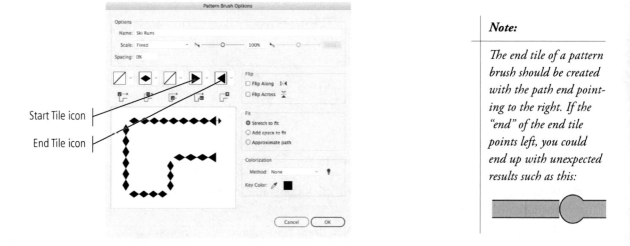

Start Tile icon

End Tile icon

Note:

The end tile of a pattern brush should be created with the path end pointing to the right. If the "end" of the end tile points left, you could end up with unexpected results such as this:

14. **Click OK to create the brush.**

15. Select all four of the paths on the visible layer and click the Ski Runs pattern brush in the Brushes panel.

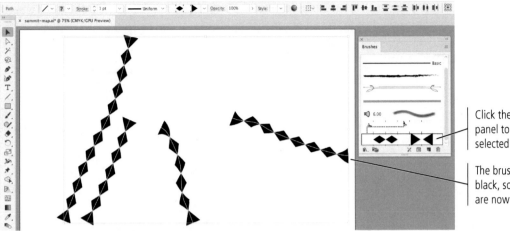

Click the brush in the panel to apply it to selected objects.

The brush artwork is black, so all four paths are now black.

Understanding Pattern Brush Options

As with art brushes, you can control the settings for pattern brushes when you first create them or by double-clicking an existing pattern brush in the Brushes panel.

Scale adjusts the size of tiles relative to their original size.

Spacing adjusts the space between tiles in the stroke.

The **Tile buttons** allow you to apply different patterns to different parts of the line.

A   Outer corner tile
B   Side tile
C   Inner corner tile
D   Start tile
E   End tile

After you define the side tile, Illustrator automatically generates four options for the inner and outer corner tiles. This means you do not need to manually create separate corner artwork (although you can if you choose).

- **Auto-Centered.** The side tile is stretched around the corner and centered on it.
- **Auto-Between.** The side tiles extend all the way into the corner, with one copy on each side.
- **Auto-Sliced.** The side tile is sliced diagonally; the pieces are reassembled similar to the corners of a picture frame.
- **Auto-Overlap.** The side tiles overlap at the corner.

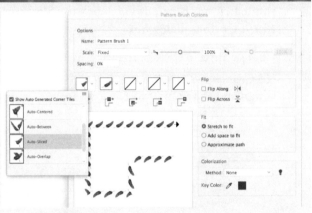

Flip Along and **Flip Across** reverse the orientation of the art in relation to the path.

In the Fit options, **Stretch to Fit** adjusts the length of the pattern tiles to fit the path.

Add Space to Fit adds blank space between pattern tiles to maintain proportions in the applied pattern.

Approximate Path fits tiles to the closest approximate path without changing the tiles.

Colorization methods determine how colors in the paths are affected by colors in the brush stroke artwork.

16. With all four paths selected, change the stroke weight to 0.5 pt.

As we explained earlier, changing the stroke size for the applied art brush and changing the stroke width of the path achieves the same result. The 0.5-pt stroke weight means the applied stroke is half the width of the defined brush.

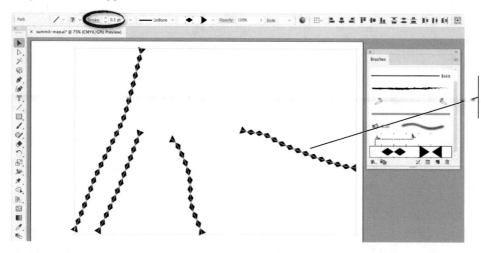

The width of the brush artwork is relative to the applied stroke weight.

17. In the Brushes panel, double-click the Ski Runs brush to open the Pattern Brush Options dialog box.

18. Choose Tints in the Colorization menu, then click OK.

The Colorization menu controls how colors in an art, scatter, or pattern brush interact with the defined stroke color.

- Select **None** to use only the colors defined in the brush.

- Select **Tints** to apply the brush stroke in tints of the current stroke color. Black areas of the brush become the stroke color, other areas become tints of the stroke color, and white remains white.

- Select **Tints and Shades** to apply the brush stroke in tints and shades of the stroke color. Black and white areas of the brush remain unaffected; all other areas are painted as a blend from black to white through the stroke color.

- Select **Hue Shift** to change the defined key color in brush artwork to the defined stroke color when the brush is applied; other colors in the brush artwork are adjusted to be similar to the stroke color. Black, white, and grays are unaffected. The key color defaults to the most prominent color in the brush art. To change the key color, click the eyedropper in the brush preview to select a different color.

Note:

Click the Tips button to the right of the menu to see a preview of colorization options.

Note:

Art brushes can produce unexpected results on sharp corners and closed paths.

Pattern brushes are the best choices for creating borders on closed paths or for other paths that have sharp corners.

19. **In the resulting dialog box, click Apply to Strokes.**

Using the Tint colorization method, black in the brush artwork is reproduced as 100% of the applied stroke color.

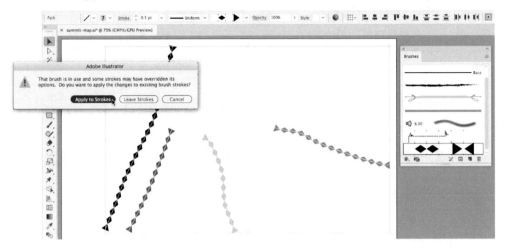

20. **Save the file and continue to the next exercise.**

Save Custom Brushes

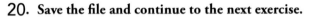

When you create custom brushes, swatches, or other elements, they are only available in the file where you create them. To access those assets in other files, you have to save your own custom libraries.

1. **With summit-map.ai open, show the Brushes panel. Open the panel Options menu and choose Select All Unused.**

Everything but the Basic brush and the Ski Runs pattern brush should be selected. (Remember, you expanded the appearance of the ski lift paths, so the Ski Lift art brush is not currently applied in the file.)

The Ski Lift art brush is selected because you expanded the appearance of the paths where the brush had been applied.

2. **Command/Control-click the Ski Lift art brush to deselect it, and then click the panel's Delete button. Click Yes in the dialog box asking if you want to delete the brush selection.**

You are not permanently deleting the brushes from the application; you are only deleting them from the Brushes panel for this file. However, Illustrator still asks you to confirm the deletion.

Command/Control-click to remove the Ski Lift brush from the active selection...

...then click the panel Delete button.

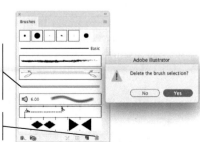

3. **Open the panel Options menu and choose Save Brush Library.**

Note:

The Basic option is an application default, which effectively removes any applied brush stroke and reverts a path to a simple 1-pt stroke.

4. **In the resulting dialog box, name the library map-brushes.ai and click Save.**

   If you're working on your own computer, the application defaults to a Brushes folder created when the application was installed.

Note:

Brush, symbol, and swatch libraries are saved with the ".ai" extension. You can also save swatch libraries in the Adobe Swatch Exchange format (using the extension ".ase") if you want to use a swatch library in another Adobe application such as Photoshop. Keep in mind, however, that swatches containing gradients, patterns, or tints are not "exchangeable" and will not be visible in other applications.

   If you are using a shared computer, you might not be able to save files in the application's default location. If this is the case, navigate to your WIP>Skiing folder to save the map-brushes.ai file.

5. **Close the Brushes panel.**

6. **Choose Window>Brush Libraries>User Defined>map-brushes.**

   If you saved the brush library file in your WIP>Skiing folder (in Step 4), choose Other Library from the bottom of the submenu, navigate to your WIP>Skiing folder, and open the map-brushes.ai file.

   The map-brushes panel opens; it contains only the brushes that were available when you saved the library. The Basic brush and Touch Calligraphic options are not included; they are, however, available in the Brushes panel of any file you open in Illustrator.

7. **Save the summit-map.ai file and continue to the next stage of the project.**

Working with CC Libraries

Managing Libraries

If you have an individual-user subscription to the Adobe Creative Cloud, you have access to CC Library functionality, which allows you to easily share assets across various Adobe CC applications. This technology makes it very easy to maintain consistency across a design campaign — for example, using the same color swatches for all pieces, whether created in Illustrator, InDesign, or Photoshop.

A Library list
B Show Items in a List
C Show Items as Icons
D Add Content
E Libraries Sync Status
F Delete

Once you create a CC library, it is stored in your Creative Cloud account so you can access the same assets in other Adobe applications. In Illustrator, you can use the menu at the top of the Libraries panel (Window>Libraries) to create new libraries, or to access libraries that already exist in your CC account.

Regardless of which application you use to create a library, you can use those libraries in any Adobe CC application. In the image below, we created the Portfolio Elements library in Adobe InDesign, and used Illustrator to add two graphic elements that are used throughout the Portfolio books.

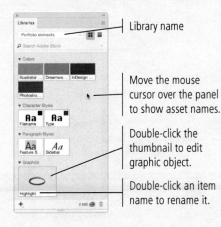

Library name

Move the mouse cursor over the panel to show asset names.

Double-click the thumbnail to edit graphic object.

Double-click an item name to rename it.

Creating Library Items

You can add new items to a library using the Add Content menu at the bottom of the Libraries panel, or by simply dragging and dropping items from the layout into the panel.

The Swatches, Paragraph Styles, and Character Styles panels also provide an easy method for adding existing assets to the active library. Clicking the Add Selected... button adds the selected assets to the active CC Library.

You can also add new elements to a CC Library when you define a new color swatch, paragraph style, or character style by checking the Add to my Library option in each dialog box.

Sharing and Collaboration

Libraries also offer a powerful opportunity to communicate assets with other users.

- If you invite others to collaborate, authorized users can edit assets in the library.
- If you share a link to a library, invited users can view a library's contents, but cannot edit those assets.

The options in the Libraries panel submenu navigate to your online Adobe CC account page, and automatically ask you to invite specific users for collaborating, or create a public link for sharing.

Working with Library Items

Graphics in CC Libraries maintain a dynamic link between the library item and placed instances of that library item.

If you double-click a graphic in the Libraries panel, the object opens in the application where it was created. If you edit the library item and save it, the changes are automatically reflected in any placed instances.

In the top image to the right, the placed object is an instance of the Highlight graphic in the CC Library.

We double-clicked the Highlight item in the Libraries panel to edit it. After changing the object's stroke color in Illustrator and saving the file, the placed instance in the first file reflects the new blue stroke color (right bottom).

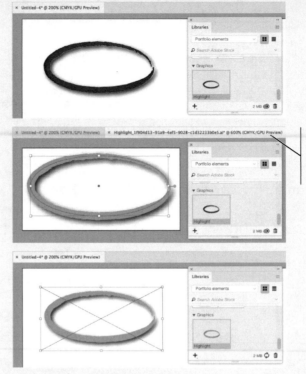

Double-clicking the library item opens that graphic in its native application.

Working with Synced Text

If a type object is selected, or if specific text is highlighted in the layout, you can use the Add Content menu button at the bottom of the Libraries panel to add the text as a new library item. (The original type object, from which you made the synced text object, is NOT linked to the new library item.)

If you drag a text item from the Libraries panel, text in the synced item is loaded into the Place cursor. Clicking in an empty space creates a new type object that contains the synced text, including applied formatting.

You can also place the text at the current insertion point by Control/right-clicking the item in the Libraries panel and choosing Place Inline from the contextual menu.

Double-clicking a text item in the Libraries panel opens a file with the synced text. Any changes you make in this file (text and/or formatting) should automatically reflect in placed instances of that object. If you had changed a placed instance, those changes will be overwritten with the edited text.

Double-clicking the item in the library opens the text in a separate file.

Important note: At the time of this writing, placed instances of synced text in Illustrator do not accurately reflect changes made to the synced object. If you make changes to the synced text, you have to manually replace the text in placed instances.

STAGE 3 / Using Symbols

In many cases, you will need to use multiple copies of a specific graphic in a complex illustration like the one in this project. You can create any element and define it as a **symbol**, which you can then use as many times as necessary in a drawing. All placed **instances** of a symbol are linked dynamically to the saved definition of the symbol; this means that you can change all instances simultaneously by changing the saved definition of the symbol. You can also isolate specific instances of a symbol, which effectively breaks the link to the saved definition of the symbol (and its other instances). Once the link is broken, changes to the original saved symbol no longer affect the isolated instances.

As with brushes and swatches, symbols are managed in panels. The default Symbols panel (Window>Symbols) has a few randomly selected symbols from various built-in libraries. You can also open other symbol libraries by choosing from the menu at the bottom of the Window menu, or in the Symbol Libraries menu at the bottom of the Symbols panel.

If you open a symbol library from the Window menu, the first library opens in its own panel. Successive panels open as separate tabs that are automatically grouped with other open symbol libraries, unless they have been intentionally moved out of the panel group and positioned elsewhere in the workspace. If you open a symbol library using the Symbol Libraries menu at the bottom of the Symbols panel, the new library replaces the active library.

Open Custom Symbol Libraries

Several elements of this project will benefit from the use of symbols. Many of the symbols for this project have already been created and saved in a custom library, which you can easily load so you don't have to recreate work that has already been completed.

1. **With summit-map.ai open, open the Symbols panel (Window>Symbols).**

2. **Click the Symbol Libraries menu button at the bottom of the default Symbols panel, and choose Other Library at the bottom of the menu.**

   If you create a custom library on your computer using the default Save location, the library appears in the User Defined submenu of the main Libraries menu. If a custom library was created on another computer, you have to choose Other Library from the menu and navigate to the file that contains the library you want to use.

3. **Navigate to `map-symbols.ai` in your WIP>Skiing folder and click Open.**

The new symbol library appears in its own panel (possibly grouped with other library panels if other symbol libraries are also open).

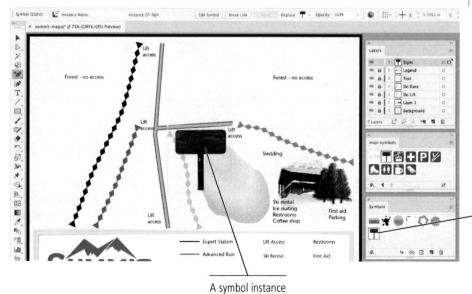

Symbols in loaded libraries are not connected to the current file unless you place an instance of a symbol from the loaded library into the file. When you place a symbol instance from a loaded library, the symbol is added to the default symbol library for the file. The same is true when working with brush libraries.

4. **Continue to the next exercise.**

Control Symbol Instances

In addition to loading built-in or custom symbol libraries, you can also create new symbols by drawing the art and dragging it into the default Symbols panel. In this exercise, you create a custom symbol to identify the different ski runs on the map — a simple road sign. You need four different signs to label the various runs.

1. **With `summit-map.ai` open, show and lock all layers. Create a new layer named Signs at the top of the layer stack and make sure it is selected.**

2. **Click and drag the Sign symbol from the Map-Symbols panel to the artboard.**

Note:

Simply clicking a symbol in an external panel copies that symbol into the file's Symbols panel.

Symbols placed from other libraries are added to the default Symbols panel for the file.

A symbol instance is a single object.

3. **Using the Transform panel, scale the placed instance to 1″ wide (proportionally).**

You can transform the instance as you would any other object, by dragging the bounding-box handles. This has no effect on the original symbol, nor on other placed instances of the same symbol.

When you transform a symbol instance, the Transform/Control panel does not offer the reference point proxy option. The symbol's registration point position, around which transformations will be applied, is defined when you create the symbol.

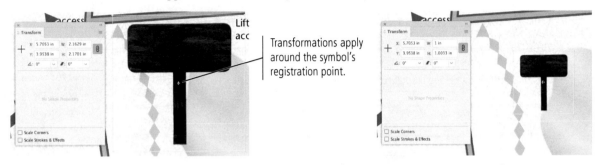

Transformations apply around the symbol's registration point.

4. **Using the Selection tool, drag the resized symbol instance near the top of the black-diamond ski path.**

5. **Clone (Option/Alt-drag) the sign symbol instance three times. Place each clone near the top of each ski run path.**

Each symbol instance is an object, which means it can be modified — transformed, rotated, stretched, etc. — as you would modify any other object. Transforming a placed instance has no effect on other placed instances of the same symbol.

Cloning an instance results in an additional instance of the symbol. All instances are linked to the original symbol.

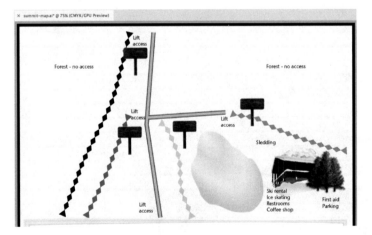

6. **Choose View>Fit Artboard in Window.**

As with the Edit Pattern mode, the symbol artwork is centered in the document window when you edit the symbol artwork. This command centers the artboard in the document window, so the artboard edges will not interfere with symbol artwork.

7. **In the Symbols panel, double-click the Sign symbol to enter into Symbol Editing mode.**

   Make sure you double-click the symbol in the regular Symbols panel and not the Map-Symbols panel.

   This opens **Symbol Editing mode**, which shows the symbol artwork centered in the active document window. The symbol artwork is the only visible item; other artwork in the file is not visible.

8. **Drag the snowdrift symbol from the Map-Symbols panel onto the artboard. Place it over the bottom edge of the signpost.**

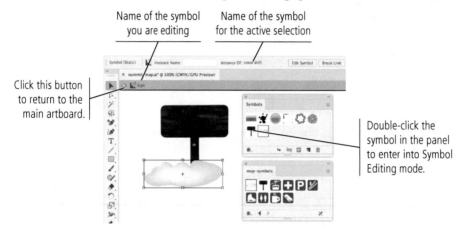

Name of the symbol you are editing

Name of the symbol for the active selection

Click this button to return to the main artboard.

Double-click the symbol in the panel to enter into Symbol Editing mode.

Note:

*Double-clicking a placed instance allows you to edit the symbol in the context of the surrounding artwork, called **editing in place**.*

Editing in place shows the symbol at full size, not the scaled dimensions of the placed instance. When you exit Symbol Editing mode, the placed instance returns to its scaled size.

9. **Choose the Type tool in the Tools panel.**

10. **Click anywhere outside the sign area to create a new point-type object. With the placeholder text highlighted, type:**

    SNOSURF [Return/Enter]
    SLOPE

11. **Choose the Selection tool.**

    When you change from the Type tool to the Selection tool, the type object where the insertion point was placed is automatically selected.

The insertion point is flashing.

The entire type object is selected.

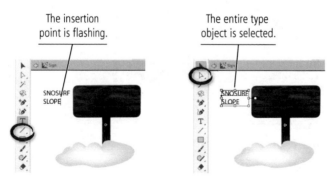

12. **With the type object selected, change the type formatting to 23-pt ATC Garnet Ultra with 21-pt leading, filled with white, with centered alignment.**

13. Move the type object to be centered in the horizontal area of the sign.

14. In the top-left corner of the screen, click the left arrow button to exit Symbol Editing mode and return to the main artboard.

Notice that the new type element has been added to all four placed instances. As we mentioned, the advantage of using symbols is that you can change all linked instances — whether there are 4 or 400 — by making changes once to the saved symbol definition.

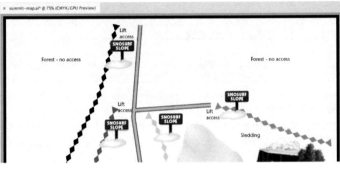

The problem, of course, is that the ski runs are not all named "Snosurf Slope". Although changing the symbol definition allowed you to add, format, and align the type object, you still need to edit it separately on each instance. To change the text on each individual sign, you have to break the link from each instance to the original symbol.

15. Select all four instances of the Sign symbol and click the Break Link button in the Control panel.

Once the links are broken, all the elements of the symbol artwork become a group in the main file. Editing the actual symbol will have no effect on instances that are no longer linked to the symbol.

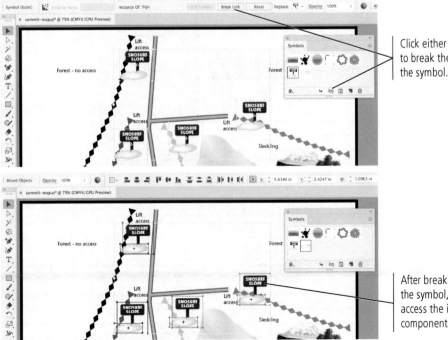

Click either option to break the link to the symbol.

After breaking the link to the symbol, you can now access the individual components of the object.

16. **Change the text of each former symbol instance as follows. Use the Return/Enter key to place each word in the titles on a separate line:**

Black run: MIDNITE HILL

Cyan run: RIPPER PEAK

Pink run: BUNNY HOLLOW

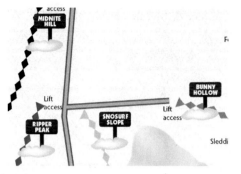

17. **Save the file and continue to the next exercise.**

Replace Symbols

The next step of this map project involves placing icons around the map to identify different services. The symbols were provided in the supplied library, so this is a relatively simple process of placing symbols in the right place.

1. **With summit-map.ai open, lock the Signs layer. Create a new layer named Amenities at the top of the layer stack and make sure it is selected.**

2. **Drag the Lift Access symbol from the Map-Symbols panel to the artboard. Place the instance on top of the matching words near the top of the artboard.**

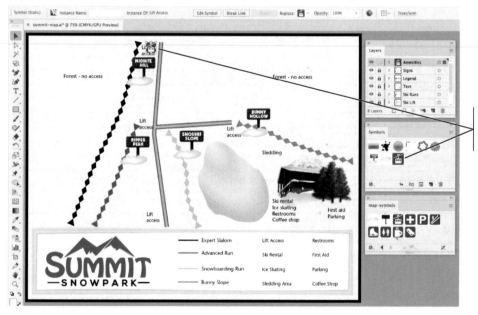

The Lift Access symbol is added to the file's Symbols panel.

3. **Clone the placed instance three times and place the clones according to the text on the original map.**

4. **Continue dragging symbols from the Map-Symbols panel to the artboard, using the text as a guide.**

   Skip the legend for now; you will create that later in this exercise.

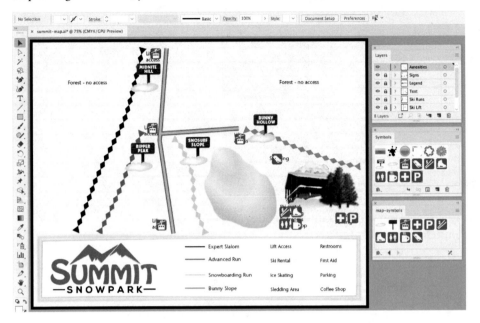

5. **Delete the Text layer from the file.**

6. **Lock the Amenities layer. Unlock the Legend layer and make it active.**

7. **Drag an instance of the Lift Access symbol from the main Symbols panel to the artboard. Place it to the left of the words "Lift Access," centered vertically with the text object.**

8. **Drag additional instances of the Lift Access symbol to appear before each label in the legend.**

   Use any method — the Align panel, Smart Guides, etc. — to align the instances to one another, as shown here:

9. **Select the symbol instance next to the Ski Rental text. Open the Replace menu in the Control panel and choose the Ski Rental symbol.**

   As soon as you select the new symbol, the selected instance changes to the new symbol.

The Replace With menu includes all symbols that are available in the file's Symbols panel.

10. **Repeat Step 9 for the remaining symbols in the legend, choosing the correct symbol to match the text.**

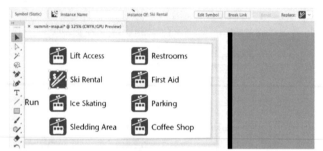

11. **Save the file and continue to the next exercise.**

Spray Symbols

The next task is to create the forest around the ski runs. The supplied file already has a perfectly good group of trees near the lodge graphic; you are going to use those trees to create a new symbol, then spray a forest around the map.

1. **With summit-map.ai open, lock the Legend layer and unlock Layer 1.**

2. **Using the Selection tool, select the trees on the right side of the artboard.**

3. **Drag the selected group onto the main Symbols panel.**

4. **In the resulting dialog box, define the following settings, then click OK:**

> **Name:** Trees
>
> **Export Type: Movie Clip**
>
> **Symbol Type: Static Symbol**
>
> **Registration: Center**

When you create a symbol from objects on the artboard, the original objects are automatically converted to an instance of the new symbol.

The selection is now an instance of the new Trees symbol.

5. **Lock Layer 1, then create a new layer named** Forest **at the top of the layer stack. Make the Forest layer active.**

6. **Double-click the Symbol Sprayer tool in the Tools panel.**

The Symbol Sprayer tool is used to spray multiple symbol instances onto the artboard. Other tools nested under the Symbol Sprayer in the Tools panel can be used to squeeze, spread, pinch, and otherwise modify the sprayed symbol instances.

Double-clicking the tool in the Tools panel opens the Symbolism Tools Options dialog box, where you can change settings that apply when you use the symbolism tools.

- **Diameter** reflects the tool's current brush size.
  The Symbol Sprayer tool defaults to the last-used size.

- **Method** determines how the symbol modifier tools (all but the Symbol Sprayer and Symbol Shifter) adjust symbol instances:

  – **Average** smoothes out values in symbol instances.

  – **User Defined** adjusts instances in relation to the position of the cursor.

  – **Random** modifies instances randomly under the cursor.

- **Intensity** determines the rate of change for modifying instances.

- **Symbol Set Density** creates more tightly packed (higher values) or loosely packed (lower values) instances in the symbol set.

If the Symbol Sprayer tool is selected in the middle of the dialog box, you can control a variety of options related to how new symbol instances are added to symbol sets. Each option has two possible choices:

- **Average** adds new symbols with the average value of existing symbol instances within the brush radius. For example, in an area where the average existing instance is rotated by 10°, new instances will be rotated by the same amount.

- **User Defined** applies specific values for each parameter, primarily based on the original symbol size, mouse direction, and current color settings.

If the Symbol Sizer is selected, you have two additional options:

- **Proportional Resizing** maintains a uniform shape for each instance as you resize.

- **Resizing Affects Density** moves symbol instances away from each other when they are scaled up, and moves symbol instances toward each other when they are scaled down.

If the **Show Brush Size and Intensity** option is checked, the cursor reflects the tool diameter.

7. **Change the Diameter field to 1.5 in, and the Symbol Set Density to 5. Click OK to apply the change.**

Diameter determines the tool's current brush size. Symbol Set Density determines how tightly symbol instances are sprayed; higher values create more instances (spaced closely together) in the symbol set.

Note:

Press the left bracket key ([ ) to decrease or the right bracket key ( ]) to increase the size of the tool (and its cursor).

8. **Click outside of the artboard to the left of the black ski path and drag down, following the ski path as a rough guide.**

When you click and drag with the Symbol Sprayer tool, you create a **symbol set** — multiple instances of a single symbol that are treated as a single, cohesive unit.

As you spray the symbols, you can see wireframe outlines of the shapes that will be added.

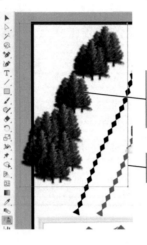

When you release the mouse button, the full-color symbol instances appear on the artboard.

This boundary shows the edge of the symbol set.

Note:

The slower you drag, the more instances will build up in a single place. We dragged at a moderate pace to place this first set of trees.

If you click and hold the mouse button without dragging, symbol instances pile on top of one another, just as spray paint builds up if you hold the can in one place.

9. **Without deselecting the symbol set, click again and drag to fill in the entire top-left corner of the artboard.**

Each click of the tool adds more instances to the set, but can also affect the position of existing instances in the set. Don't worry if your trees cover other objects on the map; you will fix that problem shortly.

By leaving the set selected, the new instances are added to the existing set.

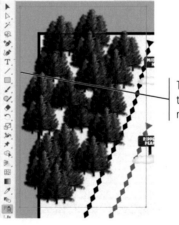

The set expands to include the new instances.

10. **Press Command/Control to temporarily access the Selection tool and click away from the symbol set to deselect it.**

Pressing Command/Control temporarily switches to the Selection tool; when you release the Command/Control key, the Symbol Sprayer tool is again active.

If you don't deselect the active symbol set, clicking again adds more instances to the selected symbol set. In this case, you want to create a second symbol set, so you have to deselect the first set before clicking again with the Symbol Sprayer tool.

When using sprayed symbols, many designs call for adjustments to individual components or instances within a symbol set. Without breaking the links between individual instances and the original symbol, you can use a number of tools (nested under the Symbol Sprayer tool) to modify symbols within a set.

The **Symbol Shifter** tool ( ) pushes instances around the artboard. The tool only affects instances touched by the tool cursor.

The **Symbol Scruncher** tool ( ) causes the cursor to act as a magnet; all instances in the set are drawn toward the cursor when you click. Pressing Option/Alt reverses the effect, pushing instances away from the cursor.

The **Symbol Sizer** tool ( ) changes the size of instances within a set. Clicking causes instances under the cursor to grow. Option/Alt-clicking causes instances under the cursor to shrink.

The **Symbol Spinner** tool ( ) rotates instances under the cursor where you click. Dragging indicates the direction of the rotation.

The **Symbol Stainer** tool ( ) changes the hue of instances under the cursor using the defined fill color.

The **Symbol Screener** tool ( ) increases the opacity of instances under the cursor. Press Option/Alt to decrease instance opacity.

The **Symbol Styler** tool ( ) allows you to apply a graphic style to symbol instances.

11. **Click the Symbol Sprayer tool above the horizontal ski lift path and drag to create the second forested area.**

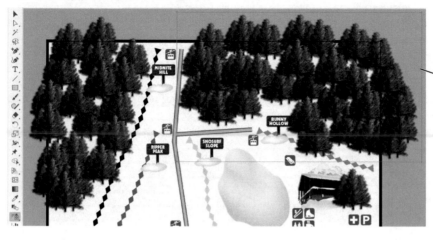

Because you deselected the first set of trees, this group is a separate symbol set.

12. **Select the Symbol Shifter tool (nested under the Symbol Sprayer tool).**

13. **Click and drag within the selected set to move all the trees away from the important objects on the map.**

14. **Press Command/Control to temporarily access the Selection tool and click the forest on the left side of the map to select that symbol set.**

15. **Use the Symbol Shifter tool to adjust the position of trees so that no objects on the map are obscured.**

Using the Symbol Shifter tool, you can click and drag within the selected symbol set to move individual instances.

Note:

Press Option/Alt and drag with the Symbol Sprayer tool to delete symbol instances from a symbol set.

Note:

Although you can't use the Direct Selection tool to access individual instances within a set, you can use the Selection tool to move the entire set all at once.

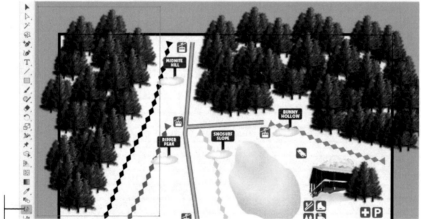

Symbol Shifter

16. **Save the file and continue to the next exercise.**

Understanding Dynamic Symbols

The symbols you used in this project are static; you can edit the master symbol to change each placed instance, but you can't access or change the individual elements of symbol artwork in specific placed instances.

Dynamic symbols, identified by a + in the symbol thumbnail, offer a more versatile alternative. If you choose the Dynamic option when you create a symbol (or open the Symbol Options dialog box using the button at the bottom of the Symbols panel), you will be able to modify certain attributes of symbol artwork without detaching the instances from the master symbol.

Using the Direct Selection tool, you can select individual elements of a placed symbol instance and change their fill and stoke attributes. Those changes do not affect the original symbol artwork or other placed instances of the same symbol.

If you do edit individual instances of a dynamic symbol, you can use the Reset button in the Control panel to restore the original symbol artwork.

Unfortunately, dynamic symbols are fairly limited at this time. You can't, for example, edit the text of a type object in an individual symbol instance. To accomplish the goal of this project, for example, you would still have to break the links to the master symbol to change the name on each sign.

Each graphic is an instance of a dynamic symbol named Book-Title. We used the Direct Selection tool to change the fill color of each instance.

Dynamic symbol

Changes to the master symbol are reflected in placed instances; transformations applied to the placed instances are not overridden.

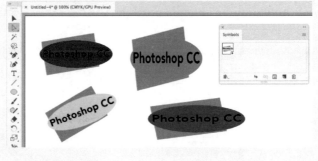

Create a Clipping Mask

The final step of this project is to save the file so it can be used in other applications. Part of this process requires "finishing off" the edges so that no objects, such as trees, hang past the artwork edges. Rather than manually cutting your artwork, you can square off the design by creating a **clipping mask** to hide the elements you don't want to see.

In this exercise, you are going to perform a few small clean-up tasks, and then create a clipping mask to show only parts of the forest inside the artboard area.

1. **With summit-map.ai open, make all layers unlocked and visible.**

2. **Rename Layer 1 as Lodge.**

   Remember, it's always a good idea to use descriptive names.

3. **Drag the Legend layer to the top of the layer stack.**

   Rearranging the layer order makes more logical sense, and prevents the legend from being obscured by the forest.

4. **Using the Selection tool, click to select the four lines in the legend. Drag the left-center bounding-box handle until the width of the selection is 1.15″.**

When all four lines are selected, a single bounding box surrounds the entire selection.

Drag the left-center handle to make all four lines longer.

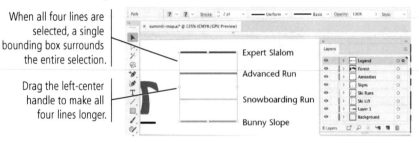

5. **In the Control panel, apply the Ski Runs brush, and then change the stroke weight to 0.5 pt.**

Use this menu to apply a different brush stroke to the selected paths...

...then change the stroke weight to 0.5 pt to reduce the size of the applied brush strokes.

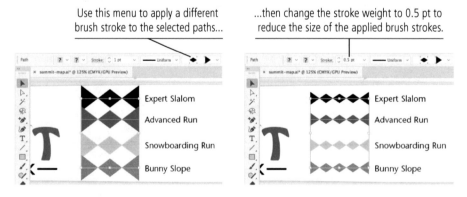

6. **Deselect everything on the artwork.**

7. **In the Layers panel, click the Forest layer to select it. Press Command/Control and click the Background layer to add it to the selection.**

8. **Open the Layers panel Options menu and choose Collect in New Layer.**

Note:

Clipping masks do not permanently affect the artwork. You can remove the mask by selecting the mask shape and choosing Object>Clipping Mask>Release.

9. **Rename the new layer Clipped Forest, then expand it in the panel.**

This option maintains the layered integrity of your finished artwork by collecting the individual layers into sublayers of the new one, allowing you to treat the finished layers as a single unit by selecting the containing layer.

The Collect in New Layer command maintains the original layer names as sublayers in the new layer.

Note:

To create a clipping mask, all the objects you want to clip should be part of the same layer as the masking object. If you create a clipping mask for objects on different layers, all affected objects are copied to the layer that contains the mask object (called **flattening***).*

10. **Drag the Background sublayer above the Forest sublayer.**

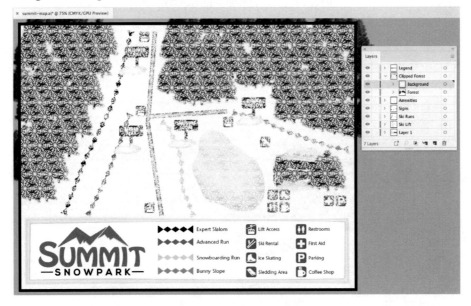

11. **Click the Selected Art icon for the Clipped Forest layer to select all objects on that layer (including the objects on both sublayers).**

12. **Choose Object>Clipping Mask>Make.**

A **clipping mask** is an object that masks other artwork; only those areas within the clipping mask shape remain visible.

This option converts the topmost selected object into a clipping path; other underlying (selected) objects are clipped by the shape of the topmost object.

Once an object is converted to a clipping mask, the defined fill and stroke attributes are removed. However, you can reapply fill or stroke attributes to any clipping mask shape, just as you would to any other object.

13. **Expand the Background sublayer in the layers panel, then expand the clip group.**

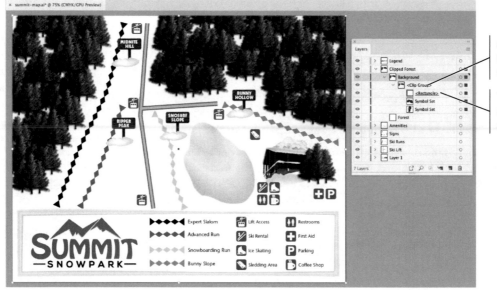

All selected objects are now part of a clip group.

The topmost selected object is converted to a clipping path.

14. **Click the Selected Art icon for only the Rectangle object at the top of the Clip Group.**

15. **Using the Control panel, change the object's fill to the Snowflakes pattern and change the stroke to 6-pt black.**

The fill attributes of a clipping path object — in this case, the snowflakes pattern — are applied behind the clipped objects. Objects on underlying layers, however, are still obscured by the clipping object's fill attribute.

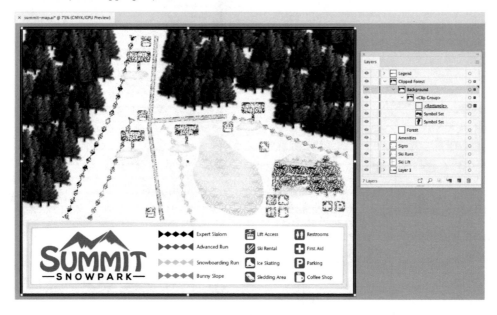

16. Drag the Clipped Forest layer to the bottom of the layer stack.

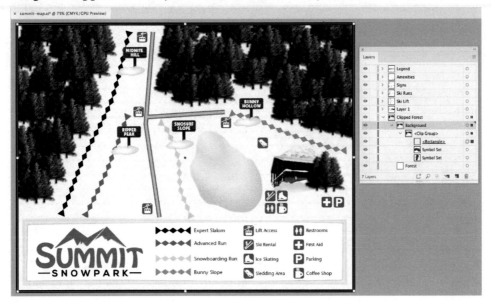

17. Save the file and close it.

PROJECT REVIEW

1. The _____ panel provides access to colors, patterns, and gradients that have been saved in the active file.

2. _____ brushes scatter copies of an object along a path.

3. _____ brushes apply a brush stroke or object shape across the length of a path.

4. _____ brushes paint a pattern of defined tiles along a path. You can define different tiles for straight edges, inner and outer corners, and the beginning and end of a path.

5. After choosing _____ in the Object menu, you can no longer access a path spine, but you can access the outlines of the resulting shapes.

6. The _____ is used to add multiple copies of a symbol with a single mouse click. When you release the mouse button, added symbol instances are contained within a group.

7. Use the _____ format to export an Illustrator swatch library for use in Photoshop.

8. After clicking the _____ button for a specific symbol instance, editing a symbol's content has no effect on that instance.

9. Double-clicking a symbol instance on the artboard, or double-clicking a symbol in the Symbols panel, enters into _____.

10. A(n) _____ is an object that masks other artwork; only those areas within the _____ shape remain visible.

1. Briefly explain the potential problem caused by using spot colors in gradients.

2. Briefly explain the differences between an art brush and a pattern brush.

3. Briefly explain two advantages of using symbols.

PORTFOLIO BUILDER PROJECT

Use what you have learned in this project to complete the following freeform exercise.
Carefully read the art director and client comments, then create your own design to meet the needs of the project.
Use the space below to sketch ideas. When finished, write a brief explanation of the reasoning behind your final design.

The Los Angeles parks and recreation director has hired you to create an illustrated, user-friendly map of the Griffith Park recreation complex.

❏ Download the park map from the park website (https://www.laparks.org/sites/default/files/griffith/pdf/GriffithParkMap.pdf).

❏ Use drawing techniques to create the basic park layout, including roads, trails, and defined paths.

❏ Create or find symbols to identify the different facilities and services.

❏ Add artwork, images, and color however you prefer to identify the different venues and attractions throughout the park.

Griffith Park is one of the largest public green spaces in the western United States. The park is home to a number of famous attractions, including the Griffith Observatory, Greek Theater, and the L.A. Zoo. It also offers equestrian trails, bike and hiking trails, and golf courses, as well as swimming, camping, concerts, and a host of other activities.

As you can guess from all of these available activities and attractions, the park is a very large place. We currently have a detailed topographic map from our master plan document, but I'd like something that is more attractive to tourists. I want to create an appealing, colorful, printed brochure that visitors can purchase for a nominal fee at park entrances and facilities so they can easily find what they're looking for.

PROJECT SUMMARY

As you completed this map project, you learned a wide range of important new skills, including managing many types of assets (swatches, patterns, and brushes), accessing built-in and custom libraries, and creating your own custom assets. You can apply these skills at any stage of an Illustrator project, saving significant amounts of time and effort.

Some of the planning work for this project was completed by the art director — including creating the icons for different elements of the artwork — and approved by the client in an earlier project meeting. Rather than taking the time to recreate those elements, you streamlined the design process by accessing that artwork as symbols that can be easily updated as necessary.

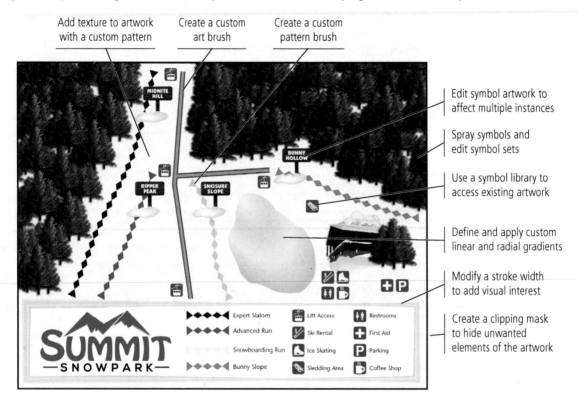

Add texture to artwork with a custom pattern

Create a custom art brush

Create a custom pattern brush

Edit symbol artwork to affect multiple instances

Spray symbols and edit symbol sets

Use a symbol library to access existing artwork

Define and apply custom linear and radial gradients

Modify a stroke width to add visual interest

Create a clipping mask to hide unwanted elements of the artwork

Letterfold Brochure

5

Your client is a non-profit artists' cooperative in San Francisco that coordinates and hosts special events throughout the year. This year they are launching a new "Art of Science" program, which will be a month-long series of special events all over the city to promote the city's artistic community. You have been hired to create the first brochure to begin advertising the new program.

This project incorporates the following skills:

❏ Creating a folding template that meets production requirements

❏ Placing and managing links to external graphics and images

❏ Importing text and controlling the flow of text across multiple frames

❏ Working with styles to automate repetitive text-formatting tasks

❏ Correcting typographic problems, such as widows

❏ Checking for and correcting spelling errors

❏ Exporting PDF files of specific artboards for print

PROJECT MEETING

I really don't have that much input on what the flyer should look like — I am relying on your expert opinion to produce an effective, functional brochure. I have the text, two logos, and several images that I want to include; you can modify those pictures as necessary to better fit the overall project.

A lot of people design folding documents incorrectly. Some people use a six-page layout with each page the size of the final folded job. Other people use two pages, each one divided into three equal "columns." In both cases, all panels on the job are the same width, which is wrong.

Paper has inherent thickness; any panel that folds "in" to the other panels needs to be smaller than the other panels. In the case of a folding brochure, the inside panel needs to be 1/16″ smaller than the other panels.

Different types of folding documents also have different facing- or non-facing-page requirements. For a letterfold, the job needs to be set up on two separate "pages" with guides and margins that mirror each other. One page has the front panel, back panel, and the outside of the folding flap; the other page has the three inside panels.

To complete this project, you will:

❏ Define folding guides and margins as required for a folding document

❏ Create an Illustrator template file so you can access a common layout again later

❏ Place images based on the panel position in the final folded piece

❏ Import and format client-supplied copy

❏ Manage the flow of copy across multiple text frames

❏ Define paragraph and character styles to simplify formatting across multiple text elements

❏ Control hyphenation and line spacing

❏ Format tabs to improve readability

❏ Check spelling in a layout

❏ Save artboards as PDF files for commercial print output

When you design entire pages, you need to be aware of several important measurements. **Trim size** is the size of the flat page (for example, a letter-size piece of paper has a trim size of 8.5″ × 11″). When pages are printed on a commercial output device, they are typically combined with other pages (possibly multiple copies of the same page) on a large press sheet. After the ink is dry, the individual pages are cut or trimmed from the press sheets to end up with the final job.

Because commercial printing is a mechanical process, there is inherent variation in the output from one page to another and in the accuracy of any given device (including the cutters that cut apart pages). **Bleed allowance** is the distance objects should extend beyond the trim. Using a bleed ensures that no unwanted white space appears around the edges of the final trimmed output (if there is variation in the cutting process). Most printers require at least a 1/8″ bleed allowance, but you should always check with the output provider who is producing a specific job.

Live area is the space within the trim area where it is safe to place important content. Live area is essentially the opposite of bleed allowance; content within the live area remains untouched during the trimming process.

Folding Document Considerations

There are several common types of folds:

 Letterfolds have two folds and three panels to a side. These are often incorrectly called "trifold" because they result in three panels. The panel that folds in should be 1/16″ to 1/8″ narrower than the two outside panels. Ask your service provider how much allowance is required for the paper you're using.

Accordion folds can have as many panels as you prefer. When it has six panels (three on each side), it's often referred to as a **Z-fold** because it looks like the letter Z. Because the panels don't fold into one another, an accordion-fold document has panels of consistent width.

 Double-parallel folds are commonly used for eight-panel rack brochures (such as those often found in a hotel or travel agency). Again, the panels on the inside are narrower than the outside panels. This type of fold uses facing pages because the margins need to line up on the front and back sides of the sheet.

> **Note:**
>
> *Some service providers give their clients folding templates to use for building a layout. You should ask your service provider if these templates are available before you waste time and effort reinventing the wheel.*

 Barrel folds (also called **roll folds**) are perhaps the most common fold for 14″ × 8.5″ brochures. The two outside panels are full size, and each successive panel is narrower than the previous one. You can theoretically have as many panels as you want, but at some point the number of fold-in panels will become unwieldy.

 Gate folds result in a four-panel document. The paper is folded in half, and then each half is folded in half toward the center, so the two ends of the paper meet at the center fold. The panels that fold in are narrower than the two outside panels. This type of brochure allows two different spreads: the first revealed when you open the outer panels, and the second revealed when you open the inner flaps.

It is important to understand that the mechanics of commercial printing require allowances for cutting and folding.

There are two basic principles to remember when designing documents that fold. First, paper sometimes shifts as it moves through a folding machine (most are accurate to about 0.0125″). Second, paper has thickness. Because of these two principles, any panel that folds into the other panels needs to be smaller than the other panels — typically at least 1/16″ smaller, but greater allowance might be required depending on variables such as paper thickness.

It is also important to understand the relationship between the front and back (or "inside" and "outside") of a folding document. If your job requires different-size panels, the position of panels on the front needs to mirror the position of those same panels on the back.

You should note that these issues have nothing to do with the subjective elements of design. Page geometry is governed by specific mechanical variables in the production process. These principles are rules, not suggestions.

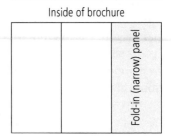

Outside of brochure

Inside of brochure

Use Artboards to Create the Panel Layout Structure

On the outside of a letterfold brochure, the left panel is the fold-in panel; it is slightly narrower than the other two panels. On the inside of the brochure, the right panel is the fold-in panel. In this exercise, you create a single Illustrator file with multiple artboards to manage both sides of the brochure.

1. **Download Science_AI19_RF.zip from the Student Files web page.**

2. **Expand the ZIP archive in your WIP folder (Macintosh) or copy the archive contents into your WIP folder (Windows).**

   This results in a folder named **Science**, which contains the files you need for this project. You should also use this folder to save the files you create in this project.

3. **In Illustrator, choose File>New. Choose the Print option at the top of the dialog box, and choose the Letter document preset.**

   Remember, using the Print category of presets automatically applies the CMYK color mode and 300 ppi raster effects.

4. **Define the following settings in the Preset Details section:**

Name:	**Rack 4x9**
Units:	Inches
Orientation:	Portrait
Width:	4 in
Height:	9 in
Artboards:	6

The brochure has 6 panels, and you are going to create each panel as a separate artboard. You are setting the dimensions of each artboard as the defined flat size of the folded brochure. Once the file is created, you will use the Artboard tool to change the size of the fold-in panels to meet print requirements.

5. **Click the More Settings button at the bottom of the Preset Details section.**

6. **In the resulting More Settings dialog box, make the following choices:**

Arrangement:	**Grid by Row**
Spacing:	**0 in**
Columns:	**3**
Bleed:	**0 in (all four sides)**

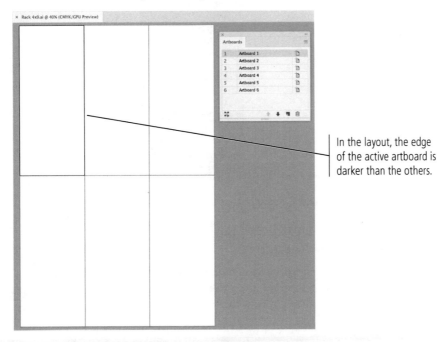

- ▦ Grid by Row
- ▨ Grid by Column
- ↔ Arrange by Row
- ↕ Arrange by Column
- → Change to Right-to-Left Layout

Make this button active to force all four fields to the same value.

The arrangement options here are the same as those you used when you arranged the two artboards in Project 3: Identity Package.

The Grid options place multiple artboards left-to-right, top-to-bottom, based on the defined number of rows. The Arrange options place all artboards in a single row or column. The Spacing value defines how much space will be created between each artboard.

With the Chain icon active, the bleed fields are constrained. In other words, changing one bleed value changes all four bleed values to the same measurement.

Note:

Although you need bleed allowance for each side of this brochure as a whole, you do not need bleeds for each panel. You will use a different method to create bleed guides later.

7. **Click Create Document to create the file.**

8. **Open the Artboards panel (Window>Artboards).**

Each artboard in the file is listed in the panel, numbered according to its position in the file — left-to-right across the first row and then the second row, as you defined in the New Document dialog box when you created the file.

In the layout, the edge of the active artboard is darker than the others.

9. **Save the file as Rack 4x9.ai in your WIP>Science folder, and then continue to the next exercise.**

Control Artboard Size and Position

As you know, you need one panel on each side of this brochure to be narrower than the other panels. When you create a file, all artboards adopt the size that you define in the New Document dialog box. You can use the Artboard tool and panel to control the size and position of individual artboards within the file.

1. **With Rack 4x9.ai open, choose the Artboard tool in the Tools panel.**

2. **With Artboard 1 active, highlight the existing artboard name in the Control panel and type Outside Fold In.**

   Artboard labels do not appear in the file output; they only appear in the document window when the Artboard tool is active. Meaningful artboard names are far more useful than the default numbered names.

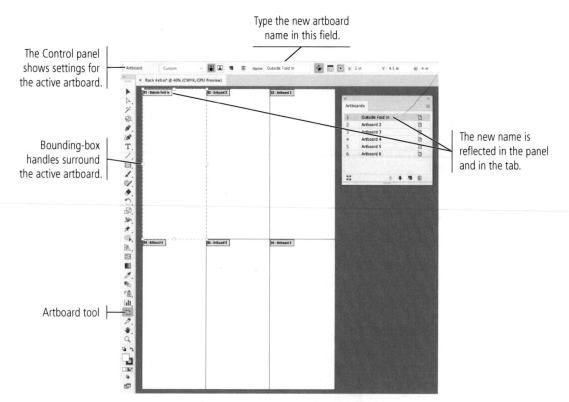

Type the new artboard name in this field.

The Control panel shows settings for the active artboard.

Bounding-box handles surround the active artboard.

The new name is reflected in the panel and in the tab.

Artboard tool

3. **Choose the right-center reference point in the Control panel.**

4. **Make sure the W and H fields are not linked. Click after the existing W (width) value and type -.125, then press Return/Enter.**

   If your Control panel does not show the W and H fields, you can use the same fields in the Properties panel, or click the Artboard Options button in the Control panel and use the Artboard Options dialog box to change the artboard width.

   Because you know the fold-in panel needs to be 1/8″ smaller than the other panels, it is easy to simply subtract that amount from the original artboard width. By selecting one of the right reference points, you make sure the two panels remain aligned with no space in between the left and center panels.

Note:

Illustrator recognizes standard mathematical operators in most panel and dialog box fields.
- *Use + to add*
- *Use − to subtract*
- *Use / to divide*
- *Use * to multiply*

Unfortunately, Illustrator only shows two decimal places in the size of an artboard. After you subtract 0.125″ from the existing 4″ width, the software rounds the new artboard width to 3.88″ (as you see in the Control or Transform panel). However, the software does store the accurate measurement of 3.875″, as you will see when you create shapes that snap to the artboard edges later in this project.

This is a significant flaw in the software, which you should be aware of in case you need to create an artboard with a specific measurement of more than two decimal places.

Select the right-center reference point...   ...then type **−.125** after the existing value and press Return/Enter.

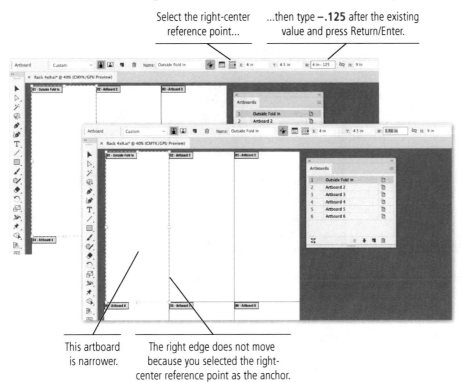

This artboard is narrower.   The right edge does not move because you selected the right-center reference point as the anchor.

5. **With the Artboard tool active, click inside the bounds of Artboard 2 to select that artboard. Use the Control panel to change the artboard name to Outside Center.**

As we stated previously, meaningful names are more useful than generic ones. This name reminds you that this panel needs to contain self-mailer information.

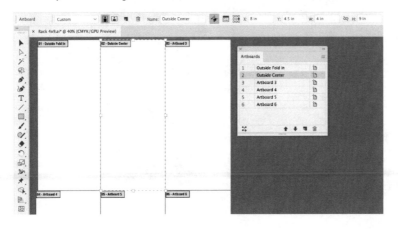

6. **Repeat Step 5 to name the remaining artboards as follows:**

Artboard 3	Outside Right – Front
Artboard 4	Inside Left
Artboard 5	Inside Center
Artboard 6	Inside Fold In

Note:

As with layers, you can double-click the art-board name in the panel to rename an artboard.

7. **With the Inside Fold In artboard active, select one of the left reference points in the Control panel, and then subtract 0.125″ from the current width.**

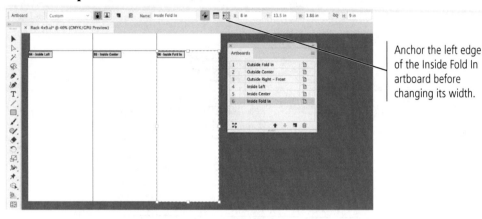

Anchor the left edge of the Inside Fold In artboard before changing its width.

8. **With the Artboard tool active and the Inside Fold In artboard active, press Shift and click the other two inside artboards.**

Pressing Shift allows you to select multiple artboards at one time. You can also press Shift and then drag a marquee to select multiple artboards.

9. **Click inside any of the selected artboard areas, then drag down and slightly right until the Smart Guides show the left edge aligning to the left edge of the Outside Fold In artboard, with at least 1/2-inch of space between the two rows.**

Make sure you click inside the artboard area to move the artboard. If you click too close to the artboard edges, you might accidentally resize the artboard instead.

Note:

You might want to zoom in to better see the smart guides when you drag the artboard.

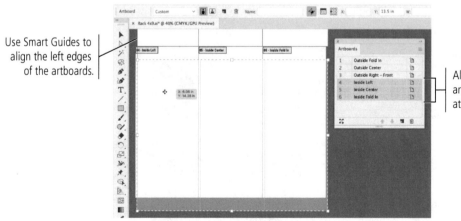

Use Smart Guides to align the left edges of the artboards.

All three selected artboards move at one time.

10. **Using the Artboard tool, click and drag a new artboard that overlaps all three of the outside-panel artboards.**

You are creating two more artboards that identify each "side" of the brochure. When the layout work is complete, you will use these two artboards to output each side of the brochure as a single PDF file.

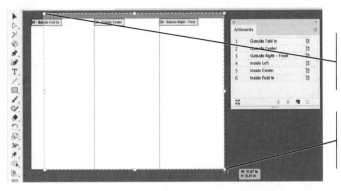

Click outside the existing artboard areas to begin drawing the new artboard.

Click and drag to create a new artboard that overlaps the three "outside" artboards.

11. **Still using the Artboard tool, adjust the corners of the new artboard to match the entire spread formed by the first three artboards.**

If you click the corner of an existing artboard, you will change the shape of that artboard instead of creating a new one. Instead, you have to create the new artboard, and then adjust its size by snapping the handles to the underlying artboards.

12. **In the Control panel, change the new artboard name to Outside.**

The new artboard is automatically added at the bottom of the list of artboards, numbered according to its top-to-bottom position.

Align the new artboard corners with the corners of the outside-panel artboards.

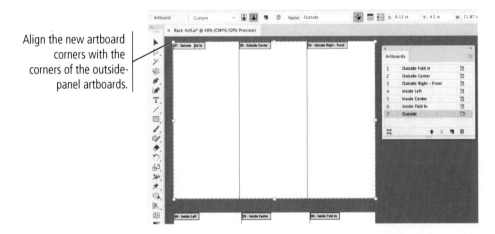

13. **Repeat Steps 10–12 for the Inside artboards and name the new artboard Inside.**

14. In the Artboards panel, Shift-click to select Artboards 7 and 8 (Outside and Inside).

15. Click either selected artboard and drag to the top of the panel.

You can rearrange the order of artboards by simply dragging in the panel, or selecting a single artboard in the panel and using the Move Up and Move Down buttons at the bottom of the panel. Moving the artboards up changes the numbers associated with each artboard in the file.

16. Save the file and continue to the next exercise.

Create Margin and Bleed Guides

A few more elements are required in your folding layout to make the actual implementation easier. First, you need to define the bleed area for each side of the brochure (not for each panel). Unfortunately, you can't define different bleed settings for individual artboards, so you have to define this area manually. Second, you need to define margin guides for each panel because Illustrator does not include an automatic margin guide option.

1. With Rack 4x9.ai open, choose the Selection tool and make sure the Outside artboard is active.

You can't change the artboard rulers when the Artboard tool is active.

2. If rulers are not already visible, choose View>Rulers>Show Rulers (Command/Control-R).

3. Control/right-click the top ruler. If the bottom option in the menu shows "Change to Artboard Rulers," choose that option.

When Global rulers are active, the zero point remains in place relative to the overall file. After you changed the width of the Outside Left panel, the left edge of that panel no longer aligns to the file's original zero point.

When using with Artboard rulers, the zero point automatically defaults to the top-left corner of the active artboard.

Note:

You can also change from Global to Artboard rulers (and vice versa) in the View>Rulers submenu.

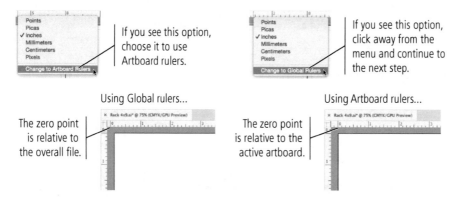

4. Choose the Rectangle tool in the Tools panel and click the Default Fill and Stroke button.

5. **Using the Smart Guides to snap to the existing artboard edges, create a rectangle that exactly matches the size of the Outside artboard.**

Note:

Remember: The software only shows two decimal places for the artboard dimensions. This Outside artboard is actually 11.875" wide.

Remember, the Outside artboard width is the sum of the three individual panel widths: 4 + 4 + 3.875 = 11.875". This should be the width of the rectangle you create.

As you drag the rectangle, the cursor feedback shows the two-digit decimal places of 11.88". Remember, this is a flaw in the software — the same flaw that rounded the artboard width to two decimal places. However, when you release the mouse button, the Transform panel shows the accurate three-digit decimal measurement of 11.875".

6. **Using the Control or Transform panel, choose the center reference point.**

7. **Break the link between the W and H fields. After the existing W value, type +.25, and then press Return/Enter to apply the change.**

Note:

Remember, if you have a small monitor or Application frame, the X and Y fields in the Control panel might be condensed into a "Transform" hot-text link that opens the Transform panel where you can define the guide positions.

Again, mathematical operators make it easy to add the required 0.125" bleed to the rectangle. Because you anchored the rectangle at the center reference point, half of the 0.25" is added to each side of the shape.

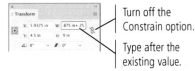

Turn off the Constrain option.

Type after the existing value.

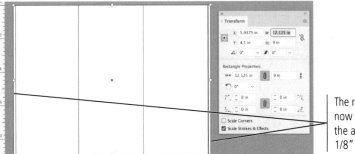

The rectangle is now 1/4" wider than the artboard, with 1/8" on either side.

8. **Repeat Step 7 to add 0.25" to the rectangle height, half on each side.**

You don't need to reselect the reference point because it retains the last-used option.

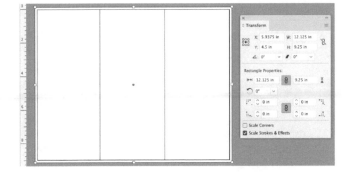

9. **With the resized rectangle selected, choose View>Guides>Make Guides.**

   You can use this command to turn any regular object into a nonprinting guide.

10. **Command/Control-click away from the selected rectangle to deselect it, then release the Command/Control key to return to the Rectangle tool.**

    When converted to a guide, the object loses its defined fill and stroke attributes.

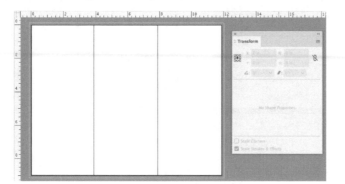

Note:

Press Command/Control-5 to create a guide from any selected object. Add the Shift key to release all guides that have been created from objects.

11. **Repeat Steps 3–8 to add a bleed guide around the Inside artboard.**

12. **Using the Rectangle tool, create a rectangle that aligns with the edge of the Outside Fold In artboard (the top left artboard).**

    Remember, this is the fold-in panel; its width is 3.875″. The rectangle should exactly match the existing panel width.

13. **With the center reference point active in the Transform or Control panel, use mathematical operators to subtract 0.5 from the height and width of the rectangle, then convert it to a guide.**

    This rectangle defines 0.25″ margins on each side of the panel.

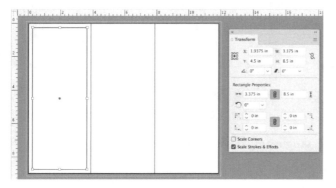

Note:

When you create the rectangle in Step 12, it should properly snap to the artboard edges. However, depending on exactly how far you drag before releasing the mouse button, the middle artboard might become the active one, indicated by the heavier artboard edge. It doesn't affect your work here, but it is something to be aware of in case you need to change an object's X/Y position based on the active artboard.

14. Repeat Steps 10–11 to add 0.25″ margin guides to all panels in the layout.

The margin-guide rectangles on the full-size panels should be 3.5″ wide by 8.5″ high.

On the fold-in panels, the margin-guide rectangles should be 3.375″ wide by 8.5″ high.

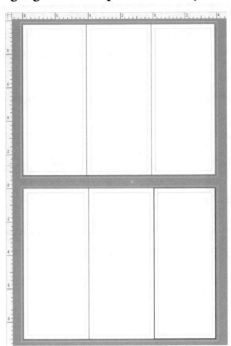

Note:

Choose View>Guides> Release Guides to convert a guide object into a regular object; the object's original fill and stroke (before you converted it to a guide) are restored. This is an all-or-nothing action. You can't release a single custom guide; you have to release all of them at once.

Note:

View>Guides>Clear Guides removes all guides from the page. If you want to remove only a single guide, you can select it (as long as it's unlocked) and press Delete.

15. Choose View>Guides, and make sure guides are locked.

If the submenu shows Lock Guides, choose that option to lock guides in the file. If the submenu shows "Unlock Guides," guides are already locked; you can click away from the menu to dismiss it.

16. Save the file and continue to the next exercise.

Create Folding Marks

The final step in establishing your folding grid is marking the location of folds. Once you have done so, you should then save your work as a template because this is a common project size and you can reuse the template whenever you need to build a new folding rack brochure.

1. With Rack 4x9.ai open, make the Outside Fold In artboard active.

You can click the artboard name in the Artboard panel, or simply click inside the target artboard with either Selection tool.

2. Choose the Line Segment tool in the Tools panel.

3. Create a vertical line that is 0.5″ high anywhere in the pasteboard area above the Outside artboard.

Use Smart Guides to create the line exactly vertical, or simply press Shift while you drag up or down with the Line Segment tool. It doesn't matter exactly where you create the line, because you will place it numerically in the next few steps.

4. **Using the Transform, Properties, or Control panel, select the top-center reference point. Change the line's X position to 3.875 in and Y position to -0.5 in.**

The line should appear to blend in with the black line that marks the artboard edges.

Because Artboard rulers are active, the zero point relates to the active artboard.

5. **With the line still selected, open the Stroke panel and change the stroke weight of the active line segment to 0.5 pt.**

6. **If you only see the Weight field in the Stroke panel, open the panel Options menu and choose Show Options.**

7. **In the middle of the Stroke panel, check the Dashed Line option. Type 3 in the first Dash field, press Tab, and type 3 in the first Gap field.**

The dash and gap fields define the specific appearance of dashed lines.

8. **Double-click the Selection tool to open the Move dialog box.**

This opens the Move dialog box, which is an easy way to move or clone the selected object(s) by exact measurements.

9. **Change the Horizontal field to 4, the Vertical field to 0, and click Copy.**

You know the center panel is 4″ wide, so copying the line 4″ to the right places the copy exactly over the panel edge. The software automatically calculates the angle of 0° because you are moving the object exactly right, horizontally.

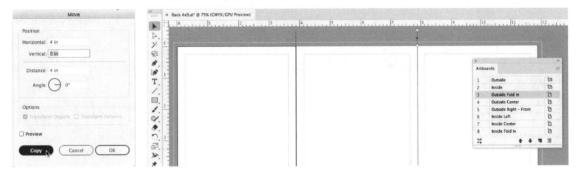

10. **Select both lines above the outside spread, then double-click the Selection tool. Change the Position Horizontal field to 0, the Vertical field to 9.5, and click Copy.**

You are moving the copy by 9.5″ because the marks are 0.5″ and the panels are 9″ high. The total movement places the copied lines immediately below the bottom of the Outside artboard. The software automatically calculates the angle of –90° because you are moving the object exactly down, vertically.

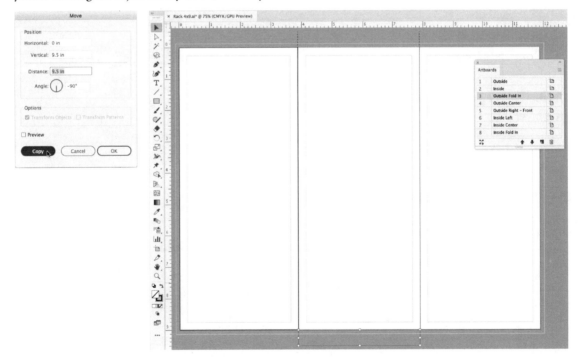

11. **With the Selection tool active, choose Select>All to select all four folding marks. Press Option/Alt, then click and drag any of the selected marks to clone all four in the same position relative to one another.**

Although the fold marks will occupy a different X position on the Inside artboard, the center panels are the same width, so the relative position of the marks is the same on both "pages" of the brochure. Rather than recreating the marks, you are cloning the existing ones, which you will precisely place in the next few steps.

12. **In the Artboards panel, activate the Inside Center artboard.**

Because you are using Artboard rulers, measurements for the selected objects are now relative to the Inside Center artboard.

13. **Choose the top-left reference point, then change the selection's position to X: 0 in, Y: −0.5 in.**

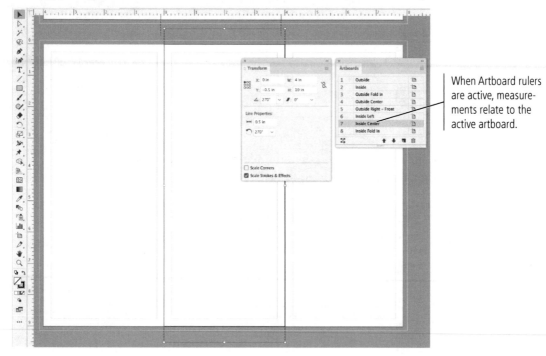

When Artboard rulers are active, measurements relate to the active artboard.

14. **In the Layers panel, rename the active layer Guides and Marks, then lock the layer.**

15. **Choose File>Save As Template. Navigate to your WIP>Science folder as the target location, and click Save.**

Since you have taken the time to properly set up these folding guides, you are saving your work as a template so you can access these same folds whenever you need them.

When you use the Save As Template command, the Save As dialog box defaults to the application's default "Templates" folder. Illustrator Template (ait) is automatically selected in the Format/Save As Type menu, and the file extension is changed to ".ait".

16. **Close the file and continue to the next stage of the project.**

Most page-layout jobs incorporate a number of different elements, including images and graphics that exist in external files. Although Illustrator does not include the sophisticated link-management options of a dedicated layout application, such as Adobe InDesign, you can place and work with a variety of common image formats. The key to creating a successful job is understanding a job's output requirements so that you use only the types of graphics that are suitable for the project you are building.

Place Layout Images

Both sides of the brochure require images that were already created — some in Illustrator and some in Photoshop. When you place external images into a file, you need to understand the concept of file linking, so you can create a complete file with all of the information necessary for high-quality, commercial print output.

1. Choose File>Open. Navigate to Rack 4x9.ait in your WIP>Science folder and click Open.

You could also use the File>New From Template menu command. However, that option defaults to the application's built-in Templates folder, so you would have to navigate to your WIP>Science folder to find your template file.

Make sure you choose the template file and not the regular Illustrator file.

When you open a template file, you are actually opening a copy of the template with the name "Untitled." This prevents you from accidentally overwriting the original template.

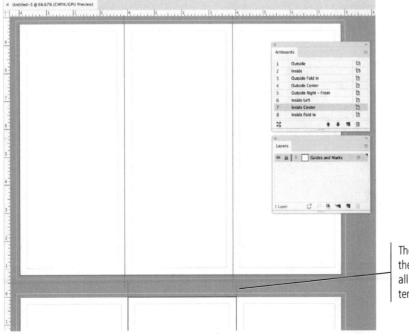

The file created from the template includes all elements in the template.

Note:

You can overwrite a template by manually typing the same file name as the original template when you save the file. You will be asked to confirm that you're sure you want to replace the existing file.

2. Add a new layer named **Graphics** above the existing Guides and Marks layer.

3. With the Graphics layer selected, choose File>Place.

4. Click **aos-logo.ai** in the WIP>Science folder to select that file.

5. Press Command/Control, then click **cac-logo.ai** and **einstein.jpg** to add those files to the active selection.

   You can press Shift to select multiple consecutive files in the Place dialog box, or press Command/Control to select non-consecutive files.

Note:

If more than one file is selected in the Place dialog box, you cannot choose the Template option.

6. At the bottom of the dialog box, check the Link and Show Import Options, then click Place.

   Macintosh users: Remember, you might have to click the Options button to reveal the check boxes.

   When the Link option is checked, the placed graphic will be a link to the original file. When Show Import Options is checked, placement options will appear for native Illustrator files.

   Press Command/Control to select multiple, non-consecutive files in the dialog box.

7. In the resulting Place PDF dialog box, choose Art in the Crop To menu and click OK.

   Because you checked the Show Import Options box in Step 6, the Place PDF dialog box shows options related to the first selected Illustrator file.

8. Review the Place PDF dialog box for the second file, then click OK again.

   The second dialog box shows the options for the second selected Illustrator file (cac-logo.ai); the dialog box defaults to the last-used option.

   After clicking OK, all three of the selected files from the Place dialog box are loaded into the Place cursor at one time. The cursor icon shows a preview of which file will be placed if you click, as well as the total the number of loaded files (e.g., "1/3").

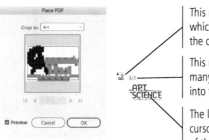

This number shows which file is active in the cursor.

This number shows how many files are loaded into the Place cursor.

The loaded Place cursor shows a preview of the active file.

Note:

No further import options are available for placed JPEG or TIFF files.

Note:

If you choose the Template option in the Place dialog box, the selected file is not loaded into the cursor; it is simply placed at the center of the document window.

9. **With the first image in the loaded Place cursor, click and drag to place that file at the top of the Outside Fold In artboard, inside the margin guides of the panel (as shown in the following image).**

   If you click and drag with the loaded Place cursor, you can define the area in which the loaded file is placed. This area retains the original aspect ratio of the file being placed.

   Use Smart Guides to begin the placement marquee at the top-left guide corner and end the marquee at the right margin guide on the Outside Fold In artboard.

   Click and drag to define the area where the loaded image will be placed. The area always maintains the original aspect ratio of the file being placed. When you release the mouse button, the placed file fills the area you drew. The next file is automatically loaded into the Place cursor.

   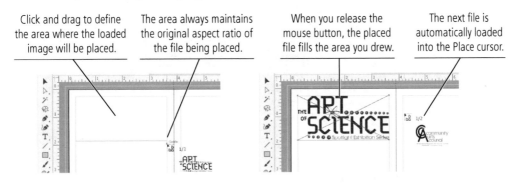

10. **With the second image loaded in the Place cursor, click and drag to place the second image within the margin guides on the Outside Center artboard.**

11. **Press Command/Control to temporarily access the Selection tool, then drag the placed image to align with the bottom and left margin guides.**

    When you release the Command/Control key, you return to the loaded Place cursor. The third loaded file automatically becomes the active file in the cursor after you place the second loaded file.

    Press Command/Control to access the Selection tool and reposition the placed image.

12. **With the third image loaded in the Place cursor, click at the top-left corner of the bleed guide for the Outside artboard.**

    Clicking without dragging places the loaded image at 100% of its original size. The top-left corner of the image is placed at the location you click.

13. **Make the Inside artboard active in the document window, then choose File>Place.**

14. **Press Command/Control, then click to select aos-logo.ai, cac-logo.ai, dna.ai, and einstein-light.jpg.**

   With the Link option still checked, uncheck the Show Import Options box and then click Place.

   The Link and Show Import Options boxes remember the last-used value. If you do not show import options, the last-used Crop To option will be applied to any selected Illustrator files.

15. **With four images loaded in the Place cursor, press the Right Arrow key until the cursor shows the fourth image (4/4) as the active one.**

   When more than one image is loaded in the cursor, the images are loaded in the order in which they appear in the containing folder. You can use the arrow keys to make a different loaded image the active one.

   Selected images are loaded in the order in which they appear in the containing folder.

   Use the arrow keys to make a different image active in the loaded Place cursor.

Note:

You can press the ESC key to remove the active loaded image from the Place cursor.

16. **Click the top-left bleed guide of the Inside artboard to place the active loaded image.**

   After you place the active image, the next image is active in the Place cursor. Because the one you just placed was image 4, image 1 is the next one to become active.

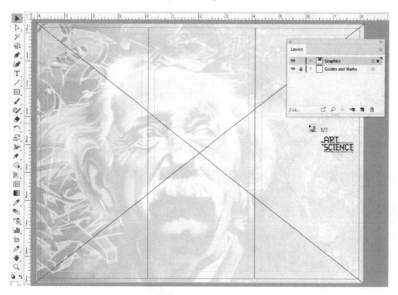

17. **Using the click-drag method, place the loaded image across the top of the Inside Left and Inside Center artboards.**

18. **Using the click-drag method, place the loaded image at the bottom of the Inside Right artboard.**

19. **Click to place the final loaded image at 100%. Drag it until it snaps to the bottom bleed guide and the right margin guide of the Inside Left artboard.**

20. **Save the file as a native Illustrator file named `aos-brochure.ai` in your WIP>Science folder, and then continue to the next exercise.**

Manage Linked and Embedded Files

As you have seen, you have the option to place a link to an external file, or embed the external file directly in your Illustrator file. There are advantages and disadvantages to each method, so you should consider what you need to accomplish before you choose.

When you link to an external file, that file needs to be available when the Illustrator file is output. If the linked file is moved or changed after being placed into the Illustrator file, you have to locate or update the linked file before output. Missing and modified images are both identified in the Links panel.

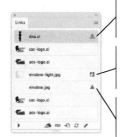

This icon means a linked file has been modified since being placed.

This icon means a file has been embedded into the Illustrator file.

This icon means a linked file is missing; it has been moved or deleted since being placed.

If you embed the external file into the Illustrator file, the physical file data becomes part of the file. This eliminates the potential problem of missing required files, but it can add significantly to the size of your Illustrator file.

Linked files make it easier to update multiple placed instances of the same file. By editing the original file, all placed and linked instances will reflect the changes when the links are up to date.

If you embed specific placed instances, they are no longer linked to the original file data; any changes in the original file are not reflected in the placed and embedded instances. This means you can independently edit the embedded instances without affecting other linked instances.

1. **With `aos-brochure.ai` open, open the Layers panel (if necessary) and expand the Graphics layer.**

   As you can see, the Graphics layer includes a number of <Linked File> items. Although each linked file appears as a separate sublayer in the panel, the way each is listed depends on the type of file that you place:

   - TIFF and native Photoshop (PSD) files are listed by file name.
   - Native Illustrator (AI), PDF, and JPEG files are listed as <Linked File> items.

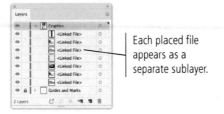

Each placed file appears as a separate sublayer.

2. **Open the Links panel (Window>Links). If the bottom half of the panel is not visible, click the Right-Arrow icon to show the information section of the panel.**

   Every file that has been placed with the Link option is listed in this panel. You can use the panel to navigate to selected images.

   - **Relink from CC Libraries** allows you to create a dynamic link to a graphic that is stored in one of your CC libraries.
   - **Relink** opens a navigation dialog box, which you can use to replace the selected file image with a different one. If a linked file is missing, you can also use this button to locate the missing file.
   - **Go To Link** selects the linked file in the layout, and changes the document view to center the selected object in the document window.
   - **Update Link** updates a modified link to show the most current version of the linked file.
   - **Edit Original** opens the linked file in its native application (for example, a placed AI file opens in Illustrator and a placed PSD file opens in Photoshop).

Every placed instance of the same file is listed separately.

Click here to show more information about the selected link.

Relink from CC Libraries

Relink

Go To Link

Update Link

Edit Original

3. **Select einstein.jpg in the Links panel list and click the Go To Link button in the middle of the panel.**

The einstein.jpg file is a raster image, which means it has a defined resolution. If you resize a raster image, the number of pixels per inch is stretched or reduced to fit into the new object dimensions; the result of factoring physical size into an image's resolution is called **effective resolution**.

The Control panel shows a number of useful data points for placed raster images, including the file name, color model, and resolution. The same information is also available in the bottom half of the Links panel.

The Control panel shows the name, color mode, and resolution of the linked file.

The file you selected in the Links panel is selected and centered in the workspace.

Linked files are identified with crossed diagonal (nonprinting) lines.

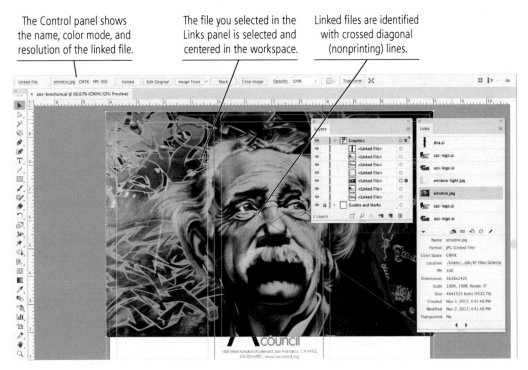

4. **Navigate to the Inside artboard. Using the Selection tool, select the CAC logo on the Inside Fold In artboard.**

As you can see in the Links panel, there are several placed instances of the same file. The panel, however, does not identify the location of each link. When you select a placed file in the layout, it is automatically selected in the Links panel as well.

You want to remove the address information from this instance, but not from the instance that is placed on the Outside artboard.

5. In the Control panel, click the Embed button.

Rather than affecting all instances, you can embed this instance of the placed Illustrator file directly into the layout. Because the placed file is an Illustrator file, the Illustrator objects become a native part of the layout file.

When you embed a previously linked Illustrator file, it is converted to a group of artwork objects. The Layers panel now shows the group, which you can expand to view the individual objects that make up the embedded artwork.

After being embedded, one instance of the Illustrator file is no longer listed in the Links panel.

The embedded artwork is automatically converted to a group.

6. In the Layers panel, click the arrow icon to the left of the new <Group> sublayer, then click the arrow icon to the left of the <Clip Group> sublayer to expand it.

Any embedded Illustrator file results in a somewhat messy stack. When you expand the group, you first see a secondary sublayer called <Clip Group>. That group contains a <Clipping Path> object and another <Clip Group> object. If you expanded the secondary Clip Group, you would see another <Clipping Path> object at the top of the stack of objects that make up the logo artwork.

Note:

*A **clipping path** defines the visible area of underlying objects in the clip group; areas outside the clipping path are hidden.*

*A **clip group** is a group comprising the clipping path object and the objects being clipped.*

7. Using the Selection tool, double-click the group on the artboard to enter into Isolation mode for the group.

8. Using the Direct Selection tool, draw a selection marquee around only the address information.

You are working in Isolation mode for the group.

Draw a marquee with the Direct Selection tool to select the address information.

The marquee will select the corner of at least one clipping path object that is part of the placed file.

9. **Press Delete/Backspace to remove the selected objects.**

Because your selection included the bottom-right corner of the clipping-path shapes, you have also deleted those points. The remaining parts of the clipping-path shapes, however, still apply to the underlying objects in the Clip Groups, which is why half of the group appears to be missing.

The clipping paths that are created by embedding other Illustrator files are almost always unnecessary, but you should be aware of their existence.

Deleting the selected points leaves only the unselected top paths of the previous selection.

Deleting part of the clipping object obscures the part of the group that is outside the new "object" shape.

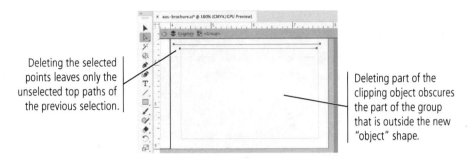

10. **Press Delete to remove the remaining portion of the clipping-path objects.**

After you deleted the selected points in Step 9, the remaining points of the clipping-path shape are automatically selected. Pressing Delete in this step removes those points and effectively removes the clipping path.

11. **In the Edit bar (at the top of the document window), click the arrow button two times to exit Isolation mode.**

You can also press the ESC key, or double-click away from the artwork, to exit Isolation mode.

12. **Using the Selection tool, drag the logo down to snap to the bottom margin guide on the Inside Fold In panel.**

13. **Save the file and continue to the next exercise.**

Warp a Graphic Object

Puppet Warp provides a way to transform and distort specific areas of a layer without affecting other areas of the same layer. It is called "puppet" warp because it's based on the concept of pinning certain areas in place, and then bending other areas around those pin locations — mimicking the way a puppet's joints pivot. In this exercise, you will use puppet warping to bend the DNA artwork to fill more of the space at the bottom of the inside left panel of the brochure.

1. **With aos-brochure.ai open, make the Selection tool active.**

2. **Click to select the DNA artwork that is placed on the inside left panel, then click the Embed button in the Control panel.**

   The Puppet Warp tool does not work with linked files. Any object you want to warp in Illustrator must be either embedded or created in the actual Illustrator file.

   Illustrator's puppet warp does not work on raster-based objects, like placed images. Since the DNA artwork is a vector graphic also created in Illustrator, you can use the Puppet Warp to bend the graphic after it is embedded.

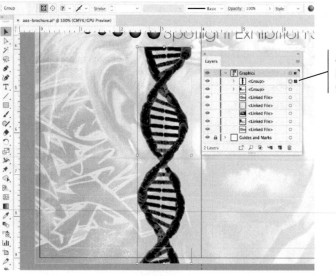

After embedding, the placed graphic is a group of Illustrator objects.

3. **In the Layers panel, expand the resulting group and both nested Clip Groups.**

   As you saw in the previous exercise, embedding a native Illustrator file results in two clip group objects that contain all of the pieces of the embedded graphic. To avoid problems in the puppet warping process, you should release both of these clip groups before continuing.

4. **Click the Selected item icon for the second (nested) Clip Group to select that group.**

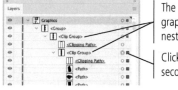

The embedded graphic includes two nested clip groups.

Click to select only the second nested Clip Group.

5. **With the Clip Group selected, choose Object>Clipping Mask>Release.**

Releasing the clipping mask removes the Clip Group object.

6. **Repeat Steps 4–5 to release the remaining Clip Group.**

Select the remaining Clip Group and release it.

7. **Click the Selected Item icon for the top Path object, then Shift-click the Selected Item icon for the second Path object to add it to the selection.**

These two paths defined the clipped areas in the two clip groups you just released. The paths are unnecessary after releasing the clipping masks; they can now be deleted.

8. **Press the Delete/Backspace key to remove the two selected objects from the artboard.**

Remember, these icons select objects on the artboard, so you delete them as you would any other object from the layout. If you try to use the panel's Delete button you will remove the entire layer and all objects on that layer instead of only the two selected paths.

Select and delete the top two Path objects.

9. **Using the Selection tool, click to select the DNA graphic on the artboard.**

10. **Choose the Puppet Warp tool.**

When you select the Puppet Warp tool, the software scans the selected object and automatically places pins in key locations. A mesh appears over the entire object; this represents the joints in the shape that can bend when you warp it.

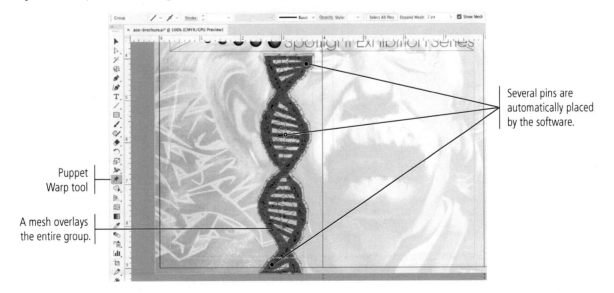

Several pins are automatically placed by the software.

Puppet Warp tool

A mesh overlays the entire group.

11. **With the mesh group selected, click the Select All Pins option in the Control panel, then press the Delete/Backspace key.**

The software automatically placed these pins based on its analysis of the graphic, but automatic options do not always meet your specific goals. In this case, it is better to remove the automatic pins, and then place your own.

12. **With the Puppet Warp tool active, click the bottom-left corner of the DNA graphic group.**

Note:

There is a bug in the software that might cause the pins to reappear after a brief pause. If this occurs, repeat Step 11.

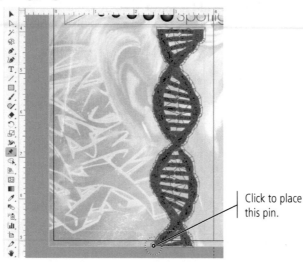

Click to place this pin.

Note:

You can toggle the mesh visibility using the Show Mesh checkbox in the Control or Properties panel.

13. **Click to place a second pin at the bottom-right corner of the object.**

These two pins anchor the bottom edge in place so that they do not move away from the bleed guide when you warp the upper portion of the graphic.

14. **Click near the top-left corner of the graphic to place a third point.**

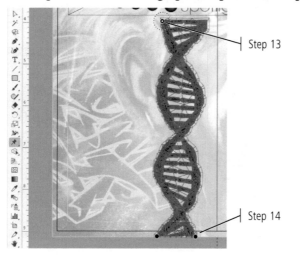

Step 13

Step 14

15. Click the third point and drag left to the left bleed guide.

You can't click and drag create a pin and move it at the same time. You must first place the pin, then click the existing pin and drag to move it.

As you drag a pin, you can see a slight bend occur near the bottom of the graphic. The two bottom pins remain anchored in place, so the bend at this point is very slight.

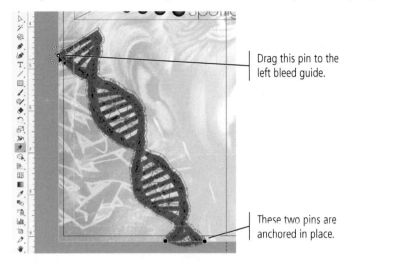

Drag this pin to the left bleed guide.

These two pins are anchored in place.

Note:

The mesh disappears while you are dragging the pin.

16. Move the cursor away from the third point until a dotted circle appears around the pin.

17. Click and drag counterclockwise to rotate the mesh and the underlying graphic. Release the mouse button when the entire top edge of the group extends beyond the left bleed guide.

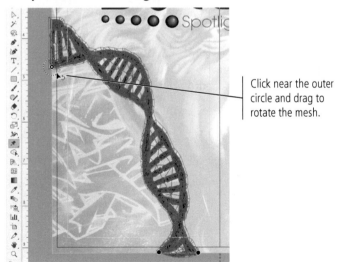

Click near the outer circle and drag to rotate the mesh.

18. Click to select the first pin, then press Shift and click the second point to select both bottom pins.

19. **Click the right selected pin and drag right until the second point aligns to the right panel edge.**

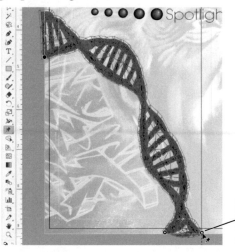

Shift-click to select both bottom points, then drag them right.

20. **Save the file and continue to the next exercise.**

Crop Images in Illustrator

The outside of the brochure you are building requires breaking the Einstein painting image into three separate pieces. Although you can't cut a raster image apart in Illustrator, you can use image cropping, along with duplication, to accomplish the same goal.

1. **With aos-brochure.ai open, make the Outside artboard visible in the document window.**

2. **Choose the Einstein image with the Selection tool, then click the Embed button in the Control panel.**

   Illustrator's image-cropping functionality requires the image data to be embedded in the Illustrator file. If you try to crop a linked image, you are warned that the linked file must be embedded and the cropping will not affect the original placed file.

3. **In the Layers panel, expand the Graphics layer (if necessary).**

4. **With the embedded image selected, choose Object>Arrange>Bring To Front.**

   Commands in this submenu affect the stacking order of selected objects:

   - **Bring to Front** moves selected objects to the top of the stacking order, above all other objects on the same layer.

   - **Bring Forward** moves selected objects up one place in the stacking order.

   - **Send Backward** moves selected objects down one place in the stacking order.

   - **Send to Back** moves selected objects to the bottom of the stacking order, below all other objects on the same layer.

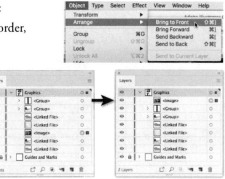

   When you paste objects — as you will do in the next step — the pasted objects are placed at the top of the layer stack. Although not strictly necessary, this step moves the original embedded image to the top of the stack on the Graphics layer, so that all three copies will appear in sequential order in the Layers panel.

5. **With the embedded image still selected, choose Edit>Copy, and then immediately choose Edit>Paste In Place two times.**

This step results in three copies of the same image in the exact same position, which you need to show different areas of the image on each of the three outside panels. The Layers panel shows each instance of the image as a separate sublayer.

Pasted objects appear at the top of the stacking order.

6. **In the Layers panel, rename the three instances of the image as follows:**

Einstein Left

Einstein Middle

Einstein Right

After embedding and duplicating the image, all three sublayers have the name <image>, which can become confusing. Renaming the individual sublayers makes it easier to understand which image is in which place.

7. **In the Layers panel, click the Eye icon for the Einstein Middle and Einstein Right sublayers to hide them.**

8. **Click to select the still-visible image on the artboard, then drag it down until it snaps to the bottom bleed guide.**

9. **With the image selected, click the Crop Image button in the Control panel.**

In cropping mode, the image's bounding-box handles turn into crop handles, which you can drag to define the portion of the image you want to keep.

Crop handles replace the regular bounding-box handles.

Note:

You can press the Esc key to exit the cropping process without cropping the image.

10. **Click the top-right crop handle on the image, then drag down and left until cursor feedback shows the image dimensions to 4″ wide and 3.1″ high.**

As you drag the crop handles, areas outside the bounding box are screened back. The area inside the bounding box remains at full strength to identify the area that will be maintained when you finalize the crop.

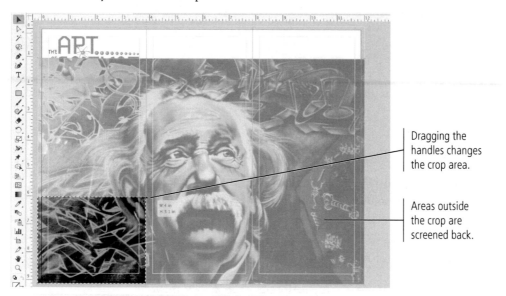

Dragging the handles changes the crop area.

Areas outside the crop are screened back.

11. **Press Return/Enter to finalize the crop.**

After cropping, pixels outside the crop area are permanently removed from the file. You can use the Undo command to reverse the process, but you cannot change the visible portion of the image at a later time after you finalize the crop.

Before image cropping was enabled in Illustrator, you had to use a clipping mask to hide areas you wanted to remove. Although a clipping mask allows you to change the visible portion of the image at a later date, the entire embedded file data is still included in the layout, which can significantly increase processing time.

After cropping, the object in the Layers panel is renamed <Image> because the cropping process essentially creates a new image.

12. **Rename the <Image> object Einstein Left.**

13. **In the Layers panel, hide the Einstein Left sublayer and show the Einstein Middle sublayer.**

14. **Select the visible image on the artboard and click the Crop Image button in the Control panel.**

15. **Drag the bottom-center crop handle up until the image height is 6.5″.**
Drag the left-center crop handle to the left edge of the center artboard, and drag the right-center crop handle to the right edge of the center artboard.

16. **Press Return/Enter to finalize the crop, then rename the resulting <Image> object** Einstein Middle**.**

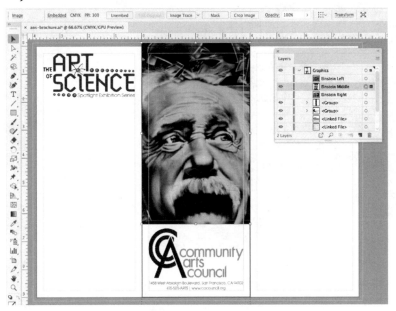

17. **In the Layers panel, hide the Einstein Middle sublayer and show the Einstein Right sublayer.**

18. **Drag the visible image down until it snaps to the bottom bleed guide, then crop it to leave only the area on the right panel with a height of 7.15″.**

19. **Press Return/Enter to finalize the crop, then rename the resulting <Image> object** Einstein Right**.**

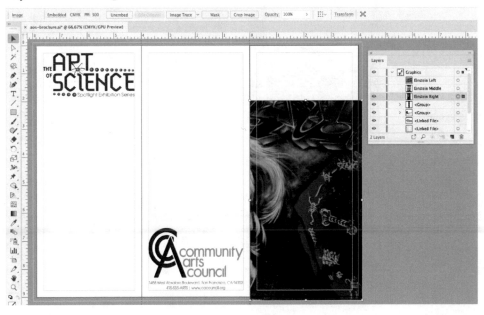

20. Show all three Einstein sublayers.

21. Clone the "Art of Science" logo from the left panel and place the clone into the empty space at the top of the right panel.

22. Save the file and continue to the next stage of the project.

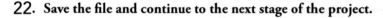

Unembedding Images

When an embedded image is selected, the Control panel now offers an Unembed button. Clicking that button opens a dialog box, where you can define a file name and choose the location where you want to save the resulting file.

JPEG and TIFF files are automatically converted to native Photoshop files (using the .PSD extension).

After you unembed an image, the placed instance in the layout becomes a linked instance to the unembedded file.

Click Unembed to convert the embedded image to a separate Photoshop image file.

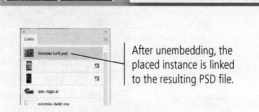

After unembedding, the placed instance is linked to the resulting PSD file.

Depending on how much text you have to work with, you might place all the layout text in a single frame; you might cut and paste different pieces of a single story into individual text frames; or you might thread text across multiple frames — maintaining the text as a single story, but allowing flexibility in frame size and position. In many cases — including this project — you will use more than one of these methods within a single file.

Import Text for the Inside Panels

Illustrator provides a number of tools and options for formatting text, from choosing a font, to automatically formatting paragraphs with styles. The first step in this project, however, requires importing the client-supplied text into the brochure layout.

1. **With aos-brochure.ai open, make the Inside artboard visible.**

2. **Collapse and lock the Graphics layer, then create a new layer named Text at the top of the layer stack.**

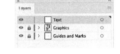

3. **With the Text layer active, choose File> Place. Navigate to cac_inside.docx in the WIP>Science folder and click Place.**

    When you import a Microsoft Word file into Illustrator, the application asks how you want to handle formatting in the file. In addition to the basic text, you can also choose to include special options such as a table of contents, footnotes, and an index.

4. **In the Microsoft Word Options dialog box, make sure the Remove Text Formatting option is not checked and click OK.**

    This dialog box appears even when the Show Import Options box is not checked in the Place dialog box.

    If the Remove Text Formatting option is checked, the imported copy will be formatted with the Illustrator default type settings only. Although you will typically reformat most imported text, it's a good idea to import text with formatting so you can review the editorial priority of the copy (i.e., where titles and headings are intended to appear).

5. **If you see a missing font warning, click OK.**

    For the text to display properly with the formatting that was applied in the Word file, Illustrator needs access to the same fonts that were used in the Word file. If you don't have the same fonts available on your system, you might see a Font Problems dialog box listing the missing fonts. In most cases, you can simply dismiss it because you will replace the original fonts with ones more suited to professional graphic design.

Note:

The Font Problems dialog box frequently appears when you import a Microsoft Word file.

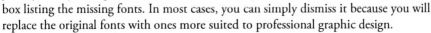

6. **With the Word file loaded in the Place cursor, move the cursor over the left margin guide on the center panel, below the placed logo.**

The Smart Guides show the word "intersect" when the cursor is over the left margin guide.

The gray line on the vertical ruler shows the Y position of the cursor.

Smart Guides show when the cursor is over the margin guide.

The gray line on the ruler shows the position of the cursor.

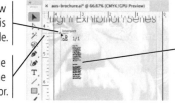

The cursor shows that a text file is loaded into the Place cursor.

7. **When the cursor is at the 4.125″ mark, click and drag to create a type area that fills the space in the margin guides below the logo.**

When a text file is loaded into the Place cursor, clicking and dragging creates an area-type object (also simply called a type area and commonly referred to as a text frame) with the text in the file you selected to import.

The small red symbol at the bottom of the area-type object is called the **overset text icon**; this indicates that the story includes more text than will fit in the available space.

Clicking and dragging creates an area-type object to contain the loaded text.

The overset text icon indicates that more text exists in the story than will fit in the area.

8. **Save the file and continue to the next exercise.**

Thread Multiple Type Areas

When a story includes more text than the current type area can accommodate, you have to decide how to solve the problem. In some cases, when only one or two words are overset, minor changes in formatting will create the additional space you need. If you can edit the text (although graphic designers are typically not permitted to do so), changing a word or two might also help.

When you can't edit the client-supplied text and you have a considerable amount of overset text (as in this project), the only solution is to add more space for the leftover text. Here again, you have two alternatives: cut some of the text and paste it into another type area, or link the existing area to one or more additional type areas (called **threading**) so the story can flow through multiple frames.

1. **With aos-brochure.ai open, choose the Selection tool and click to select the area-type object you created in the previous exercise.**

This solid handle identifies the object as an area-type object.

Double-click this handle to extend the area as high as necessary to fit all of the text.

Note:

Click and drag with the Type tool to create a new, empty area-type object.

2. Click the Overset Text icon once with the Selection tool.

The Overset Text icon appears in a small rectangle, which is the **out port** of the selected text frame. By clicking the out port of an area (regardless of whether overset text exists), you can direct the flow of text into another type area.

When you click an out port with an Overset Text icon, the cursor changes to the loaded text cursor. You can use that cursor to click any other text frame, or click and drag to create a new frame in the same thread.

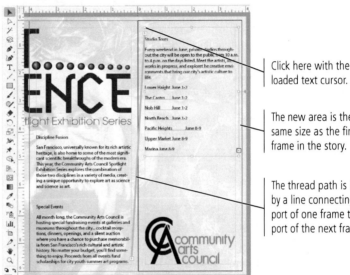

Loaded text cursor

Clicking the out port loads the rest of the story into the cursor.

3. Click the top-left margin guide on the right panel to create another area-type object.

The new frame automatically fills with more of the text from the first frame, which had been loaded into the cursor.

Click here with the loaded text cursor.

The new area is the same size as the first frame in the story.

The thread path is identified by a line connecting the out port of one frame to the in port of the next frame.

4. Using the Selection tool, click the bottom-right corner of the area-type object and drag to the bottom-right margin guide on the right panel.

Dragging a handle on an area-type object resizes the object; text inside the area reflows to match the area's new dimensions. Until you release the mouse button, the text appears in the same color as the layer on which the text object is placed.

Don't worry about the text overlapping the logo; you will fix that problem later when you format the text.

5. Save the file and continue to the next exercise.

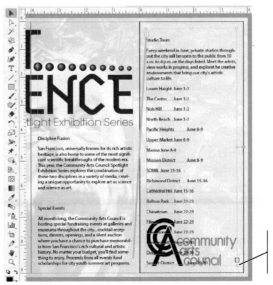

Note:

You can use the out ports to link empty frames; when you eventually place text into the frame, it automatically flows from one to another in the chain.

Use the Selection tool to resize the type area.

Work with Hidden Characters

Your layout now includes a story that threads across two separate text frames. The only obvious formatting is extra space between paragraphs. You can identify the intended headings (the short paragraphs), but the layout lacks the polish of professional design.

1. **With `aos-brochure.ai` open, choose Type>Show Hidden Characters.**

Hidden characters identify spaces, paragraph returns, and other non-printing characters. It can be helpful to view these hidden characters, especially when you are working with long blocks of text.

When you work with client-supplied text, you will frequently find each paragraph separated by two (or more) paragraph returns. Because Illustrator's typographic controls allow you to easily change the spacing of paragraphs, these double paragraph returns are unnecessary and should be deleted.

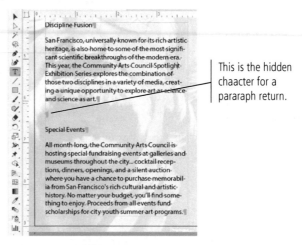

This is the hidden chaacter for a pararaph return.

Unfortunately, Illustrator's Find and Replace function is very limited. Unlike InDesign, you can't use the utility to search for a paragraph return character — you have to manually delete the extra paragraph returns.

Using the Find and Replace Dialog Box

Finding and replacing text is a function common to many applications. Illustrator's Find and Replace utility (Edit>Find and Replace) is fairly straightforward, offering the ability to search for and change text in a layout, including a limited number of special characters and options. The menus associated with the Find and Replace With fields list the special characters that can be identified and replaced.

The check boxes below the Replace With field are toggles for specific types of searches:

- When **Match Case** is active, a search only finds text with the same capitalization as the text in the Find field. For example, a search for "Illustrator" does not identify instances of "illustrator" or "ILLUSTRATOR."

- When **Find Whole Word** is active, a search only finds instances where the search text is not part of another word. For example, a search for "old" as a whole word does not include the words "gold" or "embolden."

- When **Search Backwards** is selected, Illustrator searches from the insertion point to the beginning of the story.

- When **Check Hidden Layers** is active, the search includes text frames on layers that are not visible. In this case, the hidden layer remains visible until you close the Find and Replace dialog box.

- When **Check Locked Layers** is active, the search locates text on locked layers.

2. **Using the Type tool, click to place the insertion point in the first empty paragraph in the text, and then press Delete/Backspace.**

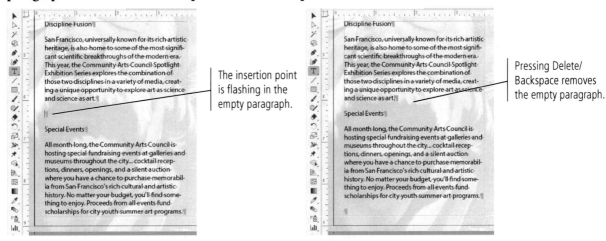

The insertion point is flashing in the empty paragraph.

Pressing Delete/ Backspace removes the empty paragraph.

3. **Using the same method, remove all extra empty paragraphs in the story.**

   You might need to use the arrow key to move the insertion point into the second frame. You can also press Command/Control to select the second frame, then click with the Type tool to place the insertion point in the empty paragraph in that frame.

4. **Save the file and continue to the next exercise.**

Define Paragraph Styles

When you work with long blocks of text, many of the same formatting options are applied to different text elements throughout the story (such as headings).

To simplify the workflow, you can use styles to store and apply multiple formatting options in a single click. Styles also have another powerful benefit: when you change the options applied in a style, any text formatted with that style reflects the newly defined options. In other words, you can change multiple instances of non-contiguous text in a single process, instead of selecting each block and making the same changes repeatedly.

1. **With `aos-brochure.ai` open, click with the Type tool to place the insertion point anywhere in the text and choose Select>All.**

   When you use the Select All command, you select the entire story in all threaded frames.

2. **Open the Paragraph Styles panel (Window>Type>Paragraph Styles).**

   Text imported from a Microsoft Word file is commonly formatted with styles in the native application; those styles are imported into Illustrator when you place the text.

   The Paragraph Styles panel shows that the selected text is formatted with the Body Copy style. The plus sign (+) next to the style name indicates that some formatting is applied other than what is defined by the style. This is a quirk of importing formatted text. Although you imported the text and chose to include formatting, Illustrator doesn't recognize something in the style, resulting in the plus sign. This will occur in almost all text you import into Illustrator.

Note:

Not every instance of a plus sign (+) next to a style name is an error, but you should always be sure that what you have is really what you want.

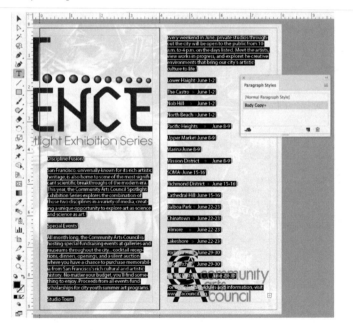

3. **With the text selected, open the Paragraph Styles Options menu and choose Clear Overrides.**

   This is an issue that you should be aware of; if you do not clear the overrides, later changes to the style might not correctly reflect in text formatted with the style. When you work with styles — whether they are imported styles or styles that you create — check the applied styles to see if a plus sign appears where you know it shouldn't.

Note:

You can also click the plus sign in the style name to clear overrides.

After choosing Clear Overrides, the plus sign is gone.

4. **Command/Control-click away from the text frame to deselect the text (and the containing frames).**

5. **In the Paragraph Styles panel, double-click the Body Copy style item away from the style name.**

   If you double-click the actual style name, you will highlight the name so you can rename it. If you want to edit the style, double-click the style *away* from the style name.

   You can also edit a style by single-clicking it in the panel, and then choosing Paragraph Style Options in the panel Options menu.

6. **In the resulting dialog box, make sure the Preview option is checked.**

   Double-clicking a style opens the Paragraph Style Options dialog box for that style, where you can edit the settings stored in the style.

   Checking the Preview option allows you to immediately see the effect of your changes in the layout before you finalize them.

7. **Click Basic Character Formats in the left list to show the related options. Choose ATC Onyx in the Font Family menu and Normal in the Font Style menu. Change the Size to 12 pt and the leading to 15 pt.**

Different options are available in the right side of the dialog box, depending on what is selected in the list of categories.

To see the effects of your changes, you have to click away from the active field to apply the new value. You can either tab to another field or click an empty area of the dialog box to preview the results.

Note:

You do not have to select text to change the definition of a style. In fact, you don't even need to select a text frame for this process to work.

8. **Click Indents and Spacing in the category list. Change the Space Before field to 0 pt and the Space After field to 10 pt.**

9. **Click Hyphenation in the category list. Click the Hyphenate check box twice to turn off automatic hyphenation.**

   When you work with styles that are imported from Microsoft Word, some style settings will be ambiguous, indicated by a dash in the check box. You might have to click a check box more than once to completely disable that option.

Note:

Later in this project you will apply hyphenation only in specific locations.

Click this check box two times to disable automatic hyphenation.

10. **Click OK to finalize the new style definition.**

11. **In the layout, use the Type tool to highlight the first paragraph in the story ("Discipline Fusion"). Using the Control or Character panel, change the formatting to ATC Onyx Bold and the type size to 13 pt.**

Note:

To open the Character panel, choose Window> Type>Character, or click the Character hot text in the Control panel.

To open the Paragraph panel, choose Window> Type>Paragraph, or click the Paragraph hot text in the Control panel.

12. **Using the Paragraph panel, change the Space After Paragraph field to 3 pt.**

   Unlike character formatting, paragraph formatting applies to the entire paragraph in which the insertion point is placed. If text is selected, paragraph formatting applies to any paragraph that is entirely or partially selected.

   If you don't see the Space Before Paragraph and Space After Paragraph fields in the Paragraph panel, open the panel Options menu and choose Show Options.

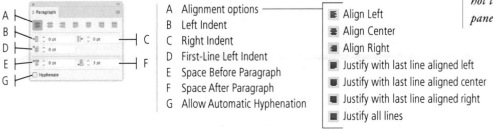

A	Alignment options			Align Left
B	Left Indent			Align Center
C	Right Indent			Align Right
D	First-Line Left Indent			Justify with last line aligned left
E	Space Before Paragraph			Justify with last line aligned center
F	Space After Paragraph			Justify with last line aligned right
G	Allow Automatic Hyphenation			Justify all lines

13. With the same type selected, click the Create New Style button in the Paragraph Styles panel.

When you create a new style, it defaults to include all formatting options applied to the currently selected text (or to the location of the insertion point, if no characters are selected).

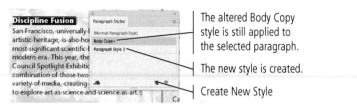

The altered Body Copy style is still applied to the selected paragraph.

The new style is created.

Create New Style

14. With the heading selected, click Paragraph Style 1 to apply the new style to the selected text.

Clicking the style name applies that style to the active/selected paragraph.

15. In the Paragraph Styles panel, double-click the Paragraph Style 1 name. Type `Heading`, then press Return/Enter to finalize the change.

16. Place the insertion point in the second heading (Special Events) and click the Heading style in the Paragraph Styles panel.

Applying a paragraph style is as simple as placing the insertion point and clicking a style. You do not need to select the entire paragraph to apply the paragraph style.

17. Using the same method, apply the Heading style to the Studio Tours heading.

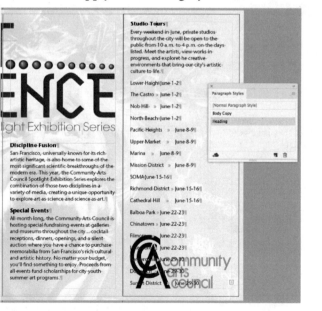

Note:

By default, every Illustrator document includes the [Normal Paragraph Style] option. The formatting applied in this style is the default formatting for new text areas created in the file. You can edit this style to change the default settings for new text areas in the existing file.

Note:

You can delete a style by dragging it to the panel Delete button. If the style had been applied, you would see a warning message, asking you to confirm the deletion. You do not have the opportunity to replace the applied style with another one, as you do in Adobe InDesign.

18. **If necessary, use the Selection tool to adjust the height of the first text frame so the third heading is forced into the second frame.**

Unfortunately, you can't use the Transform panel to change the height of the type area. If you do, you will artificially scale the height of the text within the area to match the new dimensions. This is counter to what you might expect (especially if you are familiar with working in Adobe InDesign). However, you can drag the type area's handles to resize the area. In this case, the text is not scaled; it reflows to fit the new dimensions of the area.

19. **Select the first paragraph in the story (the heading "Discipline Fusion"). Using the Fill Color menu in the Control panel, change the text color to one of the darker red swatches.**

Remember, everything between paragraph return characters (¶) is considered a paragraph, even if that text occupies only a single line.

We applied this swatch as the text fill color.

Note:

If you don't see the default color swatches, you can access them by opening the Default Swatches>Basic CMYK swatch library.

20. **With the same text still selected, open the Paragraph Styles panel Options menu and choose Redefine Paragraph Style.**

This option changes the selected style formatting to match the formatting of the current text selection in the document.

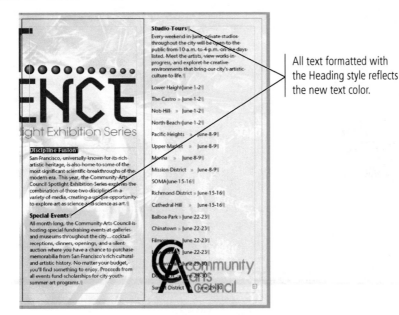

All text formatted with the Heading style reflects the new text color.

21. **Save the file and continue to the next exercise.**

Import Styles from Other Files

Once you create styles, you can apply them to any text in the file, on any artboard. You can also import styles from other Illustrator files so those styles can be used for different projects.

1. With **aos-brochure.ai** open, make the Outside artboard visible in the document window and make the Selection tool active.

2. Place the file **cac_outside.docx** into a type area on the Outside Fold In artboard (the one on the left). Include formatting in the placed file, and click OK if you see the Font Problems dialog box.

3. Using the Selection tool, drag the new text area's handles so its top edge begins approximately 1/8″ below the logo and the other edges align with the panel's margin guides.

   Don't worry about the text overlapping the bottom image. You will correct this problem as you apply type-formatting options in the remainder of this project.

4. Use the Type tool to place the insertion point in the placed text, then choose Select>All. Use the Paragraph Styles panel Options menu to clear the style overrides in the selected text.

   When the insertion point is placed, the Select All command selects all text in the active story. Text in other (non-threaded) type areas is not selected.

5. Open the Paragraph Styles panel Options menu and choose Load Paragraph Styles.

6. Navigate to the file `cac-styles.ai` (in your WIP>Science folder) and click Open.

If styles of the same name exist in the open and imported files, Illustrator maintains the definition from the active file. Unlike other applications, Illustrator does not allow you to control the import process for individual styles.

Two new styles are added to the panel.

7. Using the Layers panel, hide the Graphics layer.

Since the type objects are now in the proper position, hiding the underlying graphics makes it easier to focus on the type formatting without distraction.

8. Select any part of all but the first paragraph in the text area, and click the Sponsor Address style.

Paragraph styles relate to entire paragraphs — anything between two paragraph return (¶) characters.

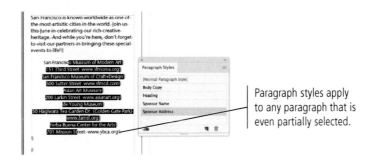

Paragraph styles apply to any paragraph that is even partially selected.

9. Place the insertion point in the first paragraph you just formatted, and then click the Sponsor Name style to apply it.

10. Apply the Sponsor Name style to every other paragraph in the list.

Make sure you pay attention to where paragraphs begin and end. Don't apply the style to every other *line*.

11. Save the file and continue to the next exercise.

Define a Character Style

As with paragraph styles, a character style can be used to store and apply multiple character formatting options with a single click. The primary difference is that character styles apply to selected text only, such as italicizing a specific word in a paragraph or adding a few characters in a different font.

1. **With aos-brochure.ai open, highlight the web address in the first sponsor listing.**

2. **Using the Control or Character panel, change the font to ATC Onyx Italic.**

3. **Open the Character Styles panel (Window>Type>Character Styles).**

4. **Click the Create New Style button at the bottom of the panel.**

    The process of creating a character style is basically the same as creating a paragraph style. The new style is created, but it is not yet applied to the selected text.

    Create New Style

Note:

You can Option/Alt-click the Create New button in most panels to automatically open the Options dialog box for the asset you are creating.

5. **Double-click the new style name in the panel. Type Web Address, then press Return/Enter to finalize the new name.**

    Because you double-clicked the style to rename it, the first click of that double-click applied the selected style. Like a paragraph style, new character styles adopt the formatting of the current selection.

6. **Highlight each web address in the list and apply the Web Address character style.**

    Unlike paragraph styles, character styles apply only to selected text.

7. **Save the file and continue to the next stage of the project.**

STAGE 4 / Fine-Tuning Text

There are still a number of typographic issues in the brochure text that should be addressed so the layout looks professional and well-polished, instead of appearing just "good enough." Although some problems will require manual intervention, many can be solved using Illustrator's built-in utilities.

Apply Smart Punctuation

When you import text from an external text file, it is possible that you are importing a number of typographic errors — both typing errors and errors of typography.

From a typography standpoint, some problems, such as straight quotes, have to do with the way text is encoded in the file you import. Other issues, such as double spaces after a period, are intentionally (but incorrectly) created by the author. In any case, Illustrator includes a utility to find and fix these common issues.

1. **With aos-brochure.ai open, make sure nothing is selected in the layout.**

2. **Choose Type>Show Hidden Characters to toggle those characters off.**

3. **Zoom in to the Inside artboard so you can clearly see the text.**

4. **Choose Type>Smart Punctuation.**

   This dialog box makes it very easy to search for and change common characters to their typographically correct equivalents. You can affect selected text only, or you can affect the entire document at once.

   - **ff, fi, ffi Ligatures** converts these combinations to the replacement ligatures.
   - **ff, fl, ffl Ligatures** converts these combinations to the replacement ligatures.
   - **Smart Quotes** converts straight quote marks into true (curly) quotes.
   - **Smart Spaces** eliminates multiple space characters after a period.
   - **En, Em Dashes** converts a double keyboard dash to an en dash and a triple keyboard dash to an em dash.
   - **Ellipses** converts three periods to a single-character ellipsis glyph.
   - **Expert Fractions** converts separate characters used to represent fractions to their single-character equivalents.

5. **In the Replace Punctuation area, check all options but Expert Fractions.**

6. **Choose the Entire Document option, make sure the Report Results box is checked, and then click OK.**

7. **Review the information in the report dialog box, and then click OK.**

8. **Save the file and continue to the next exercise.**

Control Hyphenation and Justification

The text on both sides of the brochure shows a problem called a **widow**, which is a short line at the end of a paragraph (typically one word, or two very short words). Whenever possible, these should be corrected. One way to do so is to adjust the hyphenation and justification settings in a paragraph.

Note:

*A **widow** is a very short line — usually one or two words — at the end of a paragraph.*

*An **orphan** is a heading or the first line of a paragraph at the end of a column, or the last line of a paragraph at the beginning of a column.*

1. **With `aos-brochure.ai` open, use the Type tool to place the insertion point in the paragraph after the Studio Tours heading.**

2. **Open the Paragraph panel Options menu and choose Hyphenation.**

Large, uneven gaps appear at the right side of the column.

This is a widow.

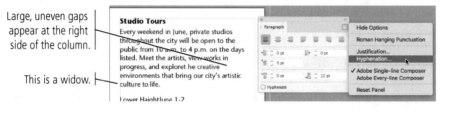

3. **In the Hyphenation dialog box, activate the Preview check box.**

4. **Check the Hyphenation option to allow automatic hyphenation based on the settings defined in the lower part of the dialog box.**

Allowing hyphenation fixes the widow.

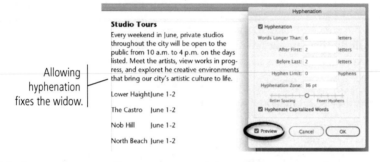

The Hyphenation options allow you to control the way Illustrator applies hyphenation.

- **Words Longer Than _ Letters** defines the minimum number of characters that must exist in a hyphenated word.

- **After First** and **Before Last** defines the minimum number of characters that must appear before or after a hyphen.

- **Hyphen Limit** defines the maximum number of hyphens that can appear on consecutive lines. Remember, you are defining the *limit*, so zero means there is no limit, allowing unlimited hyphens.

- **Hyphenation Zone** defines the amount of white space allowed at the end of a line of unjustified text before hyphenation begins.

- The slider allows Illustrator to determine the best spacing. Dragging left allows more hyphens; dragging right reduces the number of hyphens in a paragraph, but might produce less-pleasing results in line spacing.

- If **Hyphenate Capitalized Words** is checked, capitalized words (proper nouns) can be hyphenated.

5. **Click OK to apply the change and return to the layout.**

6. **Navigate to the Outside Fold In artboard and place the insertion point in the first paragraph.**

7. **Using the Paragraph panel, apply the Justify All Lines alignment option.**

8. **Open the Paragraph panel Options menu and choose Justification.**

9. **Activate the Preview option, and then change the Minimum Word Spacing field to 70%.**

The Justification dialog box allows you to control the minimum, desired, and maximum spacing that can be applied to create justified paragraph alignment.

- **Word Spacing** defines the space that can be applied between words (where spaces exist in the text). At 100% (the default Desired amount), no additional space is added between words.

- **Letter Spacing** defines the space that can be added between individual letters within a word. All three values default to 0%, which allows no extra space between letters. At 100%, an entire space would be allowed between characters, making the text very difficult to read.

- **Glyph Scaling** determines how much individual character glyphs can be scaled (stretched or compressed) to justify the text. At 100%, the default value for all three settings, characters are not scaled.

- In narrow columns, single words sometimes appear on a line by themselves. If the paragraph is set to full justification, a single word on a line might appear to be too stretched out. You can use the **Single Word Justification** menu to center or left-align these single words, instead of leaving them fully justified.

By reducing the Minimum Word Spacing value, the spaces between words in the second line are reduced. Basically, you are telling Illustrator, "Reduce the amount of word spacing down to 70% of the normal spacing that would be applied by pressing the spacebar." This setting results in smaller word spaces throughout the paragraph, and corrects the widow at the end of the paragraph.

10. **Click OK to apply the change and return to the layout.**

11. **Save the file and continue to the next exercise.**

Note:

Issues such as paragraph and word spacing are somewhat subjective. Some of your clients will break all other typographic rules to reduce loosely fitted lines, while others will absolutely refuse to allow widows, and still others will disallow hyphenation of any kind.

The specific way you solve problems will be governed by your client's personal typographic preferences.

Format Tabbed Text

On the inside of the brochure, the list of dates was created with tab characters separating the locations from the dates. Rather than leaving the list as it is — more or less unformatted and messy — you can adjust tab formatting to present a well-ordered, easy-to-read list.

1. **With `aos-brochure.ai` open, select any part of each list paragraph (the lines listing the event dates) on the Inside Fold In artboard.**

   Tab positions are technically paragraph formatting attributes, so your changes will apply to any paragraph that is even partially selected.

2. **Open the Tabs panel (Window>Type>Tabs).**

   If the top edge of the active text frame is visible, the Tabs panel will automatically appear at the top of the frame. If the top edge of the frame is not visible, the panel floats randomly in the workspace. Because these two frames are linked, the left side of the Tabs panel appears above the left text frame — the first frame in the thread.

   If the Tabs panel does not automatically open above the active type area, you can adjust the file in the document window, and then click the Position Panel Above Text button to position the panel above the active type area. Keep in mind, there must still be enough room above the frame for the panel to fit in the workspace.

   Position Panel Above Text

3. **Click the Right-Justified Tab marker at the top of the panel.**

   This defines the type of tab stop you are going to create. If an existing tab marker is already selected on the ruler, clicking a different type of marker changes the type of the selected stop.

4. **Click the ruler in the Tabs panel above the left frame to place a tab stop, then drag that stop to about the middle of the left frame.**

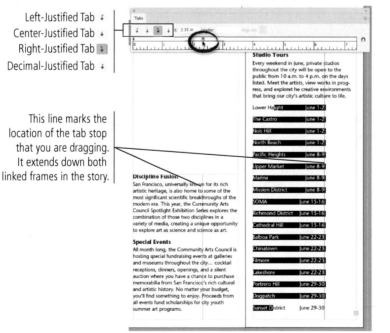

Left-Justified Tab

Center-Justified Tab

Right-Justified Tab

Decimal-Justified Tab

This line marks the location of the tab stop that you are dragging. It extends down both linked frames in the story.

Note:

If you use a Decimal-Justified Tab stop, you can use this field to determine which character is the alignment key.

5. **Click the existing tab stop and drag right until the line shows the tab located just short of the right edge of the right frame.**

Remember, these two frames are slightly different sizes due to the size difference of the artboards. You have to watch the line in the right frame to make sure the tab will be aligned properly.

6. **With the tab stop still selected, type period-space in the Leader field, and then press Return/Enter to apply the change.**

Whatever you type in the Leader field will occupy the space between tab stops.

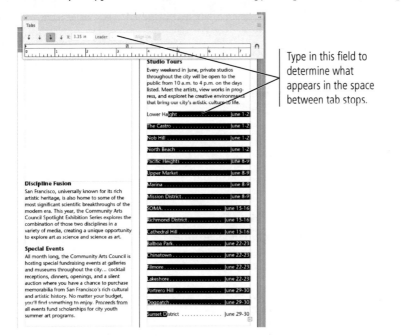

Type in this field to determine what appears in the space between tab stops.

7. **Select any part of all but the last list item, then use the Paragraph panel to change the Space After Paragraph value to 3 pt.**

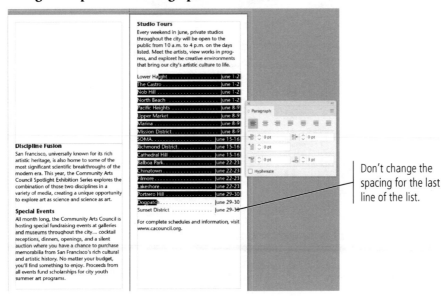

Don't change the spacing for the last line of the list.

8. **Save the file and continue to the next exercise.**

Check Spelling

Misspellings and typos creep into virtually every job, despite numerous rounds of content proofs. These errors can ruin an otherwise perfect job. As with most desktop applications, Illustrator allows you to check the spelling in a document. It's all too common, however, to skip this important step, which could result in spelling and typing errors in the final output.

You probably won't create the text for most design jobs, and you aren't technically responsible for the words your client supplies. However, you can be a hero if you find and fix typographical errors before a job goes to press; if you don't, you will almost certainly hear about it after it's too late to fix. You simply can't brush off a problem by saying, "That's not my job" — at least, not if you want to work with that client again.

Note:

Keep in mind that spell-check is not infallible; it does not check for incorrect usage or grammar — for example, incorrectly using "two many copies" instead of "too many copies."

1. **With `aos-brochure.ai` open, make sure nothing is selected in the layout.**

2. **Choose Edit>Check Spelling.**

3. **In the resulting Check Spelling dialog box, click Start.**

   As soon as you click Start, Illustrator locates the first potential problem and highlights it in the layout.

   This error ("exploret he") is a typo, but it presents a spell-checking problem: "exploret" is an error, but the second half of the typo ("he") will not be identified as a misspelling. In this case, you have to use the upper field to make the necessary correction to both words.

The suspect word is highlighted in the layout so you can review it in context.

4. **In the upper window of the Check Spelling dialog box, change "exploret he" to explore the.**

Type directly in this field to correct the error.

5. Click Change.

As soon as you click Change to correct the first error, Illustrator automatically highlights the next suspect word.

Your change from the previous step is applied.

The next suspected error is highlighted.

Studio Tours

Every weekend in June, private studios throughout the city will be open to the public from 10 a.m. to 4 p.m. on the days listed. Meet the artists, view works in progress, and explore the creative environments that bring our city's artistic culture to life.

Lower Haight	June 1-2
The Castro	June 1-2
Nob Hill	June 1-2
North Beach	June 1-2
Pacific Heights	June 8-9
Upper Market	June 8-9
Marina	June 8-9
Mission District	June 8-9

Check Spelling

Word Not Found: "Haight" (English: USA)

artistic culture to life.
Lower Haight   June 1-2
The Castro   June 1-2

Suggestions
Hight
Height
Airtight
Lightroom

▶ Options

Ignore
Ignore All
Change
Change All
Add

Done

6. Click Ignore in the Check Spelling dialog box and review the next flagged word.

In this case, the suspect word is the name of a street in San Francisco, and it is spelled correctly.

Keep in mind that Illustrator checks spelling based on the language defined for the text. (You can change the default language in the Hyphenation pane of the Preferences dialog box, or you can assign a specific language to selected text using the Character panel.) Some words, although spelled correctly, are not included in the built-in dictionaries, so they are flagged as errors when you check spelling.

As soon as you click Ignore, Illustrator automatically highlights the next suspect word.

7. Continue reviewing any potential problems, making any necessary changes to words that are not place names or web addresses.

Many of the suspected problems in this file are either place names or web addresses; both are commonly flagged as potential errors, even when they are spelled correctly.

For the sake of this project, you can assume place names and web addresses are correct. In a professional environment, those are common sources of typos; always check the accuracy of these words carefully.

The only other actual spelling error is the word "artisitic" on the Outside artboard.

8. Click Done to close the Check Spelling dialog box.

When Illustrator can't find any more potential problems, the dialog box shows that the Spell Checker utility is complete.

Check Spelling

Spell Checker Complete

Suggestions

▶ Options

Done

9. Save the file and continue to the next exercise.

Note:

Never simply click Change when you check spelling. Carefully evaluate the suspect word in the context of the layout.

Note:

If you expand the Options section at the bottom of the Check Spelling dialog box, you see a number of choices to refine the evaluation.

The Find section allows the spell checker to identify repeated words (e.g., "the the") and non-capitalized beginnings of sentences (i.e., lowercase words immediately following a period and space).

In the Ignore section, you can force Illustrator to skip words that are all uppercase, words with numbers, and Roman numerals.

Create a Job Package

As we have already stated, the images and fonts used in a layout must be available on the computer used to output the job. Now that your file is complete, you can package it to send to an output provider, or to create an archive for later use. Illustrator now includes a Package utility that makes this process very easy.

1. **With aos-brochure.ai open, show the Graphics layer.**

2. **Choose File>Package. In the resulting dialog box, change the Folder Name field to Finished Culture Brochure.**

Click here to define a different location for the packaged job folder.

Use this field to define the name of the packaged job folder.

3. **Make sure all options are checked at the bottom of the dialog box, then click Package.**

   These options determine what will be included in the packaged job folder.

   - **Copy Links.** When checked, this option copies all linked files into the resulting job package folder. The original linked file is not affected.

   - **Collect Links in Separate Folder.** When checked, the packaged job folder includes a secondary Links folder to contain all of the link files. If this option is not checked, the linked files will be placed in the main job package folder.

   - **Relink Linked Files to Document.** When checked, links in the Illustrator file are changed to refer to the new copied link files. If this option is not checked, the links still point to the original placed file, which might cause a missing-file warning when you send the job package to another user (or open the file at a later time).

   - **Copy Fonts (Except Adobe Fonts and non-Adobe CJK fonts).** When checked, this option results in a secondary Fonts folder to contain the font files that are used in the Illustrator file.

     As the name of this item suggests, Adobe Typekit and CJK (Chinese/Japanese/Korean) fonts are not copied into the job package. If you send a file to other users, they will have to license the required CJK fonts, or sync the required Typekit fonts using their own Creative Cloud subscriptions.

   - **Create Report.** When checked, this option creates a text file that includes information about the Illustrator file (color mode, linked files, etc.).

   Note:

   CJK (Chinese/Japanese/Korean) fonts contain a large number of picto-graphic characters.

4. **Read the resulting warning, then click OK.**

   As with any software, you purchase a license to use a font — you do not actually own the font. It is illegal to distribute fonts freely, as it is illegal to distribute copies of your software. Most (but not all) font licenses allow you to send your copy of a font to a service provider, as long as the service provider also owns a copy of the font. Always verify that you are not violating font copyright before submitting a job.

5. **In the resulting dialog box, click the Show Package button.**

If you don't see this dialog box, it is possible someone else has checked the Don't Show Again option. (If someone has disabled the dialog box, you can open the General pane of the preferences dialog box and click the Reset All Warning Dialogs button.) In this case, you can use your desktop Finder to view the contents of the packaged job folder.

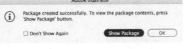

When the process is complete, all of the necessary job elements appear in the job folder (in your WIP>Science folder).

6. **Continue to the next exercise.**

Export a PDF File for Print

The Portable Document Format (PDF) was created by Adobe to facilitate cross-platform transportation of documents, independent of the fonts used, linked files, or even the originating application. The format offers a number of advantages for commercial printing workflows:

- PDF files can contain all of the information needed to successfully output a job.

- Data in a PDF file can be high or low resolution, and it can be compressed to reduce file size.

- PDF files are device-independent, which means you don't need the originating application or the same platform to open and print the file.

- PDF files are also page-independent, which means a PDF document can contain rotated pages and even pages of different sizes.

1. **With aos-brochure.ai open in Illustrator, choose File>Save As. Choose Adobe PDF in the Format/Save As Type menu.**

2. **Navigate to the Finished Culture Brochure folder (in your WIP>Science folder) as the target location for saving the PDF file.**

3. **Choose the Range option, type 1-2 in the related field, then click Save.**

Because you created separate artboards to contain each composite side of the brochure, you can use the Range option to output only those two artboards in the PDF file.

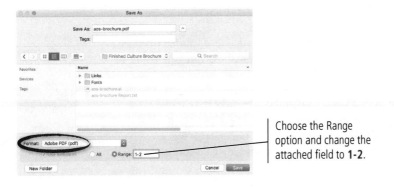

Choose the Range option and change the attached field to **1-2**.

4. **In the Save Adobe PDF dialog box, choose Press Quality in the Adobe PDF Preset menu.**

The Adobe PDF Preset menu includes six PDF presets (in brackets) that meet common industry output requirements. Other options might also be available if another user created custom presets in Illustrator or another Adobe application.

Because there are so many ways to create a PDF — not all of them optimized for commercial printing — the potential benefits of the file format are often negated. The PDF/X specification (defined in the Standard menu) was created to help solve some of the problems associated with bad PDF files entering the prepress workflow. PDF/X is a subset of PDF, designed to ensure that files have the information necessary for, and available to, the digital prepress output process. Ask your output provider whether you should apply a PDF/X standard to your files, and if so, which version to use.

The Compatibility menu determines which version of PDF you will create. This is particularly important if your layout uses transparency. PDF 1.3 does not support transparency, so the file will require flattening. If you save the file to be compatible with PDF 1.4 or later, the transparency information will be maintained in the PDF file; it will have to be flattened later in the output process (after it leaves your desk).

5. **Review the Compression options.**

The Compression options determine what — and how much — data will be included in the PDF file. This set of options is one of the most important when creating PDFs, since too-low resolution results in bad-quality printing, and too-high resolution results in long download times.

Before you choose compression settings, you need to consider your final goal. If you're creating a file for commercial printing, resolution is more important than file size. If your goal is a PDF for posting on the web for general consumption, file size is equally as important (if not more so) as image quality.

You can define a specific compression scheme for color, grayscale, and monochrome images. Different options are available, depending on the image type:

- ZIP compression is lossless, which means all file data is maintained in the compressed file.

- JPEG compression options are lossy, which means data is discarded to create a smaller file. When you use one of the JPEG options, you can also define an Image Quality option (from Low to Maximum).

If you don't compress the file, your PDF file might be extremely large. For a commercial printing workflow, large file size is preferable to poor image quality. If you don't have to submit the PDF file via modem transmission, large file size is not an issue. If you must compress the file, ask your service provider what settings they prefer you to use.

Note:

Since you chose the High Quality Print preset, these options default to settings that will produce the best results for most commercial printing applications.

6. **In the Marks and Bleeds options, check the Trim Marks option, and change the Offset field to 0.125 in.**

Most printers prefer trim marks to appear outside of the bleed area, which is 0.125″ for this project; this requires a 0.125″ offset.

7. **In the Bleeds section, make sure the four fields are not linked. Change the Top and Bottom values to 0.5 in, and change the Left and Right values to 0.125 in.**

Because you did not define a specific bleed setting for the artboards in this file, the Use Document Bleed Settings option won't work.

You have to manually define the area on each side to include in the exported file. You're including more space on the top and bottom so the folding marks will be visible in the resulting PDF file.

Note:

The Output options relate to color management and PDF/X settings. Ask your output provider if you need to change anything for those options.

If this button shows a linked chain, click to unlink the four Bleed fields.

8. **Click Save PDF. When the process is finished, close the aos-brochure.ai file.**

1. _____ is the size of a flat page before folding, and after it has been cut from a press sheet.

2. _____ is the area where it is safe to place important content.

3. _____ is the amount you must extend objects beyond the actual artboard edge for them to safely appear at the cut edge of the final job.

4. For a folding document, panels that fold in need to be at least _____ smaller than outside panels.

5. The _____ command can be used to convert any object into a nonprinting guide.

6. Using _____ rulers, measurements relate to the first artboard in the file.

7. Using _____ rulers, measurements relate to the currently active artboard.

8. The _____ icon indicates that more text exists in the story, but does not fit into the current text area or chain.

9. You can use the _____ dialog box to change all instances of a selected font in the active file.

10. You can choose the _____ command to show visible, nonprinting indicators of spaces and paragraph return characters.

1. Briefly explain how the mechanics of printing affect the layout for folding documents.

2. Briefly explain two advantages of using styles for text formatting.

3. Briefly explain the difference between linked and embedded files.

PORTFOLIO BUILDER PROJECT

Use what you have learned in this project to complete the following freeform exercise.
Carefully read the art director and client comments, then create your own design to meet the needs of the project.
Use the space below to sketch ideas. When finished, write a brief explanation of the reasoning behind your final design.

art director comments

The Painted Turtle is a camp for children with serious medical conditions. It is run entirely by donations, and children are not charged to attend the camp.

Last spring the camp was heavily damaged by fire, so the camp directors and organizers are launching a fundraising campaign to raise the funds to rebuild.

❏ Create a letterfold brochure that can be mailed, placed in stand-up rack-card holders, and handed out at community events.

❏ Look at the camp's website for inspiration (www.thepaintedturtle.org).

❏ Include a "Donate Now" section with a form to gather the donor's name, contact information, amount of donation, and method of donation (check or credit card). Be sure to include space to gather the donor's credit card information if necessary.

client comments

Our camp is one of the largest of its kind, catering to the special needs of children (and their families) who would not normally be able to experience the joy of attending summer camp. Our largely volunteer staff gives its time and expertise to make this a positive experience for every child who comes through the gates.

We estimate that it costs about $1,600 per child to attend the camp, but we never turn away a sick child whose family can't afford it. Our fundraising efforts are vitally important to provide as many children as possible with memories they will cherish. The fire last spring was devastating, and we need more funds now than ever to help rebuild.

We want the fundraising pamphlet to be happy and colorful, and reflect the overall spirit of our camp. You can find a lot of text and images on our website; use anything you want from the site as FPO images. Once you know which ones you want to use, we'll provide you with high-resolution versions for print.

project justification

To begin the letterfold layout, you built technically accurate folding guides for each side of the brochure. To speed up the process for the next time you need to build one of these common letterfold jobs, you saved your initial work as a template.

Completing this project also required extensive work with imported text, specifically, importing styles from a Microsoft Word file and controlling the flow of text from one frame to another. You also worked with several advanced text-formatting options, including paragraph and character styles, and typographic fine-tuning.

Templates and styles are designed to let you do the majority of work once, and then apply it as many times as necessary. Many different projects can benefit from these tools, and you will use them extensively throughout your career as a graphic designer.

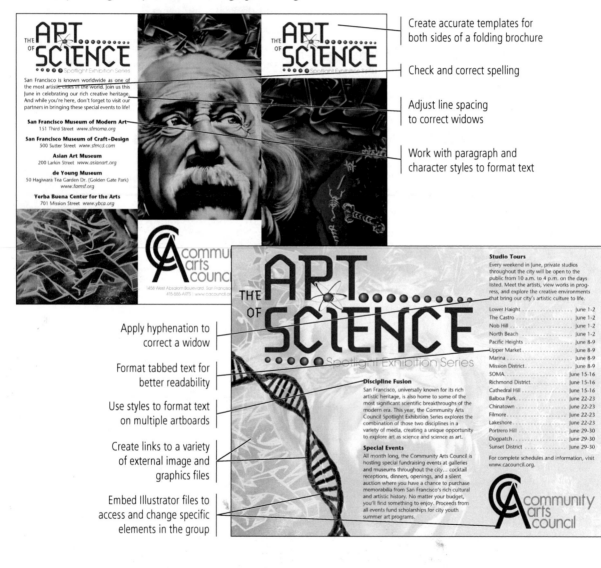

Create accurate templates for both sides of a folding brochure

Check and correct spelling

Adjust line spacing to correct widows

Work with paragraph and character styles to format text

Apply hyphenation to correct a widow

Format tabbed text for better readability

Use styles to format text on multiple artboards

Create links to a variety of external image and graphics files

Embed Illustrator files to access and change specific elements in the group

Candy Packaging

6

Your client, a candy manufacturer, has hired you to design and build the packaging for a new product launch at its anniversary party, which will be held at the annual candy expo. You will incorporate client-supplied elements and create custom graphics as you develop an attractive, modern box design.

This project incorporates the following skills:

❏ Using Image Trace to create a complex illustration

❏ Sampling colors to create custom swatches

❏ Using warp and 3D effects to add depth to artwork

❏ Creating type on an irregular path

❏ Controlling object blending modes and opacity

❏ Understanding and defining raster effect settings

❏ Previewing 3D artwork

PROJECT MEETING

client comments

We're celebrating our company's 75th anniversary this year. For the annual candy expo, we are introducing SmartTarts™ — a new product that combines different flavor profiles and textures into a single candy. Response at early focus groups has been very positive, so we're excited about the potential.

We would like to create a fun, colorful box to hand out product samples at our reception following the first day of the show. We'd like to give a larger sample size to the VIP guests who are invited to the party, so we need a box that is a 4-inch cube. Later we'll need to create a smaller box that we can use for show-floor samples, as well as final packaging that will be used for the retail product.

art director comments

We have a template from the printer with the package structure already laid out, based on an existing die that's used to cut the flat box from the press sheet. There's no need to reinvent the wheel, so use this template to build the finished box artwork.

The only thing they said they want is "fun, colorful" packaging, so we have complete artistic freedom for this project. They did send some components that need to be included: a background image, an anniversary logo, and some copy. They didn't send a company logo, so I think we'll try something creative with their company name.

Illustrator has all the tools you need to make this package technically accurate and aesthetically pleasing. When you finish the layout, you can even use built-in tools to create a comp of the final folded box.

project objectives

To complete this project, you will:

- ❏ Create the package file from a template
- ❏ Sample colors to create custom swatches
- ❏ Create warp and 3D effects
- ❏ Create type on an irregular path
- ❏ Change object blending modes and opacity
- ❏ Apply raster effects to vector objects and placed images
- ❏ Apply effects to pieces of a group
- ❏ Define raster effect settings
- ❏ Preview transparency flattening
- ❏ Flatten transparency in a PDF file
- ❏ Preview a 3D representation of the completed box artwork

STAGE 1 / Building the File Structure

When you work on a package design, it's important to realize that many types of packages have a standard size and shape. Although there is something to be said for standing out in a crowd, package design is often governed by the space allowed on store shelves, which means you probably won't have any choice regarding the size and shape of the package.

You also need to understand that packages are typically designed and printed as a flat layout, using a template to indicate edges and folds. They are then diecut, folded, and glued. The next time you finish a box of cereal, tear it apart along the glue flaps to see how the package was designed. Because many packages share common sizes, printers often have existing templates you can use.

Create the Package File from a Template

The printer for this package has provided you with a template file that includes the diecut layout and folding guides. You will use this file as the basis for the entire project.

1. **Download Candy_AI19_RF.zip from the Student Files web page.**

2. **Expand the ZIP archive in your WIP folder (Macintosh) or copy the archive contents into your WIP folder (Windows).**

   This results in a folder named **Candy**, which contains the files you need for this project. You should also use this folder to save the files you create in this project.

3. **Create a new file by opening the square-box.ait template file from your WIP>Candy folder. Resize the view so you can see the entire artboard.**

   The file has three layers: one has guides indicating the location of the folds, one has guides that define margins and bleeds for each panel, and one has the die lines for the box shape. The box's top and bottom panels are identified, as well as the flap where glue will be applied in the converting process to create the finished box shape.

4. **Save the new file as a native Illustrator file named candy-box.ai in your WIP>Candy folder, then continue to the next exercise.**

Note:

You should notice that the red bleed guide does not extend to the end of the glue flap. The printer for this job has recommended that ink should not be printed in the gluing area — a common requirement for package printing.

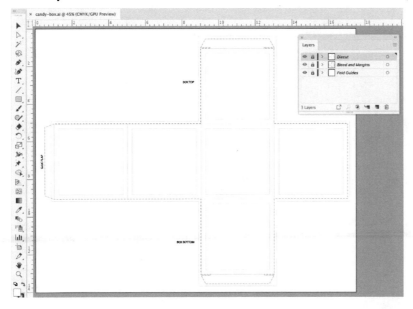

Use Image Trace to Create a Complex Image

If you have completed the other projects in this book, you should have a solid foundation for creating basic and complex vector graphics, whether based on a sketch or photograph, or from scratch.

Another option — Image Trace — makes it very easy to create vector graphics directly from an image, using a variety of options to determine how realistic the resulting illustration will be.

1. **With candy-box.ai open, create a new layer named Background.**

2. **In the Layers panel, drag the Background layer below the Diecut layer.**

   The Diecut layer shows the location of the cut lines. Although it will not be printed in the final output, this layer needs to be visible while you create the basic package.

   Be careful how you drag the layer to reposition it. If you accidentally move the layer to the wrong place in the stack, or move it to be a sublayer of another layer, simply drag it again to the top of the layer stack.

   Note:

   Even though the panel layers are above the guide layers, guides always appear in front of artwork.

   The heavy line identifies where the layer will be positioned when you release the mouse button.

3. **With the Background layer selected in the Layers panel, choose File>Place.**

4. **Select the file background.tif in your WIP>Candy folder. Make sure none of the options at the bottom of the dialog box are checked, then click Place.**

   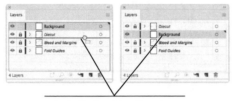

   The selected image is loaded into the Place cursor.

5. **Click the loaded Place cursor to place the selected image.**

6. **Using the Selection tool, position the placed file so the pile of candy extends across all four side panels, but does not extend into the top panel. (Use the following image as a guide.)**

As you can see in the Control panel, the placed image is only 72 ppi, which is insufficient resolution for commercial printing. Because you are going to use this image as the basis for a vector illustration, the low resolution will not be a problem.

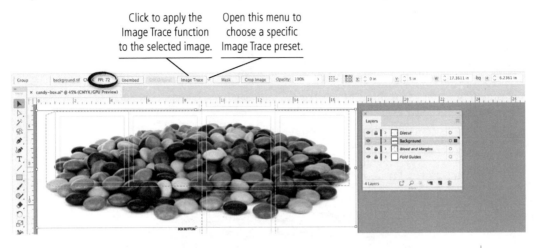

Click to apply the Image Trace function to the selected image.

Open this menu to choose a specific Image Trace preset.

7. **Hide all but the Background layer.**

You don't need these layers for this stage of the process; hiding them allows you to better see the effect of the Image Trace process.

8. **With the placed background image selected, click the Image Trace button in the Control panel.**

By clicking this button, Illustrator automatically traces the image using the default black-and-white preset.

The result is a special type of object called an **image tracing object** (which you can see in the Control panel). As long as you don't expand the tracing object, you can change the settings to produce different results from the same picture.

9. **Open the Image Trace panel (Window>Image Trace).**

When you trace an image, the original photo is hidden and the illustrated version appears in its place.

Note:

In the Layers panel, Option/Alt-clicking the Eye icon for a layer hides all other layers in the file.

Note:

You can also apply the default Image Trace settings by choosing Object>Image Trace>Make.

Choose a defined tracing preset.

Open the Image Trace panel.

Use this menu to change the visibility of the original traced image.

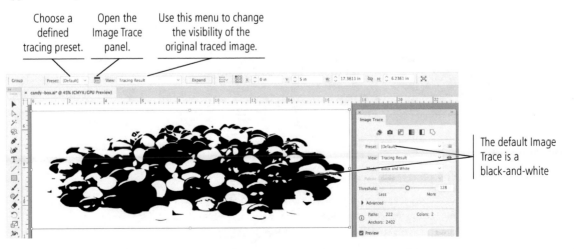

The default Image Trace is a black-and-white

10. **Open the Preset menu and choose Low Fidelity Photo.**

Illustrator includes a number of Image Trace presets that you can apply to any image. These can be accessed in the Image Trace panel or Control panel when a tracing object is selected.

As long as you don't expand the tracing object, you can change the settings that generate the illustration. However, when the Preview option is checked at the bottom of the panel, every change requires Illustrator to reprocess the image to generate the correct curves. Because this is a rather large image, processing each change could take considerable processing power and time (depending on your computer).

Use this menu to access one of the built-in presets.

Using the current settings, the resulting illustration will include 1047 distinct colors.

11. **Open the Palette menu and choose Limited.**

Using a limited color palette can reduce the complexity of the file. The Image Trace panel shows that you have reduced the tracing from 1000+ colors (from Step 10) to 30, which is the default option when using the Limited palette option. You can use the Colors slider to reduce the number of colors even further.

By allowing only a small number of colors, you force Illustrator to create larger objects of solid colors, ultimately resulting in more of a "paint-by-numbers" effect.

Note:

Increasing the number of possible colors creates a more realistic result, and a more complex illustration.

When you use a Limited palette, you can define the specific number of colors to allow in the illustration.

12. **At the bottom of the panel, uncheck the Preview option.**

Rather than waiting to preview each change, it's a better idea to activate the preview after defining your initial choices; you can then toggle the preview on and off as necessary to reduce the time you spend sitting and waiting.

13. **Click the arrow to the left of the Advanced heading to expand the panel.**

14. **Change the Paths option to 75%.**

    This controls how tightly the tracing conforms to the original image; a higher number means more tightly fitting paths.

15. **Change the Corners option to 25%.**

    This controls how corners in the original image are represented in the tracing; a higher number results in more corners instead of rounded paths.

16. **Change the Noise option to 5 px.**

    This controls the smallest-size area that is ignored in the tracing result; higher values mean fewer small spots of color in the tracing.

Click here to show or hide the advanced options.

Turn off the preview to reduce processing time every time you make a change in the panel.

Understanding Image Trace Options

With so many options and sliders, the Image Trace panel might seem intimidating at first. As with any tool, it's easier to get the desired results if you understand the options.

Buttons at the top of the panel apply specific color modes to the illustration (from left): Auto Color, High Color, Low Color, Grayscale, Black and White, or Outline.

- **Preset** includes a number of built-in groups of settings that produce specific results, such as Sketched Art or Technical Drawing.
- **View** changes what is visible in the document. You can show the tracing result with or without outlines, the source image with or without outlines, or only the source image.
- **Mode** defines the color mode (color, grayscale, or black and white) of the resulting illustration.
- **Palette**, which is available when the Mode is set to Color, defines the specific colors that can be used. The default Full Tone option allows Illustrator to use an unlimited palette to create the illustration.
- **Threshold**, which is available when the Mode is set to Black and White, defines the maximum tonal value that will remain white before an area is filled with black.
- **Colors.** When Full Tone or Automatic is selected in the Palette menu, this option defines the accuracy of illustration colors as a percentage; higher values result in a larger number of colors being used.

    When the Limited palette is selected, this option defines the specific number of colors Illustrator can use to trace the image. More colors create more depth, but also increase the complexity and number of points in the illustration.

- **Paths** adjusts how closely traced paths will follow the pixels of the original image.
- **Corners** defines the minimum angle that can be traced as a sharp corner instead of a smooth curve.
- **Noise** adjusts the smallest color area (in pixels) that can be drawn as a path.
- **Method** determines whether shapes in the illustration are created as abutting (left) or overlapping (right).
- When you use the Black and White color mode, you can use the **Create** options to define whether the illustration is created as fills, strokes, or a combination.
    - **Fills** results in solid-filled paths.
    - **Strokes** results in paths with an applied stroke color and weight. The Stroke Width field defines the maximum stroke weight that can be applied before a stroke will be recreated as a fill object.
- **Snap Curves to Lines** replaces slightly curved lines with straight lines.
- **Ignore White** does not create shapes to represent white areas in the image.

17. Check the Preview option at the bottom of the panel to review the results of your choices.

The change is subtle, but you should notice slightly more accurate path shapes (Step 14), fewer sharp corners (Step 15), and fewer small areas of isolated color (Step 16).

18. Open the View menu in the Image Trace panel and choose Tracing Result with Outlines.

By default, vector outlines that make up the image-tracing object are not visible in the document. Without expanding the image tracing object, these preview options allow you to view the resulting paths based on your current Image Trace settings.

When Tracing Result with Outlines is selected, you can see the vector paths that will make up the resulting illustration.

19. Choose Tracing Result in the View menu.

This turns off the path outlines and restores the illustration to full opacity.

20. Click the Eye icon to the right of the View button and hold down the mouse button.

You can click and hold this button to show the original image that is used to make the Image Trace. This provides a quick method for reviewing the original image, while still experimenting with the Image Trace options.

21. Save the file, and then continue to the next exercise.

Note:

To access the individual anchors and paths, you have to expand the image-tracing object.

Sample Colors and Create Custom Swatches

Using the Eyedropper tool, you can select colors from other objects in the file, which makes it easier to create a cohesive package design. In this exercise you will sample three colors from the tracing image; you will use those swatches later for other elements of the design.

1. **With `candy-box.ai` open, deselect everything in the file.**

   In many instances, sampling a color with the Eyedropper tool automatically changes the attributes of any selected objects. Although this is not the case for a tracing object, you should get into the habit of deselecting objects before sampling new colors, unless you want to purposefully change the color of a selected object.

2. **Display the Swatches and Color panels, and then choose the Eyedropper tool in the Tools panel.**

   If you don't see the color sliders in the Color panel, choose Show Options in the panel's Options menu.

3. **Click the Eyedropper tool in a dark red color of the tracing object.**

   Clicking with the Eyedropper tool changes the color in the Color panel; this method is called **sampling** color.

We clicked here to sample the dark red color.

Eyedropper tool

The template includes only four color swatches: Registration, White, Black, and CMYK Green.

Sampled color values appear in the Color panel.

4. **With the Fill icon on top (the active attribute) in the Swatches and Color panels, click the New Swatch button at the bottom of the Swatches panel.**

5. **In the resulting New Swatch dialog box, activate the Global check box and uncheck the Add to My Library option. Click OK to accept the default swatch name and color values.**

   The sampled color is saved as a swatch, so you can access it again later.

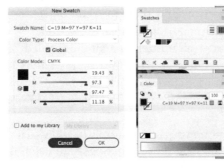

Note:

If your Color and Swatches panels are docked, drag them out of the dock so you can use them both at once.

Note:

You could also simply click the New Swatch button in the Swatches panel to create a custom color swatch.

6. **Use the Eyedropper tool again to sample a light pink color, and then add the sampled color as a second global swatch.**

We sampled the light pink color in this area.

7. **Use the Eyedropper tool again to sample a light yellow color, and then add the sampled color as a third global swatch.**

We sampled the light yellow color in this area.

8. **Save the file and continue to the next stage of the project.**

STAGE 2 / Working with Styles and Effects

When you design a complex project, such as this package, it helps to decide on a logical approach to accomplish the task. Rather than jumping around in the layout, it makes more sense to work on one panel at a time. In this stage of the project, you are going to use a number of tools and techniques to create the various pieces that are required, primarily using advanced type options and Illustrator effects.

Illustrator includes a number of effects for enhancing objects in a layout. Effects in Illustrator are live and non-destructive, which means they can be edited or removed from an object without destroying the original object.

When you work with effects, you should be aware that many of these options eventually result in rasterized elements, even when you apply them to vector objects.

Some of the Illustrator Effects — specifically Drop Shadow, Inner Glow, Outer Glow, and Feather options in the Stylize submenu — all utilize some form of graded transparency, and they all result in objects that reproduce as pixels (rasters) instead of vectors. For example, a drop shadow creates a soft-edge shadow object that blends from the shadow color to fully transparent. To achieve this effect on output, the shadow has to be rasterized into pixels that reproduce the visual effect.

In this stage of the project, you use effects and transparency controls to add visual interest to different elements of the box artwork. In Stage 3 of this project, you will learn how to control transparent objects that need to be rasterized before they can be successfully output.

Transform and Warp Design Elements

The first two side panels in this box require a banner-type object that highlights the product name. Rather than simply creating a flat banner, you're going to use built-in effects to create a three-dimensional banner that appears to wave around the box corner. You're also going to create the banner in two separate pieces so that the content for each side can be easily isolated later.

1. With **candy-box.ai** open, lock and hide the Background layer. Show the Diecut, Bleed and Margins, and Fold Guides layers.

2. Create two new layers, named **Side 1** and **Side 2**, immediately above the Background layer. Make Side 1 the active layer.

3. Create a rectangle in the center of the left panel that is 3.75" wide and 1" high. Fill the rectangle with the dark red custom swatch and set the stroke to None. Position it so the shape's right edge aligns to the right edge of the left panel.

   Use the image after Step 4 as a guide for positioning this object.

4. Using the Add Anchor Point tool, add an anchor point to the left edge of the rectangle, halfway between the corners. Use the Direct Selection tool to drag the point right, creating the basic banner shape.

We added an anchor point to a basic rectangle to create the left side of the banner shape.

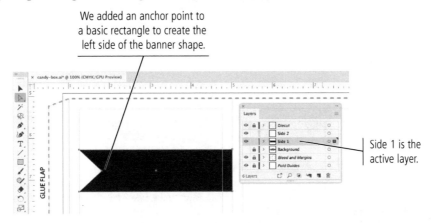

Side 1 is the active layer.

5. Click the object's fill to select the entire shape, then choose the Reflect tool (nested under the Rotate tool).

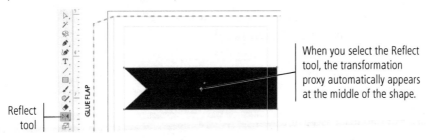

Reflect tool

When you select the Reflect tool, the transformation proxy automatically appears at the middle of the shape.

6. **Click the right edge of the selected shape to move the transformation point.**

7. **Press Option/Alt-Shift, then drag right to clone and reflect the selected shape.**

   Pressing Option/Alt allows you to clone the object while you reflect it. Pressing Shift constrains the reflection to 45° angles.

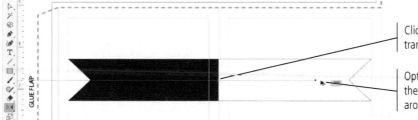

Click to move the transformation proxy.

Option/Alt-Shift-drag to clone the object while you reflect it around the transformation proxy.

8. **In the Layers panel, expand the Side 1 layer. Drag the Selected Art icon to the Side 2 layer, then expand the Side 2 layer.**

   Remember, expanding a layer shows the objects contained on the layer (called sublayers). You can further expand sublayer groups so that you can show — and select — the individual elements in a group, if necessary.

Expanding the layer shows the objects (sublayers) on that layer.

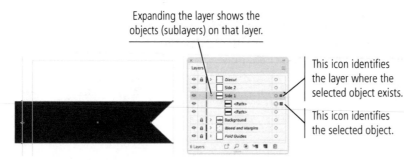

This icon identifies the layer where the selected object exists.

This icon identifies the selected object.

You can drag the Selected Art icon from the layer or from the actual selected object. If more than one object is selected, dragging from the actual layer name moves all selected objects to the new target layer.

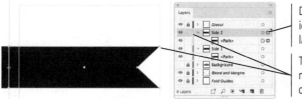

Drag the Selected Art icon from the Side 1 layer to the Side 2 layer.

The object's handles now reflect the color of the Side 2 layer.

9. **With Side 1 as the active layer, use the Type tool to create a point-type object near the center of the banner shape on the left panel.**

   Be sure the cursor is not near the existing shape edge when you click with the Type tool. If you click too close to the edge of the existing shape, clicking with the Type tool will convert the existing shape into an area-type object. Use the shape of the cursor as a guide for when you can click to create a new type area.

When you see this cursor, clicking will convert the existing shape to a type area.

   To work around this potential problem, you could also click to create a type object somewhere else, then drag it into position later.

If the cursor is far enough away from the edges of existing shapes, you can click and drag to create a new type object.

10. Type Smart to replace the default placeholder text, and then format the text as 60-pt ATC Garnet Ultra with a white fill and right paragraph alignment.

11. Position the type object so the text is centered vertically in the banner shape, 1/8″ from the right panel edge (as shown in the following image).

Side 1 is the active layer.

12. Using the Selection tool, press Option/Alt-Shift and drag the type object right until the bounding box is 1/8″ from the left edge of the second side panel.

The cloned object automatically appears on the same layer as the original. Because these objects exist on Side 1, which is lower than Side 2, the red shape on Side 2 obscures the text in the cloned type object.

The cloned object remains on the same layer as the original.

13. In the Layers panel, drag the Selected Art icon to the Side 2 layer.

When you move objects from one layer to another using the Selected Art icon, the objects are automatically moved to the top of the object stacking order on the target layer.

14. Using the Control or Paragraph panel, change the selected object to left paragraph alignment. Use the Selection tool to reposition the type object to be 1/8″ from the left edge of the Side 2 panel area.

You might want to reset the zero point to the left edge of this panel, or you can simply use the artboard rulers to place the second type object properly.

15. Change the type in the second object to Tarts.

16. Apply kerning as necessary for each type object until you are satisfied with the result.

Note:

Feel free to toggle rulers on and off (View>Rulers>Show/Hide Rulers, or Command/Control-R) as necessary to complete the exercises in this project.

17. **Place the insertion point at the end of the second type object, then open the Glyphs panel (Window>Type>Glyphs).**

18. **Scroll through the panel to find the trademark symbol (TM). Double-click that glyph to add it at the location of the insertion point.**

   The trademark symbol is a single character (glyph) even though it has two letters.

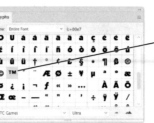

Double-click a glyph to add it at the location of the insertion point.

19. **Highlight the trademark character. In the Character panel, change the type size to 40 pt and change the baseline shift to 10 pt.**

   If you don't see the Baseline Shift field, choose Show Options in the panel Options menu.

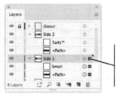

20. **In the Layers panel, click the empty space to the right of the Side 1 layer to select all objects on that layer.**

Click here to select all objects on a layer.

21. **With both shapes on the panel selected, choose Object>Group.**

22. **Repeat Steps 20–21 for the Side 2 panel.**

23. **Save the file and continue to the next exercise.**

Understanding the Glyphs panel

The Glyphs panel (Window>Type>Glyphs or Type>Glyphs) provides access to all glyphs in a font. Using the panel is simple: place the insertion point where you want a character to appear, then double-click the character you want to place.

A Show the entire font or access specific character sets

B Double-click a glyph in the chart to add it at the current insertion point

C Change the font family that is displayed in the panel

D Change the font style that is displayed in the panel

E Zoom out (make glyphs in the panel grid smaller)

F Zoom in (make glyphs in the panel grid larger)

By default, the panel shows the entire active font, but you can show only specific character sets using the Show menu.

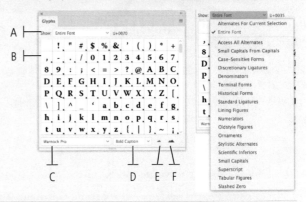

ASCII is a text-based code that defines characters with a numeric value between 001 and 256. The standard alphabet and punctuation characters are mapped from 001 to 128. Extended ASCII characters are those with ASCII numbers higher than 128; these include symbols (copyright symbols, trademark symbols, etc.) and some special formatting characters (en dashes, accent marks, etc.).

OpenType fonts offer the ability to store more than 65,000 glyphs (characters) in a single font — far beyond what you could access with a keyboard (even including combinations of the different modifier keys). The large glyph storage capacity means that a single OpenType font can replace separate "Expert" fonts that contain variations of fonts.

Unicode fonts include two-bit characters common in some foreign language typesetting (e.g., Cyrillic, Japanese, and other non-Roman or pictographic fonts).

Apply a Warp Effect

The Warp effect allows you to easily distort objects in predefined shapes, based on the selected style, direction, bend, and distortion values. The Warp effect, like most Illustrator effects, is nondestructive, which means you can change the applied settings at any time to change the resulting shape.

1. **With candy-box.ai open, select the group on the Side 1 layer.**

   You can use the Layers panel to select the group, or simply click the group on the artboard with the Selection tool.

2. **With the group selected, choose Effect>Warp>Arc. In the resulting Warp Options dialog box, activate the Preview check box.**

The icon for each warp style suggests the result that will be created.

The Bend value determines how much warping will be applied.

Distortion values change the horizontal and vertical perspectives.

The bounding box and paths reflect the original objects without the warp.

3. Choose Arch in the Style menu.

As the Arch icon suggests, the object's left and right edges are unaffected by an Arch warp.

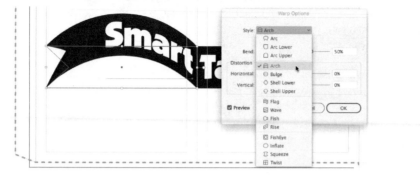

Note:

You can choose from any of the 15 styles in the Style menu (these are the same as the options listed in the Effect>Warp submenu).

4. Change the Bend value to -32 and click OK to apply the warp.

The warp effect is treated as an appearance attribute. When the warped object is selected, you can see the original object shape.

Note:

Effects dialog boxes remember the last-used settings.

5. In the Layers panel, expand the Side 1 and Side 2 layers if necessary so you can see both groups.

6. Press Option/Alt, then click the Target icon for the group in Side 1 and drag to the target icon of the Side 2 group.

The filled target icon indicates that effects and/or transparency attributes have been applied to a specific object. You can move those attributes to a different object by dragging from the filled icon to the hollow icon of another object.

By pressing Option/Alt, you are actually cloning the appearance attributes of the original object and applying those same attributes to another object.

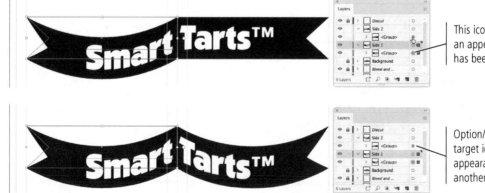

This icon indicates that an appearance attribute has been applied.

Option/Alt-drag the filled target icon to clone the appearance attributes to another object.

7. **Select the group on the Side 2 layer, then open the Appearance panel.**

Remember. effects in Illustrator are non-destructive. You can use the hot-text links in the Appearance panel to change an effect's settings at any time. You can hide a specific effect by clicking the Eye icon in the Appearance panel, or permanently remove an effect by dragging that listing to the panel's Delete button.

Use the hot-text links to change the settings of an applied effect.

8. **Click the Warp:Arch hot text to reopen the dialog box for the applied effect.**

Choosing the same option more than once in the Effect menu actually applies a second instance of that effect to the selected object. Use the Appearance panel to modify the settings of an applied effect.

9. **Change the bend value to 32% and click OK.**

10. **Save the file and continue to the next exercise.**

Create a 3D Effect

3D effects allow you to create three-dimensional objects from two-dimensional artwork. You can simulate depth by changing an object's rotation along three axes, or use extrusion settings to basically "pull" an object in three directions. You can also control the appearance of 3D objects with lighting, shading, and other properties.

1. **With candy-box.ai open, use the Selection tool to select the banner group on the Side 1 panel.**

2. **Choose Effect>3D>Extrude & Bevel and activate the Preview option.**

In the 3D Extrude & Bevel Options dialog box, the cube/preview shows the approximate position of the original object (the blue surface) in relation to the object created by the settings in this dialog box.

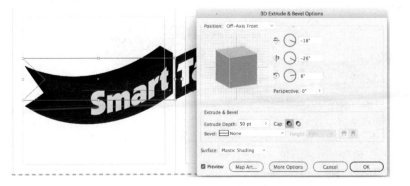

Note:

The X Axis value rotates an object around an invisible horizontal line.

The Y Axis value rotates an object around an invisible vertical line.

The Z Axis value rotates an object around an invisible line that moves from the front of an object to the back.

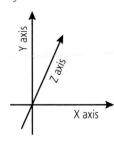

3. Click the preview icon and drag it around.

As you drag the preview cube, the values in the three fields change, based on how and where you drag. In the layout, the selected group also changes because the Preview option is active.

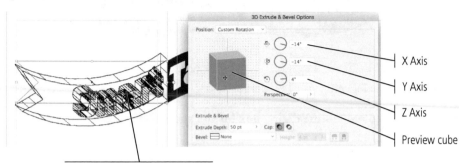

While you move the preview icon, the object appears as a wire frame (the basis of 3D artwork).

Note:

The surface of the object only appears after the wires are calculated internally.

4. When you're done experimenting with the preview, specify the following values:

X Axis = 20°

Y Axis = 0°

Z Axis = 0°

Extrude Depth = 50 pt

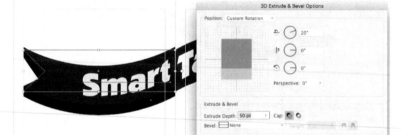

5. Click OK to apply the effect.

6. Select the banner group on Panel 2, then choose Effect>Apply Extrude & Bevel.

The top menu option shows the last-used effect. If you use this menu command, the effect will be applied with the last-used settings. You will not see the effect's dialog box.

Note:

Illustrator remembers the last-used effect, and the specific settings you used to apply that effect. The top of the Effect menu includes the option to apply the last-used effect without opening the related dialog box, or to open the dialog box for the last-used effect.

7. Using the Arrow keys, nudge the second banner group up or down until the two objects align to each other.

The Extrude & Bevel effect can slightly shift objects on the artboard. To restore the appearance of a single banner extending across both box panels, you have to nudge the extruded banners back into the correct position.

8. Save the file and continue to the next exercise.

Create Type on a Path

You can create unique typographic effects by flowing text onto a path. A text path can be any shape you can create in Illustrator, whether it's a simple shape created with one of the basic shape tools, a straight line drawn with the Line Segment tool, or a complex graphic drawn with the Pen tool.

1. **With `candy-box.ai` open, lock the groups on the Side 1 and Side 2 layers.**

   You can use the Lock icon for individual sublayers to lock those objects without locking entire layers.

2. **With the Side 1 layer active, choose the Pen tool. Change the fill to None and the stroke to 1-pt black.**

3. **Draw a curve above the banner shape, extending across both panels (as shown in the following image).**

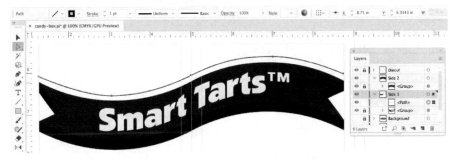

4. **Double-click the Eraser tool in the Tools panel.**

   The Eraser tool erases parts of a shape, whether from an open or closed path. When you use this tool, Illustrator automatically adds anchor points as necessary based on what you erase.

5. **In the resulting dialog box, change the Size field to `8 pt`, then click OK.**

   You can also use this dialog box to change the angle and roundness (shape) of the Eraser tool cursor.

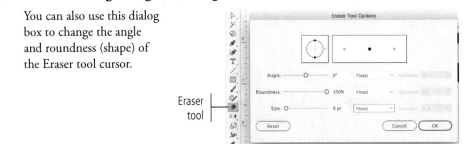

Eraser tool

Note:

The Eraser tool erases from the fill and stroke of the object. The Path Eraser tool only erases from the selected path; an object's fill is not affected.

6. **Place the cursor over the panel fold line between the first and second panels.**

The tool cursor indicates the brush size.

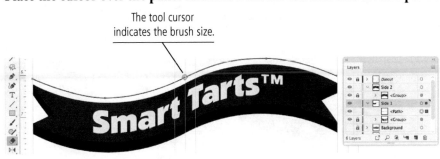

7. Click to erase 8 points of space from the path you created in Step 3.

Anchor points are added to the now-open ends of the path where you erased the previous line segment. The Layers panel shows that the result is two separate paths, each of which ends before the fold guide that separates the two panels.

8. Using the Selection tool, click away from the selected objects to deselect them, then select only the right path (in the second panel).

9. In the Layers panel, drag the Selected Art icon from the Side 1 layer to the Side 2 layer.

Move the right path to the Side 2 layer.

10. Select the Type tool in the Tools panel, and then click near the left side of the path on the left panel.

Clicking an existing path with the Type tool converts the path to a type path. You could select the Type on a Path tool (nested under the Type tool), but it's not necessary because when the Type tool cursor is near an existing path, it automatically switches to the Type on a Path tool cursor.

When the Type tool cursor is near an existing path, it switches to the Type on a Path tool cursor.

Note:

If you choose Panel Options in the Layers panel Options menu, you can change the size of thumbnails so you can better see the contents of each layer and sublayer.

11. Type A sweet, fruity trip to replace the highlighted default placeholder text.

12. Select all the text on the path (Select>All) and format it as 24-pt ATC Coral Normal, with 0 pt baseline shift and right paragraph alignment. Change the text color to the dark red swatch.

Depending on where you clicked, some of the message might not be visible after you change the formatting; the location where you clicked defined the starting point for text along the path. You will adjust the text position on the path in the next two steps.

The 1-pt black stroke attribute is automatically removed when you convert the stroke to a type path.

The text is aligned to the right end of the type path.

Note:

If you continued directly from the previous exercises, the adjusted baseline shift from the trademark character is still applied. You need to reset the baseline shift to 0 for the type on these paths.

13. **With the Type tool still active, press Command/Control and click away from the active object to deselect it.**

14. **Using the Type tool, click anywhere on the right path to convert it to a type path. Type with a sour zip!.**

    The Type tool remembers the last-used settings, so the second path also uses 24-pt ATC Coral Normal with right paragraph alignment. For some reason, however, the new type is filled with black instead of the custom red swatch.

15. **Change the paragraph alignment to left, and change the type fill color to the custom red swatch.**

Type on a Path Options

You can control the appearance of type on a path by choosing Type>Type on a Path>Type on a Path Options. You can apply one of five effects, change the alignment of the text to the path, flip the text to the other side of the path, and adjust the character spacing around curves (higher Spacing values remove more space around sharp curves).

The **Align options** determine which part of the text (baseline, ascender, descender, or center) aligns to which part of the path (top, bottom, or center).

The **Flip** check box turns type onto the other side of the path. This option is useful for putting text inside shapes.

The **3D Ribbon** effect maintains horizontal edges of type, while rotating vertical edges to be perpendicular to the path.

The **Rainbow** (default) effect keeps each character's baseline parallel to the path.

The **Stair Step** effect aligns the left edge of each character's baseline to the path without rotating any characters.

The **Skew** effect maintains the vertical edges of type, while skewing the horizontal edges around the path.

The **Gravity** effect aligns the center of each character's baseline to the path, keeping vertical edges in line with the path's center.

16. **Choose the Direct Selection tool in the Tools panel.**

When the insertion point is placed in type on a path (or type on a path is selected), switching to the Direct Selection tool reveals the start and end points of the type path. Modifying those points is the same basic concept as changing the left and right indents for text in a regular type area.

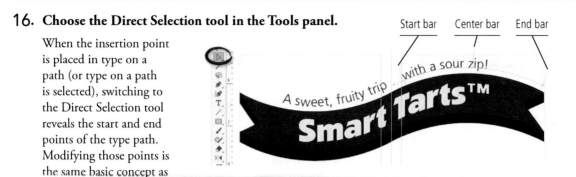

You can also click a type path with the Selection tool, or click the type on the path with the Direct Selection tool, to reveal the start and end points of the type.

17. **Click the start bar and drag near the left end of the path, until the "w" is approximately 1/8″ from the left panel edge.**

The start bar automatically appears at the point where you first click to create the type path (Step 14). Dragging the start bar repositions the starting point for text on the path.

Note:

The start bar's original location is based on where you click to convert the path to a type path.

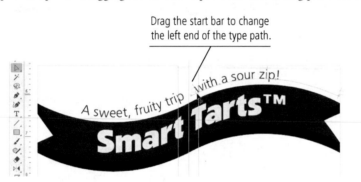

Drag the start bar to change the left end of the type path.

Note:

Make sure you click the start bar and not the white square that represents the in port of the text path.

18. **Unlock the groups on both Side layers, then show the Background layer.**

19. **Choose Select>All, then move all the selected objects up until the text is not obscured by any object on the Background layer.**

Because the Background layer is still locked, the Select>All command selects only the banner groups and type paths.

20. **Collapse the Side 1 and Side 2 layers in the Layers panel.**

21. **Save the file and continue to the next exercise.**

Place a Native Photoshop File

Native Photoshop files offer a number of advantages over other formats, including the ability to store multiple layers and even, in some cases, maintain editability directly on the Illustrator artboard.

1. **With candy-box.ai open, create a new layer named Side 3 immediately above the Side 2 layer.**

2. **Lock all but the Side 3 layer, and make sure Side 3 is the active layer.**

3. **Make the third side panel prominent in the document window.**

4. **Using the Rectangle tool, create a white-filled rectangle that fills the third side panel area.**

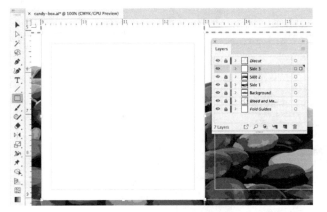

5. **Choose File>Place. Select box-copy.txt and click Place. In the resulting dialog box, click OK to accept the default text import options.**

   The TXT extension identifies a text-only file, which is a text file that has been saved without any formatting. These files can be generated in any text-editing software, from full word-processing suites to basic text apps on mobile devices.

> **Note:**
>
> *The Text Import Options dialog box appears even if Show Import Options is not checked in the Place dialog box.*

6. **Click and drag to create an area-type object that fills the margin guides on the Side 3 panel (as shown in the following image).**

7. **Select all the text in the type area, then change the type formatting to 12.5-pt ATC Coral Normal with 17 pt leading.**

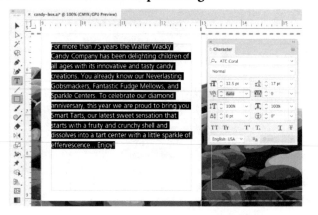

8. **Choose File>Place and select anniversary75.psd (in your WIP>Candy folder). Make sure Link is *not* checked and Show Import Options *is* checked, then click Place.**

Note:

Learn more about Adobe Photoshop in the companion book of this series, **Adobe Photoshop CC: The Professional Portfolio**.

9. **In the resulting dialog box, make sure the Show Preview option is checked.**

The Photoshop Import Options dialog box allows you to control how Photoshop elements are translated into Illustrator:

- Use the **Layer Comp** menu to import a specific layer comp saved in the file.

- If you link to the file instead of embedding it, you can use the **When Updating Link** menu to control what happens if you update the linked image.

- **Convert Layers to Objects** converts Photoshop layers to Illustrator objects. This option preserves type layers as editable type objects in Illustrator. It also preserves masks, blending modes, transparency, and slice information. Adjustment layers and layer effects are flattened into the placed objects.

- **Flatten Layers to a Single Image** combines all Photoshop layers into a single layer. The appearance of the image is preserved, but you can't edit the layers.

- **Import Hidden Layers** can be checked to include layers that are not visible in the Photoshop file.

- **Import Slices** is only available if the Photoshop file includes slices for web layouts. If this option is checked, the slices will be maintained in the imported file.

10. **Choose the Convert Layers to Objects option (if necessary) and click OK.**

This image has only one layer, which you will not edit, so this option has the same result as converting Photoshop layers to Illustrator objects.

11. **Click to place the loaded image on the artboard. Using the Selection tool, move the placed file to the top-right corner of the third side panel. Leave approximately 1/8″ between the placed art and the panel edges.**

12. **With the placed object selected, choose Object>Text Wrap>Make.**

Applying a **text wrap** to an object forces surrounding text to flow around that object instead of directly in front of, or behind it.

13. **Choose Object>Text Wrap>Text Wrap Options.**

14. **In the resulting dialog box, change the Offset field to 12 pt and click OK.**

    The **Offset** value defines the distance at which text will wrap from the object.

    If you check the Invert Wrap option, the surrounding text will flow into the wrap shape instead of flowing around it.

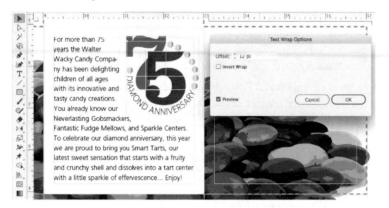

15. **If you see an Overset Text icon for the type object on the panel, use the Arrow keys to nudge the selected object (the anniversary logo) closer to the top and right edges of the panel area.**

16. **Save the file and continue to the next exercise.**

Apply Transparent Effects

Many Illustrator options allow you to add dimension and depth to virtually any design element. You can apply creative effects (such as drop shadows) that incorporate transparency, apply different blending modes so objects blend smoothly into underlying objects, and change the transparency of any object.

1. **With candy-box.ai open, expand the Side 3 layer in the Layers panel and then expand the anniversary75.psd sublayer.**

    Because you chose to convert layers to objects when you placed the native Photoshop file, the resulting object is a group. Each layer in the original file becomes a separate sublayer within the group.

2. **Click the Selected Art icon to select only the Seven object in the sublayer.**

Select only the Seven object.

3. **Choose Effect>[Illustrator Effects] Stylize>Drop Shadow.**

   Make sure you choose the option in the Illustrator Effects section
   and not the Photoshop Effects section.

4. **Activate the Preview check box, then change the drop shadow settings
   to the following:**

Mode:	Multiply
Opacity:	50%
X Offset:	0.02 in
Y Offset:	0.02 in
Blur:	0.03 in
Color:	Black

5. **Click OK to apply the drop shadow.**

6. **Open the Appearance panel (Window>Appearance).**

   The drop shadow is treated as an appearance attribute. You can edit the applied
   settings by clicking the effect hot text in the Appearance panel. You can remove the
   effect by dragging it to the Appearance panel's Delete button.

   Click the hot text to open the
   dialog box and change the
   settings of the applied effect.

   The solid target indicates that
   an effect has altered the
   appearance of the sublayer.

7. **In the Layers panel, click the target icon to select the Five sublayer in the
   anniversary75.psd object.**

8. **Choose Effect>Apply Drop Shadow.**

   This command reapplies the listed effect with the last-used settings.

Understanding Transparency Panel Options

Blending Modes

Blending modes control how colors in an object interact with colors in underlying objects. Objects are set to Normal by default, which simply overlays the top object's color onto underlying objects (i.e., the "base").

- **Darken** returns the darker of the blend or base color. Base pixels that are lighter than the blend color are replaced. Base pixels that are darker remain unchanged.

- **Multiply** multiplies (hence, the name) the base color by the blend color, resulting in a darker color. Multiplying any color with black produces black. Multiplying any color with white leaves the color unchanged.

- **Color Burn** darkens the base color by increasing the contrast. Blend colors darker than 50% significantly darken the base color by increasing saturation and reducing brightness. Blending with white has no effect.

- **Lighten** returns the lighter color (base or blend). Base pixels that are darker than the blend color are replaced. Base pixels that are lighter remain unchanged.

- **Screen** is basically the inverse of Multiply, always returning a lighter color. Screening with black has no effect. Screening with white produces white.

- **Color Dodge** brightens the base color. Blend colors lighter than 50% significantly increase brightness. Blending with black has no effect.

- **Overlay** multiplies or screens the blend color to preserve the original lightness or darkness of the base color.

- **Soft Light** darkens or lightens base colors, depending on the blend color. Blend colors lighter than 50% lighten the base color (as if dodged). Blend colors darker than 50% darken the base color (as if burned).

- **Hard Light** combines the Multiply and Screen modes. Blend colors darker than 50% are multiplied, and blend colors lighter than 50% are screened.

- **Difference*** inverts base color values according to the brightness value in the blend layer. Lower brightness values in the blend layer have less effect on the result. Blending with black has no effect.

- **Exclusion*** is similar to Difference, except mid-tone values in the base color are completely desaturated.

- **Hue*** results in a color with the luminance and saturation of the base color and the hue of the blend color.

- **Saturation*** results in a color with the luminance and hue of the base color and saturation of the blend color.

- **Color*** results in a color with the luminance of the base color, and the hue and saturation of the blend color.

- **Luminosity*** results in a color with the hue and saturation of the base color, and the luminance of the blend color (basically, the opposite of the Color mode).

*To prevent problems in the output process, avoid applying these blending modes to objects with spot colors.

Options at the bottom of the Transparency panel allow you to control transparency settings relative to grouped objects. In the examples shown here, the letter and blue shape are grouped. The yellow shape at the back of the object stacking order is not part of the group. If you don't see these check boxes, choose Show Options in the panel Options menu.

Choose Show Options in the panel Options menu to show these check boxes.

If **Isolate Blending** is checked for the group, blending changes only apply to other objects in the same group. The group effectively knocks out the underlying shapes. In this example, we applied the Multiply blending to the purple letter. When Isolate Blending is checked for the group (bottom), the blending mode does not affect the underlying yellow shape.

If **Knockout Group** is checked, transparency settings for elements within the group do not apply to other elements in the same group. The transparent effects are only applied to objects under the entire group. In this case, elements within the group knock out other objects in the same group. In the images here, the opacity of the purple letter has been reduced to 50%. When Knockout Group is checked (bottom), the opacity only affects underlying objects that are not part of the group.

If **Opacity and Mask Define Knockout Shape** is checked, the mask object's opacity creates a knockout effect. Where the mask is 100% opaque, the knockout effect is strong. In areas of lower opacity, the knockout is weaker.

An opacity mask defines the transparency of selected artwork. In Illustrator, you can create an opacity mask by selecting two or more shapes and clicking the Make Mask button in the Transparency panel. The topmost selected object (or group) becomes the masking object. Underlying objects in the selection are the masked artwork.

The best way to explain the concept of opacity masks is through example. The first image shows two separate objects: the top object (the word "OK" converted to outlines) and the gradient-filled rectangle.

When you define an opacity mask, shades in the masking (top) object determine the degree of transparency in the masked (underlying) artwork.

- Where the mask is white, the masked object is 100% visible.
- Shades of gray in the mask allow some of the underlying object to be visible.
- Black areas of the mask completely obscure underlying areas.

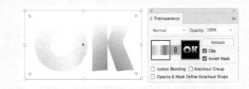

Masked artwork   Mask
thumbnail   thumbnail

When the **Invert Mask** option is checked, tones in the masking object are reversed (black becomes white and white becomes black). Transparency of the masked artwork is also effectively reversed.

When the **Clip** option is checked, the masking object also determines which parts of the masked artwork are visible; any areas outside the mask object are not visible. In this image, we turned off the Clip option to allow the gradient-filled rectangle to be visible beyond the edges of the masking lettershapes.

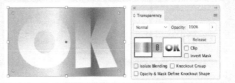

By default, the masking object and masked artwork are linked, which means you can't move one without the other. If you click the Link icon between the masked artwork and the mask thumbnails, you can move the two elements independently.

Turn off the Link option to move either object independently.

9. **With the Five object still selected, open the Blending Mode menu in the Transparency panel (Window>Transparency) and choose Multiply.**

   After changing the blending mode, the text is a blend of the original black text color and the blue gradient color of the badge object.

10. **Select the white-filled rectangle at the bottom of the Side 3 layer stack.**

11. **In the Transparency panel, change the Opacity field to 80%.**

    The Opacity value determines how much of the underlying colors show through the affected object. If an object is 80% opaque, 20% of the underlying colors are visible.

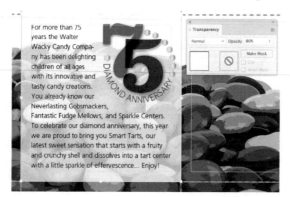

12. **Collapse the Side 3 layer in the Layers panel.**

13. **Save the file and continue to the next exercise.**

Use the Touch Type Tool

If you have completed the previous projects in this book, you've already learned a number of ways for manipulating type in an Illustrator file. As you know, you can highlight any characters and change their formatting using the Character panel options. You can also convert type to outlines, and then transform it as you would any other drawing object (using the Selection tool, Free Transform tool, etc.).

In this exercise, you learn how to use the Touch Type tool, which allows you to dynamically transform a selected character using transformation handles, all while maintaining the character as live text. This means you can simply drag in the artboard to experiment with character size and position, but still maintain the ability to edit the actual text in the type object.

1. With **candy-box.ai** open, create a new layer named **Box Top** above the Side 3 layer. Lock all other layers, and make the Box Top layer active.

2. Make the Box Top area of the artboard prominent in the document window.

3. Using the Type tool, create a new point-type object with the following text:
   alter [Return/Enter]
   Wacky

4. Format the type as 56-pt ATC Pyrite Heavy with 50-pt leading, with right paragraph alignment.

5. Position the type object so it is centered near the top of the Box Top panel area.

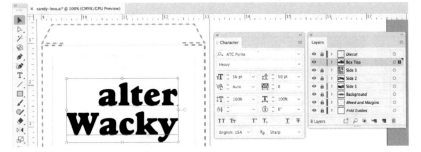

6. Choose the Touch Type tool (nested below the regular Type tool).

Note:

This tool is called the "Touch Type" tool because its options work on a touch-enabled screen.

7. **Click the W in the point-type object to select it.**

When you select a character with the Touch Type tool, you can use the resulting handles to modify the selected character in much the same way as you would transform an object that is selected with the Free Transform tool.

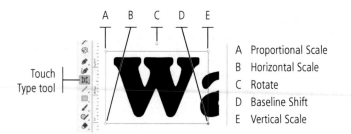

A Proportional Scale
B Horizontal Scale
C Rotate
D Baseline Shift
E Vertical Scale

Touch Type tool

8. **Click inside the character's bounding box and drag down until the bottom is slightly below the baseline of the second line.**

We aligned the top of the uppercase W with the top of the lowercase a.

Click inside the bounding box and drag to reposition the character.

Note:

You can also click the Baseline Shift handle to reposition the selected character.

9. **Click the Proportional Scale handle and drag up and left until the top of the W is higher than the tops of the letters in the first line.**

10. **Click the Horizontal Scale handle and drag right to make the scaled character slightly narrower.**

11. **Choose the Type tool in the Tools panel, then click to place the insertion point before the "a" in the second line of the type object.**

When you place the insertion point in a type object where characters have been manipulated with the Touch Type tool, it can be very helpful to use the Arrow keys to move the insertion point to the location you need.

12. **Using the Character panel, reduce the kerning between the W and the a.**

Remember, kerning adjusts the space between two specific letters. Although you modified the W with the Touch Type tool, it is still a live character, which means you can still use kerning to adjust the spacing between the characters.

13. **Continue adjusting the kerning for all letter pairs in the type object until you are satisfied with the results.**

14. **Place the insertion point at the beginning of the first line. Increase the kerning until the entire letter "a" is visible past the modified character.**

When the insertion point is at the beginning of a line, kerning moves the first character left or right relative to the end of the type path; all other letters in the line also move.

15. **Save the file and continue to the next exercise.**

Apply a Built-In Graphic Style

In addition to the numerous effects that you can apply, Illustrator includes a number of graphic style libraries, which are simply stored groups of appearance attributes that can be applied in a single click. In this exercise you will use a built-in style to create a custom logotype for the top and bottom of the box.

1. **With `candy-box.ai` open, select the logotype object (on the Box Top layer) with the Selection tool.**

2. **Move the type object to be approximately centered in the box-top panel area.**

3. **Choose Window>Graphic Style Libraries>Scribble Effects.**

   Graphic styles are managed in much the same way as swatches and other libraries.

4. **With the logotype object selected, click the top-left style in the Scribble Effects panel.**

5. **Open the Appearance panel and review the options.**

   Built-in styles are basically a combination of attributes and effects that can be applied in Illustrator. They are all nondestructive, which means the logotype object is still live text.

6. **Create another point-type object with the words Candy Company. Format the type in this object as 15-pt ATC Coral Normal, and change the type fill color to the custom pink swatch.**

7. Move the second type object until it appears as shown in the following image:

8. Select the two objects on the top panel and group them.

9. Create a new layer named **Box Bottom** above the Box Top layer.

10. Select the group on the Box Top layer. In the Layers panel, Option/Alt-click the Selected Art icon, then drag to the Box Bottom layer.

    By this point, you should realize that this clones the selected art, placing the cloned copy on the Box Bottom layer.

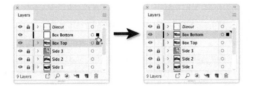

11. Lock the Box Top layer.

12. On the artboard, drag the art on the Box Bottom layer so it is centered in the box-bottom panel area.

13. Using the Layers panel, select only the logotype object in the group. Apply a 1-pt white stroke to the selected object.

    This helps the logotype to stand out from the background object.

14. Save the file and continue to the next stage of the project.

Because object opacity, blending modes, and some effects relate to transparency, you should understand what transparency is and how it affects your output. Transparency is the degree to which light passes through an object, so that objects in the background are visible. In terms of graphic design, transparency means being able to "see through" objects in front of the stacking order to objects in back of the stacking order.

Because of the way printing works, applying transparency in print graphic design is a bit of a contradiction. Commercial printing is, by definition, accomplished by overlapping a mixture of (usually) four semi-transparent inks in different percentages to reproduce a range of colors (the printable gamut). In that sense, all print graphic design requires transparency.

But *design* transparency refers to the objects on the page. The trouble is, when a halftone dot is printed, it's either there or it's not. There is no "50% opaque" setting on a printing press. This means that a transformation needs to take place behind the scenes, translating what we create on screen into what a printing press produces.

When transparent objects are output, overlapping areas of transparent elements are actually divided into individual elements (where necessary) to produce the best possible results. Ink values in the overlap areas are calculated by the application based on the capabilities of the mechanical printing process. The software converts our digital designs into the elements that are necessary to print.

Although some output devices can accurately translate transparent elements to printed elements, older equipment might have problems rendering transparency. Similarly, if the file you're creating will be placed into another layout — for example, as an ad in a magazine or newspaper — you also need to consider the capabilities of the software being used to create the larger project. Older versions of software might not be able to interpret transparent elements correctly.

For transparent elements to output properly in these workflows, the transparent elements must be converted, or **flattened**, into information that can be rendered.

The following exercises explain the concept of flattening so you will understand what to do if your file needs to work with older equipment that does not support transparent design elements.

Note:

Don't assume everyone has the most recent version of a software application or output device. For one reason or another, many professional environments still use older versions of software or older output device drivers.

Define Raster Effect Settings

Flattening means dividing transparent elements into the necessary vector and raster objects to properly output the file. In some cases, flattening results in the creation of new rasterized objects (for example, where transparent text overlaps a raster image).

If you are going to create raster objects — either manually or allowing Illustrator to manage the process — you need to be able to control the resolution of those elements. For high-quality print jobs, you should use at least 300 pixels per inch.

This white text has been set to 80% opacity.

Flattening creates raster images with the pixels altered to create the same apparent effect as the semi-transparent text. The vector outlines of the original type mask the new raster elements.

This text has a drop shadow applied.

Flattening the text object results in a separate raster object to create the drop shadow.

1. **With candy-box.ai open, choose Effect>Document Raster Effects Settings.**

2. **Review the settings in the resulting dialog box.**

   These settings, applied in the printer's original template, are already optimized for high-quality output. However, it's a good idea to check the settings when you work.

   The **Color Model** menu determines the mode that will be used for new rasterized objects (CMYK, Grayscale, or Bitmap for a document in CMYK mode; an RGB option replaces CMYK if the file uses the RGB color mode).

   The **Resolution** options include three basic settings: 72 ppi for low-resolution screen display, 150 ppi for medium-resolution desktop printers, or 300 ppi for high-resolution print output. You can also assign a custom resolution in the Other field.

   The **Background** options determine how unfilled areas of the file will be handled when placed into another file. If White is selected, underlying objects will not be visible through empty areas of the file.

   In the **Options** area:

   - **Anti-alias** helps to create smooth transitions, reducing stair-stepping around the edges of rasterized objects.

   - **Create Clipping Mask** creates a vector mask that makes the background of the rasterized image appear transparent.

   - **Add _ Around Object** creates a specific-sized border around a rasterized image. If you use the White Background option, this area will be filled with white.

   - **Preserve Spot Colors** allows spot-color objects to be maintained as spot colors instead of being converted to CMYK.

3. **Click OK to close the dialog box.**

4. **Continue to the next exercise.**

Note:

Note the warning at the bottom of the dialog box that says, "Changing these settings may affect the appearance of currently applied raster effects."

Preview Transparency Flattening

If you are designing with transparency, it's a good idea to know exactly what elements will be affected when the file is flattened for output. Illustrator provides a Flattener Preview panel that you can use to review the file for potential problems.

1. **With candy-box.ai open, choose Window>Flattener Preview.**

2. **If nothing appears in the white space of the panel, click the Refresh button.**

Drag this corner to make the panel larger, and then click Refresh to enlarge the preview image.

3. **In the Highlight menu, choose All Affected Objects.**

The red areas in the preview show all objects that are affected by transparency in the file; all of these objects will somehow be affected by flattening. You can use the Flattener Preview to highlight different kinds of areas to determine which settings are best for the entire file or for a specific object.

- **None (Color Preview)** displays the normal layout.
- **Rasterized Complex Regions** highlights areas that will be rasterized based on the Raster/Vector Balance defined in the applied preset.
- **Transparent Objects** highlights objects with opacity of less than 100%, blending modes, and/or transparency effects (such as drop shadows).
- **All Affected Objects** highlights all objects affected by transparency, including the transparent objects and the objects overlapped by transparent objects. All of these objects will be affected by flattening.
- **Affected Linked EPS Files** highlights all EPS files that are linked (not embedded) in the file.
- **Expanded Patterns** highlights patterns that will be expanded by flattening. Pattern effects must be expanded if they are affected by transparency; this takes place automatically when you output the file.
- **Outlined Strokes** highlights all strokes that will be converted to filled objects when flattened. For example, a 5-pt stroke with the Screen blending mode will be converted to a 5-pt-high rectangle filled with the underlying object when the file is flattened.

4. **In the Highlight menu, choose Transparent Objects.**

The highlighted areas reduce to only the objects where transparency is actually applied.

5. **Choose Show Options in the panel Options menu, and then click Refresh.**

The options show the specific settings that will be used to flatten the artwork, based by default on a flattener preset.

6. **Close the Flattener Preview panel, and then continue to the next exercise.**

Expanding Appearance Attributes

When you print a file, the raster-image processor (RIP) processes the PostScript stream to create the print. Extremely complex designs can take a long time to output, depending on the processing capability of the output device, and can even crash the device or cause an output error. To prevent output problems, you might want to expand appearance attributes after the design has been finalized.

If you select an object and choose Object>Expand Appearance, the object is permanently altered to mimic the appearance of applied effects. Raster effects are converted to raster objects, which are grouped with the converted vector objects.

After expanding effects, the file will output faster, but you won't be able to change the effect settings. We highly recommend saving the original and expanded versions as separate files so you can make changes if necessary.

Two effects have been applied to this object: Warp (Arch) and 3D Extrude & Bevel.

The paths show the new objects created by expanding the effects. The effects are no longer editable.

Flattening Individual Objects

Although flattening is typically managed for you when you output a file, you can also flatten selected objects manually. Flattening is a permanent action — you can no longer edit any effect or setting that caused the transparency. This process should only be done at the very end of a project. Again, we recommend maintaining your original file and saving a new version with the manually flattened artwork.

When a transparent object is selected, you can choose Object>Flatten Transparency to define settings that will be used to create the necessary raster object.

Flattening the object created a new raster object to reproduce the Drop Shadow effect. (If Preserve Alpha Transparency is not checked, the flattened artwork will have a white background; the effect will not blend into the background color.)

Understanding Flattener Presets

Illustrator includes four default flattener presets. You can also choose Edit>Transparency Flattener Presets to create your own presets or load presets that might be provided by other users, such as your output service provider.

- **Raster/Vector Balance** determines how much vector information will be preserved after flattening, from 0 (all vectors will be rasterized) to 100 (maintains all vector information).

- **Line Art and Text Resolution** defines the resulting resolution of vector elements that will be rasterized, up to 9600 ppi.

- **Gradient and Mesh Resolution** defines the resolution for gradients that will be rasterized, up to 1200 ppi.

- **Convert All Text to Outlines** converts all type to outlines. The text will not be editable or selectable in a PDF file.

- **Convert All Strokes to Outlines** converts all strokes to filled paths.

- **Clip Complex Regions** forces boundaries between vector objects and rasterized artwork to fall along object paths, reducing potential problems that can result when only part of an object is rasterized.

- **Anti-Alias Rasters** helps to create smoother edges in the raster images that are created from vector graphics.

Export a PDF File for Proofing

Although packaging such as this box is commonly printed directly from the Illustrator file, you should still create a proof that your client can review either on screen or printed. The PDF format is ideal for this use because the client doesn't need Illustrator to open or print the proof file.

1. **With `candy-box.ai` open, choose File>Save As.**

2. **Navigate to your WIP>Candy folder as the destination and choose Adobe PDF in the Format/Save As Type menu.**

3. **Click Save.**

4. **Choose High Quality Print in the Adobe PDF Preset menu.**

   The Adobe PDF Preset menu includes six PDF presets that meet common industry output requirements.

5. **Choose Acrobat 4 (PDF 1.3) in the Compatibility menu.**

   The Compatibility menu determines which version of the PDF format you will create. Not all clients will have the latest versions of technology, so you should consider saving all proof-quality PDFs to be compatible with the earliest version of PDF possible.

6. **Click Advanced in the list of options.**

   PDF 1.3 does not support transparency, so the file will require flattening. If you save the file to be compatible with PDF 1.4 or later, the transparency information will be maintained in the PDF file; it will have to be flattened later in the process.

7. Choose High Resolution in the Preset menu.

Even though this PDF is for proofing purposes, high-resolution produces better results. If file size is not a concern, it's a good idea to use the high-resolution flattener even for proofs.

8. Click Save PDF to output the file.

9. Close the PDF file, then continue to the final stage of the project.

STAGE 4 / Previewing the Box in 3D

In Stage 2, you used the 3D Extrude & Bevel feature to add depth to the banners on the front of the box. This effect can also be used to create a box shape, and preview your flat box artwork in three dimensions, which is especially useful for showing a client how the art will look when the final piece is printed and folded.

Export Artboards for Screens

As you know, the background image for the box artwork currently extends across multiple panels in the folding template. To map artwork to a 3D box mock-up, you need to cut that background image into separate pieces for each box panel. Although there are many ways to accomplish this goal, the easiest is to use artboards to define the different sides of the box.

1. Open candy-box.ai from your WIP>Candy folder. Zoom out so you can see the entire artboard.

Make sure you open the Illustrator file and not the PDF file that you created at the end of the last stage.

2. Show all layers except the Diecut and Bleed and Margins layers, then lock all layers.

3. Choose the Artboard tool in the Tools panel. Click to the right of the existing artboard and drag to create a new artboard.

If you click inside the existing artboard area, dragging will move the existing artboard instead of creating a new one. Instead, you are using the pasteboard to create the new artboard; you can then move it into the correct position overlapping the existing artboard.

4. In the Control panel, change the new artboard name to **box-top.**

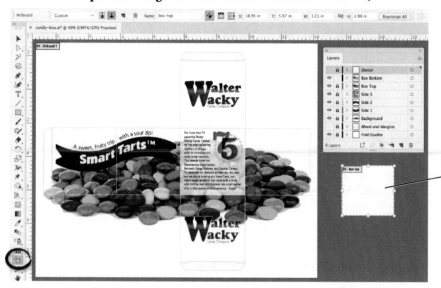

Create the new artboard away from the original one.

5. Move the Artboard tool cursor inside the new artboard area and drag it to be on top of the box top area in the layout.

Click inside the artboard boundary and drag to reposition it.

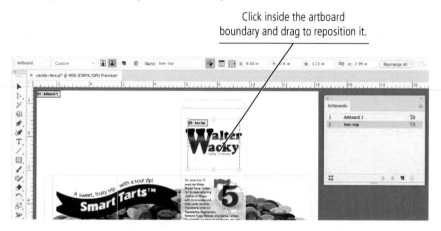

6. Drag the artboard corner handles to snap to the guides that mark the box top area in the layout.

After adjusting the handles, the box-top artboard should be 4″ wide × 4″ high.

Snap the artboard edges to the guides that mark the box panel sides.

The artboard should be 4″ wide and 4″ high.

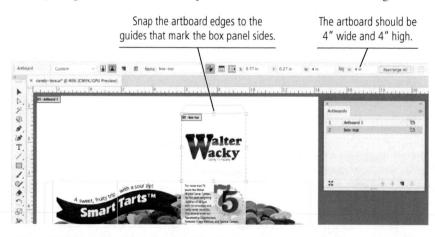

7. **In the Control panel, turn off the Move/Copy Artwork with Artboard option.**

8. **Click the box-top artboard and hold down the mouse button, then press Option/Alt-Shift and drag down to clone the artboard. Place the cloned artboard over the box-bottom area of the layout.**

Clone the artboard and position it over the box-bottom panel.

Move/Copy Artwork with Artboard is toggled off.

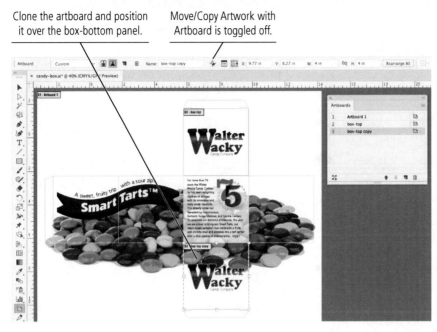

9. **Change the selected artboard's name to box-bottom.**

10. **Using the same general process outlined in the previous steps, create new artboards for the remaining four sides of the box. Use the names shown in the following image.**

   You can draw new artboards, or simply clone the existing ones and drag them into place for each side of the box.

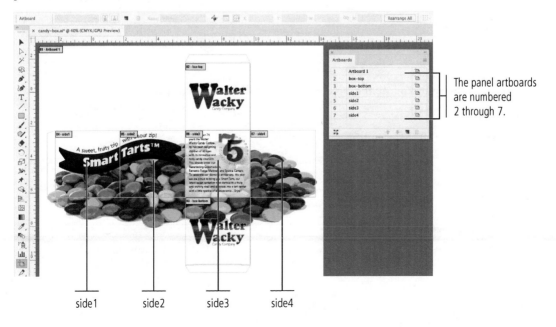

The panel artboards are numbered 2 through 7.

side1   side2   side3   side4

11. **Choose File>Export>Export As.**

12. **In the resulting dialog box, create a new folder named side-panels in your WIP>Candy folder.**

13. **Choose JPEG in the Format/Save As Type menu.**

Illustrator can export a number of different formats. The JPEG format creates a single flat file with a white background for each artboard you choose to export.

14. **At the bottom of the Export dialog box, choose the Use Artboards option. Choose the Range radio button, and type 2-7 in the attached field.**

You do not need to export the overall artboard with the diecut layout (Artboard 1). You need to export each of the artboards you just created as a separate file, which you will later use to create the 3D box preview.

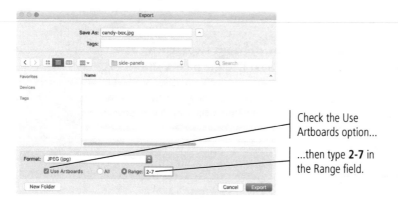

Check the Use Artboards option...

...then type **2-7** in the Range field.

15. **Click Export. In the resulting dialog box, define the following settings:**

Color Model:	**CMYK**
Quality:	**10 (Maximum)**
Resolution:	**High (300 ppi)**

16. **Click OK to export the necessary files.**

17. **When the export process is complete, save and close the candy-box.ai file.**

18. **On your desktop, review the contents of your WIP>Candy folder.**

Six new files, one for each side of the box, should appear in the side-panels folder. The file names are made up of the original file name (which appeared in the Save As field of the Export dialog box) and the artboard name (which you defined earlier).

19. **Continue to the next exercise.**

Create Symbols for Box Panels

For this process to work, you first have to do a bit of setup work. The artwork for each panel has to be saved as a symbol before it can be applied to the 3D box shape. This means you have to do some cutting and cleanup work so that you have the exact shapes you need before you create the 3D box preview.

1. **Create a new file for print that uses Inches for the unit of measurement and contains two letter-sized artboards. Save it as box-folded.ai in your WIP>Candy folder.**

2. **Choose File>Place. Navigate to your WIP>Candy>side-panels folder. Select all six images in the folder. Make sure none of the options at the bottom of the box are checked, then click Place.**

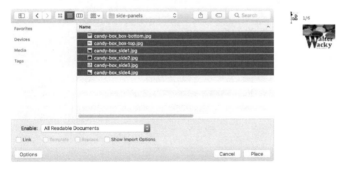

3. **When the images are loaded into the Place cursor, click to place each loaded image onto the artboard.**

Don't worry if all the files don't fit into the artboard. You are only using them to create symbols, after which you will delete the original images from the artboard.

4. **Open the Symbols panel (Window>Symbols) and float it away from the panel dock if necessary.**

5. **Open the panel's Options menu and choose Large List View so you can see the symbol names.**

6. **Open the Symbols panel Options menu and choose Select All Unused.**

7. **With all the default symbols selected, click the panel's Delete button. Click Yes when asked to confirm the deletion.**

Although this is not strictly necessary, removing the unnecessary pieces makes it easier to manage the remaining symbols.

8. **Select the box-bottom image on the artboard, then click the New Symbol button in the Symbols panel.**

The Control panel shows which image is selected.

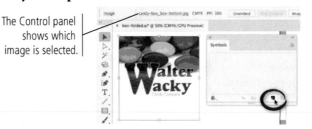

9. **In the resulting dialog box, name the symbol box-bottom and click OK.**

The other options in this dialog box have no effect on this project, so you can leave them at the default settings.

10. **Repeat Steps 8–9 for the remaining five images on the artboard, naming each symbol appropriately.**

11. **Select all of the placed images on the artboard and delete them.**

12. **Save the file and continue to the next exercise.**

Map the Art to a 3D Box

Now that you have symbols for each side of the box, you have to create a shape that you can turn into a three-dimensional box. This shape needs to be the correct size for the existing artwork, so you will again use the panel folding guides to build the shape.

1. **With box-folded.ai open, use the Rectangle tool to create a shape that is 4″ wide by 4″ high, with a white fill and no stroke.**

Each panel on the box template is 4″ square. A shape of this size will be the basis for your three-dimensional box sample.

2. **With the new rectangle selected, choose Effect>3D>Extrude & Bevel. Make sure the Preview option is checked.**

3. **In the Extrude Depth field, type 4" and press Tab to apply the change.**

Because the shape is 4" square, you are using this measurement as the depth to create a cube with equal height, width, and depth. Illustrator automatically makes the necessary conversion to points.

4. **Define the following parameters in the Position area:**

X axis:	**70°**
Y axis:	**40°**
Z axis:	**-13°**

5. **Uncheck the Preview box, and then click the Map Art button.**

When the Map Art dialog box is open, the object in the layout displays as a 3D wireframe preview, even when the Preview option is unchecked. The red line around the preview shows which side (surface) of the shape is being mapped.

The red line indicates the side where art is being mapped.

Use this menu to choose which symbol to place on the active surface.

Use these options to navigate the surfaces that can have mapped art.

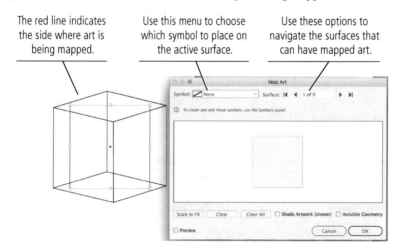

6. **Choose box-top in the Symbol menu, then turn on the Preview option in the Map Art dialog box.**

Illustrator renders a preview of the symbol on the 3D box shape (this might take a few seconds to complete).

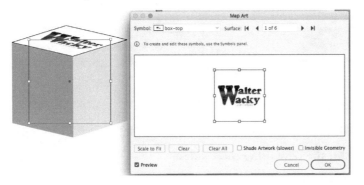

7. **Click the right Next Surface arrow, then choose box-bottom in the Symbol menu.**

The preview shows the box-bottom panel is selected. No other change is apparent because the bottom of the box is not visible using the existing shape position.

The box-bottom surface is not visible in this position.

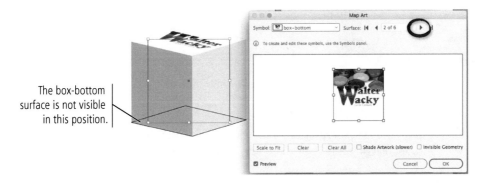

8. **Click the right Surface arrow to select the next side, then choose side4 in the Symbol menu.**

The thumbnail is placed in the wrong orientation, so you need to rotate it. You can click an object in the Map Art preview and drag to move the symbol artwork, or you can use the bounding-box handles to resize or rotate the symbol until it fits the gray surface shape.

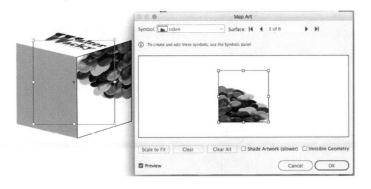

Note:

Rendering 3D artwork takes time and must be redone every time you make a change in the dialog box. If you prefer, you can turn off the Preview option while you're making changes, and then turn it on only when you want to review your progress.

9. **Place the cursor near one of the top corner handles. Click when you see the rotate cursor, press Shift, and drag around to rotate the artwork 180°.**

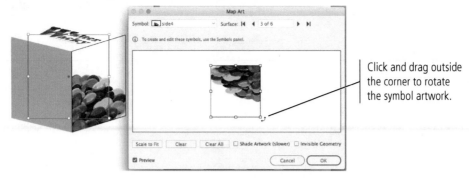

Click and drag outside the corner to rotate the symbol artwork.

10. **Repeat Steps 8–9 to add the artwork for the remaining three sides.**

Make sure you place the symbols in the correct order. Because the side4 artwork is on the first side panel, you should place side3 on the next panel, then side2, then side1.

You won't see any difference in the artboard for surfaces 5 and 6 because they are not visible in this position. You will create another object to show those sides in the next few steps.

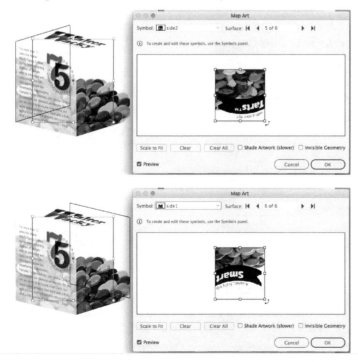

11. Click OK to close the Map Art dialog box, and then click OK again to finalize the 3D box preview.

12. Using the Selection tool, clone the existing shape and place the clone on the second artboard.

13. In the Appearance panel, click the 3D Extrude & Bevel hot-text link to open the dialog box for that effect.

14. Check the Preview option at the bottom of the dialog box. In the preview proxy, place the cursor over one of the vertical lines and drag until the other two sides of the box are visible.

Dragging one of the vertical lines in the proxy changes only the Z rotation.

15. Click OK to apply the change.

16. Save the file and close it.

PROJECT REVIEW

1. You can use the _____ tool to sample colors from placed images.

2. The _____ can be used to review all the available characters in a font.

3. Checking the _____ option when you place a native Photoshop file results in a single object on a single layer in the Illustrator file.

4. The _____ determines the left-indent position of type on a path.

5. You can use the _____ panel to review and edit applied effects.

6. Applying a _____ to an object forces surrounding text to flow around that object instead of directly in front of or behind it.

7. The _____ is the specific method used to blend the color of one object into the colors of underlying objects.

8. _____ refers to the degree to which light passes through an object.

9. A(n) _____ can be used to restrict opacity to selected objects; colors in the topmost object determine which areas of the underlying object are visible.

10. The _____ effect can be used to preview a box 3D shape.

1. Briefly explain how the concept of a diecut relates to package design in Illustrator.

2. Briefly explain the concept of sublayers, including at least one example of their potential benefit.

3. Briefly explain how transparency settings relate to Illustrator files created for commercial printing.

PORTFOLIO BUILDER PROJECT

Use what you have learned in this project to complete the following freeform exercise.
Carefully read the art director and client comments, then create your own design to meet the needs of the project.
Use the space below to sketch ideas. When finished, write a brief explanation of the reasoning behind your final design.

art director comments

You have been hired to create a label design for a new energy water called triUMPH. It is going to be marketed throughout the United States, so it must incorporate the required elements for food packaging and retail sales.

❑ Use the label template that has been provided in the **Triumph_AI19_PB.zip** archive on the Student Files web page.

❑ Create a compelling type treatment for the product name. Find or create imagery as necessary to support the overall package design.

❑ Include the nutrition information and the barcode that have been provided by the client. Also include the package size (16.9 FL OZ/500 mL) somewhere in the label design.

❑ Include the "Recycle" logo in the design.

❑ Include the following text in the design:
ME-HI-5¢ CA CRV

client comments

The energy drink market is huge in the United States, so we've decided to branch out from our traditional soda manufacturing. We need you to create an energetic logotype for the new product, as well as a complete label design for the bottles.

Our printing company has provided us with a template that is standard for this type of packaging. The pressroom manager wanted me to make sure to remind you to keep important design elements away from the glue area that is indicated on the template.

Because this is a consumable product, there are a lot of elements that must be incorporated in the package design. Make sure nothing important is left out, or we won't be able to meet our ship date.

project justification

PROJECT SUMMARY

The flexible artboard size and layer controls, coupled with the extensive set of creative tools, make Illustrator ideally suited to meet the complex needs of packaging design. You can design sophisticated artwork that can be wrapped or folded into virtually any shape to package virtually any product.

This project combined the technical requirements of packaging design — specifically using a custom diecut template supplied by the output provider — with the artistic capabilities necessary to create the final design for a custom candy package. You composited a number of existing elements and created others, then used a number of features to modify artwork, adding interest and depth to unify the different pieces into a single, cohesive design.

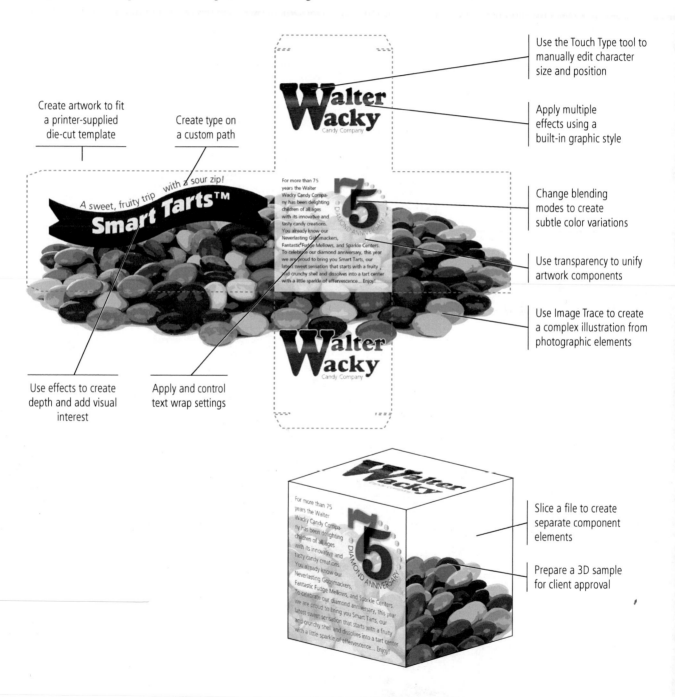

Create artwork to fit a printer-supplied die-cut template

Create type on a custom path

Use the Touch Type tool to manually edit character size and position

Apply multiple effects using a built-in graphic style

Change blending modes to create subtle color variations

Use transparency to unify artwork components

Use Image Trace to create a complex illustration from photographic elements

Use effects to create depth and add visual interest

Apply and control text wrap settings

Slice a file to create separate component elements

Prepare a 3D sample for client approval

Consumer Infographics

7

As the illustrator for a magazine publisher, it's your job to create interesting graphics for articles in a variety of magazines. Next month's feature article is about trends in the food and beverage industry. You need to create several graphs and one illustration to accompany the article.

This project incorporates the following skills:

- ❏ Creating graphs to present data in a visual format
- ❏ Editing graph data to change the appearance of a graph
- ❏ Importing data from an external file
- ❏ Managing fills, legends, and labels to make graphs more visually appealing
- ❏ Defining a perspective grid
- ❏ Putting objects into the correct perspective

One feature article in next month's trade magazine for the food and beverage industry is about trends in coffee production and drinking.

We need three different graphs:

- Historical coffee pricing data
- Coffee-drinking habits as reported by consumers (from a long-term survey)
- Coffee preferences (from the same survey)

This is a general interest consumer magazine and not a cut-and-dry financial report. I'd like something more than just a set of plain graphs. I'd like you to put the graphs into some kind of context, or overall illustration, to make the presentation more interesting.

Finally, we want some kind of illustration showing the seven top coffee producing countries in the world. I don't want just a boring table of numbers.

Before you start creating the graphs, you should evaluate the kinds of data you have; that way, you can determine which type of graph will best suit the data. Illustrator's graphing tools support many graph types, but you probably won't need more than a few. Bars and pies are the most common types, but the others have important uses, too.

You might want to look at some other consumer and personal financial magazines to see how different kinds of graphs and charts are typically used, and how they are incorporated into illustrations to make the data appear more attractive and interesting.

I sketched a "coffee dispenser" idea that I think will be a good container for the final illustration. I already put it into an Illustrator file and created the pieces I want you to use in the perspective artwork.

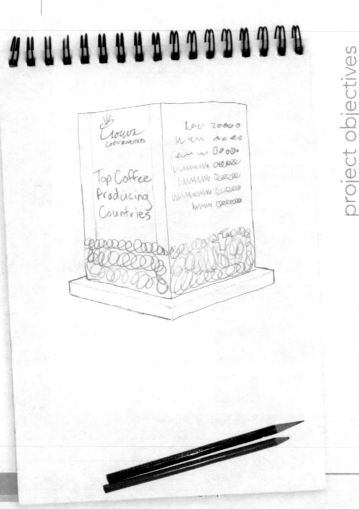

To complete this project, you will:

- ❏ Create line, bar, and pie graphs to present different types of data
- ❏ Edit live graph data to change the segment breakdown in a graph
- ❏ Import data from an external file to create a graph
- ❏ Edit fills, legends, and labels to create aesthetically pleasing, technically accurate graphs
- ❏ Create a perspective grid for complex, three-dimensional artwork
- ❏ Draw new objects on different perspective planes
- ❏ Move and transform perspective objects
- ❏ Create type objects in perspective
- ❏ Place existing artwork and symbols in perspective

STAGE 1 / Creating Charts and Graphs

The first stage of this project revolves around one of the more powerful, but least-used functions in Illustrator — the ability to generate graphics based on data. Information graphics (referred to as "infographics") are illustrations that deliver information; bar graphs, pie charts, and area charts are all examples of information provided in a visual format that makes it easier to understand.

Successfully designing infographics requires knowing which kind of chart best shows which type of information. Once you know what kind of chart you need, Illustrator provides the tools to generate the chart.

Distinguishing Types of Graphs

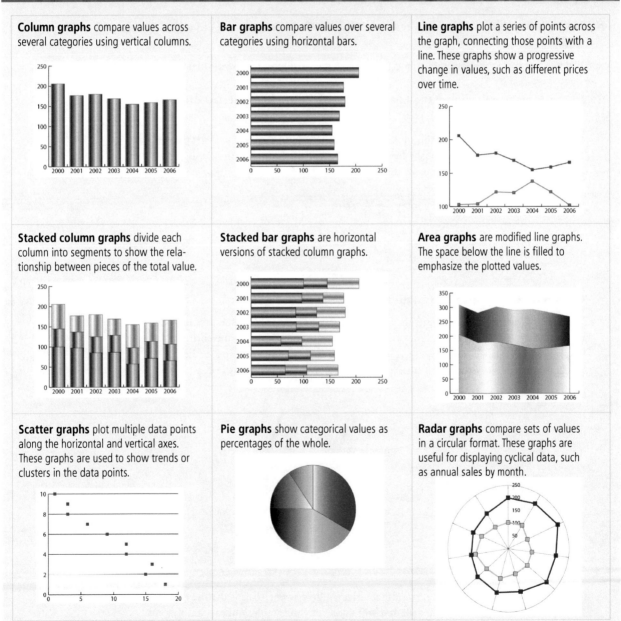

Column graphs compare values across several categories using vertical columns.

Bar graphs compare values over several categories using horizontal bars.

Line graphs plot a series of points across the graph, connecting those points with a line. These graphs show a progressive change in values, such as different prices over time.

Stacked column graphs divide each column into segments to show the relationship between pieces of the total value.

Stacked bar graphs are horizontal versions of stacked column graphs.

Area graphs are modified line graphs. The space below the line is filled to emphasize the plotted values.

Scatter graphs plot multiple data points along the horizontal and vertical axes. These graphs are used to show trends or clusters in the data points.

Pie graphs show categorical values as percentages of the whole.

Radar graphs compare sets of values in a circular format. These graphs are useful for displaying cyclical data, such as annual sales by month.

Create a Line Graph

The first graph for this project is based on historical data of coffee prices. Because this data tracks a change in value over time, a line graph is the best way to represent this information visually.

1. Download **Coffee_AI19_RF.zip** from the Student Files web page.

2. Expand the ZIP archive in your WIP folder (Macintosh) or copy the archive contents into your WIP folder (Windows).

   This results in a folder named **Coffee**, which contains the files you need for this project. You should also use this folder to save the files you create in this project.

3. Create a new file by opening the file **chalkboard.ait** in your WIP>Coffee folder.

   You will use this artwork as the "frame" for each of the graphs you build in this project.

4. In the Tools panel, choose the Line Graph tool (it might be nested under one of the other graph tools).

   When you choose a specific graph tool, it becomes the default tool in the Tools panel. Depending on what was previously done in your version of the application, your default graph tool might be different than ours.

5. Click and drag an area that snaps to the guides on the artboard.

   The size you define here represents the size of the graph shape only; it does not include the legend or axis labels. If you know the amount of space available for the entire graph (including labels and legend), you should define a smaller graph size so the labels and legend fit within the available space.

Note:

If you click once with a graph tool, a dialog box opens where you can define the height and width of the new graph, just as when you single-click with one of the basic drawing tools.

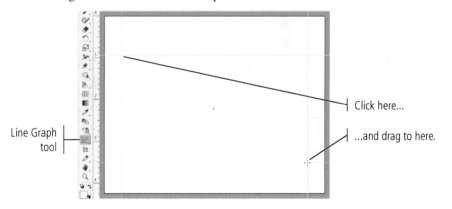

Line Graph tool

Click here...

...and drag to here.

When you create a new graph, a spreadsheet-like window opens. This is the Illustrator Data panel, where you enter the data that will make up your graph. You can simply type in the various data cells, but many graphing projects will involve importing data from an external file, as you will do in this project.

6. **In the Data panel, click the Import Data button. Navigate to the file prices.txt in the WIP>Coffee>Data folder and click Open.**

This data was originally a Microsoft Excel file, but it was exported as a tab-delimited text-only file. You cannot directly import an Excel file into Illustrator; if you try, you will see either an error message or incomprehensible data that is useless for making a graph.

Import Data button

7. **Click the Apply button in the Data panel.**

As you can see, there is clearly a problem in the resulting graph. The imported data has two columns of numbers, but the first column actually shows the years associated with the data in the second column. By default, Illustrator's Data panel treats all numbers as parts of the data. In cases like this — when you want certain numbers to be treated as regular text, rather than actual data — you have to enclose those numbers within quotes in the Data panel.

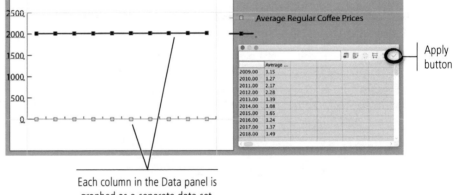

Each column in the Data panel is graphed as a separate data set.

Apply button

8. **Click the 2009.00 cell in the Data panel to select it.**

9. **In the text field at the top of the panel, add quote characters on both sides of the number.**

You can't use the arrow keys on your keyboard to move the insertion point within the Data panel text field. You have to click in the appropriate location to add a new character.

Enclosing the years in quotation marks enables Illustrator to properly translate the numbers as data labels.

Note:

Unlike traditional spreadsheet applications, you can't drag data cells to a new location in the panel. You can, however, cut cells and paste them into a new position if you need to add new data between existing data.

10. Press Return/Enter to highlight the next cell down, and then add quote characters around the 2010 text.

Pressing Tab moves to the next cell in the row. Pressing Return/Enter moves to the next cell down in the column. You can also use the arrow keys to move through the cells.

11. Repeat this process for all years in the table, then click the Apply button at the top of the Data panel.

Unfortunately, there is no way to speed up this process. You simply have to type the quotes for each year in the data.

After clicking apply, you can see the effects of revising the graph data. Because the first column is now treated as labels, the graph has only one data set (one line).

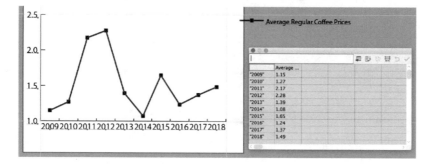

Note:

Pressing the Enter key on your numeric keypad has the same effect as clicking the Apply button.

12. Click the Cell Style button at the top of the Data panel. In the resulting dialog box, change the Number of Decimals field to 3, then click OK.

By default, the Illustrator Data panel shows the first two decimal points in the imported data. The Number of Decimals option changes the number of digits that are visible after the decimal point. If the data does not include as many decimals as you allow, Illustrator adds zeros at the end of the existing values.

Note:

The Column Width field can be changed to make longer data points visible in the Data panel cells.

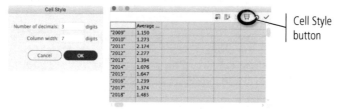

13. Click the Data panel Close button to close the panel. When asked if you want to save changes to the data, click Save/Yes.

Adding the extra decimal is technically a change, even though you won't see a significant change in the actual graph.

14. Save the file as price-graph.ai in your WIP>Coffee folder and then continue to the next exercise.

Change Graph Formatting Options

When you create a graph in Illustrator, all of the elements within the graph are grouped together in a special graph object. If you ungroup the graph, the data is no longer editable, which means you can no longer replot data points in the graph design. As a general rule, you should maintain a graph object as a graph object as long as possible in case you need to change some aspect of the graph data, which happens far more often than you might expect.

1. **With price-graph.ai open, click any part of the graph object with the Selection tool.**

2. **In the Character panel, change the character formatting to 9-pt ATC Onyx Normal with 90% horizontal scale.**

   Type objects in a graph object are originally formatted with Illustrator's default type settings. When a graph object is selected, changes to type formatting options apply to all type elements within the graph object.

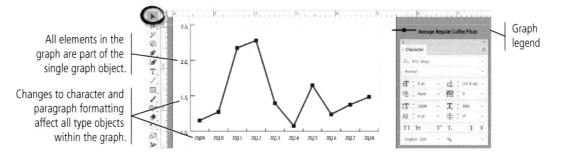

All elements in the graph are part of the single graph object.

Changes to character and paragraph formatting affect all type objects within the graph.

Graph legend

3. **Control/right-click the graph and choose Type in the contextual menu.**

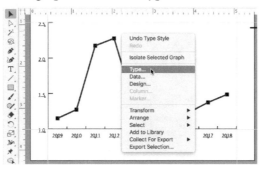

4. **Choose Value Axis in the menu at the top of the resulting dialog box.**

   This dialog box has different options depending on the type of graph you are creating. The value axis (in this case, the vertical axis on the left) is the one that marks the range of values that are depicted in the data. The current axis labels are automatically generated based on the data in the table. This graph shows prices in dollars, so you are going to change the axis labels to more accurately reflect those prices.

5. **Choose Full Width in the Tick Marks Length menu.**

   By default, tick marks are short lines on the inside of the graph area. You can choose Full Width to extend the tick marks across the full width of the graph, or you can choose None to turn off the value axis divisions.

6. **In the Add Labels area, type $ in the Prefix field and type 0 [zero] in the Suffix field.**

   The prefix will be added before the existing axis labels; the suffix will be added at the end of the existing axis labels.

Note:

You can access the same graph-editing options in the Object>Graph submenu.

Note:

Unfortunately, the Graph Type dialog box does not include a Preview check box. You can't see the results of your choices until you click OK. As long as the graph object remains a graph object, you can always make changes.

7. **Choose Category Axis in the top menu and change the corresponding Tick Marks Length menu to None.**

   By default, categories are separated by tick marks (just as values are).

Note:

If you are including divisions in your graph, you can add subdivisions using the Draw _ Tick Marks Per Division option.

8. **Click OK to apply your changes.**

The value labels now include the prefix and suffix, clearly showing that they are prices.

Value-axis tick marks now extend the full width of the graph.

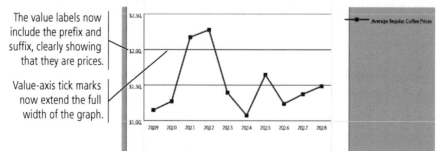

9. **Save the file and continue to the next exercise.**

Transform Graph Objects and Graph Components

The special nature of a graph object makes changing the individual elements a bit tricky, but you can change the formatting of various pieces within the graph as long as you understand how to access them.

You cannot resize a graph object by dragging bounding-box handles or using the Transform panel. You can, however, use the transformation tools (Scale, Rotate, Reflect, and Shear) or the transformation dialog boxes that are available in the Object>Transform submenu. You can also use the Direct Selection tool to access and edit individual elements within a graph.

1. **With `price-graph.ai` open, use the Selection tool to select the graph object on the artboard.**

   Remember, the Selection tool selects entire objects.

2. **With the graph object selected on the artboard, double-click the Scale tool in the Tools panel.**

   Double-clicking a transformation tool opens the related dialog box, where you can numerically define the transformation. This is the same dialog box you would access by choosing Object>Transform>Scale; double-clicking the tool provides a faster method for accessing the dialog box.

3. **Choose the Uniform Scale option and type 90% in the field.**

Scale tool

Use the Uniform scaling option.

4. **Click OK to return to finalize the change.**

   Transformations applied to a graph object apply to every element of the graph, including the type. By reducing the graph size to 90%, you also changed the type to 90% of the 9 pt you defined in the previous exercise.

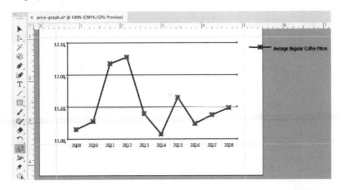

5. **Choose the Selection tool again. With the graph object selected, change the type size back to 9 pt.**

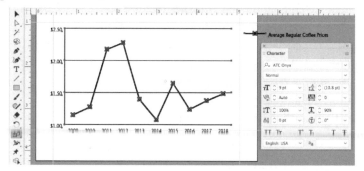

6. **With the graph object still selected, use the arrow keys to nudge the graph until it fits entirely within the guides.**

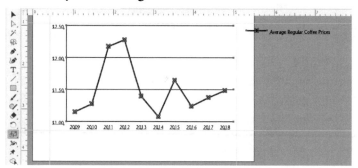

7. **Choose the Direct Selection tool in the Tools panel.**

The Direct Selection tool is the key to changing individual elements within a graph. You can't double-click to "enter into" the graph, as you can with a regular group. The Direct Selection tool can be used to select the individual components of a graph.

8. **Drag a selection marquee that selects only the three legend objects (including the type object).**

Make sure your selection marquee selects all anchor points of all three objects.

When the first row of your data defines labels for each column, the graph automatically includes a legend with a marker of the assigned color and the related label.

9. **Using the Direct Selection tool, drag the legend objects entirely outside the artboard area.**

Because this graph has only a single line, you don't really need a legend. However, you can't delete the legend icon objects because they are technically part of the graph object.

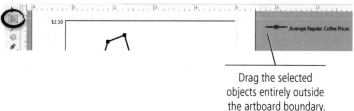

Drag the selected objects entirely outside the artboard boundary.

Anything entirely outside the artboard area is excluded when an Illustrator file is placed into another file. This technique effectively removes the legend icon, without breaking apart the graph.

10. **Save the file and continue to the next exercise.**

Note:

In a later exercise, you will add a title to the graph using a type object that is built into the template file.

Format Graph Markers

Rather than using plain squares to mark data points on a graph, you can use any existing artwork in place of the default data-point markers. In this exercise, you will use artwork provided in the template to plot data on your line graph.

1. **With `price-graph.ai` open, use the Direct Selection tool to select the first square on the data line.**

    Be careful when you use the Direct Selection tool to select these small squares. You have to click the fill to select the entire object instead of an individual anchor point on the shape. It can be helpful to zoom in to complete this part of the project.

     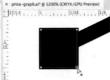

    Click inside the shape's fill to select the entire object.

    Make sure you don't select only one point of the shape.

2. **Double-click the Scale tool to open the Scale dialog box. Change the Uniform Scale field to `300%`, then click OK.**

    When you replace the default markers with custom artwork, the artwork defaults to the same size as the marker it is replacing. You are enlarging the markers now so that the custom markers will be more easily distinguishable on the graph.

    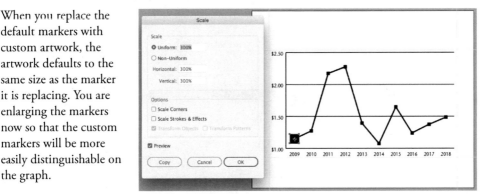

3. **Press Command/Control to access the Direct Selection tool, and click to select the second square on the line.**

4. **Release the Command/Control key, then double-click the Scale tool to reopen the Scale dialog box.**

5. **With the Scale Uniform field still set to 300%, click OK to apply the change to the second data point.**

    You might have noticed that the dialog box remembers the last-used settings when it is reopened. These steps provide a faster method of accomplishing the repetitive task of scaling each graph marker.

    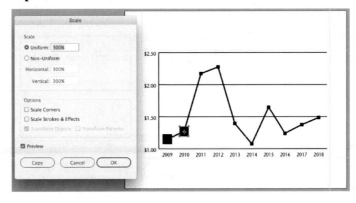

> **Note:**
>
> *Unfortunately the Transform Again command does not work correctly on graph markers.*

6. **Repeat Steps 3–5 for each data point on the line.**

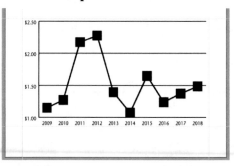

7. **Choose the Selection tool, then click away from the graph to deselect it.**

8. **Show the Design Elements layer. Using the Selection tool, click to select the small coffee cup artwork to the right of the artboard.**

   You want to select the entire group, so you need to use the Selection tool and not the Direct Selection tool.

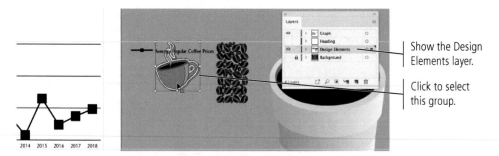

Show the Design Elements layer.

Click to select this group.

9. **With the artwork selected, choose Object>Graph>Design.**

   Nothing appears in the Graph Design dialog box until you intentionally define one or more designs.

10. **Click New Design in the Graph Design dialog box.**

   The artwork that was selected is added to the list of available graph designs.

11. Click Rename. Type `Coffee Cup` in the dialog box and click OK, then click OK to close the Graph Design dialog box.

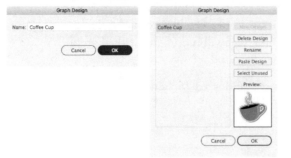

12. Using the Selection tool, click to select the graph object. Control/right-click the selected graph object on the artboard and choose Marker in the contextual menu.

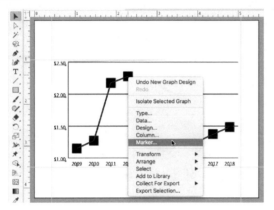

13. Choose Coffee Cup in the Graph Marker dialog box, then click OK.

The selected design replaces the squares that mark data points on the graph. The design you choose as the marker is the same size as the original square.

Remember, you have to use the Direct Selection tool to select individual pieces of a graph (including the markers). If you tried to select the cup artwork instances after they become the graph markers, you would only be able to select individual elements that make up the cup artwork instead of the entire marker instance. Scaling the markers before defining the design works around this problem.

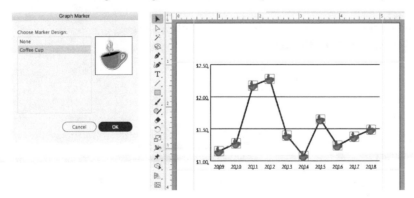

14. Save the file and continue to the next exercise.

Unify Template and Graph Elements

For all intents and purposes, your line graph is complete. However, the provided template includes a background image reminiscent of a chalkboard menu that you might see at a local coffee shop. In this exercise, you will modify individual graph elements to appear clearly on the provided background.

1. **With price-graph.ai open, make sure guides are locked (in the View>Guides submenu).**

2. **Deselect the entire graph object and then use the Direct Selection tool to click and drag a marquee around the vertical line at the left side of the graph.**

   It can be helpful to zoom in to the line to make this selection, so that you select exactly (and only) the elements you want. Make sure none of the type objects are selected.

   Because you dragged the marquee, you also selected the left endpoints of the four horizontal tick-mark lines; those lines are now also selected.

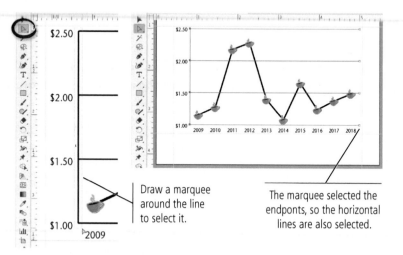

Draw a marquee around the line to select it.

The marquee selected the endponts, so the horizontal lines are also selected.

3. **Use any method you prefer to change the color of the selected lines to 0.5 pt using 20% black as the stroke color.**

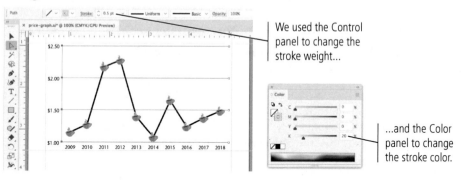

We used the Control panel to change the stroke weight...

...and the Color panel to change the stroke color.

4. **Repeat this process to select the type objects on the left and bottom edges of the graph, then change the type fill color to white.**

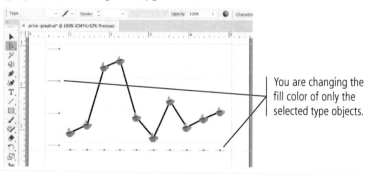

You are changing the fill color of only the selected type objects.

5. **Using the Direct Selection tool, click to select the first connecting line on the graph. Press Shift and click the other connecting lines to add them to the selection.**

6. **Use any method you prefer to change the selected lines to 1.5 pt using white as the stroke color.**

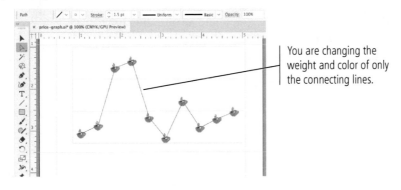

You are changing the weight and color of only the connecting lines.

7. **Click away from the graph to deselect everything.**

8. **In the Layers panel, delete the Design Elements layer, then show the Background and Heading layers.**

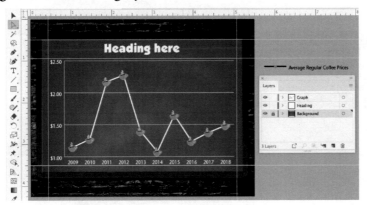

9. **Click the Heading layer to make it active.**

10. **Using the Type tool, replace the placeholder text on the Heading layer with the text from the graph legend.**

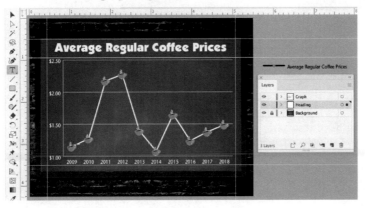

11. **Save the file and close it.**

Create a Bar Graph

The second required graph is based on data from a survey that asked 500 people why they drink coffee. Respondents were allowed to select one or more answers. Because this data shows a comparison of values for different categories, a bar graph will accurately represent the data.

Orientation is the only real difference between a bar graph and a column graph. Bbar graphs represent each data set as a horizontal bar, while column graphs use vertical columns. Because the chalkboard you're using as a background is horizontally oriented, a bar graph is more appropriate for this project.

1. **Create a new file by opening chalkboard.ait from the WIP>Coffee folder. Choose the Bar Graph tool in the Tools panel.**

2. **Click and drag an area that snaps to the guides on the artboard.**

3. **Click the Import Data button in the Data panel. Navigate to reasons.txt in your WIP>Coffee>Data folder and click Open.**

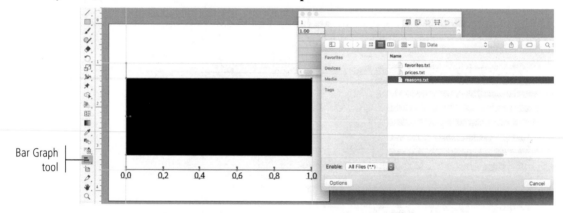

4. **Click the Apply button in the Data panel to generate the graph.**

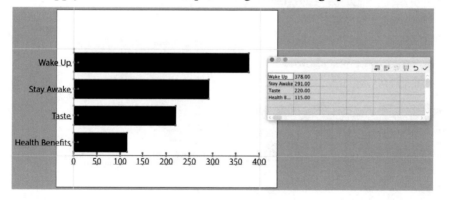

5. **Close the Data panel, clicking Save if asked.**

6. **Double-click the Scale tool. Change the Scale Uniform field to 90%, then click OK.**

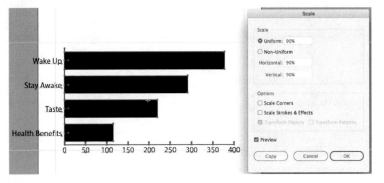

7. **With the graph object selected, change the type formatting to 9-pt ATC Onyx Normal with 90% Horizontal Scale.**

8. **Choose the Selection tool, then nudge the graph object as necessary until it fits inside the sign area (excluding the category labels on the left).**

9. **Control/right-click the graph object with the Selection tool and choose Type in the contextual menu.**

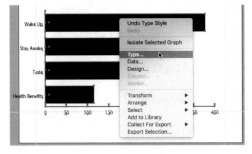

10. **Choose Value Axis in the Graph Options menu. Check the Override Calculated Values box, then type 4 in the Divisions field.**

For bar graphs, Illustrator uses a range, beginning with 0 and extending in increments as necessary, to show all of the defined data. You can use the Min and Max fields to define the values of a specific axis, such as always extending to 100 instead of ending at 70, or any other lower value.

The Divisions field determines how many labels are added to the value axis (the horizontal axis for this bar graph). The number of labels will always be one more than the number of divisions you define.

11. **Choose None in the Tick Marks Length menu.**

12. **Choose Category Axis in the Graph Options menu, and choose none in the Tick Marks Length field.**

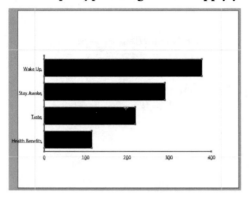

13. **Click OK to close the Graph Type dialog box and apply your changes.**

14. **Save the file as reasons-graph.ai in your WIP>Coffee folder, then continue to the next exercise.**

Define Graph Column Graphics

When you created the line graph, you defined a graph design object to use in place of the data markers. Those markers can be applied to any graph that plots individual data points (line, scatter, and radar). You can use a similar technique to apply custom graphics as the fill for bar and column graphs, as you will do in this exercise.

1. **With reasons-graph.ai open, use the Layers panel to show the Design Elements layer.**

2. **Using the Selection tool, click to select the coffee-bean artwork, then choose Object>Graph>Design.**

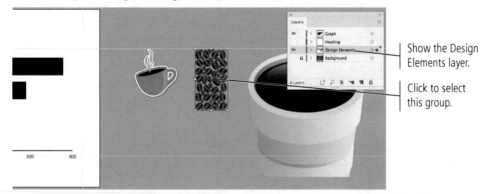

Show the Design Elements layer.

Click to select this group.

3. **Click New Design in the Graph Design dialog box.**

   This is the same process you used to define an available graphic for the data markers. You have to define the graphic first before you can apply it to the fills on a bar or column graph.

4. **Click the Rename button, then type** `Coffee Beans` **in the Graph Design field. Click OK to return to the primary Graph Design dialog box.**

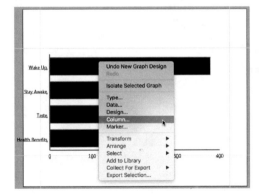

5. **Click OK to return to the artboard.**

6. **Using the Selection tool, click to select the graph. Control/right-click the selected graph on the artboard and choose Column in the contextual menu.**

7. **In the Graph Column dialog box, choose Coffee Beans in the list of designs.**

8. **Make the following choices in the lower half of the dialog box:**

Column Type:	Repeating
Each Design Represents:	50
For Fractions:	Chop Design

The Column Type menu determines how the graph will be extended across the length of the bar or height of the column.

- **Vertically Scaled** stretches a single instance of the graphic across the length of the entire column. The graphic is distorted to exactly fit the space defined by the bar or column.

- **Uniformly Scaled** places a single instance of the graphic, scaled as necessary to fit proportionally across the entire height of the bar or length of the column. Although the graphics are not distorted, the scaling can enlarge individual bars so that they overlap other bars.

- **Repeating** creates a pattern from the graphic, based on additional settings defined below the Column Type menu:

  - **Each Design Represents** determines the amount of space that will be occupied by each instance of the graphic.

  - **For Fractions** determines how the last instance of the graphic will appear in the column. If you choose Scale Design, the last instance will be disproportionally scaled to fit into the space defined by the bar or column. You can choose Chop Design to simply cut off the unscaled graphic at the end of the bar or column.

- **Sliding** places a single instance of the graphic in the bar or column. The ends of the graphic are not affected. The middle is stretched or compressed to fit the defined space.

9. **Click OK to apply your choices and return to the artboard.**

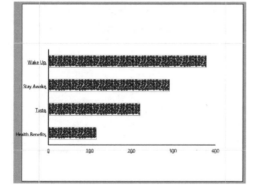

10. **Delete the Design Elements layer from the file,**

11. **Save the file and continue to the next exercise.**

Edit Graph Data

As long as you maintain a graph object without ungrouping it, you can edit both the parameters and the data that make up the graph. Any changes in the data are automatically reflected in the graph object on the artboard.

1. **With reasons-graph.ai open, select the graph object with the Selection tool.**

2. **Control/right-click the graph object and choose Data in the contextual menu.**

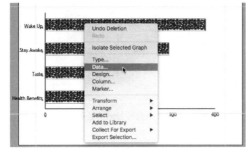

3. **Click the cell below the "Health Benefits" cell and type Social Experience.**

4. **Press Tab to highlight the cell to the right and type 215.**

5. **Click the Apply button in the Data panel.**

   The graph automatically changes to include the new data. The height of existing bars changes to accommodate the new fifth category in the defined space of the graph.

6. **Close the Data panel.**

7. **Using the Direct Selection tool, select the two lines at the left and bottom edges of the graph. Using any method you prefer, change the selected lines to 0.5 pt with a 20% black stroke.**

   Dragging a small marquee around the area where the two lines meet is the easiest way to select only the two lines.

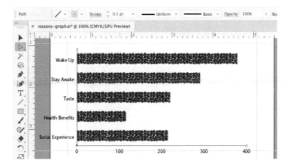

8. **Select only the type objects at the bottom edge of the graph. Change the type fill color to white.**

9. **Select only the type objects on the left side of the graph. Change the type formatting to left paragraph alignment.**

10. **Drag the selected type objects so they appear immediately above each bar on the graph.**

    It is easier to position the type objects while you can still see the actual text.

11. **Change the fill color of the selected type objects to white.**

12. **Show the Background and Heading layers.**

13. Change the heading placeholder text to **Why do you drink coffee?.**

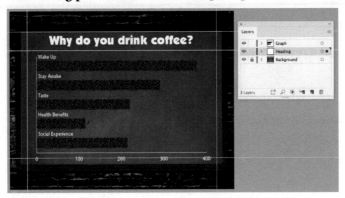

14. Save the file and close it, then continue to the next exercise.

Create a Pie Graph

The final required graph is based on data from a survey of 500 people who were asked their favorite type of coffee. Each person gave a single response to the question, so the combined percentages of responses will equal 100%. A pie graph is the best way to show values as percentages of the whole.

1. Create a new file by opening **chalkboard.ait** from the WIP>Coffee folder. Choose the Pie Graph tool in the Tools panel.

2. Click and drag an area that snaps to the guides on the artboard.

Regardless of the shape you draw, pie graphs are always circles.

3. Click the Import Data button in the Data panel. Navigate to **favorites.txt** in your WIP>Coffee>Data folder and click Open.

Note:

Pie graphs always present numbers as percentages of the whole. If data is provided as actual numbers instead of percentages, Illustrator calculates the necessary percentages based on the entered data.

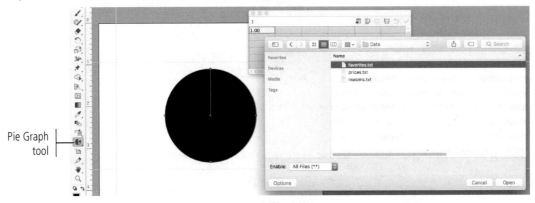

Pie Graph tool

4. Click the Apply button in the Data panel.

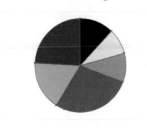

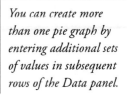

Note:

You can create more than one pie graph by entering additional sets of values in subsequent rows of the Data panel.

5. **Close the Data panel.**

6. **Choose the Direct Selection tool, then click away from the graph to deselect it.**

7. **Using the Direct Selection tool, click to select only the top-left wedge in the graph.**

8. **Open the Swatches panel. Make sure the Fill Color icon is active, then click the lightest brown swatch to change the selected wedge's fill color.**

    This template file includes six different built-in swatches, which you will use to format the graph elements in this exercise.

    Changing the wedge color does not affect the color of the related legend object. You would have to manually select the legend object and change its fill color to match. In the following steps, however, you will create a different type of legend, so you don't need to worry about the legend objects.

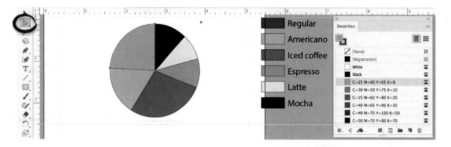

9. **Change the fill color of each wedge, using a different built-in swatch for each.**

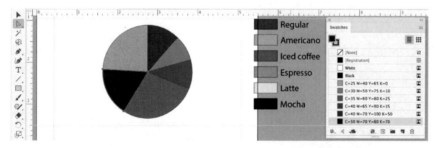

10. **Choose the Selection tool in the Tools panel, then click to select the entire graph object.**

11. **Control/right-click the graph and choose Type in the contextual menu.**

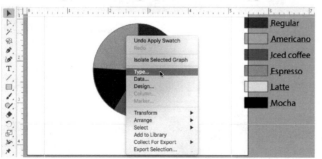

12. **In the Options area of the Graph Type dialog box, choose Legends in Wedges in the Legend menu.**

You can use the Legend menu to remove the legend completely, create a standard stacked legend (the default), or place the legend labels inside the associated wedges.

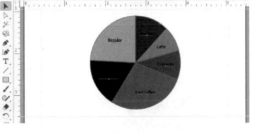

Note:

If you check Add Legend Across Top when the Standard Legend option is selected, the legend appears as a row above the graph.

13. **Click OK to return to the document.**

Using the Legends in Wedges option, the legend type objects move into the related wedges. The color-filled squares are removed.

14. **Save the file as favorites-graph.ai in your WIP>Coffee folder, then continue to the next exercise.**

Edit Pie Graph Elements

Pie graphs are very common, but they present several unique formatting challenges and opportunities. In this exercise, you manipulate the graph legend to add information, and then apply gradients to the wedges to add visual interest.

1. **With favorites-graph.ai open, Control/right-click the graph and choose Data from the contextual menu.**

2. **Select the first label field in the Data panel, then place the insertion point at the end of the existing text (Mocha) in the field at the top of the panel.**

3. **Type |12%, then click the Apply button.**

The pipe character (Shift-Backslash) is used to create a new line in the graph label.

Use this field to add to the selected label.

4. **Using the same method, add the appropriate values to each label in the Data panel, click the Apply button, and then close the Data panel.**

   The point of infographics is to make data easy to view and understand. The labels now reflect the actual data that was used to create the graph wedges.

   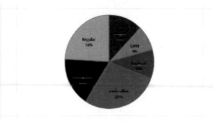

5. **Using the Layers panel, show the Design Elements layer.**

6. **Drag the large coffee-cup artwork onto the artboard. Position the bottom edge of the cup at the bottom edge of the artboard, and center it horizontally (as shown here).**

   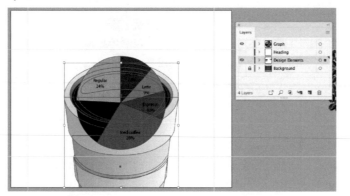

7. **Lock the Design Elements layer.**

8. **Using the Selection tool, drag the graph object so its top center aligns with the top center of the "coffee" in the cup artwork.**

   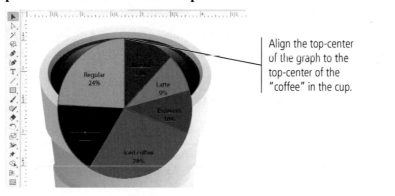

   Align the top-center of the graph to the top-center of the "coffee" in the cup.

We zoomed in to complete the scaling process outlined in the next few steps.

9. **Choose the Scale tool in the Tools panel, then click the top-center point of the graph to reposition the transformation point.**

   Remember, when you use the transformation tools, the transformation point is the "anchor" around which transformations are made.

10. **Click the bottom-center of the graph and drag up to scale the graph vertically. Release the mouse button when you see a pink horizontal smart guide.**

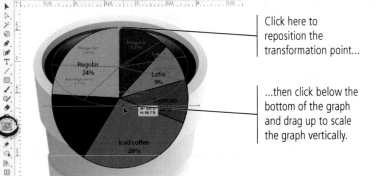

Click here to reposition the transformation point...

...then click below the bottom of the graph and drag up to scale the graph vertically.

11. **Click the right edge of the graph and drag out until the graph fills the area that represents the coffee in the cup artwork (as shown here).**

Because the top-center of the graph is anchored, dragging the right side out applies an equal change to the left side of the graph.

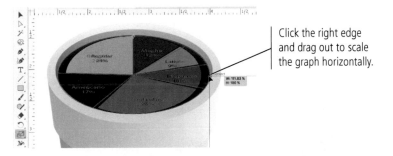

Click the right edge and drag out to scale the graph horizontally.

12. **With the graph object selected, open the Character panel.**

As you can see, the disproportionate scaling you applied to the graph had a significant effect on type objects within the graph.

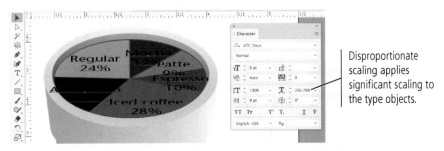

Disproportionate scaling applies significant scaling to the type objects.

13. **With the entire graph selected, change the type formatting to 9-pt ATC Onyx Normal with 100% vertical and horizontal scaling.**

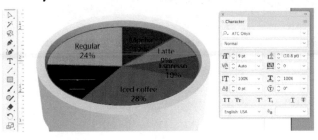

14. **Deselect the graph, then choose the Direct Selection tool.**

15. **Click each legend in the graph and drag it just outside the cup artwork, as shown here:**

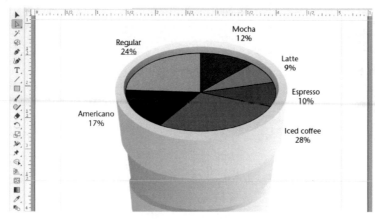

16. **Shift-click to select all 6 legend type objects, then change the type fill color to white.**

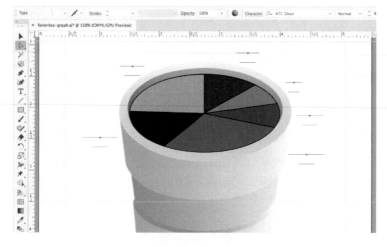

17. **Show the Background and Heading layers. Change the heading placeholder text to What is your favorite coffee?.**

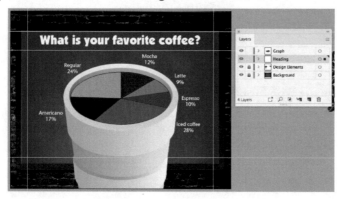

18. **Save the file and close it, then continue to the next stage of the project.**

STAGE 2 / Drawing in Perspective

The second half of the word "infographics" means adding visual elements that make data more attractive and accessible. The graphs from the first half of this project use a "chalkboard" background to present data in a visual manner that makes sense with the magazine article they illustrate.

Infographics can be as basic as graphs and charts, or as complex as any type of art you can conceive. In the second half of this project, you will create a coffee-dispenser box like you might see at a meeting or volunteer event. One side of the box will display the infographic heading, while the other will show the data being presented.

Define the Perspective Grid

In this series of exercises, you will create artwork based on a flat pencil sketch. Objects in the real world have depth, which means the box you are drawing should reflect that same level of dimension.

To recreate this effect using two-dimensional drawing tools, you need to understand the basic artistic principle of perspective. The concept of perspective means that all lines on the same surface (or plane) eventually appear to meet at a single point in the distance, called the **vanishing point**. Lines move closer together as they approach the vanishing point, creating the illusion of depth.

Illustrator includes a Perspective Grid tool that makes it very easy to define the perspective planes that will guide your drawing.

1. **Open the file box.ai from your WIP>Coffee folder.**

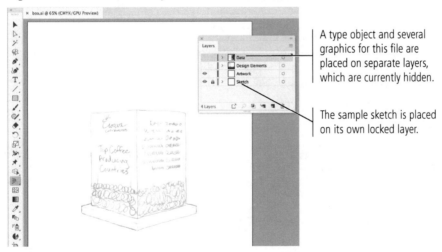

A type object and several graphics for this file are placed on separate layers, which are currently hidden.

The sample sketch is placed on its own locked layer.

2. **Choose the Perspective Grid tool in the Tools panel.**

   When you first choose this tool, the default two-point perspective grid appears in the file. You can change the grid to one- or three-point perspective by choosing the appropriate option in the View>Perspective Grid menu.

Note:

Press Shift-P to access the Perspective Grid tool.

3. If you can't see all handles of the perspective grid, zoom out slightly.

In two-point perspective, there are two vanishing points — left and right — and three planes — left, right, and ground. Illustrator's perspective grid shows the left plane in blue, the right plane in orange, and the ground plane in green.

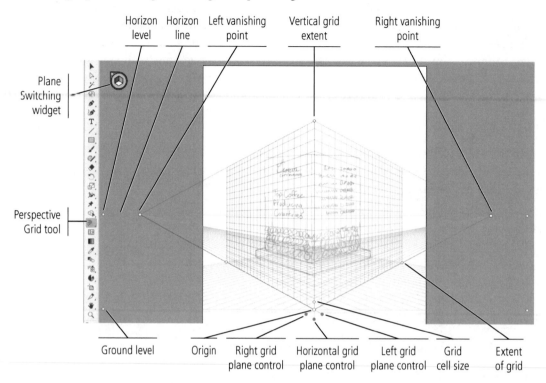

Horizon level · Horizon line · Left vanishing point · Vertical grid extent · Right vanishing point · Plane Switching widget · Perspective Grid tool · Ground level · Origin · Right grid plane control · Horizontal grid plane control · Left grid plane control · Grid cell size · Extent of grid

If you have never worked with perspective drawing, the grid might seem intimidating at first. However, once you understand the various elements, you will see how this grid makes it very easy to draw in correct perspective. To begin, you should also understand several basic terms related to dimensional drawing:

- A **plane** is a flat surface (even if it is only theoretical).

- A **vanishing point** is the location where all lines on a plane appear to converge.

- The **horizon line** is the height of the theoretical viewer's eye level.

- The **origin** is the zero point for perspective objects. For objects on the horizontal plane, the origin point is X: 0, Y: 0. For objects on the left or right plane, the origin point is X: 0.

- The **ground level** is the position of the theoretical ground in relation to the planes in the perspective grid.

You can change the position of the Plane Switching widget by double-clicking the Perspective Grid tool to open the Perspective Grid Options dialog box.

4. **With the Perspective Grid tool active, click either Ground Level handle and drag until the origin aligns with the corner in the sketch (as shown here).**

   You can use the Ground Level handles to move the grid without affecting the perspective.

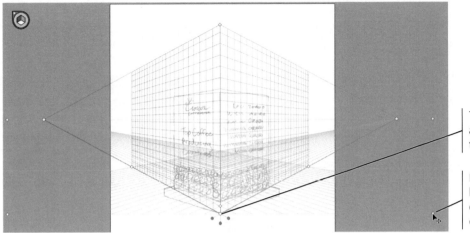

The origin should align to the corner in the sketch.

Drag the Ground Level handles to move the entire grid without changing perspective.

5. **Click either Horizon Level handle and drag up until the horizon line matches the top-left and -right corners of the box in the sketch.**

   Changing the horizon line changes the height of both vanishing points. All three perspective planes are affected by the change.

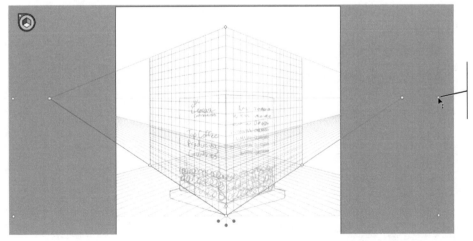

Drag the Horizon Level handles to change the eye level and adjust the perspective.

6. **Zoom out if necessary to show more area around the perspective grid.**

7. **Click the Right Vanishing Point handle and drag right until the bottom line of the orange grid aligns with the bottom line in the sketch.**

Keep in mind that you're working from a sketch, which is probably not exact. The ultimate goal is to create accurate perspective artwork, using the sketch as a *rough* guide.

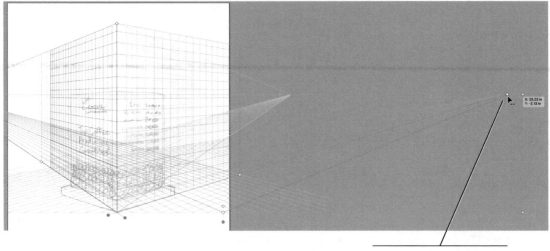

Drag the Horizon Level handles to change the eye level and adjust the perspective.

8. **Click the Left Vanishing Point handle and drag left until the bottom line of the blue grid aligns with the bottom line in the sketch.**

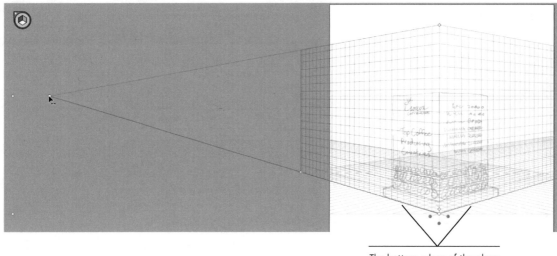

The bottom edges of the plane grids should align to the bottom lines in the sketch.

If you choose View>Perspective Grid>Lock Station Point, both vanishing points move when you drag either. They are effectively locked in position relative to each other. The origin point becomes a pivot, around which the vanishing points rotate.

9. **Click the Extent of Grid handle for the right plane and drag left until the right-most orange gridline aligns with the right edge of the box.**

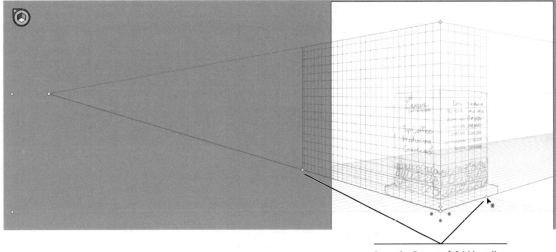

Drag the Extent of Grid handles to change the horizontal area that displays gridlines.

10. **Click the Extent of Grid handle for the left plane and drag right until the left-most blue gridline aligns with the left edge of the box.**

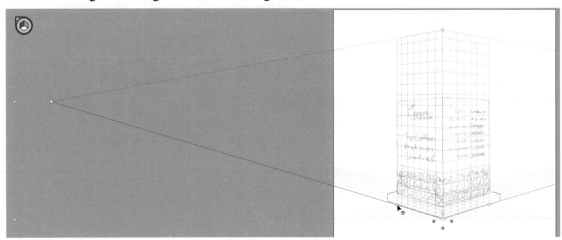

11. Click the Vertical Grid Extent handle and drag down until the top edge of the grid aligns with the top edge of the sketched box.

It is important to realize that the perspective grid is only a visual guide; the extent of the grid planes does not limit the location of the planes. Each plane is theoretically infinite.

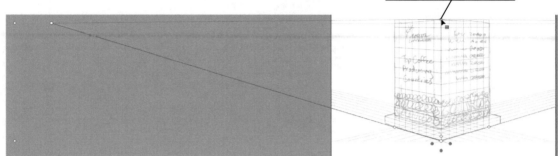

Drag the Vertical Grid Extent handle to change the vertical area that displays gridlines.

12. Zoom in to the sketch. Click the Grid Cell Size handle and drag up until the first row of the grid appears to match the height of the box's platform.

The grid cell size is the same for all planes on the grid. Although you are basing the grid size on the right plane, all three grids change to reflect the new grid size.

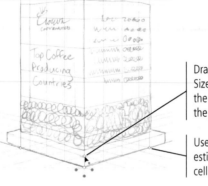

Drag the Grid Cell Size handle to change the size of squares in the perspective grid.

Use this surface to estimate the grid cell size.

13. Choose View>Perspective Grid>Define Grid.

You can use this dialog box to define very specific, numeric grid settings, which can be useful for precise technical illustration.

This field shows the grid size that resulted from dragging the Grid Cell Size handle.

Use these options to change the appearance of the grid on the artboard.

Understanding Default Perspective Grids

Illustrator supports one-, two-, and three-point perspective grids, all of which can be accessed in the View>Perspective Grid submenus.

Only one perspective grid can exist in a single file regardless of the number of artboards in the file. If you choose a different preset from one of the submenus, you replace any grid that already exists in your file.

If you have established a grid that you think you might need again, you can save it as a preset by choosing View>Perspective Grid>Save Grid As Preset. The resulting dialog box has most of the same options as the Define Perspective Grid dialog box, but you can type a name in the top field for easier recognition. Your saved grid presets will then be available in the View>Perspective Grid submenus.

Default one-point perspective grid

Default two-point perspective grid

Default three-point perspective grid

14. **Change grid Opacity to 30%, then click OK to apply your change.**

Reducing the grid opacity makes it easier to see what you're building.

Note:

Some users report a bug that causes the perspective grid to disappear after defining the grid properties. If this is the case, simply choose View>Perspective Grid>Show Grid.

Note:

If you choose View> Perspective Grid>Show Rulers, the Y position of gridlines appears near the edge of each vertical perspective plane.

15. **Save the file as coffee-producers.ai in your WIP>Coffee folder and then continue to the next exercise.**

Draw in Perspective

Once you have defined a perspective grid, creating objects in perspective is a fairly simple process. The most important issue is determining which plane you should draw on, and making sure that plane is active when you draw.

1. **With coffee-producers.ai open, choose the Rectangle tool in the Tools panel and reset the default fill and stroke attributes.**

2. **In the Layers panel, make the Artwork layer active.**

3. **In the Plane Switching widget, click the Right Grid proxy to make it the active plane.**

4. **Using the Rectangle tool, click near the corner of the sketch, then drag right to create a shape that represents the right-front edge of the box platform.**

Although you are drawing with the basic Rectangle tool, the new shape automatically adopts the perspective defined by the active plane in the grid.

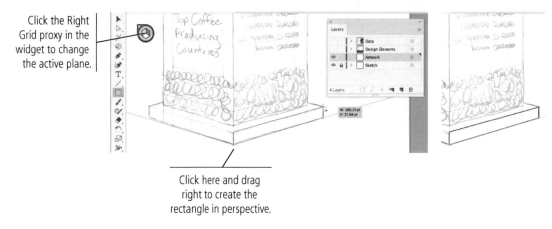

Click the Right Grid proxy in the widget to change the active plane.

Click here and drag right to create the rectangle in perspective.

5. **Click the Left Grid proxy in the Plane Switching widget.**

6. **Starting at the top-right corner, draw another rectangle representing the left-front edge of the platform.**

   Smart guides work in perspective drawing mode just as they do in regular drawings. You can snap to existing objects to align edges and corners when you draw new objects. However, the perspective grid also acts magnetic by default, so it might be difficult to snap to exactly the right location.

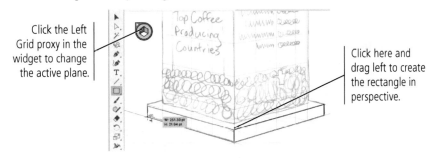

Click the Left Grid proxy in the widget to change the active plane.

Click here and drag left to create the rectangle in perspective.

7. **Click the Horizontal Grid proxy in the Plane Switching widget.**

8. **Using the Rectangle tool with the default fill and stroke attributes, draw another rectangle representing the top surface of the platform.**

   Start at the left corner and drag to the right corner, snapping to the existing points to create the top surface of the sign platform.

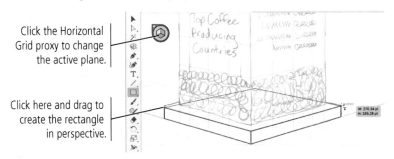

Click the Horizontal Grid proxy to change the active plane.

Click here and drag to create the rectangle in perspective.

9. **Use the Layers panel to hide the Sketch layer, and then choose View>Perspective Grid>Hide Grid.**

10. **Using the Selection tool, select the top-surface shape.**

11. **Use any method you prefer to change the object's stroke weight to 0 and the fill color to the CCR Brown1 swatch provided in the file's Swatches panel.**

    To move or resize a perspective object within the perspective grid, you have to use the Perspective Selection tool (nested under the Perspective Grid tool). This is a very important distinction, and one that is easy to forget. If you move or resize a perspective object with the regular Selection tool, the object's perspective is not maintained in the transformation.

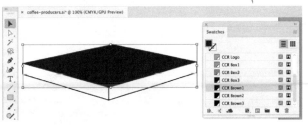

    In this case, you are only changing a property of the object — not its actual dimensions — so you do not need to use the Perspective Selection tool.

Note:

It might be helpful to turn off the snapping behavior by choosing View>Perspective Grid>Snap to Grid.

Note:

Click the background area in the Plane Switching widget to select No Active Grid if you want to draw objects that aren't attached to the perspective grid.

12. **Using any method you prefer, change the fill and stroke properties of the other two objects as follows:**

> **Right-front surface:**
> Fill: CCR Brown2
> Stroke: 0 pt
>
> **Left-front surface:**
> Fill: CCR Brown3
> Stroke: 0 pt

13. **Click the Perspective Grid tool in the Tools panel.**

When you choose the Perspective Grid tool, the grid automatically reappears. You can also choose View>Perspective Grid>Show Grid.

14. **Show the Sketch layer, save the file, then continue to the next exercise.**

Moving Objects in Perspective

One of the most powerful advantages of drawing in Illustrator's perspective grid is the fact that it is mostly nondestructive. Perspective objects can be moved around on their planes, and even moved to different planes, without degrading their quality.

Note:

A perspective drawing object is still a drawing object. You can use the Control panel, Swatches panel, or Color panel to change the fill and stroke colors of the selected shape.

1. **With coffee-producers.ai open, choose the Perspective Selection tool (nested under the Perspective Grid tool).**

Remember, to move or resize a perspective object within the perspective grid, you have to use the Perspective Selection tool.

2. **Press Option/Alt-Shift, then click the rectangle on the right-front face of the platform and drag up until the top edge aligns with the top edge of the sketched box.**

The same keyboard shortcuts for transforming objects work for transforming objects in perspective. Press Shift to constrain an object's movement to 45° angles (including exactly horizontal or vertical). Press Option/Alt to clone the object that you are dragging.

As you move the clone, you can see how the object adopts the appropriate shape based on the active perspective plane.

Note:

Press Shift-V to access the Perspective Selection tool.

Note:

The perspective grid does not need to be visible to transform objects in perspective; in fact, it is sometimes easier to make fine changes when the grid is not visible.

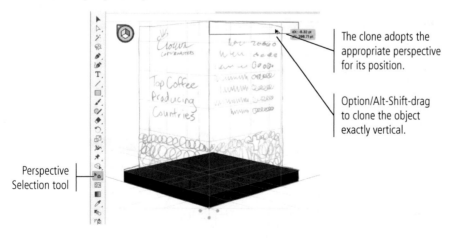

Perspective Selection tool

The clone adopts the appropriate perspective for its position.

Option/Alt-Shift-drag to clone the object exactly vertical.

3. **Change the selected object's fill color to the CCR Box1 swatch.**

4. **Using the Perspective Selection tool, click the bottom-center handle of the rectangle, and drag down until it meets the top edge of the first shape.**

   Remember, to resize an object in perspective, you have to use the Perspective Selection tool and not the regular Selection tool.

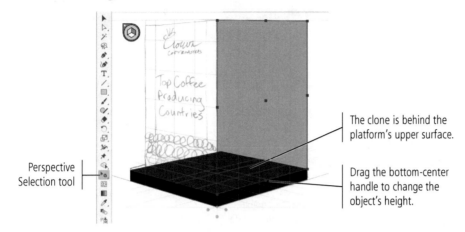

Perspective Selection tool

The clone is behind the platform's upper surface.

Drag the bottom-center handle to change the object's height.

5. **Choose Object>Arrange>Bring To Front to move the second rectangle above the top edge of the platform.**

   Object stacking order in perspective drawing follows the same rules as in regular drawing. New objects are automatically created at the top of the stacking order on the active layer. When you clone an object, the new clone is stacked immediately above the object you cloned.

6. **Press and hold the 5 key, then click the light-brown rectangle and drag approximately 1/4″ left.**

   Pressing the 5 key while dragging an object moves the object perpendicular to the plane on which it sits. In other words, the object moves nearer or farther away without changing its horizontal (X) position on that plane.

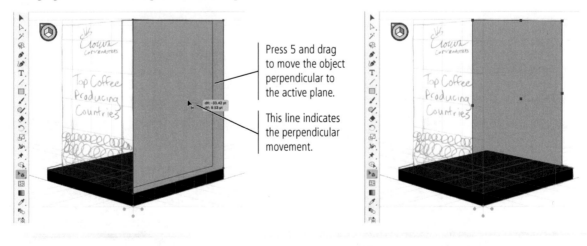

Press 5 and drag to move the object perpendicular to the active plane.

This line indicates the perpendicular movement.

7. **Choose Object>Arrange>Bring To Front to move the second rectangle back in front of the top edge of the platform.**

When you move an object perpendicularly on its plane, a bug in the software might move that item to the back of the stacking order.

8. **Using the Perspective Selection tool, drag the left-center handle until the left edge aligns with the left edge of the lower shape.**

The sketch appears to show the exact corner of the box, so the corners of the two surfaces should appear to align.

9. **Drag the right-center handle left to bring the box edge in slightly from the platform edge.**

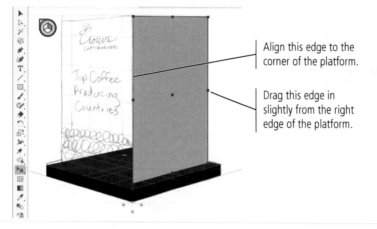

Align this edge to the corner of the platform.

Drag this edge in slightly from the right edge of the platform.

Note:

When the Perspective Selection tool is active, arrows in the cursor icon remind you which plane is active.

⬡ ˙ *Left Grid*

⬡ ˙ *Right Grid*

⬡ ˙ *Horizontal Grid*

⬡ ˙ *No Grid*

10. **Press Option/Alt, then click and drag the rectangle to clone it to the left. While still holding the Option/Alt key and the mouse button, press 1 to move the clone to the left perspective plane.**

You can move an object to a different plane by pressing the appropriate shortcut key while you drag the object:

- Left plane: 1
- Horizontal (ground) plane: 2
- Right plane: 3
- No plane: 4

These keyboard shortcuts relate only to the main numbers on the keyboard; the numeric keypad numbers do not work for switching planes.

Note:

On Windows, you have to be actively dragging the clone to move the object to another plane.

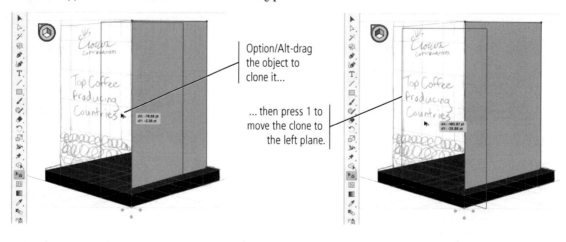

Option/Alt-drag the object to clone it...

... then press 1 to move the clone to the left plane.

11. **Using the Perspective Selection tool, resize the object to the appropriate shape by dragging the object handles.**

If necessary, turn off the Snap to Grid feature to resize the object appropriately.

12. **Change the selected object's fill color to the CCR Box2 swatch.**

Note:

Using the Perspective Selection tool, you can only select and group multiple objects if they exist on the same plane.

Using the regular Selection tool, you can select and group objects on different perspective planes. If you do, selecting an object in the group with the Perspective Selection tool only affects the object you click. You can't move or transform objects on different planes at the same time.

13. **With the left-plane object selected, choose Edit>Copy, then immediately choose Edit>Paste-in Place.**

14. **Using the Perspective Selection tool, drag in the left- and right-center handles of the pasted shape. Leave approximately 1/4″ between the edges of the front and back shapes.**

15. **Change the color of the select object to the CCR Box3 shape.**

16. **Save the file and continue to the next exercise.**

Work with Type in Perspective

Most drawing objects can be placed in perspective, with a few exceptions (notably, graphs). Adding existing artwork to the perspective grid is a fairly simple process.

1. With **coffee-producers.ai** open, show the **Design Elements** layer.

2. Using the regular Selection tool, click to select the group of coffee beans to the right of the artboard.

3. Choose the Perspective Selection tool (if necessary) and choose the Left Grid proxy in the Plane Switching widget.

4. Click the group of coffee beans to the right of the artboard, then drag the group into perspective on the left surface of the box.

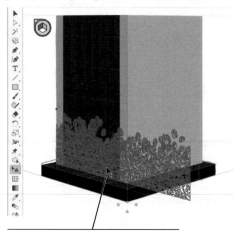

Drag with the Perspective Selection tool to place the object onto the active plane.

5. Using the Perspective Selection tool, drag the group so its bottom edge appears to sit on top of the upper surface. Adjust the group's corner and side handles so it fits into the box area, as shown here:

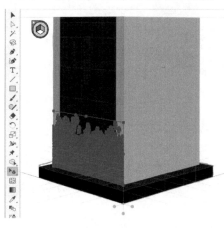

6. Press Option/Alt, then click and drag the group to clone it to the right. While still holding the Option/Alt key and the mouse button, press 3 to move the clone to the right perspective plane.

Note:

Some users, especially on Windows, have noted problems switching an object to a different perspective plane. You might need to hold down the 3 key, or press it several times, for the cloned object to accurately change planes.

7. Using the Perspective Selection tool, drag the group so its bottom edge appears to sit on top of the upper surface. Adjust the group's corner and side handles so it fits into the box area, as shown here:

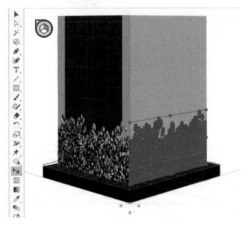

8. Choose the Left Grid proxy in the Plane Switching widget.

9. Click the group that includes the client's logo (to the right of the artboard) and drag it into perspective on the left surface of the box. Adjust the group's handles so it fits into the darker brown area above the coffee beans.

10. Show the Data layer.

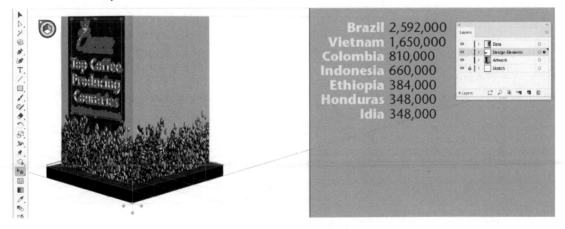

11. **Choose the Perspective Selection tool and choose the Right Grid proxy in the Plane Switching widget.**

12. **Click the type object to the right of the artboard and drag until it appears on the right face of the box.**

    Both point-type and area-type objects can be applied to a perspective grid. The text remains editable unless you release the object from the perspective grid.

13. **Drag the left- and right-center handles to fit all the text into the width of the box face.**

Edit Text button   Edit Perspective button

14. **With the type object selected, click the Edit Text button in the Control panel.**

    When a perspective type object is selected, you have to enter into the text to change the color of the text. Unlike other objects, you can't change the fill or stroke attributes of a perspective type object without first entering Edit Text mode.

15. **In Edit Text mode, use the Type tool to change the word "Idia" to "India."**

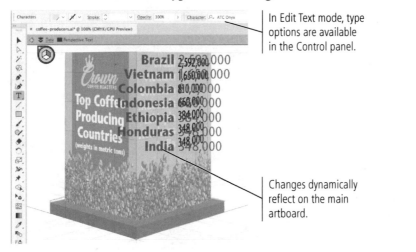

In Edit Text mode, type options are available in the Control panel.

Changes dynamically reflect on the main artboard.

Note:

You can also double-click the type object to enter the Edit Text mode.

16. Click the arrow button at the top of the document window two times to exit Edit Text mode.

17. Deselect everything on the artboard, delete the Sketch layer, then choose View>Perspective Grid>Hide Grid.

18. Save the file and close it.

Transforming Perspective Type Objects

Make sure you use the Perspective Selection tool and not the regular Selection tool to transform perspective type objects.

If you try to resize a perspective type object with the regular Selection tool, the object is detached from the perspective grid and expanded into a group of shapes that represent the letters. The appearance of perspective is maintained, but the object is no longer attached to the perspective grid; the text is no longer editable.

The warning you see does not have a Cancel button, so you have to simply click OK. If the action was an error, you can use the Undo command to restore the perspective type object.

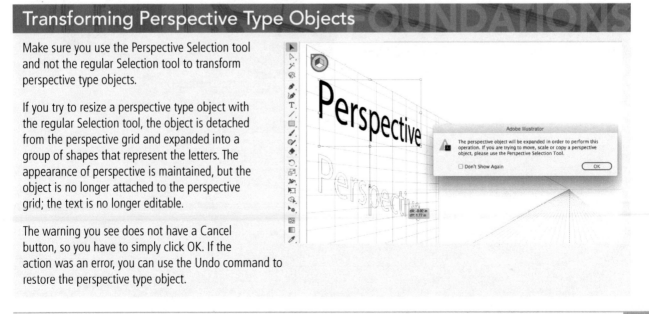

Other Perspective Grid Options

FOUNDATIONS

Attaching Objects to the Perspective Grid

If you create a regular drawing object that is not attached to a perspective plane, you can attach it to a specific plane by selecting it with the Perspective Selection tool and choosing Perspective>Attach to Active Plane in the object's contextual menu (or by choosing Object>Perspective>Attach to Active Plane). The object's shape is maintained, but the bounding box changes to reflect its new perspective boundaries.

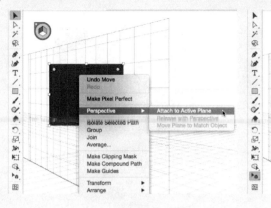

Releasing Objects from the Perspective Grid

To convert an object from a perspective object to a regular object, you can choose Perspective>Release with Perspective in the object's contextual menu (or choose Object>Perspective>Release with Perspective). The selected shape becomes a regular drawing object. The apparent perspective is maintained, but the object is no longer attached to a plane. The object's bounding box reveals the outermost edges of the flat artwork.

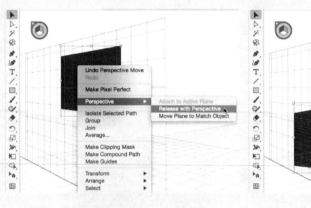

Moving the Plane to Match Perspective

If you have moved objects perpendicularly away from the active plane, you can adjust the grid plane to meet the position of the selected object by choosing Perspective>Move Plane to Match Object in the object's contextual menu (or by choosing Object>Perspective>Move Plane to Match Object). The active plane snaps to the face of the selected object, which makes it easier to create or place new objects along the same plane as the existing object.

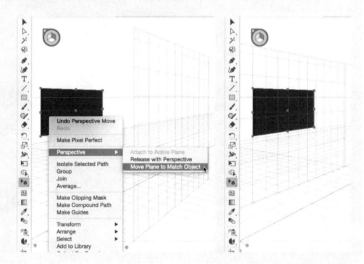

PROJECT REVIEW

fill in the blank

1. A _____ graph shows values as percentages of the whole.

2. A _____ graph plots values as a series of connected points, showing progressive change in value.

3. You must use _____ to enter numbers as text in the Data panel.

4. You must use the _____ to select one segment of a graph without ungrouping the entire graph.

5. You can click the _____ button in the Data panel to increase the number of decimals that are included in each data cell.

6. The _____ is the height of the theoretical viewer's eye level.

7. The _____ is the spot at which multiple lines on the same perspective converge.

8. The _____ tool is used to define the position of various attributes of the perspective grid.

9. The _____ is used to determine which perspective plane is active.

10. The _____ tool is used to move or resize objects in perspective.

short answer

1. Briefly explain what is meant by the term "infographics."

2. Briefly explain the concept of two-point perspective.

3. Briefly explain the difference between the Selection tool and the Perspective Selection tool.

PORTFOLIO BUILDER PROJECT

Use what you have learned in this project to complete the following freeform exercise.
Carefully read the art director and client comments, then create your own design to meet the needs of the project.
Use the space below to sketch ideas. When finished, write a brief explanation of the reasoning behind your final design.

art director comments

The main theme for next month's magazine is "Living Green." The main articles all focus on some aspect of environmental conservation, such as renewable energy, recycling strategies, and landfill reduction. Your job is to create infographics for data that will accompany the cover story.

To complete this project, you should:

❏ Download the **Info_AI19_PB.zip** archive from the Student Files web page.

❏ Use the supplied data to create three infographics that present the data in visually interesting way.

❏ Create illustrations for each set of data that support the overall theme of the article.

client comments

The main focus of next month's cover story is the different methods that are being explored to supply affordable electricity in large metropolitan areas, such as New York City and Los Angeles.

The author has compiled three different sets of data about renewable energy — wind power, water power, and so on — that will support the ideas and facts in the article. We need some type of illustrated graph for each of these data sets.

We want our readers to see the graphs even if they only flip through and skim the article. Create a compelling illustration for each one, so they are more than just graphs. However, keep in mind that the data is the most important element — it needs to be clear and understandable.

Use a consistent color scheme in all three graphs; green should play a prominent role because people naturally associate that color with environmentalism and natural resources.

project justification

PROJECT SUMMARY

Infographics like the ones you created in this project are frequently used in newspapers, magazines, and presentations to visually represent complex statistics or other numerical data. Infographics range from simple pie charts and line graphs to elaborate full-color images.

When you create this type of illustration, keep in mind that the information or data being presented is always the priority. Although aesthetic appeal is a primary concern of most graphic designers, the integrity of the information is the most important aspect of creating infographics.

Create and format
a line graph

Create and format
a pie graph

Create and format
a bar graph

Move and transform
perspective objects

Place type objects
in perspective

Place existing objects
into perspective

Draw objects on different
perspective planes

Define a perspective
grid based on a sketch

Website Interface

As an in-house designer for a multimedia services company, your job is to create the pieces that are required for a client's new home page. The basic site structure has already been designed; you need to make changes that were requested by the marketing manager, and then export the necessary pieces and information that is required for the HTML page to function properly.

This project incorporates the following skills:

❑ Working with color groups to unify the overall composition

❑ Using Live Color to edit vector elements

❑ Preparing page elements for export to use in a web page

❑ Defining cascading style sheets (CSS) to properly format various page elements in the final HTML file

client comments

We are very happy with the overall site layout. There are just a few things we'd like to change.

The guitar illustration in the original comp was a bit overpowering. We like the idea, but can you darken the colors in that illustration a bit so that the logo stands out more?

The blue color from the old site doesn't really work with the new illustration behind the navigation links. Can you change all the blue to something that works better with the guitar illustration?

Finally, can you change the bottom-half of some of the squares in the focus illustration? We're aiming for something that looks like the digital bars on a mixing board, but we want all the pieces to work together better.

art director comments

Illustrator color groups should make it fairly easy to meet all three of the client's requests. You can use them to universally lighten the illustration, change blue objects to red in just a few clicks, and even cut apart squares and paint only certain areas of vector shapes.

While you're making the aesthetic changes, I'll have the Dreamweaver developer start working on the web page code. By the time you get to that point, you will have an HTML page that you can use as a reference when you define names in Illustrator to create the necessary CSS and image files.

project objectives

To complete this project, you will:

- ❏ Create color groups to manage the color swatches in the file
- ❏ Adjust global color attributes in all selected artwork
- ❏ Adjust individual colors in a group to change all objects where the color is applied
- ❏ Work with Live Paint groups
- ❏ Explore HTML page code
- ❏ Examine the pixel grid
- ❏ Define object names to create CSS class selectors
- ❏ Create a gradient page background
- ❏ Define character styles to create CSS tag selectors
- ❏ Export CSS and image files

As you should already know, you can use Illustrator to create virtually any type of illustration — from a basic vector drawing to a complex, realistic illustration. You can also use Illustrator to design an entire composition, whether a letterfold brochure that will be printed or a website interface that will be used as the map for an HTML page. In the first stage of this project, you are going to use color groups and Live Color to adjust global and specific colors to unify various elements of the existing site design.

Use a Color Group to Change Multiple Swatches

Color groups are useful for organizing color swatches into logical and manageable collections. You can make changes that affect all colors within a group; this takes the concept of global color swatches one step further. In this exercise, you create a group from the tracing object swatches, so you can make changes that affect the entire illustration.

1. Download **Studio_AI19_RF.zip** from the Student Files web page.

2. **Expand the ZIP archive in your WIP folder (Macintosh) or copy the archive contents into your WIP folder (Windows).**

   This results in a folder named **Studio**, which contains the files you need for this project. You should also use this folder to save the files you create in this project.

3. **Open the file site-design.ai from the WIP>Studio folder.**

4. **In the Layers panel, expand all five layers if necessary and review the various elements.**

   The basic site layout follows a structure that is fairly common in website design. Four layers — Navigation, Header, Main, and Footer — represent the various sections of a basic HTML page. A fifth layer, named Background, contains a single path with a solid gray fill, representing the background color of the entire page.

> *Note:*
>
> *As you work through the exercises in this project, the importance of the structure used in this file will become apparent.*

5. **In the Layers panel, click to the right of the Target icon to select the bottom group on the Header layer.**

Remember, clicking in this area reveals the Indicates Selected Art icon.

The selected group was created by applying the Image Trace function to a photograph of a flaming guitar; this results in a group of vector objects that can each be selected and manipulated individually to achieve the designer goal.

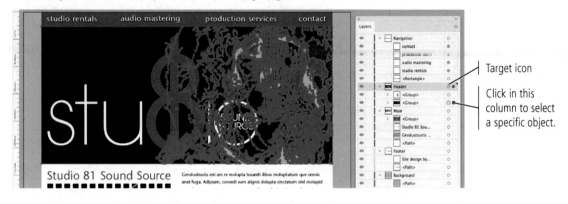

Target icon

Click in this column to select a specific object.

6. **With the group selected, click the New Color Group button at the bottom of the Swatches panel.**

New Color Group button

7. **In the resulting dialog box, type Guitar Colors in the Name field. Choose the Create From Selected Artwork radio button, check the Convert Process to Global option, and turn off the Include Swatches for Tints option.**

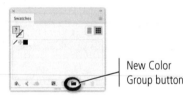

8. **Click OK to create the new color group.**

By checking the Selected Artwork option, every color used in the selection is added as a separate swatch in the group. Each is a global swatch, which means editing the swatch will affect the appearance of any object where that swatch is applied.

New color group

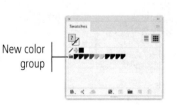

Note:

It is helpful to view the Swatches panel in Swatch view instead of list view

9. **With the artwork still selected, click the color group folder icon to select the entire group.**

If you click a swatch instead of the group folder, you will change the fill/stroke attribute (whichever is active) of the selected objects.

10. **Click the Edit or Apply Color Group button at the bottom of the Swatches panel.**

Click the folder icon to select the color group.

Edit or Apply Color Group button

11. **Change the Recolor Artwork dialog box to Edit mode, and make sure the Recolor Art option is checked in the bottom-left corner.**

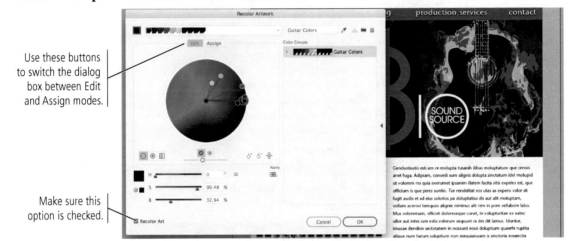

Use these buttons to switch the dialog box between Edit and Assign modes.

Make sure this option is checked.

12. **Make sure the Link Harmony Colors button is active. Drag the Brightness slider (below the color wheel) slightly right to lighten all colors in the image.**

The Link Harmony Colors button is a toggle. When it is already active, the tool tip for the button shows "Unlink Harmony Colors" (and vice versa).

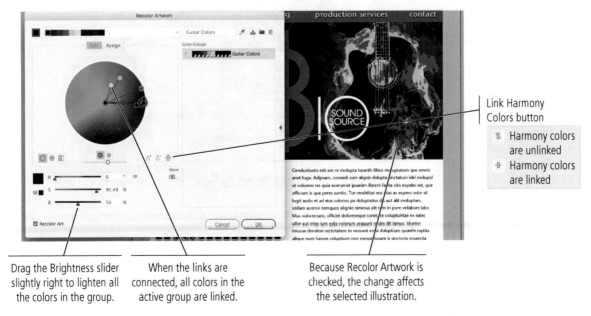

Link Harmony Colors button

Harmony colors are unlinked

Harmony colors are linked

Drag the Brightness slider slightly right to lighten all the colors in the group.

When the links are connected, all colors in the active group are linked.

Because Recolor Artwork is checked, the change affects the selected illustration.

13. **Click OK to apply the change. Click Yes when asked if you want to save the changes to the color group.**

14. **Save the file and continue to the next exercise.**

Use a Color Group to Manage File Colors

In addition to managing universal changes to all swatches in a group, color groups can also be useful for simplifying a design and managing the individual colors included in specific areas of a file. In this exercise, you use a color group to combine similar colors into tints of a single color swatch.

1. **With site-design.ai open, use the Layers panel to lock the guitar illustration group.**

   The blue accent color in the rest of the site elements does not suit the predominant reds in the guitar illustration. You are going to use another color group to manage the site colors, changing the blue to a red color that better suits the new main image.

2. **Choose Select>All to select all unlocked artwork.**

   The color group you create in the next few steps will only include colors in the selected objects. Because the guitar-illustration group is locked, you can't select that group; colors in that illustration will not be included in the second color group.

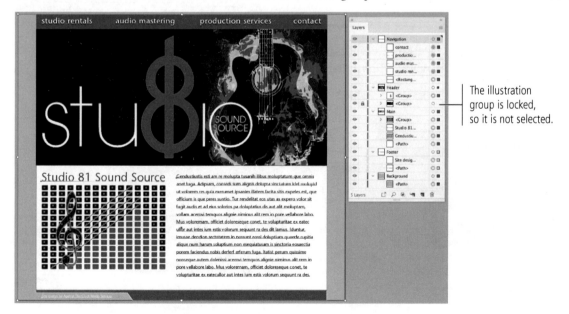

The illustration group is locked, so it is not selected.

3. **With the artwork selected, click the New Color Group button at the bottom of the Swatches panel.**

4. In the resulting dialog box, type Site Colors in the Name field. Choose the Create From Selected Artwork radio button, and make sure both check boxes are selected.

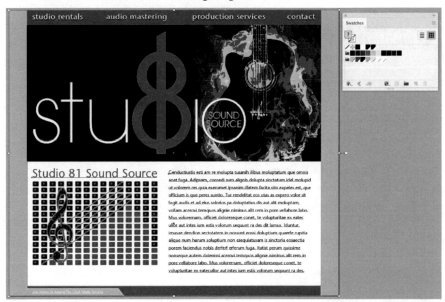

5. Click OK to create the new color group.

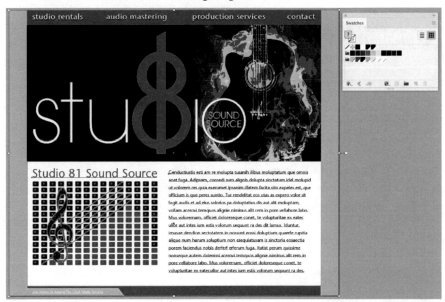

6. With the artwork still selected, click the Site Colors color group folder to select the entire group, and then click the Edit or Apply Color Group button.

This group currently contains seven colors, four of which are tints of black. It will be easier to manage the group if you combine the different gray swatches into tints of a single black swatch.

7. If necessary, change the Recolor Artwork dialog box to Assign mode.

Note:

Unchecking the Include Swatches for Tints option does not solve this problem because the artwork was not created with tints of a swatch.

8. **Click the third color in the list of current colors and drag it into the black row.**

Basic black and white appear at the bottom of the list, and do not have a swatch in the "New" column. You are using the Assign dialog box to convert the other shades of gray (including the white in the top half of the list) into shades of the default Black swatch.

 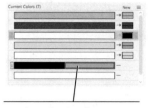

Click the first gray bar and drag it onto the black bar.

After releasing the mouse button, the Current Colors area shows that two original colors will result in a single new color.

9. **Repeat Step 8 to combine the other gray shade and the white swatch above the black one into the black color.**

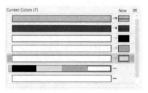

10. **Display the Recolor Artwork dialog box in Edit mode, and show the Smooth Color Wheel. Below the color wheel, click the Unlink Harmony Colors button to disconnect the color spokes from one another.**

11. **Select the blue color spoke. In the bottom area of the dialog box, display the color sliders in RGB mode and then define the spoke to be R=166 G=29 B=22.**

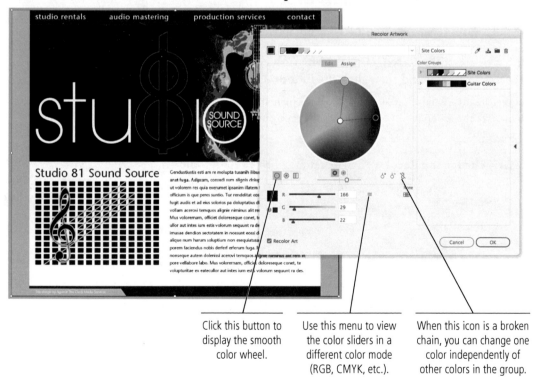

Click this button to display the smooth color wheel.

Use this menu to view the color sliders in a different color mode (RGB, CMYK, etc.).

When this icon is a broken chain, you can change one color independently of other colors in the group.

12. **Click OK to change the color group, and click Yes when asked if you want to save changes to the current group.**

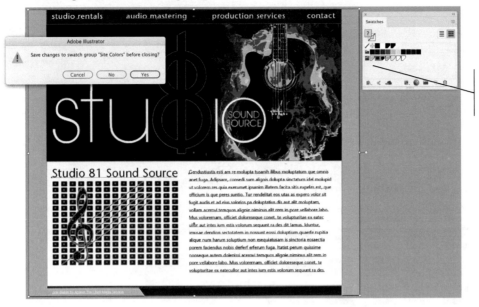

One of the Site Colors swatches is the red that you just defined.

13. **Save the file and continue to the next exercise.**

Work with Live Paint Groups

A Live Paint Group is a special type of Illustrator group. Using the Live Paint Bucket tool, you can navigate through swatches in a color group and apply those colors to different areas of the selected group. In this type of group, fills are not necessarily defined by object edges; rather, Illustrator identifies overlapping areas and allows you to treat separate areas as distinct objects, even though they are part of the same vector shape.

1. **With site-design.ai open, deselect everything in the file.**

2. **Using the Selection tool, double-click the artwork below the "Studio 81 Sound Source" subheading to enter into Isolation mode.**

   Working in Isolation mode makes it easier to work with a specific group without affecting other objects on the artboard.

3. **Choose the Live Paint Bucket tool (nested under the Shape Builder tool), and then click one of the swatches in the Site Colors group in the Swatches panel.**

Live Paint Bucket tool

Click to make the Site Colors group active.

The Live Paint Bucket tool includes three sample swatches from the active color group. The center swatch is the active swatch.

4. **Press the Right Arrow key until the red swatch in the Site Colors group appears selected in the tool cursor.**

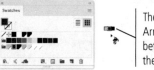

The Left and Right Arrow keys navigate between the swatches in the active color group.

Note:

If no color group is selected, the Live Paint Bucket tool shows the default ungrouped swatches.

5. **Choose Select>All to select all elements of the artwork in the group.**

6. **Zoom into the area where the yellow lines bisect the black squares.**

7. **Using the Live Paint Bucket tool, click the lower part of the last black square that intersects the bottom yellow line.**

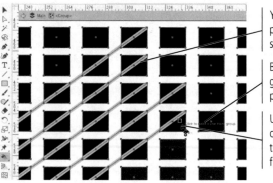

You can see the vector paths of overlapping shapes in the selection.

Before you click the group, cursor feedback provides helpful tips.

Use the point of the cursor arrow to identify the object you want to fill with the tool.

The Live Paint Bucket tool identifies divisions in the selected artwork, even though they are not technically divisions.

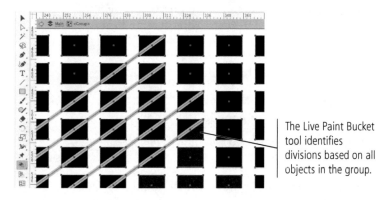

The Live Paint Bucket tool identifies divisions based on all objects in the group.

8. **Using the Direct Selection tool, click away from the active group to deselect it, and then click only the object you filled with the red swatch.**

9. **Click the selected object and drag right.**

   Moving objects that are part of a Live Paint group is different than moving individual objects in a regular vector group. Illustrator recognizes the original placement of the fill color, almost as if there is an underlay of the fill color, and the "filled" object is revealing that area of the color. Moving the individual object changes which part of the color "underlay" is visible.

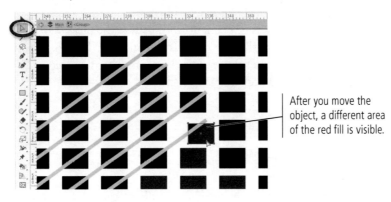

After you move the object, a different area of the red fill is visible.

10. **Choose Edit>Undo Move to reposition the object that you moved in Step 9.**

11. **Using the Selection tool, select the entire group again.**

12. **Using the Live Paint Bucket tool, fill the bottom half of each square that is bisected by a yellow line.**

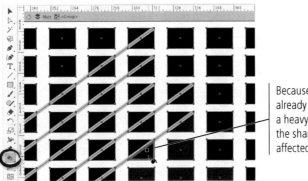

Because the selection is already a Live Paint group, a heavy border outlines the shape that will be affected if you click.

Note:

When working with the Live Paint Bucket tool, press Shift to paint the stroke of an object instead of the fill.

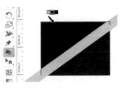

13. **Deselect the logo artwork, then press the ESC key to exit Isolation mode.**

Note:

Use the Live Paint Selection tool to select pieces of a Live Paint group.

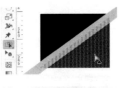

14. **Save the file and continue to the next stage of the project.**

It is common practice to create the look and feel of a website in Illustrator, and then hand off the pieces for a programmer to assemble in a web-design application, such as Adobe Dreamweaver. In the second half of this project, you complete a number of tasks to create the necessary pieces for the final website, including the different styles that will be used to properly format various elements in the resulting HTML page.

This site is a very simple example, using only a few page elements to illustrate the process of properly mapping Illustrator objects to create the pieces that are necessary in an HTML page. We kept the site design basic to minimize the amount of repetition required to complete the project. The skills and concepts you complete in this project would apply equally to more complex sites.

Examine an HTML Page

You do not need to be a web programmer to design a site in Illustrator. However to best take advantage of some of the tools that are available for moving your work into a functional HTML page, you should understand at least the basics of HTML:

- An HTML page contains code that defines the **elements** that make up a page.

- Individual page elements are defined with **tags**. For example, a <div> tag identifies a division or area of the page, and a <p> tag identifies a paragraph of text. Available tags are defined by the version of HTML being used; you can't simply make up tags.

- HTML5, the most current version of the language, adds new structural elements for common layout practices, such as <header>, <nav>, and <footer> for the header, navigation, and footer sections of a page (respectively).

- Specific elements can be identified with user-defined classes, which helps to differentiate them from other, same-type elements. For example:

    <div class="feature-image">
    <div class="text-area">

- Cascading Style Sheets (CSS) are used to define the properties of HTML elements. CSS files define **selectors**, which contain **property:value pairs** to control the appearance of specific elements in an HTML page. For example:

    header {
        width: 780px;
        height: 75px;
    }

- Two types of CSS selectors are relevant to site design in Illustrator:

  - **Tag selectors** define the appearance of HTML tags. These selectors simply use the same tag name as the selector name; for example, the **div** selector defines the appearance of all **<div>** tags.

  - **Class selectors** define the appearance of any tag that is identified with the defined class. These selector names always begin with a period. For example, the **.text-area** selector would apply to any element that has the **class="text-area"** attribute.

> **Note:**
>
> This is hardly an exhaustive explanation of HTML and CSS. We focus here on only the issues you should understand when working with Illustrator to create a website layout. To learn more about HTML tags and CSS selectors, we recommend **Adobe Dreamweaver CC: The Professional Portfolio** (the companion book to this one).

1. **Open the file index.html (from your WIP>Studio folder) in a browser window. If possible, use the Google Chrome or Opera browser.**

   This HTML page contains a number of elements, including links to images that don't yet exist. You will create those images from your Illustrator file. You will also use objects in the Illustrator file to define background images and text formatting for various HTML elements so that the HTML page more closely resembles the Illustrator file.

Note:

You might see different results depending on which browser you use. The important point is that very little has yet been done to format the various page elements.

Content is in the correct position, but its appearance is based only on default HTML rendering.

2. **If possible, open the page source code.**

   Every browser has a different method for viewing a page's source code. Using the Chrome browser on Macintosh OS, for example, you can choose View>Developer> View Source.

   You can also open the HTML file in Adobe Dreamweaver, Edge Code, or another HTML editor application.

Note:

If you cannot access the page code, use our screenshot and the following explanation as a guide.

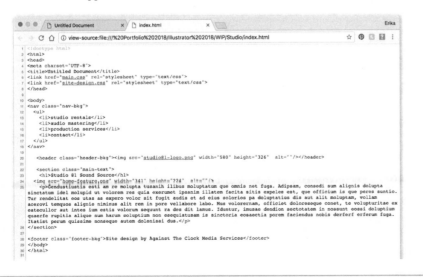

The top of the code shows the <head> tag, which contains two link elements (lines 6 and 7 in our example). Each link element refers to a different CSS file.

- The first link, **main.css**, was created by the person who created the HTML code. Selectors in that file define the size and position of various elements, which you saw in Step 1.

- You will create the second link, **site-design.css**, from the Illustrator file that you have been using in this project.

```
3  <head>
4  <meta charset="UTF-8">
5  <title>Untitled Document</title>
6  <link href="main.css" rel="stylesheet" type="text/css">
7  <link href="site-design.css" rel="stylesheet" type="text/css">
8  </head>
```

The **body** element, defined by opening <body> and closing </body> tags (Lines 10 and 29), contains all elements that are visible in the browser window.

Lines 11–18 define the **nav** element, which is further identified by the **class="nav-bkg"** attribute. Inside the opening <nav> and closing </nav> tags, an unordered list contains the text of each navigation link.

```
10  <body>
11  <nav class="nav-bkg">
12    <ul>
13      <li>studio rentals</li>
14      <li>audio mastering</li>
15      <li>production services</li>
16      <li>contact</li>
17    </ul>
18  </nav>
```

Line 20 defines the **header** element. The code for this element includes a nested image element (using the **<img>** tag). The src attribute (**src="studio81-logo.png"**) defines the file name of the image that should appear in this element.

```
20     <header class="header-bkg"><img src="studio81-logo.png" width="580" height="326"  alt=""/></header>
```

Lines 22–26 define a **section** element, which is further identified by the **class="main-text"** attribute. It contains an image element with the **src="home-feature.png"** attribute, and text content that is identified as heading 1 (**<h1>**) and paragraph (**<p>**) elements.

```
22     <section class="main-text">
23       <h1>Studio 81 Sound Source</h1>
24     <img src="home-feature.png" width="341" height="224"  alt=""/>
25       <p>Gendustiustis esti am re molupta tusanih ilibus moluptatum que omnis net fuga. Adipsam, consedi
sum alignis dolupta sinctatum idel molupid ut volorem res quia exerumet ipsanim illatem facita sitis
expeles est, que officium is que peres suntio. Tur rendelitat eos utas as expero volor sit fugit audis
et ad eius solorios pa doluptatius dis aut alit moluptam, vollam acerovi temquos alignie niminus alit
rem in pore vellabore labo. Mus volorernam, officiet doloreseque conet, te volupturitae ex eatecullor
aut intes ium estis volorum sequunt ra des dit lamus. Iduntur, imusae dendion sectotatem in nossunt
eossi doluptium quaerfe rupitia alique num harum soluptium non esequiatusam is sinctoria eosaectia porem
faciendus nobis derferf erferum fuga. Itatist perum quissime nonseque autem doleniasi dus.</p>
26     </section>
```

Line 28 defines the **footer** element with the **class="footer-bkg"** attribute.

```
28  <footer class="footer-bkg">Site design by Against The Clock Media Services</footer>
29  </body>
```

3. **Close the browser and return to Illustrator.**

4. **Continue to the next exercise.**

Note:

*Line 3, <head>, is called an **opening tag**. It represents the beginning of the element.*

*Line 8, </head>, is called a **closing tag**. It represents the end of the element.*

Examine the Pixel Grid

When you export images for a website interface, vector objects will be converted to raster files so that they display properly on-screen. As you learned at the beginning of this book, raster objects are composed of pixels. Illustrator includes a number of tools for making sure you achieve the best possible quality in the output raster files.

1. **With site-design.ai open in Illustrator, unlock all layers and sublayers.**

2. **Zoom in to the first letters of the logo in the header area. With the view percentage at least 600%, choose View>Pixel Preview.**

   This option shows the pixel grid that will be used when the artwork is converted to raster images. The grid represents 72-ppi resolution; each square is 1/72 of an inch.

   Objects are obviously bitmapped because you are viewing at such a high view percentage. However, you can see how the edges of shapes are defined by the position of pixels in the grid. This is an accurate representation of the pixel content that will exist in the final exported images.

Note:

The pixel grid appears at 600% or higher view percentage.

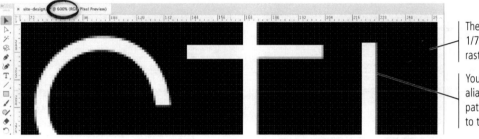

The grid shows the 1/72-inch pattern for rasterization.

You can see the anti-aliasing that results if paths are not aligned to the pixel grid.

3. **Make the Selection tool active, and then choose Select>All.**

4. **Click the Align Selected Art to Pixel Grid button in the Application/Menu bar.**

   When objects align to the pixel grid, straight lines reproduce more sharply because they no longer require anti-aliasing to fill the pixel grid. The shift is very slight — but it can make a significant difference in the sharpness of exported raster images.

Align Selected Art to Pixel Grid

Align Art to Pixel Grid on Creation and Transformation

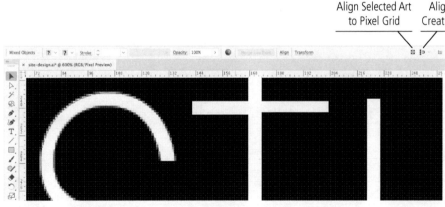

Note:

You can toggle on the Align Art to Pixel Grid on Creation and Transformation to automatically create "pixel-perfect" art when it is first drawn.

Click the arrow to the right of that button to determine which actions cause objects to snap to the grid.

5. **Choose View>Fit Artboard In Window, and choose View>Pixel Preview to turn off this option.**

6. **Deselect everything in the file, save it, and continue to the next exercise.**

Define Object Names

When you export CSS from Illustrator, object names in the Layers panel determine the resulting selector and file names. The first step in completing this stage of the project is to define object names that match the class names in the HTML file, as well as the file names of images that will be exported.

As you complete the following exercises, make sure you use the exact names we define in the steps. If you use different object and file names — including misspellings or different capitalization — the final CSS code will not function properly.

1. **With site-design.ai open, expand all layers in the Layers panel (if necessary). Unlock the locked group on the Header layer.**

2. **Click to select the red-filled rectangle at the top of the page.**

3. **Open the CSS Properties panel and review the lower half of the panel.**

   The selected object is a live shape, recognized by Illustrator as a <Rectangle>. Illustrator does not automatically generate CSS from live shapes.

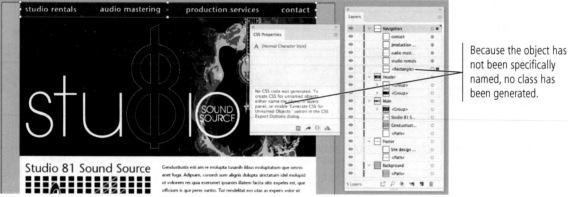

Because the object has not been specifically named, no class has been generated.

4. **In the Layers panel, double-click the selected <Rectangle> name.**

5. **Type nav-bkg, then press Return/Enter to finalize the new object name.**

The CSS Properties panel now shows the ".nav-bkg" selector name — the same as the object name you just defined. This also matches the class that is defined for the nav element in the HTML code.

When you export the CSS file later in this project, this selector will define a red background color. Two different properties define the background color so that different browsers will be able to interpret at least one of these values.

- #A61D16 is the hexadecimal color value for the red background color.
- rgba(166, 29, 22, 1) defines color based on four values: red, green, blue, and alpha transparency.

The object name is adopted as the matching class name.

6. **Click to select the guitar illustration. In the Layers panel, double-click the selected <Group> name in the Layers panel.**

7. **Type header-bkg, then press Return/Enter to finalize the object name.**

In this case, you are defining both the class name and the name of the raster image that will be generated from the selected artwork.

The Properties panel shows that the .header-bkg class defines two properties:

- **background-image : url(header-bkg.png)** defines the image that will be placed in the background of any element that is identified by the header-bkg class.
- **background-repeat : no-repeat** says that the defined background image will appear only once in the element.

The CSS Properties panel also includes an important note reminding you that the referenced image must be exported as well as the CSS file. You will accomplish this later in the project.

Note:

If you select an object that is filled with a pattern swatch, the CSS would not define a background-repeat property. This allows the background image to repeat (tile) horizontally and vertically to fill the containing element.

8. **Repeat Steps 6–7 to rename the white-filled path object (behind the secondary logo artwork and text) as** `main-text`.

The object in this section has the default name <Path>, which means it is not recognized as a live shape. The default CSS class selector for this object uses a default generic name. You need to change the object name — and thus, the selector name — so that it matches the class that is defined for the <section> tag in the HTML code.

This object represents the background behind the primary content area. In the HTML code, the section element is identified with the .main-text class, so you are using the same text as the object name.

9. **Select the red-filled shape at the bottom of the page.**

In the CSS Properties panel, you see a message that "No CSS code was generated..." for this object. Because it is an irregular shape, Illustrator has difficulty determining what to do.

10. **In the Layers panel, rename the selected object as** `footer-bkg`.

The CSS Properties panel now shows two properties that define a background color for the element. Unfortunately, there is no code that defines the irregular shape. If you leave the object and code as they are now, the resulting CSS would display the entire element background color as red. To solve this problem, you need to convert the irregular shape to a raster object that will serve as the element's background image instead of a solid background color.

11. **With the red-filled object selected, choose Object>Rasterize. In the resulting dialog box, choose Screen (72 ppi) in the Resolution menu and select the Transparent Background radio button.**

You can use this dialog box to intentionally rasterize a vector object in an Illustrator file.

- **Color Model** and **Resolution** define the settings that will be used in the resulting raster object.

- **Background** options determine what will appear in unfilled areas of the selected bounding box.

    - White fills in those areas so underlying objects will not be visible.

    - Transparent allows unfilled areas in the selection to show underlying objects.

- **Anti-Aliasing** can be used to help minimize blurry edges in the resulting raster object.

- **Create Clipping Mask** can be used to add a vector-based clipping object over the resulting raster object.

- **Add _ Around Object** adds a defined number of pixels around all four edges of the resulting raster image.

- **Preserve Spot Colors** maintains spot-color information as a separate channel in the resulting raster object.

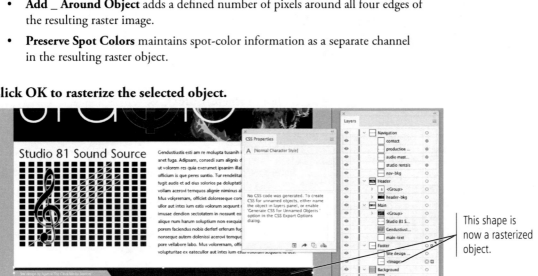

12. **Click OK to rasterize the selected object.**

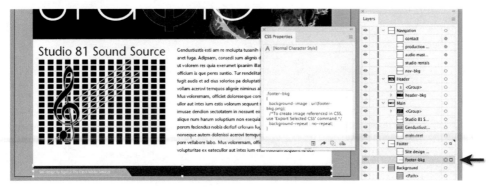

This shape is now a rasterized object.

13. **In the Layers panel, change the name of the <image> object to footer-bkg.**

After renaming the object, the CSS Properties panel now shows the code that will be generated for this class.

14. **Click to select the logotype in the header area of the layout. In the Layers panel, change the selected <Group> name to `studio81-logo`.**

The <img> tag src attribute in the header element calls for the file **studio81-logo.png**. The name you define in the Layers panel is the file name that will be used when the image is generated during the export process. You do not need to include the file extension in the object name; that will be added for you when the images are exported.

As you can see in the CSS Properties panel, a class will be created for this object. Although you don't need this class, you do need the image file that will be created. The extraneous class will not affect the HTML page because that class has not been applied to any of the HTML elements on the page.

15. **Repeat Step 14 to rename the artwork to the left of the text block as `home-feature`.**

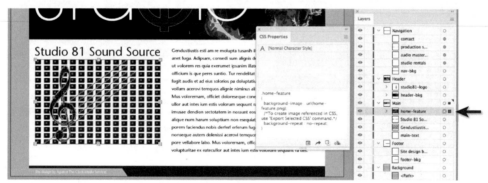

16. **Save the file and continue to the next exercise.**

Create a Gradient Page Background

The HTML body element — contained by <body></body> tags — defines everything that will be visible in a browser window. Basically, you might think of the body element as the overall page background. In this exercise, you are going to change the solid-gray background color to a gradient and define the object name so that the resulting CSS selector properly defines the appearance of the page background.

1. **With site-design.ai open, select the gray-filled object on the Background layer.**

2. **Using the Gradient panel, apply the default white-to-black linear gradient and define a –90° angle.**

3. **Drag the yellow swatch from the Site Colors group in the Swatches panel onto the left gradient stop on the gradient ramp.**

The <path> object on the background layer is selected.

Drag the yellow swatch from the Site Colors group to the left gradient stop.

4. **Drag the red swatch from the Site Colors group in the Swatches panel onto the gradient ramp in the Gradient panel. Define the stop's Location as 50%.**

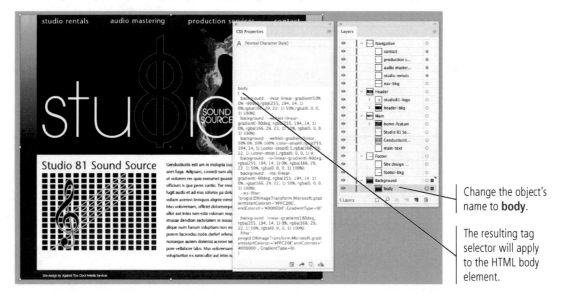

Drag the red swatch from the Site Colors group to the 50% location on the gradient ramp.

5. **In the Layers panel, rename the selected object as body.**

6. **Review the CSS Properties panel.**

If you define an object name using the name of a known HTML element, Illustrator creates a CSS tag selector instead of a class. The selector's name exactly matches the element name without a preceding period.

This selector will define the appearance of the body element in the HTML page. The gradient will appear behind all other elements. In other words, it will be the page background.

As you can see, the CSS code for a gradient is fairly complex. It defines the color (including transparency) and position of each stop in the gradient.

Change the object's name to **body**.

The resulting tag selector will apply to the HTML body element.

7. **Save the file and continue to the next exercise.**

Create Character Styles

The final required piece for this project is to control the appearance of text in various elements of the site design. This is accomplished by creating character styles that define the tag or class name to which each set of formatting options should apply.

Keep in mind that character styles only store character formatting options; they do not store paragraph formatting options, such as space before/after. Character leading, which controls the space from one baseline to the next and is a character formatting option, is mapped to the line-height property of CSS.

Paragraph spacing must be defined using the margin and padding CSS properties; this cannot be accomplished in Illustrator at the time of this writing.

1. **With site-design.ai open, open the Character Styles panel (Window>Type>Character Styles).**

2. **Using the Selection tool, select the type object with the word "contact" in the Navigation area at the top of the artboard.**

   The CSS Properties panel shows a class selector that will define the formatting in this object. Because no specific character style is defined, the application generates a class based on the Normal Character Style that is applied by default. Class names cannot include space characters, so the default class name is .NormalCharacterStyle.

Note:

If you use individual type objects for each paragraph with the same character style applied, the resulting CSS would create separate classes for each item, such as .nav1, .nav2, and so on. To avoid these unwanted classes, you should create each item as a paragraph in the same Illustrator type object.

These properties maintain the applied formatting in language that can be understood in CSS.

3. **With the type object selected, click the Create New Style button at the bottom of the Character Styles panel.**

4. **Double-click the resulting style and change its name to nav.**

   The first click of the double-click applies the new style to all text in the selected type object. The second click highlights the style name so that you can type to rename it.

   When you rename the style, the selector name in the CSS Properties panel should automatically change to reflect the new name. Unfortunately, it does not change until you click away from the selected object. This is a minor bug in the application, but you should be aware of the issue.

Note:

On Windows, the type object's drop shadow property is not reflected in the CSS. There is currently no work-around for this problem.

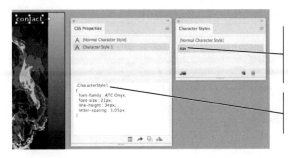

The nav character style is now applied to all type in the selected object.

The selector name does not yet reflect the new name.

5. **Click away from the selected object, then click to select it again.**

After reselecting the type object, the CSS property accurately reflects the new name. If you look at the property values in the lower half of the panel, however, you might notice that the CSS does not include character color values. This is a bug in the software that requires a minor work-around to solve.

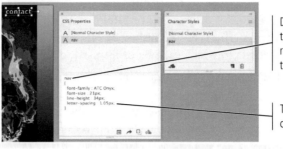

Deselect and then reselect the object to show the revised selector name in the CSS Properties panel.

The CSS does not include character color values.

6. **In the Character Styles panel, double-click the nav style away from the style name to open the Character Style Options dialog box.**

7. **Display the Character Color options in the dialog box and make sure the Fill Color swatch is active. Click to select any existing swatch other than the white one, then click to reselect the white color swatch.**

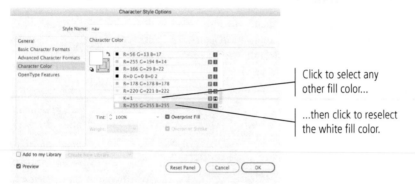

Click to select any other fill color...

...then click to reselect the white fill color.

8. **Click OK to apply the change, then click the nav item in the CSS Properties panel.**

After changing, and then reapplying the correct color to the character style, the color properties are added to the related CSS selector.

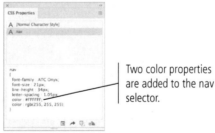

Two color properties are added to the nav selector.

Note:

If a type object includes paragraphs with different formatting, you have to select specific paragraphs before creating new character styles.

9. **Click to select the "studio rentals" type object, then shift click to select the "audio mastering" and "production services" type objects. With all three type objects selected, click the nav style in the Character Styles panel.**

If you don't apply the character style, additional CSS would be generated for each of the type objects.

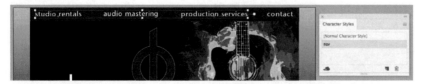

10. Repeat this process to create a new character styles named h1, based on formatting applied to the type object above the artwork in the main-text area.

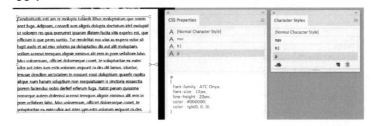

11. Open the Character Style Options dialog box for the h1 style, and reapply the R=166 G=29 B=22 swatch to the h1 character style.

12. Click OK to finalize the style change, then click the h1 item in the CSS Properties panel to see the new color values.

Note:

You can copy selector text in the CSS Properties panel, and then paste it into an HTML or CSS file in an HTML editor application, such as Adobe Dreamweaver.

13. Repeat this process to create a new character style named p, based on formatting applied to the multi-line type object to the right of the feature art. Reapply black as the character color.

14. Repeat this process to create a new character style named footer, based on formatting applied to the type object in the footer area. Reapply R=220 G=221 B=222 as the character color.

15. Save the file and continue to the next exercise.

Export CSS and Image Files

Now that you have defined the object names and created the necessary character styles, the final step is to create the CSS file and export the necessary images for the HTML page to display properly in a browser window.

1. **With site-design.ai open, deselect everything in the file.**

2. **Choose Effect>Document Raster Effects Settings.**

   The document color mode and resolution are established in the Advanced section of the New Document dialog box. You can use this dialog box to review and, if necessary, change those settings.

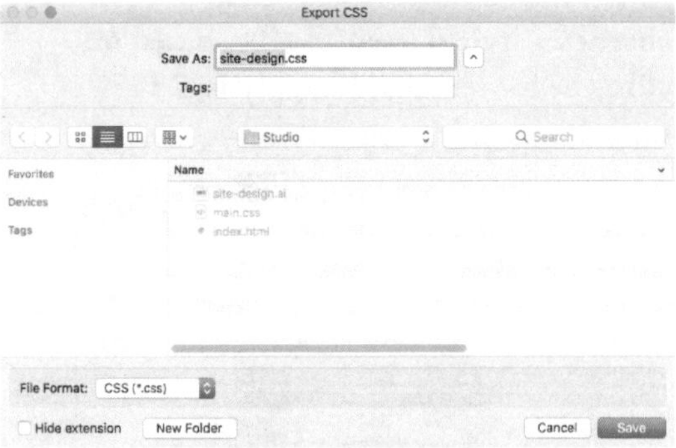

Note:

Some devices (specifically, tablets and some laptops) can display higher than 72 ppi images. We are using 72 ppi in this project for simplicity, but you might want to include higher-resolution images depending on your content.

3. **Click OK to close the dialog box.**

4. **Open the CSS Properties panel Options menu and choose Export All.**

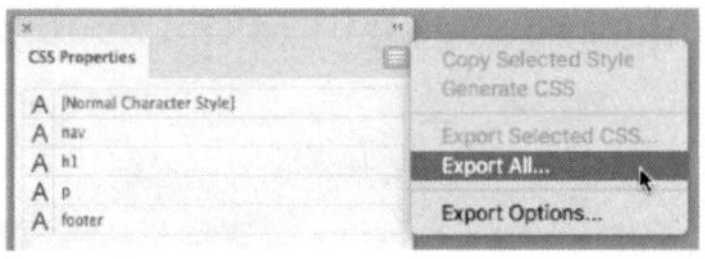

Note:

You can select specific styles in the panel and choose Export Selected CSS to create a file with only certain selectors.

5. **In the resulting Export CSS dialog box, make sure your WIP>Studio folder is selected as the target, then click Save.**

   When you export a CSS file, the file name defaults to be the same as the active Illustrator file. The HTML file in this project uses that name, so do not change it.

6. **Review the options in the resulting dialog box.**

The CSS Export Options dialog box determines exactly what is included in the export process.

- **CSS Units.** This defines the units of measurement that will be used for CSS properties. Because websties are viewed on monitors, which display pages using pixels, Pixels is the default selection.

- **Object Appearance.** These options determine whether fill, stroke, and opacity values are included in the CSS selectors. All three options are selected by default.

- **Include Absolute Position.** By default, HTML element positioning is relative to the container; for the overall page, that means relative to the browser window. This option can be used to add position properties based on the top-left corner of the artboard, which means elements will not move when the browser window gets larger or smaller. For example:

  position : absolute;
  left : 50px;
  top : 400px;

- **Include Dimensions.** This option can be used to add width and height properties to a selector so that the related element in the HTML page has the same size as the object in the Illustrator file. For example:

  width : 780px;
  height : 50px;

- **Generate CSS for Unnamed Objects.** When checked, Illustrator creates class selectors for all objects in the file, including those you did not specifically name in the Layers panel.

- **Include Vendor Pre-fixes.** Not all browsers provide the same support for some CSS properties. CSS includes a method for defining different properties for different browsers so that all browsers can come as close as possible to rendering a page as close as possible to what you intend. When this option is checked, Illustrator includes all the necessary variations in the exported CSS file.

- **Rasterize Unsupported Art.** When this is checked, Illustrator automatically generates raster images for vector artwork that can't be properly linked in an HTML file. Exported files automatically use the PNG file format and extension.

- **Resolution.** This menu defines the resolution that will be used for exported images. By default, Illustrator uses the resolution setting that is defined in the Document Raster Effects Settings dialog box.

7. **Click OK to generate the CSS for the site-design file.**

Note:

You can click the Export Options button at the bottom of the CSS Properties panel to open this dialog box at any time.

8. **On your desktop, examine the contents of the WIP>Studio folder.**

As you can see, the folder now includes a second CSS file (site-design.css) which contains the selectors based on content in the Illustrator file. Three PNG image files have also been generated.

9. **Using any browser, open index.html from your WIP>Studio folder.**

The image files generated by the Illustrator Export process should appear properly in place of the broken-link icons that you saw when you first viewed this file. The classes in the new CSS file correctly define the background images, colors, and most type formatting options that are defined in the Illustrator layout.

However, you might notice several problems; specifically, the footer background image is missing.

10. **Continue to the next exercise.**

Manually Export Site Assets

Several manual steps are required to correct the problem you saw when you opened the HTML file. To complete this project, you need to manually export the image for the footer background area.

1. **With site-design.ai open in Illustrator, make sure nothing is selected in the file.**

2. **Using the Layers panel, click to select the footer-bkg image object, then click the Collect for Export button at the bottom of the panel.**

   Using the Collect for Export button in the Layers panel automatically adds the selected object(s) to the Asset Export panel, which provides an easy interface to create the files you need for specific Illustrator graphics.

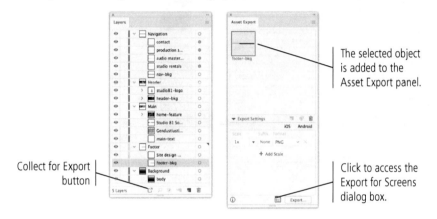

Collect for Export button

The selected object is added to the Asset Export panel.

Click to access the Export for Screens dialog box.

3. **Click the button at the bottom of the Asset Export panel to open the Export for Screens dialog box.**

   If you simply click the Export button in the Asset Export panel, these defined files are exported using the default location settings. It is a good idea to be sure of where you are exporting files, however; you can verify those settings in the Export for Screens dialog box.

4. **On the right side of the dialog box, click the Folder icon. Navigate to your WIP>Studio folder as the target location, then click Choose/Select Folder.**

5. **Uncheck the Open Location after Export and Create Sub-Folders options.**

   The HTML and CSS for this project call for images to be placed in the same location as the index.html file. You do not want the exported images to be placed into subfolders.

Click this icon to select the target location for the exported file.

Uncheck both of these options.

6. **Click Export Asset.**

7. **In a browser, open or refresh the index.html file.**

8. **Close the browser and return to Illustrator.**

9. **Save the Illustrator file and close it.**

Responsive web design, or creating pages that are optimized for the actual size of the device being used to display those pages, often calls for a number of different files for each image. For example, you would use one image for an extra-small device (a smartphone) and another image for a large display (a desktop monitor).

In addition to using the Collect for Export button in the Layers panel, you can drag an object into the Asset Export panel, determine what settings you want to use for the resulting files, and export all the defined assets in a single process.

Use the Selection tool to drag any object into the panel.

Double-click the asset name to define the resulting file name.

The lower half of the panel defines settings that will apply to exported files. The Scale menu includes most of the common sizes that are used. If you choose the Width or Height options, you can define the specific size of the exported file. If you choose the Resolution option, you define the resulting file's resolution (ppi) at 100% of the asset's original size.

When you choose one of the scaling options (2x, 3x, etc.) in the Scale menu, the Suffix field defaults to industry-standard suffixes that are added to the file name you define for each asset. You can also use the field to define custom suffixes, such as "-small" or "-xlarge".

The format menu lists common formats used in web design. The default PNG option supports continuous color and alpha transparency, which means it is suitable for most images; PNG 8 limits the file to 256 colors, so it is best suited to logos or images that do not have a wide range of color variation.

The various JPEG options determine the quality of the file; for example, JPG 100 is maximum quality/lowest compression while JPG 20 is minimum quality/highest compression.

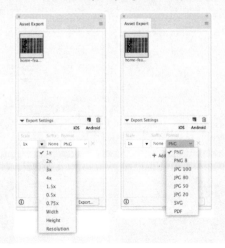

Once you have defined the settings you want to use, you can click the Export button to export files for assets selected in the top half of the panel.

You can also click the Launch... button to open the Export for Screens dialog box, where you can accomplish the same export tasks for defined assets or artboards.

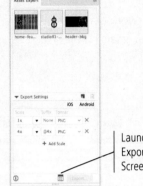

Launch Export for Screens

Click here to open the Format Settings dialog box.

To change the options related to individual file formats, you can choose Format Settings in the Asset Export panel Options menu, or click the Advanced Settings button in the Export for Screens dialog box.

1. You can check the _____ option in the Recolor Artwork dialog box to reflect color changes in selected objects.

2. If the _____ option in the Recolor Artwork dialog box is active, you can make universal changes (such as brightness) to all colors in a group.

3. The _____ tool can be used to apply color swatches from selected groups based on overlap areas rather than entire vector objects.

4. When the _____ option is active, straight lines reproduce more sharply because they no longer require anti-aliasing in the resulting raster image.

5. In CSS, a(n) _____ selector defines properties for a specific HTML element. The name is exactly the same as the element name.

6. In CSS, a(n) _____ selector defines properties for any element identified with that attribute. The name always begins with a period.

7. In HTML, the _____ element contains all elements that will be visible in the browser window.

8. Choose _____ to convert a vector object to a raster image on the artboard.

9. True or false: The document color mode and resolution are fixed in the New Document dialog box; you cannot change them once you create the file. _____

10. You can check the _____ option to override the default relative positioning of HTML elements. If this option is checked, elements will not move if a user makes the browser window larger or smaller.

1. Briefly define an HTML element, and provide at least two examples.

2. Briefly explain the concept of a CSS class.

3. Briefly explain two advantages of designing a website interface in Illustrator.

PORTFOLIO BUILDER PROJECT

Use what you have learned in this project to complete the following freeform exercise.
Carefully read the art director and client comments, then create your own design to meet the needs of the project.
Use the space below to sketch ideas. When finished, write a brief explanation of the reasoning behind your final design.

art director comments

All professional designers need a portfolio of their work. If you have completed the projects in this book, you should now have a number of different examples to show off your skills using Illustrator.

The eight projects in this book were specifically designed to include a broad range of *types* of projects; your portfolio should use the same principle.

client comments

For this project, you are your own client. Using the following suggestions, gather your best work and create printed and digital versions of your portfolio:

❏ Include as many types of work as possible.

❏ Print clean copies of each finished piece that you want to include.

❏ For each example in your portfolio, write a brief (one- or two-paragraph) synopsis of the project. Explain the purpose of the piece, as well as your role in the creative and production process.

❏ Design a personal promotion brochure — create a layout that highlights your technical skills and reflects your personal style.

❏ Create a PDF version of your portfolio so you can send it via email, post it on job sites, and keep it with you on a flash drive at all times — you never know when you might meet a potential employer.

project justification

Web design typically involves a partnership between the site designer and a web developer. The designer creates the look and feel of the site, and the developer creates the code that makes the page function properly. The new options in Illustrator CC make it much easier to translate an Illustrator file into the necessary pieces that are required by the developer, including the cascading style sheets (CSS) that translate Illustrator objects into code that a browser can read to render the HTML elements as closely as possible to what you intend.

As we mentioned previously, the site design you used in this project is a very simple example, using only a few page elements to demonstrate how Illustrator translates artboard elements to HTML and CSS elements. The skills you learned in this project would apply equally to more complex sites.

We also explained a number of concepts related to HTML and CSS in general. To improve your marketability and skills beyond using Illustrator for website design, we highly encourage you to pursue a more thorough and detailed knowledge of these topics.

Use color groups to manage and change colors in selected artwork

Use Live Paint to add a highlight color to specific artwork elements

Define object names to export CSS class selectors

Define names to generate required image files from vector artwork

Define a gradient background for the page body element

Define character styles to generate CSS tag selectors for type formatting

Rasterize an object to create a CSS background image

INDEX

INDEX

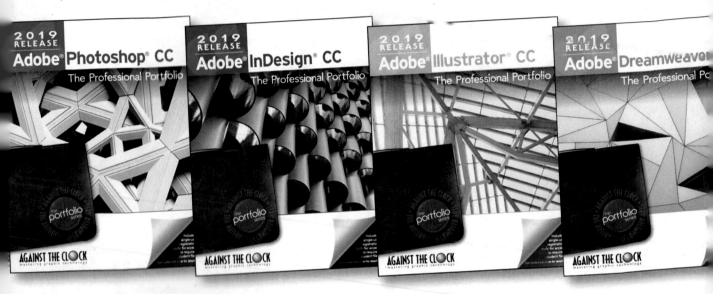